Contemporary Literary Scholarship

CONTRIBUTING AUTHORS

GEORGE K. ANDERSON, *Brown University*

GEORGE ARMS, *University of New Mexico*

JACQUES BARZUN, *Columbia University*

GERALD E. BENTLEY, *Princeton University*

BRADFORD A. BOOTH, *University of California*

JAMES L. CLIFFORD, *Columbia University*

LESLIE A. FIEDLER, *Montana State University*

RICHARD HARTER FOGLE, *Tulane University*

LENNOX GREY, *Teachers College, Columbia University*

PATRICK D. HAZARD, *University of Pennsylvania*

MERRITT Y. HUGHES, *University of Wisconsin*

CHARLTON LAIRD, *University of Nevada*

LEWIS LEARY, *Columbia University*

R. W. B. LEWIS, *Rutgers University*

FRED B. MILLETT, *Wesleyan University*

WILLIAM VAN O'CONNOR, *University of Minnesota*

HENRY POPKIN, *Brandeis University*

LIONEL STEVENSON, *Duke University*

Contemporary
Literary Scholarship

A CRITICAL REVIEW

Edited by LEWIS LEARY

for THE COMMITTEE ON LITERARY SCHOLARSHIP
AND THE TEACHING OF ENGLISH

of the NATIONAL COUNCIL OF TEACHERS OF ENGLISH

NEW YORK

Appleton-Century-Crofts, Inc.

Preface

THIS VOLUME HAD ITS ORIGIN IN
papers presented under the sponsorship of the Committee on Literary Scholarship and the Teaching of English at meetings of the National Council of Teachers of English in 1955 and 1956 and during the summer session at Columbia University in 1956. Addressing themselves to the problem of the teacher of English in high school or college who is of necessity so involved in other things that he is unable to keep up with trends and achievements in scholarship, the papers surveyed several of the areas into which the study of literature is traditionally divided. At the first meeting Gerald E. Bentley spoke on "Shakespeare and His Times," Fred B. Millett on "Trends in the Study of Recent Literature," and Lennox Grey gave a preliminary survey of problems concerning "The Literary Audience." At the second, Merritt Y. Hughes spoke on "Milton and Donne in Recent Scholarship," Randall Stewart read a paper, which has since appeared in *College English* (1957), on "Developments in the Study of American Literature," and William Van O'Connor discussed "Trends in Literary Criticism." During the summer of 1956, an open meeting and a round-table conference were devoted to problems confronting the teacher of literature: James L. Clifford presented the viewpoint of the teacher in the graduate school, John Middendorf of the teacher of undergraduates, and Patrick D. Hazard of the high school teacher.

So enthusiastic was the response to these papers and these meetings that the Committee was encouraged to invite other specialists to survey developments in other areas in order to provide as complete a survey as possible of contemporary trends in literary scholarship. Contributors were chosen, not only because of competence in areas of special interest, but because of mature critical awareness and broad acquaintance with fresh approaches toward their subject. Effort was made to enlist representatives of every major point of view as well as every area of study, and thus to place responsibility for the survey in the hands of scholar-critics who avoid pedantry, who recognize the pluralism of life and consequently of art which expresses life, as well as the various avenues which lead toward the study or teaching of literature. Each was encouraged to present more than a simple bibliographical account: to put forward his own critical view, and to express, among other things, convictions concerning the effectiveness for the teacher of current trends in criticism and investigation.

The result has happily been some disparity of opinion and some inevitable overlapping. Mr. Arms, Mr. Lewis, and Mr. O'Connor, for example, all comment on contemporary critical trends, and all differently. Mr. Bentley and Mr. Popkin do not say the same things about Shakespeare studies. Mr. Booth and Mr. Clifford both speak of Fielding and Sterne, the first briefly, as a student of fiction in general, the second more at length because of the position of prominence which these novelists occupy in the eighteenth century. Little effort has been made to avoid duplication of this kind or to edit the essays to conformity with preconceived notions of what they should have contained. Both conviction and common sense argued that the varieties of approaches toward literature and of opinions about literature could best be represented by allowing each author freedom in defining and interpreting the area he was asked to discuss. If one is austere and another excessively tolerant, one adamantly historical and another scornful of historical scholarship, this disparity of itself represents something characteristic of the study of literature today.

There is, however, behind the book something of plan, which is briefly this: to provide an informal discussion of trends and specific achievements in the study of literature during the past thirty years; to present a useful guide for teachers through areas which their own specialization or their absorption in other duties has not allowed them to roam as often as they have wished; and to underline the ancient axiom that neither pedagogical method nor enthusiasm can effectively replace knowledge of the subject to be taught. First, the problem of the teacher who is scholar and critic also is presented in two essays which say something of his nature and responsibilities. Then scholarship in the periods into which the study of literature is usually divided is considered in nine essays. Five essays are devoted, next, to the literary genres, including the study of comparative or general literature, and two essays to consideration of the literary audience, in its relation to literature and also to popular arts, such as radio, television, and the motion picture. Finally, there is a selected bibliography listing fifty books which in the opinion of scholars represent outstanding recent literary studies.

Each essay has been read critically by the editor and by at least one disinterested scholar with special competence to judge the area discussed. Special thanks in this connection is due to my colleagues at Columbia University, Jerome H. Buckley, Elliott V. K. Dobbie, S. Frederick Johnson, and Marjorie H. Nicolson, to Herbert Davis of Oxford, and Daniel G. Hoffman of Swarthmore, none of whom, however, is in any way responsible for opinions expressed. Something more than gratitude must be expressed to members of the Committee on Literary Scholarship and the Teaching of English, to Lennox Grey, its Associate Chairman, Gerald E. Bentley, Fred B. Millett, and Patrick D. Hazard, and also to T. A. Barnhart, chairman of the College Section of the NCTE, under whose direction the Committee operates, to Max J. Herzberg, the NCTE's late Director of Publications, and J. N. Hook, its Executive Secretary, whose enthusiasm and goodwill have made this book possible.

L. L.

Columbia University

Contents

THE AUDIENCE

THE PROBLEM

1

The Scholar-Critic

JACQUES BARZUN

PEOPLE OUTSIDE THE ACADEMIC profession as they know it today are always surprised to hear the distinction made between the scholar and the critic. Not only do they associate the names of leading critics with colleges and universities, but they take it for granted that scholarly method is nothing if not critical, and that all critics must deal with fact in a scholarly manner or lose their character for reliability.

Yet it was not much more than thirty years ago that inside the university the name of critic was a bar to advancement. None but scholars were wanted, and the scholar was defined negatively as one who, if he wrote or should write, would not be accepted by any of the journals known as critical.

This definition contradicted an older one, according to which the scholar acknowledged no limits to his interests, but wrote and lectured on whatever subjects attracted his fancy, from history to morals and from literature to mathematics. It has been said of such universal professors that they occupied not chairs but settees. The historical fact is that down to the middle of the nineteenth century the intellectual life tended toward unity; it was a specialty in itself and as a whole. Classical scholars wrote poetry, poets carried on scientific experiments, statesmen translated Homer, lawyers wrote metaphysical inquiries, and men of science were deep in theological controversy.

With the shift in the meaning of the word *science* due to the successfully enlarged study of nature, the unity of knowledge was broken up into ever more categories, and specialization became truly a categorical imperative. As a result, and by imitation, the treatment of literature and the arts underwent a series of transformations. First, the study of the ancient classics ceased to be

3

encyclopedic and became exclusively philological. Next, the modern literatures and the fine arts changed status: from being sources of diversion they became objects of study. English literature, for example, entered the British and American curriculum in the 1880's, but only after much resistance from those who thought it no subject at all. Finally, thanks to the spread of literacy through public schooling, and the cheapening of the printed word through technological progress, the general public grew accustomed to the attitude and methods of scholarship, at least in their surface manifestations. Just as the scholar was used to seeing an error creep into a text, so the layman saw the footnote creep into journalism. The habit of citing sources, of "giving the background," of reporting accurately ("and I quote . . . .") grew commonplace, until today scholarship, would-be scholarship, and pseudo-scholarship co-exist indiscriminately in the worlds of education, literature, art, government, industry, journalism, and advertising.

The currents that propelled this cultural change were obviously strong enough to sweep the critic back into the university, and with him came the poet, painter, and musician. They landed on the campus in two capacities—as refugees from economic competition: the free lance could no longer earn a living; and as welcome missionaries: the academic mind had lost some of its "scientific" austerity and become touched with aesthetics.

Before we can appreciate why this came about we must recall the way in which the humanities had managed in the late nineteenth century to turn themselves "scientific." They did this by adopting the historical attitude and applying the literal part of the historical method—the part that stops short of intuition and imagination. Success was immediate: as soon as the system was applied, the same desiccation that had overcome the classics began to overtake the study of modern literature and the fine arts. Academic promotion and prestige were to be had for the writing of little papers in which a point was made about a text, or an unnoted similarity teased out into an "influence." It was "shown" that Shelley and Keats had both used the image of boat, rock, and wave in poems a few years apart. In other words, the scholar could be distinguished from the critic by his unwillingness, and soon by his inability, to interest anybody but his alter ego at another university. Whatever was not factual and "shown," whatever was imaginative and readable, was unscholarly. The critic, on the contrary, was a man with ideas, an excrescence comparable to the prehensile tail which man as scholar had lost.

The intellectual asceticism of the scholar was, of course, not wholly stupid and futile. It led to genuine discoveries which enlarged knowledge, and it resisted in the name of evidence, soberness, and truth the frequent intellectual libertinism of the critic. For during the same decades, the Impressionist and Symbolist movements had triumphed in literature and inspired a criticism in their own image: the impressionist critic recorded his sensations under the spell of a masterpiece and re-created its mood or meaning. But there was no way to make him accountable; he might invent experiences in order to entertain and he often drew attention away from the work to fix it on his fascinating self.

After the first world war, a reaction set in against both the literal scholar and the introspective critic. It condemned both history and impressionism as irrelevant and useless, and asserted that the work itself was the thing—not its genesis and not its effect. Within the tangible confines of the poem or painting there was need for the application of intelligence and imagination equalling, perhaps, that required for the original creation.

The so-called new critics advocated the old method borrowed by the French lycée from the medieval scholastics—*explication de texte*, or the unfolding of true or hidden sense from words, sometimes renamed "close reading." In literature this criticism tended to be verbal and philosophical; in the fine arts, it supplemented the discovery of similarities by the interpretation of symbols; in music, it tried to isolate the ingredients of a style by discerning hidden forms beneath the obvious devices. Stylistics and exegesis were in fact the common aims of the new criticism in literature and the arts, even though it is usually assumed that the movement was exclusively literary.

In repudiating the historical method and what might be called the sociological interest, the new criticism was also expressing a distaste for the world and paying homage to art as the true reality. "Explication" suggested that material forms are not to be taken at face value, that art is seldom what it seems. But owing to the continuance of specialization, few noticed that in taking this new path criticism was but following the general evolution of thought; it was still in the wake of the physical science and the "sociology" which it rejected. For the "hidden-meaning" postulate was a derivative of the new physics and the new psychology which could also be seen at work in anthropology, semantics, philosophy, mythology, and folklore. Indeed many experts in these disciplines, themselves caught by the new hunger for fine art, fell upon its products like starved augurs, dismembering each specimen to show by their several "methods" what it *really* meant.

The attitude in these demonstrations was far more clinical than before, and the language as barbarous as ever it had been under the historical dispensation. The very word *method* showed that the intent was to reach verifiable truth by systematic devices, though this base technology was concealed from practitioners and followers by the novelty of the discourse. Because each writer spoke from a well-defined point of view and brought forward evidence from outside the common range of vision, he was deemed a critic and not merely a scholar. He passed judgment, wrote in literary quarterlies rather than scholarly periodicals, and showed (or claimed) sensitiveness to aesthetic experience. Not for him the mere cataloguing of boats, rocks, and waves: he developed their symbolism, their ambiguity, their architectonic relations to the whole and to the infinitude of parts discernible in the work once the right method was applied. No effort was spared or concealed, until it was hard to say which was the work of imagination—the poem or the gloss upon it.

The energy of the new criticism and the far vistas it seemed to open recommended it to the young, and soon it rivaled within the academy the older historical scholarship. Departments of literature first took on one critic, with mixed doubt and pride; after which "our critic" was matched by others, their specialties of method being equally acceptable provided that when laid end to end they covered the historical sequences and traditional genres.

In the enthusiasm for the new its points of likeness to the old were scarcely seen. Because meaning was the goal, the same preoccupation with textual and verbal minutiae impugned in the former historical scholarship was now felt to be justified. It was not seen that a new literalism was developing as destructive of art as the old, and more congenial only because it was more anarchic. Everyone could preach and contemn, no one could argue or refute, for symbols were ambiguous and elusive and each vaunted method was at bottom arbitrary, indeed "impressionistic." Anyone brought up on *explication de texte* knows how much is "found" by visceral fiat.

Again, the interpretation which lighted up the refreshing new "facts" was secretly loaded with history; for it is evident that to explain anything by reference to the special or ancient meaning of words, by the play of allusion and symbol, by the echoes of tradition and myth, by the recorded ideas and experience of the artist, is to rely on historical sources, whether the search for them is original or second-hand. The dictionary is a historical compendium, as is also Freudian doctrine based on case histories, or Frazer's *Golden Bough*, compiled from the written survivals of prehistory.

The pretense, moreover, of remaining "inside the work" is an illusion; while the boasting about it is as doubtful a sign of artistic sensibility as it is a clear one of low reasoning power. Either a work stands by itself, intelligible and potent, and then it needs no explaining; or else it requires explicating, and then something has to be brought to it from outside, were it only the beholder's experience of life and residue of education.

Finally, practice has shown that it is not in the methods themselves but in the few who have invoked them with talent and tact that the merits of the new criticism reside. Theme analysis and image hunting and myth decipherment, when carried on by persons of ordinary parts, have yielded the same results as the discredited historical method—dullness and triviality. The net gain, apart from the decrial of piddling irrelevance in historical "studies" and the astringent use of close reading after a surfeit of loose impressionism, has been the reinstatement of the critic as a member of the academic company. But this still leaves the burden on each lover of literature to find out for himself who are the critics that deserve the name otherwise than formally.

It also leaves the question whether the historical method is not, after all, the only one that the critic can use. It is, as we saw, the one that he has always used, even when he concealed it under new ideologies. And it may be the only one because it is least a method. Unlike the systems that try to rival the rigor of science, the historical method regulates imagination without enforcing literalism; it suits art because it was devised to seek meaning in the records of human life. If art presents, as we know it does, obscurities of text and difficulties of style; if it seems to say but a few things when it actually says many; if students and readers come to it inexperienced, inattentive, or insufficiently informed, then the critic's role is plain and we can use its definition as a test of any critical writer's work: as close to the object as to the mind of its beholder, the critic must act as go-between; he is the midwife of understanding.

From this it follows that the critic must speak with clarity and even with charm; his work must in any case not present a greater riddle than it tries to solve. Besides being clear, the book or essay or article must be graspable: it must yield a conclusion or leave a form in the receiving mind. A list of themes and images, a paper hunt for mythic symbols, even if they explain each puzzle on the way, destroy the unity and coherence achieved by the artist, giving in exchange only a confusion of loose data. Such an investigation buries not reveals; criticism is not mere annotation, hence beside the critic as analyst must dwell the critic as synoptic mind.

The critic, without being earthbound, must stick to facts, knowing how they are sought and ascertained. To that extent he must be a scholar-critic. He may conjecture hidden nuances and possible intentions, suggest subtle relations and secret influences, but he must not steadily invent and consider his fancy proved for lack of disproof. This is simply bad impressionism disguised, just as text analysis is rudimentary history disguised. The critic must slough off the one and transcend the other.

The critic having shown himself an accurate scholar will hardly be able to avoid being a good historian, for his critical interest—his interest in art and literature as manifestations of spirit—will make him see that the historical method rightly conceived is nothing but the sense of life duly ordered for communication. And he knows that without an extended, an educated, sense of life—almost a worldliness about the inextinguishable pluralism of life—there is no adequate perception of art. There is only pedantry and parochialism, precious literalism and excess of words. When a culture permits its scholars or critics to relapse into this logomachy, they are, regardless of name or academic title, no more than "blind mouths," to whom "the hungry sheep look up and are not fed."

2

Literary Scholarship and the Teaching of English

LEWIS LEARY

JUST AS THERE IS NO LONGER reason for invidious distinction between the scholar and the critic, so there is also not reason to distinguish between the scholar-critic and the teacher. He who is one is to some large but varying degree the other. Whether the classroom-audience is made up of readers of a coterie magazine, graduates in seminar, or a group of tenth-graders, the task is the same: to communicate something which he knows and about which he is enthusiastic to an audience which does not know or properly appreciate. The enterprise is trifurcate: to discover as scholar, to analyze as critic, and to communicate as teacher. No one of these activities is effective without the qualifying support of each of the other two.

I

We resent, because we find it unrealistic, the suggestion recently set forth by Robert Graves who, writing of "Diseases of Scholarship" in the *New Republic* (1957), said that we are divided into two groups, the scholar and the educationalist, the latter "a man of enthusiasm, character, humility, gifted with the art of exposition, a genuine love of teaching, but little intellectual curiosity or ambition," satisfied with being "an honored and responsible State official, trained to teach students the facts and theories generally approved by the State and required for public examination." We may chuckle over what he says because it is effective caricature, with just enough truth in it to make us squirm, but both experience and common sense remind us that our function, like so many things besides, is not a matter of this *or* that, but of this *and* that. The ancient stereotype of the man in the ivory tower, a busy squirrel hoarding acorns of fact against the long winter of his mediocrity or, as John Mason Brown has put it, acting as chiropodist to other men's footnotes, has just about as much validity as the public image if Mr. Chips, Miss Dove, or Ichabod Crane.

Because it takes all manner of people to fill up a world, or even a profession, we do in honesty admit that there are, even among our acquaintances, some squirrel-scholars who dislike teaching and therefore do it badly—like the professor who was so dull that the other professors noticed it. There are also critics who talk excitedly to themselves, just as there are teachers who rely on know-how rather than knowledge. But scholars need not be dull —on the contrary, as the Selected Bibliography at the end of this volume will indicate, their best products are often lively indeed. Nor need critics, as Jacques Barzun has suggested, be consistently irresponsible. As for the teacher, it was Anatole France who warned, "Let our teaching be full of ideas. Hitherto it has been stuffed with facts." We have learned, I think, that scaffoldings of date or incident or ideology need not be erected in such pattern that they obscure or even blur the outlines of a work of literary art. Nor need we encourage the teacher who is only personable and enthusiastic, and therefore dangerous directly in proportion to the contagion of his enthusiasm and the innocence of his learning.

Ideally, that is, our scholar-teacher-critic is a skilled professional, trained as effectively for what he is to do as is the professional in any other area, in law or medicine. He has learned techniques of presentation; he has studied the history and the background of his subject, so that he knows it of itself and can relate it to other fields of knowledge; he is acquainted with the best which has been thought and said about it, not only last year, but this year also; he keeps abreast, that is to say, with current interpretations, new trends, and with the latest in opinion and research. With sane good judgment we hesitate to put ourselves or our families into the hands of a physician who fails to keep up with techniques and discoveries set forth in the medical journals. We should indeed be naïve if we relied on a lawyer who did not keep himself informed through advance-sheet reports of decisions and transcripts of legislation. It seems reasonable, then, to suggest that the teacher of literature, on whatever level, who overlooks the criticism of T. S. Eliot or the fictional techniques of Henry James, Joyce, or Faulkner is roughly equivalent to the teacher of physics who ignores the quantum theory or the family doctor who knows nothing of Salk vaccine. And Shakespeare or Goethe, though here the analogy is less apt, is the Blackstone, the Newton, or the Pasteur whose elemental truths are daily tested.

Teachers are right when they take pride in their profession. They are exactly right when they expect the same measure of respect from contemporaries that professionals in other areas command. But they are wrong, I think, when they demand that respect without examining their professional qualifications or accomplishments. Only the cynical or the self-comforting imagine that excellence in this or any other enterprise is not recognized. The teacher who approaches his subject as if he were a masseur or a process-server can expect only that degree of respect due to a subprofessional. And, among the thousands on thousands of us, there are subprofessionals loud in their demand for recognition without remembering professional responsibilities.

It may very well be true that the teacher today is distracted with more complicating activities than ever before, but the teacher is also rising to a position where his services are more in demand and more appreciated than ever before. Our shortage of teachers and increase in number of students make for a kind of rise toward power, bargaining power, on the part of the teacher. It is about time, you say. And it is heartening indication of good things to come, but it is a trap also, and a testing. The teacher's position is better and, in the public eye, more important, but it is also more difficult than it has been for many years.

For the teacher today is faced with a profound and radical decision: whether he is to remain a professional or submit to the temptation of organizing into protective groups which will regulate hours and duties, elements which all experience demonstrates can only be self-regulated when the aim is toward excellence. His decision, in short, is whether he is to remain scholar, critic, and teacher or be satisfied with the designation of skilled worker, whether his effort will be toward the protection of masseurs and process-servers or toward concern with standards rigorously examined and maintained.

The choice is not easily made, but it is because of our conviction that it must be made, and in the right direction, that this book has been put together as an aid, not toward the easy acquisition but toward the maintenance of professional standards. It is offered in recognition of a situation which discovers the teacher so involved in dissipating activities that he has little leisure in which to invite more than recognition of what, if life were longer and less cluttered, he might do.

Even as I prepare to write it, I smile at the absurd oversimplification of the statement which I am to make: that a teacher's life is never simple. This would be a fitting time for a pause, a laying aside of this book, just to contemplate how amazingly unsimple a teacher's life is. Each has his own particular variety of entangling alliances, probably no two of us bedeviled by exactly the same confusing pattern. That, I think, we accept as a condition of our profession, a penalty perhaps for our commitment to learning. We battle against it, but inevitably—and I think rightly—eventually submit. And then we go on from there.

Because our subject is literature, our task is immensely difficult—more difficult than that of other teachers we think, though probably it is most wise not to vaunt the conviction publicly because of the distracting argument it would embroil us in with colleagues in other areas. Not only is teaching itself an art, but literature is an art, and complicated by ideas which, among other things, have what is called social significance. But beyond that, and beyond any assumption of the efficacy of pedagogical method or the intransigence of fact, lies our conviction that literature speaks effectively only to and of the spirit of man. Whatever that is, you say. And that's precisely the point, and the reason for literature.

Expressed like that, it seems perhaps an excessively simple thing, beguiling in its apparent confidence that the essence of a literary work or the spirit of an individual is easily come upon. Both are often overlarded with gross elements, sometimes of much the same kind: lack of attention to the matter under consideration, failure of observation or perception, limitation of experience, insistence on a single view—all sins to which flesh and literature are equally heir. For literature is not a simple thing, nor are people.

The best books, it has been said, "are rich fruits encased in thick and bitter rind." Olives and martinis without olives, it has been said, are acquired tastes. The intense but ordered and, in the better meaning of that word, genteel world revealed in much which is conventionally admired as literature may seem unattractively bland beside the quick world of thrill and easy titillation available in television or motion pictures, or even in what our students challenge us with by calling real life. Our responsibility to ourselves, our profession, and our student-audience is prodigiously large as we struggle with imperfect equipment to discover, as Emerson put it, the facts which endure amid transient appearances.

II

But this is not a book about the nature of literature or the art of teaching, subjects complex beyond the ability of most of us to explain. It is a modest reminder of our initial commitment and our perhaps ultimately unattainable goal. It is dedicated to two simple propositions: (1) that in order effectively to teach a subject one must know it, and (2) that the teacher's life in the United States is so involved with so many apparently necessary things and the proliferation of scholarship and criticism has become so great that it is really impossible for him to know all of the best which has recently been thought and said on his subject.

In my own university, it is a common saying that one either spends all of his time reading the works of his colleagues and therefore gets nothing done himself, or he does his own work with no time for discovering what his colleagues are doing. Though a quip passed casually in coffee shop or faculty club, this represents something of horrendous truth. Volume-sized reviews of literary studies even within special areas—Victorian literature, the Romantic poets, selected major American authors—have been numerous during the past decade. Just the bookkeeping of scholarship requires so many man-hours that compilers of the various annual or quarterly bibliographies of work published or in progress have little time for any activity besides.

When the specialist is weighted down by the task of keeping up, as we say, with his small area of literary investigation, what then is the plight of the beleaguered teacher whose responsibility is to the whole of literature, and who, in addition, has a play to direct, a school library to manage, a student paper or a yearbook to sponsor, a debating team to coach, weekly themes to correct, and other tasks which are extra-curricular, co-curricular, or service functions, depending on which school of education produced his principal or his dean? And what of the singleness of our purpose? Someone once counted 1,581 different aims set forth for the teaching of English, and an enlightened commentator has recently suggested that the number could be more reasonably placed at two thousand. To one who has run the whole gamut as I have—from grade school, to high school, college, and graduate school teaching—there remains no question that the teacher of English leads a complicated and an interesting life.

The complications, even the interest, need not distract him from remembering his first function, which has been variously stated. He may, if he prefers those terms, agree with Harold A. Anderson who, in writing in the *Bulletin of the National Association of Secondary School Principals* (1946) of "English Instruction in Education for Democracy," defined the goal of English instruction in American education as "universal literacy on a high plane and the employment of the written and spoken word for high purpose."

He may wish to spell it out more explicitly, as Louise M. Rosenblatt does in *Literature as Experience* (1938) where she enumerates seven aims:

(1) The experience of literature helps to develop the kind of imagination most needed in a democracy—the ability to understand the personality and needs of others and to envisage the possible effect of our own actions upon the lives of others. (2) Literature acts also as one of the social agencies through which the culturally accepted images of behavior, the constellations of emotional attitudes clustering about different relationships, and the culturally accepted social and moral standards, are transmitted. (3) In our heterogeneous democratic society, literature can enlighten the adolescent concerning the wide diversity of possible ways of life, possible patterns of relationship, and possible social and moral philosophies, from which he is free to choose. (4) Literature may thus also offer him a means of carrying on imaginatively some of the trial-and-error eliminations of patterns of behavior necessary for a sound choice. (5) Literary experiences may help the reader to see his own personality and problems objectively, and thus to under-

stand and manage them better. (6) Through contact with the diversity of personalities and varied experiences of his fellow-men expressed in literature, the adolescent reader may also be freed from the neurotic fears and obsessions of guilt that often accompany the feeling that somehow he is unique and queer. (7) Literature also may suggest socially acceptable channels of expression for emotional drives that might otherwise take an anti-social form.

Perhaps he will be repelled by what may seem an excessively sociological, remedial, or even medicative emphasis in Professor Rosenblatt's description and turn with relief to Oscar James Campbell's confident assertion in *The Teaching of College English* (1936) that "literature should not serve as a crutch for a crippled life, but as both energy and guide to an abundantly eager one." Either way, it is another phrasing of what Percival Chubb, long principal of the high school department of the Ethical Culture School in New York, said more than half a century ago in his remarkable book on *The Teaching of English* (1902):

The supreme aim of literary and linguistic training is the formation of character. This includes and transcends all other aims. . . . The springs of a man's character are in his loves and hates, his tastes and de- sires, his ideals and aspirations; and the life of these depends much upon the light and the perspective with which they have been invested by the imagination. This imaginative exaltation of life, of noble longings and ideals, it is the province of art, and especially of literature as the highest art, to achieve, and, in turn, foster and communicate.

Speaking in the same voice for another generation, President Nathan M. Pusey of Harvard has declared: "The best teacher is not life, but the crystallized and distilled experience of the most sensitive, reflective, and most observant of human beings, and this experience you will find preserved in our great books and nowhere else." Other voices use other words, as they have through re- corded time, to say much the same thing. Thus the Commission on the English Curriculum of the National Council of Teachers of English in its report on *The English Language Arts* (1952) lists among the ends for which the teacher of literature must strive, the creation of "personal integrity, clarity of thought and expression, depth and breadth of understanding based upon sound knowledge and appreciation of moral, spiritual, and aesthetic values which comes from the association with the best men have thought, felt, and put into words throughout the ages."

Perhaps the poets say it best. Milton in *Areopagitica* spoke for all time when he called a great book "the precious life-blood of a master spirit," which by miraculous transfusion enriches other spirits. For our time, Stephen Vincent Benét in *They Burned the Books* (1942) speaks of literary masterworks as

> . . . man's memory and his aspiration,
> The link between his present and his past,
> The tools he builds with, all the hoarded thoughts
> Winnowed and sifted from a million minds,
> Living and dead, to guide him in his way.

III

All of these things are true, and require sober consideration. "We teachers of English," I. A. Richards has said, "have a great responsibility. We are guardians of the main channel through which has come down to us whatever is high-hearted, courageous, noble, passionate in its hopes for man, whatever is faithful, whatever is honorable, whatever is serious and sincere, whatever is most aware of man's nature and fate." Yet when confronted with so correct a statement of our responsibility, which we would modify only to supply the word *literature* in place of the word *English*, in order to make room for Confucius, Plato, Dante, Goethe, and the rest who have reached effectively toward definition of the spirit of man, we may recoil from it, much as Mark Van Doren, one of the supremely great teachers of our time, recoiled when he said, "That is fine, but few teachers of English deserve it."

Literature, written or properly read, shows forth man's continuing quest to understand himself. "For all our present shallowness of thought about the matter," says Mr. Van Doren in discussing *Liberal Education* (1943), "we do still recognize that man's distinguishing feature is his inability to know himself. He is a creature doomed to desire more knowledge, at least on this one point, than he will ever have. As a result, he is both more than he need be and less than he would be. If he could slay his desire he might be content to exist rather than live. But he wants to live;

and yet he never lives enough; that is, he never knows enough, for in proportion as he knows, he lives." When Pascal described man as an incomprehensible monster, when Emerson called him a glorious impossibility, they said much the same thing. The point is that as teachers, scholars, critics of literature our responsibility is larger than we. Yet, if we can not say with Melville's Ishmael, "I try all things; I achieve what I can," then we face only defeat which, in Mr. Van Doren's terms, is existence rather than life.

Among the things which must be tried, as I have suggested, is the impossible task of knowing not only, as Thoreau said, the best books, but also the best which has been discovered about them. The first quality of a good teacher, says Gilbert Highet in *The Art of Teaching* (1950), is knowledge of his subject: "He must know what he teaches. This sounds obvious; yet it is not always practiced." Therefore teaching is inseparable from learning, from scholarship, from critical reading. It is true, as Mr. Highet goes on to say, that

one cannot understand even the rudiments of an important subject without knowing its higher levels—at least not well enough to teach it. Every day the grossest and most painful blunders are made not only by teachers but by journalists and radio commentators who have the public ear, because they confidently state a half-truth which they have read in an encyclopedia article, or because they lay down as gospel a conjecture once uttered by an authority they admired. And many teachers, trying to explain certain problems in their own subject, fall into explanations suggested to them by a colleague or thrown up by their imagination, which are nevertheless totally wrong, and which an extending knowledge of the field would have corrected long ago.

Blunders will continue to be made, even—I almost said, especially—by the most dedicated of teachers. But blunders of ignorance are different in kind from blunders of aspiration. The first are static but self-perpetuating. The latter correct themselves as an inquiring mind continues to inquire, secure in its knowledge that a foolish consistency really is the hobgoblin of little minds. It is for this reason that this volume presumes to stand out against the notion put forward by one of our most distinguished authorities on the teaching of English—namely, that the problems of the teacher are not those of scholarship, but of attention and understanding. Attention and understanding are problems of essential importance, to be sure; they demand knowledge of method and they demand rich personal qualities without which any teacher would be handicapped. I shall not forget the conversation which my wife had many years ago with the wife of another graduate student who, like mine, was working while her husband completed an advanced degree. "I am sorry for you," the second wife said to mine. "When my husband receives his degree in Education, he can teach anything, but yours can teach only English."

If, as Gilbert Highet suggests, one of the chief duties of the teacher is to stimulate, we pause immediately to question: stimulate toward what? The first answer will inevitably be: toward learning, but the essence of the question remains: toward learning what? Even if Budd Schulberg had not brought the lesson forcefully home in *A Face in the Crowd*, we should still know enough of measures of persuasion to recognize that stimulation is in our culture easily managed. One of the most frightening travesties on education of which I know is committed by an otherwise respectable teacher who through his plausible ingenuity and astounding energy has risen perilously high in what are known as national educational circles. His claim to success is that he has developed a method of teaching which depends to no degree upon content: use his method, and you can teach anything—anything. I am told that the army is interested in his technique, which has been presented at the War College; agencies entrusted with pyschological warfare are interested; there is even something of it which Madison Avenue can be taught. The implications are paralyzing. Having seen the effective operation of techniques of persuasion in areas which are merely political, in this country as well as in Europe, it is terrifying and not naïve at all to consider, not just what has been done and is being done, but also what can effectively be done toward corruption of the spirit.

However he fancies up the word in telling of it, the teacher of English is or can be, perhaps even should be, a brain-washer, which is a coarser but more direct way of saying that he molds character. *Brainwashing* is a term of opprobrium used to describe what people we dislike do to people whom we think should view the world as we do. When Shakespeare or Milton, Albert Schweitzer or Billy Graham, tempts them to a view similar to ours, we call it something else. But the results, though not always the methods, are the same. Power over another's mind, even to a simple degree, can be enormously dangerous. But that is education, and that is literature also.

Potentially dangerous, but also potentially productive of the only good, persuasion by stimulation must be managed with care. Our defense against its malevolent forms is simply stated, but difficult beyond measure in execution. Louise M. Rosenblatt gets close to the center of it, but only close, when she says:

> Pre-eminently, we must ourselves possess a love of literature and a living sense of all it offers. And we should strive chiefly to avoid unconscious inculcation of our own bias, our own personal preoccupations, and our own unrecognized assumptions concerning human beings and social values. Our task is sincerely to re-enforce the student's own efforts to acquire a valid understanding of the factors that pattern human life. We must encourage and aid him to create for himself the flexible mental habits and the humane system of values that will be relevant to the life he himself must live under the complex and fluid conditions of contemporary society.

Love is great and will endure, and sincerity is the most precious of virtues. "If you don't love 'em," I was told by a wise teacher early in my career, "you can't learn 'em"—and, except that he had a strange theory about *The Canterbury Tales*, this wise teacher was usually, and in this instance certainly, right. But precisely because they are precious and very great, these best of human attributes require large energies if they are to be effectively maintained. And large energies require feeding, which is one of the things which scholarship does.

What to do is so much easier to know than how to do it. When we are best, we deal in subtle intangibilities which our words search desperately to express. To know what Keats meant by a "still unravished bride of quietness" means the labor of a lifetime. It means ferreting facts, some of which will be silly or inconsequential. It means understanding words and what they spoke to him and how differently they may speak to us, and the relation of what his words say to what other men have said. It means also knowledge of the unhappiness which allowed him to write so beautifully, with tantalizing meaning suspended from tantalizing meaning, and of the ecstatic moments when he saw truth and beauty briefly face to face. And it means an honest appraisal of the continuing impact of his irony or his idealism as it impinges on our own quest. It has never been possible to know Keats fully without knowing Spenser, and it is necessary now to know Faulkner also. These are some of the things toward which scholarship strives. And there are many more.

For scholarship, which is honest intelligence at work, is our only defense against all the versions of vulgarity which tempt to tranquility. There are books in plenty on method, and there are courses on teaching which are good to take not only because of what they accomplish toward salary increases. Beyond them, there is experience which alone can discover how techniques must be adapted to variations among individuals or groups. And beyond that are sincerity and love, a conscience and a healthy personality —all the fine human traits which make a fine teacher. But beyond all these, giving body to the skeletal structure, lies knowledge of, interest in, and enthusiasm for what one is to teach. Nothing can take its place, and the student is quicker than the supervisor in detecting its absence.

This book, then, is not against anything, except sloth. It exists because of a recognition of the tremendous difficulty and the importance of the labor which teachers of English have undertaken. In one sense, it is a series of statements about respect for their profession, presented by scholars who are also teachers and critics; and it is an invitation to teachers everywhere, who are their associates in a joint enterprise, to share with them something of this respect. For scholarship is certainly the business of the teacher, and criticism his function. Scholarship offers returns directly in proportion to the intelligence dedicated to it. It may not always be what is sometimes too facilely called original research, resulting in original contributions to knowledge. Originality in scholarship or anything else is the rarest of commodities.

Nothing, I think, better illustrates the variety of approaches toward literature than the differences in tone and temper, attitude and assumption, set forth by the essays in this volume. No two of the scholar-critics who discuss areas in which they are actively at work speak with the same voice. Almost every school of interpretation is represented, except the Spinach School which says that literature is good for you and that you must take it whether you like it or not, the Pedestal School which demands that each reader walk softly and with hushed reverence bow before the effigy of a master, or the Gold Mine School which finds literature productive of nuggets for quotation or subjects for student themes.

For literature is so richly diverse that it submits finally to no party line, and scholarship is so various that it belongs to everyone with will intelligently to pursue it. What emphasis each places on that part of him which is scholar, or critic, or teacher will differ as greatly as do the physical, intellectual, and emotional qualities which make men, who are so much alike, each so very different. Scholarship appears in many guises. What is sometimes called pure research, the kind that engages the theoretical physicist or the mathematical logician, probably does not exist in the humanities, which are man-centered and man-structured. The scholar's single foundation is honesty, a willingness to recognize and face up to fact, and to follow wherever it seems to lead. He may investigate historical background or biographical detail, be Freudian, Marxian, or just his own quizzical self; he may be intrigued by linguistics, which is the history of mankind; he may be concerned with structural analysis or the quest for mythic archetypes; or he may simply test in classroom or study the findings of other men.

In the largest sense, scholarship is a state of mind. Some of the busiest young men in libraries who ape the gestures of scholarship are not scholars at all but pack rats hoarding bright materials which belong to other men. But all the glitter is not gold, and we sometimes think they might be more gainfully employed. When honest and inquisitive, every teacher is a scholar, and a critic as well. If he is not—if, as Henry James said of a not unrelated subject, he has not the root of the matter in him—then he is not teacher, but something else: a skilled mechanic, a drillmaster, or—to return to our former analogy—an adept and soothing masseur or a ruthlessly accomplished process-server. Our confidence that many teachers share our conviction of the dignity of our profession and of the teacher's multiple responsibility—to himself, to society, and to the art to which he is dedicated—have encouraged us to present this collection of critical essays on contemporary scholarship.

THE PERIODS

3

Beowulf, Chaucer, and Their Backgrounds

GEORGE K. ANDERSON

SINCE 1930 THE ATTENTION OF scholars has been directed more than ever before to medieval literature as literature, and not as merely a source of information concerning the Old English language and the Middle English language and their dialects. Perhaps the most noteworthy accomplishment of their scholarship has been the way in which, while accepting, consolidating, and improving on the achievements of the great German linguists of the nineteenth century, it has tended to break away from the often stultifying effects of their overwhelming emphasis upon language and has turned to a renewed study of the important monuments of Old and Middle English literature not only as social documents but also as works of art.

Not unnaturally, it is Chaucer who has been the main object of research, criticism, and appreciation, for disregarding the statement that the *Beowulf* Poet is as great an artist as Chaucer, we are safe in calling Chaucer the greatest English writer before Shakespeare. In the past twenty-five years or so, more than one thousand studies of Chaucer have in one way or another found their way into print, as articles, extended notes, bibliographies, and full-length books—for supplementary purposes, see Albert C. Baugh's "Fifty Years of Chaucer Scholarship," *Speculum* (1951). But Old English literature in general, and *Beowulf* in particular, has not been exactly ignored, and it is convenient to begin this chapter with a consideration of some of the studies of this period at the dawn of English literature, which in spite of the illumination cast upon individual works of the period, remains on the whole still a dawn.

I

The first consideration of any scholar who approaches a given field is, of course, to ascertain what there is to study. Since 1930 there have been four most helpful bibliographies of Old English literature, beginning with Arthur H. Heusinkveld and Edwin J. Bashe's *A Bibliographical Guide to Old English* (1931), and followed by those in W. L. Renwick and Harold Orton's *The Beginnings of English Literature* (1939), the *Cambridge Bibliography of English Literature* (1941), and George K. Anderson's *The Literature of the Anglo-Saxons* (1949). The Old English Group in the Modern Language Association of America is at present preparing what should be a definitive bibliography, in so far as any such bibliography ever can be definitive. Obviously we are not likely to acquire many more primary texts in the field, and the collecting of bibliographical and critical data about these surviving primary texts, while difficult, is not impossible. It is well to remember, nevertheless, that our knowledge of the total product of Old English writers will always be incomplete, as R. M. Wilson has shown in his challenging articles on "Lost Literature in Old and Middle English" and "More Lost Literature in Old and Middle English," *Leeds Studies in English and Kindred Languages* (1933, 1936, 1937).

The archaeologists, however, refuse to admit that there is not more to learn, at least about Old English civilization, if not about its literature: the researches of G. Baldwin Brown on *The Arts in Early England* (1903–37) have been extremely valuable, as have the studies by R. H. Hodgkin in *The History of the Anglo-Saxons* (1935), R. G. Collingwood and J. N. L. Myres in *Roman Britain and the English Settlements* (1936), and F. M. Stenton in *Anglo-Saxon England* (1943). The ethnology and ethnography of the Germanic nations in general and of the Anglo-Saxons in particular have been the subject of a magnificent work by G. Schütte, *Our Forefathers—the Gothonic Peoples* (1929–33); the religion of these people and their application of magic and superstition to ritual has engrossed G. Storms in *Anglo-Saxon Magic* (1948). The excavations at Sutton Hoo, described by R. L. S. Bruce-Mitford in *The Sutton Hoo Ship-Burial* (1947) and in an article in the *Scientific American* (1951), as well as other excavation elsewhere, have thrown light not only upon Anglo-Saxon ship-building but also upon Anglo-Saxon technical arts and musical instruments. Many useful if somewhat tenuous interpretations of the backgrounds of the Old English language and its literature have come out of the labors of Scandinavian scholars of the past generation, such as Eilert Ekwall, O. S. (Andersson) Arngart, E. Wadstein, and others. It is amazing how much about Anglo-Saxon culture, at least at certain levels, can be gleaned from R. F. Jessup's *Anglo-Saxon Jewellery* (1950).

As to the Old English literature itself, recent scholars seem to have found the poetry more rewarding than the prose, although the studies of Dorothy Whitelock, Kenneth Sisam, and Dorothy Bethurum[1] in the homiletic prose of Aelfric and Wulfstan have done much to establish the often neglected fact that English prose begins in the Old English age. And no student of medieval English literature should overlook R. W. Chambers's essay *On the Continuity of English Prose from Alfred to More and His School* (1932). We must give high place to the most important recent contribution to textual scholarship in Old English poetry—the series of "Anglo-Saxon Poetic Records," initiated by George Philip Krapp in 1931, and continued by Elliott Van Kirk Dobbie—for in these excellent publications we come as close as we probably can to a final text of Old English poetry, not only as it is found in the four important repositories (the *Beowulf* MS., the Junius MS., *The Exeter Book*, and *The Vercelli Book*) but in the scattered pieces as well. On the basis of these imposing pieces of textual scholarship, we are now in a position to discuss more cogently the matter of Old English poetic style, and this scholars are doing in an interesting if often necessarily speculative manner.

As a matter of fact, the actual materials of Old English poetry have during the past generation been receiving close scrutiny. The question of the unity of those two fine elegiac poems, *The Wanderer* and *The Seafarer*, as well as other considerations relating to them, are treated satisfactorily by Bernard Huppé in "*The Wanderer*: Theme and Structure," *JEGP* (1943), and O. S. (Anders-

---

[1] See, for instance, Dorothy Whitelock's edition of Wulfstan's *Sermo Lupi ad Anglos* (1939), Kenneth Sisam's "MSS. Bodley 340 and 342: Aelfric's *Catholic Homilies*," *RES* (1931), and especially Dorothy Bethurum's "Archbishop Wulfstan's Commonplace Book," *PMLA* (1942).

son) Arngart in *The Seafarer: An Interpretation* (1937). Cecilia
Hotchner's *Wessex and Old English Poetry: With Special Consideration of The Ruin* (1939) shows evidence of literature
in Wessex before 800 and suggests that *The Exeter Book* was
compiled at Glastonbury. Apart from the question of the structure of a given piece, however, there is the larger question of
style. The old idea that the Anglo-Saxon poet drew upon a
large storehouse of metaphor and kenning, alliterative formulas
and repetitive stratagems, has been brought into sharp focus
by the article by F. P. Magoun on "Oral-Formulaic Character
of Anglo-Saxon Narrative Poetry," *Speculum* (1953), and the
matter is being carried further by Robert Creed in *PQ* (1956).
The obvious surface result of such study has been a confirmation of the critic's point of view that the Old English poetic
style (and, by extension, all Old Germanic poetic styles) was as
rigid and exacting as that of any major period of English literature,
not excluding the notable exigencies of neoclassical poetical requirements. To continue with this kind of research, moreover, will
enable us to understand better the texture of Old English poetry.
We should then have all the more reason for accepting the *Beowulf*
Poet, for instance, as a superior artist, although to take seriously
Kemp Malone's lopsided statement, in *MLN* (1949), that the
Beowulf Poet is as great an artist as Chaucer is to lose sight of the
primary requirements of range, versatility, and humanity.

All the same, there is no doubt that the *Beowulf* Poet is receiving a greater due, as a poet, than heretofore, and this is true also
of Cynewulf and the poets of his and the Caedmonian cycles. We
hear much less today about the faulty structure of *Beowulf* or its
lax architectonics; indeed, the repetitious elements in the poem,
which are there for even the neophyte to see, have been given
a defense which is probably excessive. In other respects, too,
Beowulf has undergone much discussion and been subjected to
much hypothesizing—the general origins of the poem, as outlined
by J. R. Hulbert in "Surmises Concerning the *Beowulf* Poet's
Source," *JEGP* (1951), though equally important is his "The
Genesis of *Beowulf*: A Caveat," *PMLA* (1951); the folkloristic
elements, as in J. R. Tolkien's challenging statement in *Beowulf:
The Monsters and the Critics* (1937); the question as to the possible date of the composition of the poem, as in Ritchie Girvan's

study of *Beowulf and the Seventh Century* (1935), a date which cannot be far removed from the 700–750 area; the applicability of the poem as a "Mirror" poem, deriving from L. L. Schücking's address, printed in the *Bulletin of the Modern Humanities Research Association* (1929).

How were these Old English poems of the Golden Age from 700 to 850 delivered? For there were supposedly no readers of them until the time of the manuscripts, and those manuscripts which have survived do not date from before the tenth century— or before 850 at the earliest. The reconstruction of an Old English "gleewood" as a horsehair-strung instrument, as the Sutton Hoo investigators have postulated, contributes something to the picture, but we must still rely very much on guesswork. Here the important work of the past generation is unquestionably John C. Pope's *The Rhythm of Beowulf* (1942), for his analysis gives the harp its proper place and establishes the recitative manner as the probable one by which the *scop* entertained his audience.

Considering all these circumstances, a general history of Old English literature, as of any period in English literature, for that matter, becomes a precarious undertaking, to be dated on the day of its publication. If we omit consideration of the sketchy *Chapters on Old English Literature* (1935) by Elizabeth Wardale, then the only modern full-length treatment of Old English literature as a whole is that by George K. Anderson in *The Literature of the Anglo-Saxons* (1949); that is less than ten years old and already stands in need of revision. Another, in the series of Oxford histories, has been promised by John Pope. In the one-volume Oxford *History of English Literature* (1950), edited by Hardin Craig, Anderson has taken the position that Old English literature should be treated as part of medieval English literature, although it obviously deserves a separate chapter, and although Kemp Malone and A. C. Baugh have divided Old and Middle English literatures into separate "books" in the Appleton-Century *A Literary History of England* (1948), their combined efforts, in spite of Malone's noted distrust of the effects of the Norman Conquest, have had much the same general effect. Both of these general histories, incidentally, are good performances, although many have found the somewhat shorter Oxford book the more readable for the general student.

There have been a few translations of Old English literature since 1930, but only Charles Kennedy's translation of *Beowulf: The Oldest English Epic* (1940) has gained any particular prominence. Otherwise old wine has been better than new.

II

The gap between 1066 and Chaucer, no matter how fashionable it is becoming to treat all English literature before 1500 as "medieval," is nevertheless so considerable, and the intervening literature so neglected, that one might well hope for a little less time henceforth given over to Chaucer and a little more to Walter Map and the literary progeny of Geoffrey of Monmouth. Not that this neglect is inexplicable. Chaucer, who has quite deservedly been experiencing a great vogue for over a generation, is still one of the most thoroughly civilized writers in all English literature and—as Raymond Preston points out in an otherwise crotchety book, *Chaucer* (1952)—one of the best balanced. His range of human insight can continually amaze us. A general tendency has persisted throughout the past quarter-century to reappraise both his works and his life, so that the portrait emerging differs in many respects from that which was recognized at the beginning of the present century. Instead of an easy-going, gentle dilettante, we see him now as a hard-working and successful man of affairs, who was far from indifferent to his own times, even though he did not write much about them. Of the many studies of this phase of his character, in so far as we can judge them through his more personal works, the most impressive is probably Roger Loomis's "Was Chaucer a Laodicean?" in *Essays and Studies in Honor of Carleton Brown* (1940), to which I must refer later, but many passages in more extensive studies bring us to the same conclusion.

It is doubtful how much more we shall discover in the way of biographical facts about Chaucer, but there is no question that the continuing compilation of Chaucer's Life-Records, under the direction of Martin Crow and Clair Olson, and described by Olson in *The Emerging Biography of a Poet* (1953), is of enormous value, for whatever scraps of information can be picked up will add just that much more to the story. In a short compass, however, it would be difficult to improve upon the biographical sketch in the latest edition of F. N. Robinson's Cambridge Edition of *The*

Complete Works of Geoffrey Chaucer (1933, revised 1957). Suffice to say that the definitive biography of Chaucer, if one is at all possible, must await the further findings of the Life-Records.

The past third of a century, at any rate, has given us the magnificent one-volume edition of Chaucer by Robinson, just mentioned; the definitive *The Text of The Canterbury Tales* (the 1940 "Chicago" edition by John M. Manly and Edith Rickert); the comparably excellent edition of *Troilus and Criseyde* (1926) by Robert K. Root; the completely renovated *Sources and Analogues of The Canterbury Tales* (1941) edited by W. F. Bryan and Germaine Dempster, although this last-named, in view of the fact that it is a compilation of the work of many authors, must remain uneven. Besides, any such study of sources and analogues, particularly analogues, must be constantly kept up to date, especially when it deals with those works of Chaucer for which there is no known primary source—for example, *The Pardoner's Tale*. New analogues are always turning up; since the publication of the new *Sources and Analogues*, I have found a new analogue to *The Pardoner's Tale* in the course of my study of something altogether different (see my *"Die Silberlinge des Judas* and the Accursed Treasure," *SP*, 1951), and others have had a similar experience. This objection, however, is obvious and cannot detract from the solid worth of the volume which Bryan, Dempster, and their numerous contributors have assembled.

Editions and source-studies are one thing; individual considerations of special topics in Chauceriana are another. Whoever examines the mass of academic brain-children—and brainstorms—produced in this field since 1930 will be thoroughly disheartened by their sheer numbers. On an average we have had between 40 and 50 books or articles about Chaucer each year, to say nothing of the reviews and comments concerned with these various items. A remarkable thing is the steadiness of output; seldom, even during the war-years, were there less than 35, and on the other hand never more than 55. Now statistics are of no great significance in such a survey, but they make evident one point, and that is that there have been more publications by American scholars than by English in the ratio of about three to one. Nor is this difference to be accounted for primarily by the war, for the ratio held good in the 1930's, as it holds good today. Is this because Chaucer appeals more to Americans, who find in him a freshness and novelty because they have never had a medieval tradition? Or do his forthrightness and his deceptive simplicity produce the appeal? Perhaps, however, the preponderance of American contributions loses some of its significance when it is realized that the total from the American side comprises many more studies of minutiae than the total from across the Atlantic; and many of these items, not precisely worthless, are not very important.

A complete bibliography of Chauceriana since 1930 could be assembled from the usual sources: the annual bibliographies of the Modern Humanities Research Association (since 1920), suspended during the second world war, now resumed and brought up through 1947; the annual bibliographies of the Modern Language Association of America, published in *PMLA;* the *Cambridge Bibliography of English Literature;* the revised bibliographies in John E. Wells's *Manual of the Writings in Middle English, 1050– 1400* (1916, revised 1945 by Beatrice D. Brown, Eleanor K. Henigham, and Francis L. Utley). But we now have the excellent performance by D. D. Griffith in his *Bibliography of Chaucer, 1909–1953* (1955).

By and large, most of this output of scholarly and critical research has busied itself primarily with Chaucer as artist, poet, official, man of affairs, and humanist. These are basically literary and critical studies, as is only appropriate to one who in the opinion of many is second only to Shakespeare. Relatively little of this scholarship has dealt with Chaucer's language, and it is a pleasure to report that the old-fashioned college course in Chaucer which was first of all a course in Middle English has been virtually supplanted today by the course which considers Chaucer's language as only a means to an end, and that end the study of a literary artist. The most notable works of the period to treat his language would probably be F. Karpf's *Studien zur Syntax an den Werken Geoffrey Chaucers* (1930); the revised edition of Samuel Moore's *Historical Outlines of English Morphology and Phonology* (1925) by A. H. Marckwardt, under the new title of *Historical Outlines of English Sounds and Inflections* (1951)—note the concession to the ignorant reader implied in the change; and H. Kökeritz's *A Guide to the Pronunciation of Chaucer* (1954). Even so, there is nothing especially startling in these soundly conceived books.

As a matter of fact, the most lively controversy in the field of Chaucerian linguistics actually has more to do with Chaucer's prosody, in particular the disposition of the final *e*'s, in which Ruth B. McJimsey in *Chaucer's Irregular -e* (1942) and James G. Southworth in *Verses of Cadence* (1954), but particularly in "Chaucer's Final -e in Rhyme," *PMLA* (1947), depart rather radically from the older tradition of pronouncing the final *e* at the end of a line or before the main caesura. Southworth was answered by E. Talbot Donaldson in "Chaucer's Final -e," *PMLA* (1948), and he replied energetically in "Chaucer's Final -e (Continued)," *PMLA* (1949). His theory that the final *e* need not be pronounced at the end of the line may be acceptable enough metrically, but does not solve the problem of the *e* elsewhere in the line, where it must obviously be pronounced at times to make the line metrically sufficient. There is no inclination among Chaucerians today to assume that Chaucer was a slovenly metrical artist (even if he himself did reproach Adam Scriveyn); rather it would appear that Chaucer, like other English poets of his time, was a rather grim prosodist. There is undeniably a tendency, however, in the light of this dispute about the essential matter of the final *e*, to be much less dogmatic about the reading of Chaucer's verse, although few would agree with the late Karl Young, who on more than one occasion was heard by the present writer to remark that since we know nothing except theory about Chaucer's pronunciation, it would make little difference how we read him, provided we made our reading metrical. It is true that we are ignorant, but not that ignorant.

In another linguistic corner, Joseph Mersand, in *Chaucer's Romance Vocabulary* (1937), points out that Chaucer's use of words of French origin is twice as frequent as that of his (on one occasion) Francophile friend Gower, but he observes also that the peak of this romance vocabulary occurs around the Troilus years (1385–86) and recedes in *The Canterbury Tales*.

The studies of individual works by Chaucer are concerned for the greater part with *Troilus and Criseyde*, certain of *The Canterbury Tales* (especially those of the Knight, the Clerk, the Squire, the Merchant, the Man of Law, and the Pardoner, but scattered studies can be found of any one of the individual tales), *The House of Fame*, *The Parliament of Fowls*, *The Legend of Good Women*, and the *Boethius*. Many of the individual pilgrims have been the subject of various interpretations, but on the whole it is rather surprising that there has not been more discussion of the *Prologue* to *The Canterbury Tales* itself.

Of course anyone dealing with *Troilus and Criseyde* must deal also with the whole matter of the courtly lover. This is therefore a good time to mention C. S. Lewis's admirable study, *The Allegory of Love* (1936), to my mind the soundest treatment of this nebulous topic. The tendency to treat *Troilus and Criseyde* as merely a skillful and original adaptation of Boccaccio's *Filostrato* has been swept away by the helpful analysis of R. M. Lumiansky, "The Story of Troilus and Briseide according to Benoit and Guido," *Speculum* (1954). When Robert A. Pratt publishes the results of his investigation into the possible use by Chaucer of a French prose version of the *Filostrato*, it may be that we shall have a much clearer picture of the way Chaucer proceeded in the writing of his masterpiece and perhaps be in a position to explain Chaucer's peculiar silence about his Italian contemporary (see Pratt's "Chaucer and *Le Roman de Troyle et de Criseida*," *SP*, 1956). Yet when it comes to the interpretations of the leading characters in *Troilus and Criseyde*, one finds that little of any great novelty has been added in the present generation—the older studies of Kittredge, Root, Tatlock, Lowes, and Young, still of surprising vitality, have not been moved from their pedestals. Even before 1930 the number of good studies of the personality of Criseyde alone was large. In the main, though, we should praise Thomas A. Kirby's *Chaucer's Troilus: A Study in Courtly Love* (1940), which is an extremely helpful summation, although the author is probably unsuccessful in tracing the development of Criseyde from Book I through Book V. But what can one do about this? Chaucer was condemned by the requirements of his well-known narrative to make Criseyde do what she did. Besides, her actions, no matter how attractive she has been shown to be, are conceivable enough in real life. Karl Young's "Chaucer's *Troilus and Criseyde* as Romance," *PMLA* (1938), takes sharp issue with the often quoted description of the work as a psychological novel. This is an able and provocative article, though difficult to square with the poem as it stands, with two-thirds of the work in direct discourse, Criseyde assigned a notable interior monologue, and the development of character throughout three-dimensional and dynamic, even in the case of the unadventurous Troilus—see B. J. Whiting, "Troilus and Pilgrims in Wartime," *MLN* (1945). The conspicuous use of proverbs throughout the work, both in the direct discourse and also in the interior monologues, has been discussed in convincing manner by R. M. Lumiansky in "The Function of the Proverbial and Monitory Elements in Chaucer's *Troilus and Criseyde*," *Tulane University Studies in English* (1950), where it is shown that the proverbs have direct bearing upon the characterization and are not employed as a mere stylistic device. Gordon H. Gerould, in *Chaucerian Essays* (1952), takes an optimistic view of Troilus in the eighth sphere at the end of the poem; indeed, a host of scholars have come to the defense of Chaucer's harshly criticized conclusion to the poem—unfortunately too many to list here.[2] The generally favorable comment on Chaucer's use of his source-material is typified by Donald C. Boughner's "Elements of Epic Grandeur in the *Troilus and Criseyde*," *ELH* (1939), which demonstrates how, even by employing common medieval rhetorical devices, Chaucer makes his work a much more philosophical poem than the *Filostrato*. This preference for the English poet over his Italian contemporary is surprisingly seconded by an Italian scholar, Alberto Castelli, whose *Geoffrey Chaucer* (1946) is, incidentally, very good as an exposition of the Continental attitude toward Chaucer. At that, however, his willingness to accept Chaucer as a greater artist than Boccaccio is unusual for a Latin critic.

A few words should be said about a new interpretation of *Troilus and Criseyde* by George G. Williams in "Who Were Troilus, Criseyde, and Pandarus?" *Rice Institute Pamphlet Honoring George Wesley Whiting* (1957). According to him, the poem is in effect a *roman à clef*. The narrative was inspired by John of Gaunt's affair with Katharine Swynford, Chaucer's sister-in-law. Troilus is, then, John of Gaunt; Criseyde is Katharine Swynford; and Pandarus is none other than Chaucer himself. To be sure, there is no reason why Chaucer's work should not be based upon some real situation, however much one might wish to think that this true masterpiece of the Middle English era was not just a

---

[2] See, however, the 1957 edition of F. N. Robinson's *The Complete Works of Geoffrey Chaucer*, p. 837, note to 11. 1835—1855.

roman à clef. Some of the many points of argument which Williams adduces are certainly admissible; others are notably weak—if Chaucer is coy about Criseyde's age (one of the oldest humorous clichés in the Occidental world), it does not mean that he is coy because he is thinking of a real person. He could be fully as coy about a fictional character, Chaucer being Chaucer. There are similar objections to other arguments in his article, but space forbids any elaboration of them here. Suffice it that the theory stand the test of time. Who Diomed was in this real situation, Williams deponeth not.

As I have already observed, most of the recent studies of *The Canterbury Tales* have been either interpretations of the various pilgrims or attempts to approach what may have been Chaucer's original design in the collection—the order of the tales, especially with reference to the order of the Groups following the Epilogue to *The Man of Law's Tale* (Skeat's Group B1, Robinson's Fragment II): the so-called Bradshaw shift. In this knotty and highly technical business of textual scholarship, Germaine Dempster has been brilliant: she has contributed at least five important studies. It should be remarked in passing that the momentum for most of this technical investigation was furnished by the labors of Manly and Rickert in their preparation of the Chicago text already mentioned. But a few years before the Chicago text, J. S. P. Tatlock had indicated, in his "*The Canterbury Tales* in 1400," *PMLA* (1935), his belief that the titles, headings, and groupings are not Chaucer's, although perhaps some of the marginal notes may be. It is, of course, impossible to find the archetype manuscript of *The Canterbury Tales* among the dozens of extant manuscripts. But Mrs. Dempster tells us much about the methods of medieval scribes in "Manly's Conception of the Early History of *The Canterbury Tales,*" *PMLA* (1946). According to her, the nearest we can get to Chaucer's original manuscript would be a scribe's copy of the holograph, which may have been made on wax.

It is beyond the scope of this review even to attempt to follow the details of the possible rearrangement of the tales, especially since Robert A. Pratt's "The Order of *The Canterbury Tales,*" *PMLA* (1951), suggests pretty clearly that Chaucer himself had not settled upon the order. The subject, however, remains fascinating not only to the specialist but also to anyone concerned with the workings of a great writer's architectonic sense. An older study by Marian L. S. Lossing, "The Order of *The Canterbury Tales*," *JEGP* (1938), is remarkably perceptive but has been superseded by the following four articles by Germaine Dempster: "A Chapter of the Ms. History of *The Canterbury Tales*," *PMLA* (1948); "A Period in the Development of *The Canterbury Tales*," *PMLA* (1953); "Chaucer's Manuscript of Petrarch's Version of the Griselda Story," *MP* (1943); and "The Fifteenth-Century Editors of *The Canterbury Tales* and the Problem of Tale-Order," *PMLA* (1949). Carleton Brown's "Three Notes on the Text of *The Canterbury Tales*," *MLN* (1941), is of special interest because of its description of passages which may have been revised by Chaucer. Brown followed this with a more general study, "Author's Revision in *The Canterbury Tales*," *PMLA* (1942).

To the layman the problem of interpretation is always of greater appeal than the question as to which tale came where, especially since attempts to argue any over-all design for *The Canterbury Tales* have come to grief in the past. Of course the obvious pairing of tales through a quarrel (the Miller-Reeve and the Friar-Summoner combinations) needs no comment. The Marriage Group still has strong support, although it is under heavy fire at present and certainly does not seem to stand in so compact a position as it did when Kittredge first described it in 1912.

III

In a moment I shall comment again upon the Marriage Group, but first I should like to touch upon some of the studies of individual tales, with the understanding that it will be impossible to consider all of them. The *Prologue* to *The Canterbury Tales* has had two good, quite different treatments. Muriel Bowden has done a full-length book on the subject, *A Commentary on the General Prologue to The Canterbury Tales* (1948),[3] sometimes brash, sometimes downright stuffy, sometimes uncertain how to approach its audience, but full of good material and unquestionably worth consulting. H. M. Lumiansky's *Of Sondry Folk* (1955) comes near to being an outright popularization, but that is no sin, especially since Lumiansky is a remarkably discerning analyst.

---

[3] The work, however, does not confine itself solely to the *Prologue*, but rather to characters described in the *Prologue*.

Otherwise, as remarked earlier, the studies of the *Prologue* have been overshadowed by those of the individual tales and of the pilgrims who tell them.

The Knight's Tale has, of course, become a favorite topic, not only because it is the longest and most elaborate in the collection, but also because it lends itself best to abstract speculation, even allegory, which certain present-day critics can smell a mile away. Moreover, it veers from Boethian philosophy to what seems at times a travesty on the medieval romance, with all sorts of sly humor which some have seen as almost sacrilegious. At least one notable attempt has been made to displace the generally held belief that the work was written about the time of *Troilus and Criseyde*— that is, about 1385–86. This is the article of Johnstone Parr, "The Date and Revision of Chaucer's *Knight's Tale*," *PMLA* (1945); he places the tale some time after the middle of 1390, on the internal evidence which points to the triumph of Gloucester (Saturn) in 1387–89 and the coronation of Isabella of France in 1389, as well as the grand tournament sponsored by Richard II in May, 1390. But Robert Pratt in "Was Chaucer's *Knight's Tale* Extensively Revised?" *PMLA* (1948), has rejected Parr's theory and has been supported on this point by most Chaucerians. The contrast between the two young knights, Palamon and Arcite, which suggested to Hoxie Fairchild[4] the difference between the contemplative and the active life, respectively, has been impossible to miss. Courtland D. Baker in "A Note on Chaucer's *Knight's Tale*," *MLN* (1934), argued that Palamon, who sees Emily first, and who should therefore, according to the chivalric formula of love at first sight, have priority, is more Platonic than the more earthy Arcite; and the fact that Palamon ultimately wins Emily seemed to him a vindication of sacred over profane love. But this, it seems to me, is going too far.

Of the many ingenious interpretations of *The Knight's Tale*, that of William Frost stands out. In "An Appreciation of Chaucer's *Knight's Tale*," *RES* (1948), he observes that the work develops out of three widening concentric circles of interest. First, there is the human interest itself. In reference to this, one could hardly do better than quote Robinson's comment on the critical writing

[4] This appeared before 1930; see *JEGP*, XXVI, 285 ff. But it started a discussion.

that swirls about *The Knight's Tale*. In speaking of an article by J. R. Hulbert in *SP* (1929), which takes the position that the real purpose of the tale was to set forth a typical "question of love" as to "which of two young men of equal worth and with almost equal claims shall (or should) win the lady," Robinson gives this warning:

> This problem is doubtless involved in the story, and would have been more apparent in the Middle Ages than today. But *The Knight's Tale* would never have engaged, as it does, the sympathy of the reader if it had been written primarily as a discussion of such an academic problem. And the *Teseida*, we are assured, grew out of Boccaccio's emotional experience.[5]

Nor, I might add, would *Troilus and Criseyde* still be considered a masterpiece if it were to be reduced solely to the level of a *roman à clef*.

I trust I may be pardoned for the parenthesis. The first of Frost's circles, then—the human interest, is extremely important, and it would be a good thing if more present-day Chaucerians, or general critics of literature, for that matter, would give more attention to this kind of interest. The second circle of interest is that which considers two young noblemen as rivals in love and the ethical conflict between love and comradeship. The third circle of interest is the theological one, attaching itself to the way Theseus demonstrates how a just Providence stabilizes a disintegrating human situation.

It is a rather discouraging thing to say, but with few exceptions, the bulk of the smaller studies of the individual tales leaves one with the impression of individual attacks upon difficult if not insoluble problems, though occasionally one hits the target squarely. A good example would be Germaine Dempster's "On the Source of the Deception Story in *The Merchant's Tale*," *MP* (1936), in which she shows pretty conclusively that Chaucer used a lost French *fabliau*. Too many of the others, however, are too often subjective interpretations. Perhaps, because of our imperfect grasp of the facts of Chaucer's times, his life, and his artistic intent, this subjectivity is inevitable. Sometimes, too, one may feel that the author would have done better if he had had more space and time in

---

[5] *The Complete Works of Geoffrey Chaucer* (1957), p. 670.

which to work. It is always a pleasure to come upon a sound and spacious kind of study such as J. Burke Severs's monograph, *The Literary Relationship of Chaucer's Clerk's Tale* (1942)—full, accurate, an excellent sequel to his contribution concerning *The Clerk's Tale* in the Bryan-Dempster *Sources and Analogues*. Effective in smaller compass is the study by Haldeen Braddy, "The Genre of Chaucer's *Squire's Tale*," *JEGP* (1942). *The Squire's Tale* has, of course, been a puzzle from the beginning. It is Braddy's contention that the real story starts in Part II, and that Chaucer intended to tell tales within tales, in the manner of *The Arabian Nights*. Presumably, then, Part I is to set up some kind of framework. He wonders whether Chaucer broke off this enormous project, which would assuredly have entailed a work of large dimensions separate from *The Canterbury Tales*, because Cembalo fought for his sister Canacee out of incest (bearing in mind *The Man of Law's Headlink*, 78)—in other words, for moral reasons. Or did he simply underestimate the inordinate length of his Oriental original, whatever that may have been? For, as Braddy had pointed out in another article on "The Oriental Origin of Chaucer's Canacee-Falcon Episode," *MLR* (1936), the episode in Part II is originally a Persian tale.

Most of the discussion of *The Man of Law's Tale* has concentrated on the Epilogue (and its authenticity) and the order of the tales following—the Bradshaw shift already mentioned—and need not concern us further, but it should be noted how the tendency is growing among Chaucerian scholars to continue the tales after the Epilogue with *The Shipman's Tale*. Alfred L. Kellogg in "An Augustinian-Interpretation of Chaucer's Pardoner," *Speculum* (1951), sees the Pardoner as an exemplification of the Augustinian belief in secret punishment: he is a degenerate spirit whose evil gnaws away at his vitals. A less drastic interpretation would be fairer, since, as Kellogg admits, Chaucer does not seem to feel quite so condemnatory about the Pardoner's manifest moral shortcomings. I wish to commend in passing the thoughtful comments in R. M. Lumiansky's "A Conjecture Concerning Chaucer's Pardoner," *Tulane Studies in English* (1949). Too often, as in G. H. Gerould's *Chaucerian Essays* (1953), we are treated with elaborate explanations of the obvious. And so the Pardoner is a drunkard, and the Wife of Bath is sex-obsessed.

More valuable are those writings which point up the possibilities of a new concept of a Canterbury pilgrim. Thus Chaucer's treatment of the Prioress may not be so good-humored as we had once been taught, for she clearly did not follow strictly the rules of her convent against the keeping of animals—see John M. Steadman, "The Prioress's Dogs and Benedictine Discipline," *MP* (1956). And is she not a vapid anti-Semite? A casual word or phrase in an obscure review can often be most revealing. Again, however, exigencies of space must limit my allusions. We all recognize Chaucer's expert knowledge of the astronomy of his time, but his grasp of alchemy is certainly not strong, as Pauline Aiken demonstrates in "Vincent of Beauvais and Chaucer's Knowledge of Alchemy," *SP* (1944), for most of the knowledge of that recondite pseudo-science which Chaucer parades in *The Canon's Yeoman's Tale* is derivative; worse than that, Chaucer did not by any means always understand his source. Yet even if his interest in alchemy was due to his having been swindled by William Shuchirch, there is no denying the fact that he was the leading astronomer of England in his lifetime. When, therefore, a treatise, *The Equatorie of the Planetis*, was recently discovered, it was assigned automatically if somewhat tentatively to Chaucer.[6]

The Marriage Group is going to have to withstand some assaults of no mean proportions in the future. It already had its enemies forty years ago, notably H. B. Hinckley (see *PMLA*, 1917), and considerably later Clifford P. Lyons in "The Marriage Debate in *The Canterbury Tales*," *ELH* (1935). At any rate, it would seem now that it can hardly be restricted to the four tales originally named by Kittredge—the Wife of Bath's, the Clerk's, the Merchant's, and the Franklin's—but should include also at least the *Melibeus* and *The Nun's Priest's Tale*. This was the point of the article by Germaine Dempster on "A Period in the Development of *The Canterbury Tales* Marriage Group and of Blocks B_2 and C" *PMLA* (1953). The slightly facetious suggestion might be made, moreover, that other tales dealing with marriage (the Miller's, the Man of Law's, the Shipman's, The Summoner's, and the Manciple's) might also be grist for Chaucer's matrimonial grinding.

[6] Derek J. Price, *The Equatorie of the Planetis* (1955); see also G. Herdan, "Chaucer's Authorship of *The Equatorie of the Planetis*: The Use of Romance Vocabulary as Evidence," *Language* (1956).

If this were true, we might as well dismiss the whole theory.

The real difficulty at present is, as I see it, that it no longer suffices to assume that *The Franklin's Tale* represents Chaucer's own theory of what the marriage relation should be. For one thing, it is doubtful that it can be as old as the magnificent *Merchant's Tale* or *The Wife of Bath's Prologue*, both of which are extremely severe on marriage. Of course, it could still have been placed after these by Chaucer for his own artistic and intellectual purposes. Another problem lies in the fact that the *Envoy to Bukton* brings in a discord. One of the last pieces, in all probability, that Chaucer ever wrote, its strictures on marriage are harsh, yet they have never been given recognition as such. A characteristic remark in reference to it is Robinson's; he says in his edition of *The Complete Works of Geoffrey Chaucer* (p. 864) that the anti-matrimonial sentiments are all familiar and traditional and are "not to be taken too seriously." All the misogynistic tradition of the Middle Ages, however, could not in itself engender the ironic personal bitterness that exudes from every line of the poem. It would appear that Chaucer, as he grew older, became more and more anti-clerical and evidently more anti-matrimonial also. That is his privilege; there is no reason why this should not be admitted, nor is there any reason why a great writer should be obliged to end up with an Everlasting Yea.

The remaining poems of Chaucer have drawn less attention to themselves. The enigmatic *House of Fame*, to be sure, has undergone further investigation. Paull F. Baum, in "Chaucer's *The House of Fame*," *ELH* (1941), divides the work into four parts instead of the usual three—that is, he divides the last book at the point where Aeolus has finished blowing his two trumpets of praise and slander. This may be a matter of reader's convenience, for it certainly does not help us to relate the first two books to the "litel laste" one any better than we can do it now. In a word, this kind of tinkering is of little value. But an older speculation by B. H. Bronson, in *Chaucer's House of Fame: Another Hypothesis* (1934), is decidedly useful. It is his theory that the "newe tydinges" in Book III may have been discreditable to some one "of greet auctoritee." If so, the unfinished state of the work may have been deliberate, and the piece is therefore scarcely to be termed a fragment. At that, there has been an undercurrent of belief that there was not much more left to Book III in any case. In the meantime I should mention another stimulating monograph by Bronson, *In Appreciation of Chaucer's Parlement of Foules* (1934), in which he considers the possibility that *The Parliament of Fowls* was primarily an ironic presentation rather than a mere love-vision. Its core was in effect, then, a debate between the idealistic and the realistic, and contained no political allegory as such. As time goes on, many Chaucerians today are adopting an attitude of skepticism towards the importance of the political allegory in the poem, which older scholars had pretty well taken for granted. Other articles on *The Parliament of Fowls* which will be found of interest are G. Stillwell's "Unity and Comedy in Chaucer's *Parlement of Foules*," *JEGP* (1950), and C. O. McDonald's "An Interpretation of Chaucer's *Parlement of Foules*," *Speculum* (1955).

As to *The Legend of Good Women*, Margaret Galway, in "Chaucer's Sovereign Lady: A Study of the Prologue to the 'Legend' and Related Poems," *MLR* (1938), has proposed that Alceste, who requires the "legendary" from the poet as penance for having written against love, was not Anne of Bohemia, first wife of Richard II, but the Queen-Mother Joan of Kent, who died in 1385. If an earlier date than that usually assigned the F-text of the *Prologue* to this work (1385) can be accepted, then Miss Galway's theory has much to commend it, but the matter is still obscure.

In the inevitable category of the miscellaneous, we should note that, according to V. L. Dédeck-Héry's "Jean de Meun et Chaucer, traducteurs de la Consolation de Boèce," *PMLA* (1937), and his "Le Boèce de Chaucer et les manuscrits français de la Consolation de Jean de Meun," *PMLA* (1944), Chaucer used Jean de Meun's translations from the original Latin quite freely. Since this had long been suspected, it serves merely as confirmation. In reference to this same point, there is also James M. Cline's "Chaucer and Jean de Meun: *De Consolatione Philosophiae*," *ELH* (1936). Something of a flurry arose in the 1930's over an article by Carleton Brown, "Chaucer's *Wreched Engendring*," *PMLA* (1935). The work referred to is that mentioned in the G-text (Skeat's A-version) of the *Prologue* to *The Legend of Good Women*, 414. Brown was of the opinion that *A Holy Meditacioun*, usually assigned to Lydgate's prose, was the missing piece of Chauceriana. This was disputed by J. S. P. Tatlock in "Has Chaucer's 'Wreched Engendring' Been Found?" *ELH* (1936), and although Brown reasserted his theory in rebuttal, his views have not been generally accepted.

IV

There still remain some of the most important studies of all— what I may call works on the general background of Chaucer, dealing with his times, his education, and his reading, whence the literary influences exerted upon him. There are also those studies which consider what J. S. P. Tatlock so felicitously called the mind and art of Chaucer.

It is a pity that two of the books in these general categories should have been left incomplete because of the deaths of their authors. Edith Rickert's *Chaucer's World* (1948) is an absorbing by-product of the researches which she and John M. Manly carried out through the whole range of fourteenth-century English life; it should definitely be classed as belonging to the "diplomatic" school of historiography, for its substance is in reality a series of documents contemporary with Chaucer—legal writs and wills, doctor's bills, figures on the cost of food, and more of the like. In a way it reminds one of G. G. Coulton's various collections of miscellaneous material, of which his *Medieval Panorama* (revised 1948) is very likely the best, but Miss Rickert's book is organized far more systematically than Coulton's. Even so, her material could have been presented with more expository tact; it is as if a large mass of informational matter had been dumped on the table before us, and we had then been asked to sort it out for ourselves. I regret to say that this is too often the method of far too many present-day scholars. The other truncated torso is J. S. P. Tatlock's *The Mind and Art of Chaucer* (1950). This book contains a valuable summary of the known facts of Chaucer's life, plus some of the author's typically incisive comment; some pertinent information about Chaucer's world; and observations, partly historical and partly critical, on some of the Minor Poems and some of *The Canterbury Tales*. But in most respects Tatlock is at his best in his discussion of *Troilus and Criseyde*. His most unusual suggestion, first made in his *Development and Chronology of Chaucer's Works* (1907), concerning the Chaucer Canon is that *Troilus and Criseyde* may well have been written before *The House of Fame*—a theory which, while not untenable, is certainly doubtful on metrical grounds alone.

We have seen already that there has been investigation into Chaucer's relationship to French writers in the case of Jean de Meun. Haldeen Braddy's *Chaucer and the French Poet Graunson* (1947) shows that the influence of this comparatively minor French contemporary poet was perhaps deeper on Chaucer than has hitherto been suspected. We have long been in need of a restatement of the influence of Deschamps, Machaut, and Froissart on Chaucer, and a thorough rechecking of Chaucer and the *Roman de la Rose*, for Dean S. Fansler's not too strong contribution on the latter subject in 1914 has become seriously outdated. This need seems to have been at least partially filled by Charles Muscatine's excellent *Chaucer and the French Tradition* (1957), which is useful for its discussion of poetic styles on a comparative literature basis, but its purpose to seek the "meaning" of Chaucer is impossibly over-ambitious, and its aim to dislodge the assumptions of "post-Victorian Chaucerians" (who were giants) falls short, so far as reaching the target is concerned.

As early as 1946 Robert A. Pratt, in "Karl Young's Work on the Learning of Chaucer," *A Memoir of Karl Young* (1946), commented on the likelihood that much of Chaucer's learning may have been derived from individual books, two of which were of special interest—(1) a standard medieval school reader, which included Dionysius Cato, Maximian, Statius, and Claudian; and (2) a collection of anti-marriage material—Valerius (Walter Map), Theophrastus's *Liber Aureolus*, and Jerome against Jovinian. In reference to this second collection, I note that Pratt is preparing an anthology of medieval misogynistic writings under the title of *The Jankyn Book*. In two trenchant articles[7] on Chaucer's use of sources, he insists on the need of examining the sources of Chaucer's works in the forms as near as possible to those which

[7] See his "Chaucer's Claudian," *Speculum* (1947), and "Chaucer's Use of the *Teseida*," *PLMA* (1947). See also his "The Importance of Manuscripts for the Study of Medieval Education, as Revealed by the Learning of Chaucer," *Progress of Medieval and Renaissance Studies* (1949).

would be available to Chaucer. Nothing could possibly be more "available" than a schoolbook. In passing, we should remember that a pioneer in the account of Chaucer's education was George A. Plimpton, in his *The Education of Chaucer* (1935).

In addition, we have had several full-length treatments of Chaucer's life and works. Some are good and some are indifferent, although it is difficult to say that any serious work on this poet is an absolute failure. A somewhat popularized example is Henry D. Sedgwick's *Dan Chaucer* (1934), which labors under its affected title; a more serious objection is that it tends to oversimplify and to be doctrinaire; for instance, it is scarcely adequate to divide the Pilgrims into "sympathetic" and "unsympathetic." A book like Marchette Chute's *Geoffrey Chaucer of England* (1946) is more difficult to classify, because it contains good scholarship and makes good reading; but it is of much greater value to the neophyte than to the experienced reader of Chaucer. Besides, while a woman can write perceptively and well about Chaucer's poetic art, as Dorothy Everett did in her Gollancz Memorial Lecture, "Some Reflections on Chaucer's 'Art Poetical,' " *Proceedings of the British Academy* (1952), and can be distinguished in textual scholarship, as Germaine Dempster and Edith Rickert are or have been, it remains an open question whether she can appreciate fully the robust, masculine, even Rabelaisian qualities of Chaucer's humanity—so necessary a part of the total picture, or whether she can understand and give proper attention to the reasons for anti-feminism, which even in the Middle Ages were not entirely a matter of theology.

One particularly exasperating book is G. K. Chesterton's *Chaucer* (1932), because it labors the obvious and is factually on uncertain ground all too often. Besides, it overstresses Chaucer's being a Catholic. Who has ever questioned the fact? Indeed, it tends to argue that since Chaucer was a Catholic, he was therefore a great writer, which is a *non sequitur*. Chesterton gratuitously informs us that the great-souled Shakespeare must also have been a Catholic, as if this were relevant to a study of Chaucer. And in similar condemnatory vein, although for entirely different reasons, we should pass over Kemp Malone's *Chapters on Chaucer* (1951), which is a pedestrian and superfluous performance. At that, however, neither of these works is quite so bad as that of H. H. Glunz who, in *Die Literaturästhetik des europäischen Mittelalters: Wolfram, Rosenroman, Chaucer, Dante* (1937), apparently does not believe that Chaucer was a poet of humor.

Not all of these general works, however, are so unsatisfactory. Percy Van D. Shelley's *The Living Chaucer* (1940) is an excellent all-round introduction, even if it is unpretentious and unheralded, for it stresses what is not too often stressed, although I suppose it is usually taken for granted: namely, the fact that Chaucer is a vital personality, not just a quaint and kindly story-teller. Even so, it illustrates the inevitable problem posed by the disconcerting detail that we are dealing with one whose life we can never know intimately, and so must needs fall back for our chief stimulus upon the writer's mind and art as he reveals it to us. Perhaps that is why Nevill Coghill's *The Poet Chaucer* (1947) is in my opinion a successful book; he faces the problem and recognizes it for what it is. It is true that one is not obliged to agree with Coghill that Chaucer's wit is always affirmative, but the author's faith in Chaucer's acceptance of things as they are; in his sensibility (*pitee*); in his delicate feeling for beauty, which, however, he never allows to obtrude too sensuously upon his business of narrative poet; and in his liquid musical line—all this makes for a generally sound and sensitive estimate, even if he may make Chaucer's affability too pronounced. Compared to this, D. S. Brewer's *Chaucer* (1953) is a run-of-the-mill but at least adequate study.

Within a somewhat narrower range, however, William Witherle Lawrence's *Chaucer and The Canterbury Tales* (1950) accomplishes far more than a run-of-the-mill critique. Perhaps Lawrence magnifies unduly the importance of the *fabliaux* in the collection as a whole, although it is time that these tales should come into their own. Perhaps he may appear heretical to some in his preference for internal evidence over the order in the best manuscripts as a way of fixing the sequence of the tales. After all, internal evidence, particularly in Chaucerian studies, while always interesting, can be notably ambiguous. Lawrence is of the opinion that Chaucer experienced a religious crisis in his later years and hence wrote the *Retraction* at the end of *The Canterbury Tales* in all sincerity. There is no reason to question this sincerity, but it still is worth remembering that there is something of a tradition for such a tail-piece. Moreover, there is nothing in Chaucer's demonstrably later works to suggest any such spiritual crisis. But Lawrence's book is at any rate a considerable help to Chaucer's critics.

So, too, is John Speirs's *Chaucer the Maker* (1951). No doubt the author is at times rather consciously unacademic, but that does no harm; he sometimes strains toward an elaborate exposition of metaphor in the manner of a New Critic when there is no crying need for it—even an ignorant layman will recognize what Criseyde meant when she called Pandarus a fox. But it is stimulating writing, all the same. A word of praise is due Howard R. Patch's *On Rereading Chaucer* (1939), which is pleasant reading and which shows much critical insight. While he is pointing out parallelisms and paradoxes, C. A. Owen, Jr., in his "Chaucer's *Canterbury Tales*: Aesthetic Design in the Stories of the First Day," *English Studies* (1954), is entertaining; but one can only wonder how many of these Chaucer knew he was making when he wrote. Paull F. Baum's "Chaucer's Puns," *PMLA* (1956) may be accepted as a legitimate listing of plays on words, whether for humor or for demonstrating virtuosity is uncertain. Some are clever; some are dull; and even the author must concede that some of them are decidedly farfetched.

Finally, there is a group of works of varying dimensions which will serve as useful pointers in the direction from which Chaucerian scholars of the future may derive profit. W. Héraucourt's *Die Wertwelt Chaucers* (1939) in a formidably Teutonic topical organization, is one of the few Continental studies of our generation to present in even balance Chaucer's poetic style and diction as well as his moral perceptions, which, the author insists, are *both* medieval *and* modern. Too many critics today treat Chaucer as if he actually were a modern. Another German publication, that of Wolfgang Clemen, *Der junge Chaucer* (1938), speaks in praise of Chaucer's humanity, evident even in his more immature works, of his loosening of traditional literary forms, and of the emergence of his unmistakable personality. Florence R. Scott's "Chaucer and the Parliament of 1386," *Speculum* (1943) explains that the poet's silence on contemporary events, for which he has often been reproached, is a diplomatic silence. It is not likely that a successful man of affairs who depended upon royal patronage could be expected to head crusades in either the political or the religious field. Roger Loomis's "Was Chaucer a Laodicean?" to which I have already referred, is an excellent statement of the fact that Chaucer was by no means a man of indifference but rather a hardworking public servant and a wise, observant, and sympathetic man.

I add here a brief note about translations of Chaucer, of which I must in principle disapprove, for it seems to me that any lover of literature should be willing to make the minimal amount of sacrifice of time and energy necessary to read Chaucer in the original. Although the translations mentioned here are all of them good enough, and at least one is brilliant, still Chaucer's poetic art cannot be fully appreciated if we read him in someone else's version, any more than we can in this way appreciate Homer or Dante. But in Chaucer's case there seems to me even less excuse, for he wrote in English—a remarkably expressive and musical kind of English. For the record, however, I should call attention to the prose translations by Lumiansky of both *The Canterbury Tales* (1948) and *Troilus and Criseyde* (1951), and the verse translations by Hill, Nicolson, Coghill, and Morrison.[8] Morrison's translation is a remarkably successful effort to reproduce in modern English, standard as well as colloquial and taking into account Americanisms, as many of the effects of the original as is possible. I believe that he suceeds as well as anyone could hope, although the result is still not Chaucer.

Ingenious, industrious, and dedicated to their subject—that is the net impression left by the more than 1000 pieces of writing about Chaucer which have been extant since 1930. Of course many of them are unnecessary, just as many of the multitudinous writings about Shakespeare are unnecessary, but the great majority of even these superfluous items are undoubtedly written with sincerity and conviction. Most of these 1000 items have been the work of what I call the historicists—if the scholarly world is to be divided between historicists and analysts—and I know of no better evidence than this to demonstrate that historicists not only can but must be analysts as well. In the meantime let the research and criticism go

---

[8] Frank E. Hill, *The Canterbury Tales: Translated into Modern English Verse* (1935); J. U. Nicolson, *The Canterbury Tales* (1935); Nevill Coghill, *Chaucer* (1952); and Theodore Morrison, *The Portable Chaucer* (1949).

on unconfined, but over all this activity I should like to cast this warning, written by J. S. P. Tatlock in his posthumously published *The Mind and Art of Chaucer* (1950):[9]

> But what is the ultimate reality of persons created by a poet's imagination? It is not the same as that of people who have really lived. In such people there were depths and unexpected peculiarities which leave uncertain traces but may be guessed at, contradictory traits which leave us bewildered but may have to be accepted as due to unknown complexities. No such unknown traits should be postulated in characters created by a poet, for the ultimate reality of such characters is solely what was intended by the poet-creator; *what he shows no sign of intending is not the reality, however attractive.*

V

After reviewing the mass of material concerning Chaucer, one could almost believe that there were no other Middle English writers of importance. But our generation of scholars cannot be called idle in other areas of the medieval. Their activities are beyond the scope of this chapter, but the bibliographical aids I have already mentioned will give some idea of their range. Especially important is Eugene Vinaver's edition of Malory's *Morte Darthur* (1947), in my opinion the best yet published. George R. Coffman and others have attempted valiantly, though I regret to say without conspicuous success, to rehabilitate John Gower.[10] A great deal has been done with Arthurian material, such as the investigations into many aspects of the Grail legend by Roger Sherman Loomis: for instance the magnificent study of the art portrayals of the Legend by himself and his wife, Laura Hibbard Loomis, as well as his study of the part played by Chrétien de Troyes.[11] A. C. L. Brown's *The Origin of the Grail Legend* (1943) is of great value, although it strikes me that the author tends to stress too much the Irish contribution at the expense of the Welsh. And even passing attention to Arthurian studies must take into account the superb

[9] Pp. 41–42. The italics are mine.

[10] See, for example, G. R. Coffman's "John Gower, Mentor for Royalty: Richard II," *PMLA* (1954).

[11] Roger S. Loomis and Laura Hibbard, *Arthurian Legends in Medieval Art* (1938); Roger S. Loomis, *Arthurian Tradition and Chrétien de Troyes* (1949); for a good summary of his ideas about the Grail legend, see "How Did the Grail Legend Arise?" *History of Ideas News Letter* (1955).

performance by J. S. P. Tatlock, *The Legendary History of Britain: Geoffrey of Monmouth's "Historia Regum Britanniae" and Its Early Vernacular Versions* (1950), which gives us virtually the final word on Geoffrey of Monmouth. Some progress has been made on the thorny problem of *Piers Plowman;* E. Talbot Donaldson's *Piers Plowman, the C-Text and Its Poet* (1949) is brilliant. There has been a shift, justifiable enough, in the dating of the A-Text from Skeat's postulated date of 1362 to some time after 1370—see Josephine W. Bennett, "The Date of the A-Text of *Piers Plowman*," *PMLA* (1943); and the evidence seems to place the B-Text in close proximity to the death of Edward in 1377—see Bernard Huppé, "*Piers Plowman*: The Date of the B-Text Reconsidered," *SP* (1949). Here H. S. Bennett's book, *Chaucer and the Fifteenth Century* (1947), should be mentioned: it is excellent for background though not particularly notable for its appreciation of the poet, and it contains one plaintive sentence which could stand as the epilogue for this present essay: "It is particularly ironic that this most humane of English poets should be in peril of being buried under a mass of erudition."

There has been a brief flurry in the vogue of John Skelton,[12] and Sir David Lyndsay was brought again to life for a time when his morality-play, *A Satire of the Thrie Estaitis*, was presented at the Edinburgh Festival of 1949. But with Lyndsay we are almost past the Tudor period and well into the English Renaissance, and so we may close with mention of the useful book by Edwin T. Casady, *Henry Howard, Earl of Surrey* (1938).

The hierarchical structure of medieval society and the centripetal force of medieval thought have given that great age an enormous appeal during and after the years of the Second World War, when stability and order seemed to have disappeared for good; and its fashionableness at that time can be measured by the number of general works which appeared in those years about all things medieval—works which I must reluctantly omit from present consideration, although it is always possible for the reader to go to the bibliographies to find out about them. Now that we

---

[12] For example, see William Nelson's "Skelton's *Speke, Parrot*," *PMLA* (1936) and his *John Skelton, Laureate* (1939), and G. S. Fraser's "Skelton and the Dignity of Poetry," *Adelphia* (1936). The vogue burnt itself out in the early 1940's.

have become accustomed, or, as the psychologists say, negatively
adapted, to an age of uncertainty and strife, we can see that the
Middle Ages also was an age of uncertainty and strife. Now there
seems to be already a kind of reaction against the medieval, save
in the hearts and minds of its enthusiatic defenders; but no reaction can invalidate the contribution of the Middle Ages, which is
not easily measured. Perhaps it is enough to remind ourselves of
something that runs as an undercurrent throughout J. W. Atkins's
fine book, *English Literary Criticism: The Medieval Phase* (1943);
we have no longer the right to refer to any past ages as Dark Ages,
much less to refer in this way to the age which produced Dante
and Chaucer.

4

Shakespeare and His Times

G. E. BENTLEY

THE VAST BULK OF WRITINGS about Shakespeare and his times is always intimidating to students when they begin to consider the plays with any seriousness. Many of their teachers have long since given up all attempt to make a selection from the flood of Shakespearean publications. Perhaps their loss is not so great as some of us who contribute to the flood would like to think, for the plain truth is that of the many thousands of books and articles about Shakespeare that have been produced in the twentieth century, the majority are not worth reading.

But many of them are. The problem of the conscientious teacher is, of course, to find out the helpful publications and to make their contributions available to students. For any teacher at any level, the first task is to find out what the publications are. If he proposes to be very comprehensive, or if he seeks obscure material, he will turn to the annual bibliographies, which attempt to list most of the writings about Shakespeare and his time as they appear each year. The most useful of these bibliographies are:

"Recent Literature of the English Renaissance," published annually since 1920 in _Studies in Philology_; since 1923 always in the April issue.

The Year's Work in English Studies. Published annually by the Oxford University Press for the English Association. The first year surveyed was 1919–1920.

"Shakespeare: An Annotated Bibliography for 19–," published annually in _The Shakespeare Quarterly_ since 1949, and in an earlier form in _The Shakespeare Association Bulletin_, 1926–48.

The teacher who needs a more selective list can turn to the series of summaries of modern Shakespeare studies which have been appearing since 1948 in the annual volumes of the *Shakespeare Survey*, published by the Cambridge University Press. Each of these summarizing articles reviews and relates the more significant publications of the last half century on a given Shakespearean topic. The articles in the order of their appearance in the *Shakespeare Survey* are:

1948 "Studies in the Elizabethan Stage since 1900" by Allardyce Nicoll
1949 "Fifty Years of Shakespearian Production" by M. St. Clare Byrne
1950 "Studies in the Life and Environment of Shakespeare since 1900" by Charles J. Sisson
1951 "Fifty Years of Shakespearian Criticism: 1900–1950" by Kenneth Muir
1953 "Shakespeare's History Plays: 1900–1951" by Harold Jenkins
1954 "Fifty Years of the Criticism of Shakespeare's Style: A Retrospect" by M. C. Bradbrook
1955 "The Interpretation of Shakespeare's Comedies 1900–1953" by John Russell Brown
1956 "Studies in *Hamlet*, 1901–1955" by Clifford Leech
1957 "Shakespeare's Roman Plays: 1900–1956" by J. C. Maxwell

For the teacher whose time and needs are still more limited, a few books of the last twenty-five or thirty years can be recommended as good, and useful under varying circumstances. They are here selected to represent various aspects—by no means all—of the study of Shakespeare's accomplishment and his environment.

I

Rather outdated now are the old standard biographies of Shakespeare: Sir Sidney Lee's often reprinted *A Life of William Shakespeare* (1898, revised 1925) and Joseph Quincy Adams's *A Life of William Shakespeare* (1923). The best collection of biographical information is to be found in Sir Edmund Chambers's *William Shakespeare: A Study of Facts and Problems* (1930).[1] This

[1] A combined index to the four volumes of *The Elizabethan Stage* and the two volumes of this study is available in Beatrice White, *An Index to . . .* (1934).

work constitutes the prime reference book for biographical material, a monument of accurate, comprehensive, and judicious scholarship. It provides more precise and relevant factual information than any other book about Shakespeare, but, as the title indicates, it is a study of facts and problems, not a "life"; it is valuable for reference, not for student reading. A much more attractive biography for beginners is Marchette Chute's *Shakespeare of London* (1949). Miss Chute does not print her documentation in footnotes, but the book is more accurate and scrupulous than many of those which do. All her facts are reliable; she makes no assertions for which there is not good evidence; and she is less guilty of reading her own predelictions into the evidence than most of the other biographers—including Lee and Adams.

Various scholarly studies have considered not Shakespeare's life as a whole but some particular phase or period. One good example is T. W. Baldwin's two-volume work entitled *William Shakespere's Small Latine & Lesse Greeke* (1944). These volumes set forth in a comprehensive but somewhat prolix way the materials and disciplines of the petty schools and the grammar schools of sixteenth-century England—materials and disciplines which deeply influenced the thought and interests of Shakespeare and his audiences.

Many books of the last twenty-five years have presented the conditions of life and belief in which Shakespeare and all his English contemporaries worked. One of the more comprehensive is Louis Booker Wright's *Middle-Class Culture in Elizabethan England* (1935). As its title indicates, this book is primarily concerned with one particular class in the society of Shakespeare's day, but it is the class to which he belonged, as did most of his audience. A series of volumes, now published as two, which provide understanding of the time by another means are those compiled by G. B. Harrison, *The Elizabethan Journals, 1591–1603* (1938), and *A Jacobean Journal, 1603–1606* (1941). They record the popularly discussed current events of these years, mostly in the words of extant pamphlets, letters, broadsides, reports, and other contemporary documents which show what Shakespeare's fellow citizens in London were actually talking about, not what modern novelists or critics or historians would like to think they were talking about. The *Journals* provide a good antidote for those romantic students (and teachers?) who think of all Elizabethans as Raleighs and Jane Greys, and who constantly ask, "Did *all* Elizabethan audiences understand Latin?"

A different sort of book on the Elizabethan background is Don Cameron Allen's *The Star-Crossed Renaissance: The Quarrel about Astrology and Its Influence in England* (1941). This study shows "that everybody who lived during the Renaissance believed to some extent in astrology," and it sets out the bases of their belief, the degrees of their disbelief, and the points at issue. No one can read very far in the plays of Shakespeare without coming upon repeated examples of the dramatist's assumption that his audiences were accustomed to a consideration of celestial influences, at least in the lives of the great. Allen's book analyzes the backgrounds of this belief.

Another book on the ideas and modes of thought of the time is Theodore Spencer's *Shakespeare and the Nature of Man* (1942). Spencer tries to show the normal assumptions about man, God, and the universe which lay behind Shakespeare's thought and which he could assume to be—in varying degrees of awareness—in the minds of his audience. The book is not so learned, or, in some respects, so accurate, as others on the subject that have appeared in the last two decades, but it is readable, and it emphasizes the basic principle so often ignored in the criticism of the last two centuries, namely, that Shakespeare's preconceptions, judgments, and motives were Elizabethan, not Augustan, or Victorian, or twentieth-century, as is so frequently assumed.

In the last half-century scholars and critics have been paying a little more attention to a condition of Shakespeare's work which has long been generally ignored, or even tacitly denied: namely, the fact that all his plays were written to be performed by Elizabethan or Jacobean actors in the theaters of their own time. This obvious fact necessarily conditioned all that he wrote except *Venus and Adonis, The Rape of Lucrece,* and the sonnets. Yet the majority of critics have written about the plays (and too many teachers have taught their students to think about them) as if they were composed by Spenser or Milton with a sublime indifference to that vulgar commercial enterprise, the Elizabethan theater.

The growing awareness of the importance of the theater for a proper understanding of Shakespeare's work is reflected in the number of studies of his fellow actors and their playhouses which have appeared in the last few decades. The most detailed and comprehensive analysis of all aspects of the theater, including plays, players, playwrights, regulations, and theatrical economics, is Sir Edmund Chambers's *The Elizabethan Stage* (1923).[2] This reference work is one of the most comprehensive and accurate in the entire field of English and American literature, but it is not suitable for extended readings by any but the most determined students.

Numerous books and articles on the physical characteristics of Elizabethan theaters are available, particularly on the more minute features of the stage, like the music room, the tarras, the heavens, and so forth. The difficulty of the subject, both for the beginning student and for the mature scholar, is that no detailed and reliable contemporary picture of the interior of any Elizabethan theater is extant, nor any detailed and reliable description either. Modern scholars are forced to rely on inferences from stage directions and lines in the plays themselves and on casual allusions in non-dramatic poetry and prose of the time. Inferences are always unreliable, and are particularly suspect in this field, since the theaters were by no means all alike and the allusions to them are seldom precise about either the particular theater intended or the date. Under such circumstances it is not surprising that one of the most detailed, fully documented, and commonly cited studies is one of the more unreliable. For the general student, the most satisfactory book on the subject was written by a theater architect and designer, C. Walter Hodges, *The Globe Restored: A Study of the Elizabethan Theatre* (1953). Mr. Hodges knows the literature of the subject, but he relies more on his imagination and his theater experience than on Elizabethan stage directions and allusions. Ordinarily such reliance would be fatal, but fortunately Mr. Hodges' imagination is beautifully disciplined and his theater experience is varied. His own illustrations drawn for his book are pleasing and helpful.

Another recent book in the movement to return Shakespeare to his proper theatrical environment is Alfred Harbage's *Shakespeare and the Rival Traditions* (1952). Mr. Harbage notes that in London during the reigns of Elizabeth I and James I there were two

[2] The years covered are 1558–1616. The survey is continued to the logical termination of the period in the closing of all English theaters by law in 1642 in G. E. Bentley's *The Jacobean and Caroline Stage*, 5 volumes (1941–56).

quite different types of theater, patronized by two different types of audiences. One type was the so-called private theater, like the Blackfriars, comprising small, expensive houses patronized by a small, well-to-do, exclusive audience—a coterie audience. The other was the public theater, like the Globe, large, cheap, and popular, patronized by an audience made up of a cross-section of the population of London, but dominantly middle class. Harbage tries to generalize about the type of play and the kind of moral assumptions characteristic of each type of theater and audience. He contends that Shakespeare was always concerned with the large popular audience whose healthy moral attitudes are reflected in the plays written for them. I myself think that Harbage oversimplifies the case, and that certain of Shakespeare's plays show a concern for the coterie audience of the Blackfriars type,[3] but this is a rather minor criticism of a good book.

Shakespeare in his professional environment is also the basis of one of the most influential pieces of criticism of our time, Harley Granville-Barker's *Prefaces to Shakespeare* (1946, 1947).[4] The author's own experience as a poet, translator, playwright, and actor, and as the most distinguished producer of his time provided him with more of Shakespeare's own professional experience than any other critic has ever had. He attempts to make the reader see what Shakespeare intended to appear on the stage and what his theatrical problems were. In this attempt Granville-Barker's acute perceptions, his wide knowledge, his experience, and his Johnsonian common sense combine to make his *Prefaces* most illuminating.

Another part of Shakespeare's professional environment was provided by the other playwrights who also contributed to the great distinction of the Elizabethan drama. On the greatest of his professional contemporaries, Christopher Marlowe and Ben Jonson, two works of distinction have appeared in recent years: Paul Kocher's *Christopher Marlowe: A Study of His Thought, Learning, and Character* (1946) and the magnificent edition of

[3] See "Shakespeare and the Blackfriars Theatre," *Shakespeare Survey* (1948).

[4] A collection and revision of essays on *Hamlet, King Lear, The Merchant of Venice, Antony and Cleopatra, Cymbeline, Othello, Coriolanus, Romeo and Juliet, Julius Caesar* and *Love's Labour's Lost*. The essays originally appeared in a variety of forms from 1923 through 1946.

Jonson in eleven volumes by C. H. Herford, Percy Simpson, and Evelyn Simpson, *Ben Jonson* (1925–52).

A different kind of study of Shakespeare's fellow dramatists, a study of perhaps even greater distinction, is Sir Walter Greg's two-volume *A Bibliography of the English Printed Drama to the Restoration* (1939 and 1951).[5] These volumes give a bibliographical analysis of "all editions down to 1700 of all dramatic compositions which were either written before the end of 1642 . . . or printed before the *beginning* of 1660," together with a census of the copies to be found in seven English libraries and seventeen American libraries. These volumes are among the most valuable aids for every scholar of the period.

II

Indirectly related to the study of Shakespeare in the theater is another type of investigation probably less familiar, a scrutiny of his pronunciation. Pronunciation is an even more important consideration for Shakespeare than for most great English poets, for, unlike Spenser or Milton or Wordsworth or Shelley, he intended all the lines in all his major works to be spoken by actors from a stage and to be taken in by the ear, not, as with the others, necessarily read on the printed page. (We can find no evidence that Shakespeare himself ever made any attempt to get any of his plays into print.) Therefore the sounds he expected his audience to hear become doubly important for that complete understanding which is the goal of all Shakespearean research. In the last two centuries there have been various half-hearted investigations into the pronunciation of Elizabethan speech, and many half truths have been promulgated. One investigator said that twentieth-century man could have understood very little of what Richard Burbage said in a performance of *King Lear* at the Globe; another said that it would have been easier for Shakespeare to understand Chaucer's speech than it would be for us to understand Shakespeare's.

A few years ago a really thorough study of pronunciation was published after fifteen years of investigation. The book is Helge

---

[5] The volumes are printed for the Bibliographical Society by the Oxford University Press. Two further volumes are promised in the near future, but they will add no more plays to those listed.

Kökeritz's *Shakespeare's Pronunciation* (1953).[6] The book itself is a highly technical linguistic investigation, much too scientific for undergraduates and probably for many teachers. But Professor Kökeritz has issued also two long-playing records of passages from *Macbeth, Hamlet, Julius Caesar, Richard II,* the sonnets, and other popular favorites, in which the lines are pronounced as his investigations show they would have been pronounced on Shakespeare's stage. These long-playing records, issued by Columbia, ought to be illuminating for many students.

One of the enlightening features of Kökeritz's pronunciation of the lines is its revelation of many puns which modern pronunciation conceals. Shakespeare, like so many of his contemporaries, was versatile in his punning—the Elizabethans all tended to be more adroit and sophisticated in their use of language than we are, and for them a pun had many uses. Many of the plays on words which Kökeritz points out suggest overtones of meaning generally unnoticed, meanings not always so decorous as some Bard-lovers would wish—but then neither was Shakespeare.

These indecorous puns are most avidly pursued by Eric Partridge in his *Shakespeare's Bawdy* (1947, revised 1955). Occasionally this book leads the reader to feel that he is getting a more convincing picture of Partridge's Shakespeare than he is of Shakespeare's bawdy, but the majority of the puns elucidated were clearly intended by the dramatist. A more recent and more varied study of Shakespeare's puns is M. M. Mahood's *Shakespeare's Wordplay* (1957), a book which gives close attention to the punning in *Romeo and Juliet, Richard II,* the sonnets, *Hamlet, Macbeth,* and *The Winter's Tale.* Though there can be no doubt whatever that Shakespeare was more ingenious and more confirmed in his punning than most readers realize, both these writers tend, like so many modern critics (and Baconians), to be dazzled by their own ingenuity. When a critic makes frequent condescending exposures of "Shakespeare's unconscious mind," his readers are well advised to proceed with caution.

The recent critical interest in Shakespeare's wordplay is closely allied to the interest in his imagery, which has been one of the most

[6] Some of Kökeritz's assertions have been questioned by other writers on linguistics. For other conclusions see E. J. Dobson, *English Pronunciation, 1500–1700,* 2 volumes (1957).

popular subjects of critical investigation in our time. Perceptive critics of Shakespeare's poetry have always noted the effectiveness of many of his images, but the modern passion for image collection and analysis for the sake of a fuller understanding of the life of the poet or of his mental processes or of his purpose in a given play is a new development of such proportions that it suggests a response to some sort of need of our times. A few studies in this mode appeared in the late twenties and early thirties, but the first elaborate analysis of imagery to attract wide attention was Caroline F. E. Spurgeon's *Shakespeare's Imagery and What It Tells Us* (1935). Miss Spurgeon did a great deal of classifying of images in all the plays, and she seemed more interested in revelations of Shakespeare's life and development than in anything else. Her actual contribution to an understanding of Shakespeare and his work (as distinguished from her method) seems much less significant today than it seemed twenty years ago, but she did much to spread imagery study into the epidemic it became in the forties and early fifties. One sentence in her introduction indicates the insidious aspect of the imagery-study appeal: "In the case of the poet, I suggest it is chiefly through his imagery that he, to some extent unconsciously, 'gives himself away.'" Unfortunately the writers of too many of the hundreds of imagery studies—published and unpublished—show a fatal susceptibility to this appeal of the esoteric, and, rather as the Baconians and Oxfordians do, they lose contact with reality. Many of their studies betray the secret conviction of the writers that William Shakespeare was really another John Donne; comparatively few of them ever envisage the plays as intended for performance before a large popular audience at the Globe theatre. Often the writer's thwarted ambition to practice psychiatry is more apparent than his understanding of plays. But such aberrations always appear when any critical approach or scholarly method becomes a fad. Probably the best of the imagery studies is Wolfgang H. Clemen's *The Development of Shakespeare's Imagery* (1951), a revision, expansion, and translation of his *Shakespeare's Bilder* (1936). Clemen is perceptive and thorough, and he consistently shows a sense of proportion and an awareness of Shakespeare's milieu which are unusual. More impassioned studies like G. Wilson Knight's series, *The Wheel of Fire* (1930, reissued 1949), *The Imperial Theme*

(1931, reissued 1951), *The Shakespearean Tempest* (1932), *The Crown of Life* (1947), and *The Mutual Flame* (1955) often show brilliant flashes of insight which are valuable for the reader who can keep his feet in the wild torrent of words and can refuse to be swept away.

Critical studies of Shakespeare often derive advantage from the isolation of one particular type of his work. The forties and early fifties saw a notable revival of interest in Shakespeare's history plays, which are now seen to deserve more serious consideration as works of art and as coherent presentations of political problems than they formerly have had. Prominent among the pioneers in this new evaluation was Miss Lily B. Campbell, whose series of studies concerned with Tudor conceptions of history and with ideas of what historical writing should do had begun in 1934; her *Shakespeare's Histories: Mirrors of Elizabethan Policy* (1947) was the culmination of her work. Her absorption in the political theory sometimes warps her judgment of the plays, but the book is a valuable study. Somewhat more general in its appeal is E. M. W. Tillyard's *Shakespeare's History Plays* (1944), which considers first the background of history and historical writing and then the two tetralogies and *King John* and *Macbeth*. A broader study of the genre, in which Shakespeare's histories are set in the context of other historical plays of his time (not simply historical writing in general), is Irving Ribner's *The English History Play in the Age of Shakespeare* (1957). This book presents the whole development of English historical writing for the stage before 1642, including Shakespeare's contribution, and in this sharply circumscribed context Shakespeare's proper place in the development appears more clearly than it ever has before.

Though nearly one-third of the plays Shakespeare wrote are histories, most high school and college students devote more time to other types, especially the tragedies. One of the older but still widely used books on the tragedies is A. C. Bradley's *Shakespearean Tragedy: Lectures on Hamlet, Othello, King Lear, and Macbeth* (1904, and frequently reissued). Bradley was a very perceptive critic, but he almost totally ignored the theatrical context of the plays, and some of his comments seem old-fashioned now. More modern analyses of the most frequently studied tragedies are to be found in J. Dover Wilson, *What Happens in Hamlet* (1935), an exciting but very speculative book; in Henry N. Paul, *The Royal Play of Macbeth: When, Why, and How It Was Written by Shakespeare* (1950); and in R. B. Heilman, *This Great Stage: Image and Structure in King Lear* (1948).

One of the more inclusive recent books on the comedies is Thomas Marc Parrott's *Shakespearean Comedy* (1949), a book which considers comic material in all the plays and is necessarily limited in the attention devoted to any one. *All's Well That Ends Well, Measure for Measure,* and *Troilus and Cressida* are discussed, mostly in terms of their medieval backgrounds, in William Witherle Lawrence's *Shakespeare's Problem Comedies* (1931). An interesting but rather doctrinaire book on Shakespeare's last four plays is Derek Traversi's *Shakespeare: The Last Phase* (1955).

III

For the majority of school and college students, the most perplexing and generally the dullest phase of Shakespearean studies is text. But textual studies have been published in great numbers in the last three or four decades, most of them far too minute and involved for any reader whose textual appetite is not already well developed, and most are concerned with only one play. Among recent textual studies the most notable variety is that which attempts to find precisely what happened in the printing shop when a given play of Shakespeare's was set up and printed, particularly those in the folio of 1623. Such studies are unintelligible unless the reader has already trained himself to follow the details of printing-house practice. The research of Fredson Bowers and Charlton Hinman and others is rapidly extending our knowledge of what happened between the printer's receipt of the copy for, say, Shakespeare's *Othello,* and its appearance on the bookstalls in the folio of 1623. But the general reader must wait for the digestion of the results into a more readable form than they have yet received. Sir Walter Greg's *The Shakespeare First Folio: Its Bibliographical and Textual History* (1955) is a magnificently learned and accurate summary, but it cannot be called very readable.

A good guide to these highly specialized textual studies is provided by J. G. MacManaway in the reviews of each year's work, published annually in *Shakespeare Survey* since 1948.

Finally, it may be useful to note four or five miscellaneous volumes which can be of value for teachers. Very helpful for brief reference is F. E. Halliday's *A Shakespeare Companion, 1550–1950* (1952). The book is a condensed encyclopedia which attempts "to cover all aspects of Shakespeare and the people who have been most intimately associated with his works, in whatever capacity, in the course of more than three and a half centuries." It has forty-five well selected illustrations. For the quick identification of characters, theaters, plays, actors, scholars, places, poets, and other facts which slip the best of memories, this book is an invaluable aid.

Halliday's handy reference book can often be supplemented by Phyllis May Hartnoll, editor, *The Oxford Companion to the Theatre* (1951) which, of course, lists more of Shakespeare's predecessors and successors and often provides convenient notes on persons and places of incidental rather than primary Shakespearean interest.

Teachers who often wish to show their students what an original edition of Shakespeare's plays looked like will find a very convenient facsimile in Helge Kökeritz and Charles Tyler Prouty, editors, *Mr. William Shakespeares Comedies, Histories & Trage-dies: A Facsimile Edition* (1954). The facsimile is about four-fifths the size of the original, and its price is very much less than that of earlier facsimiles, so that it can easily be made part of a school library. The book has been attacked by the scholarly reviewers for its faulty introduction and for the treatment of the photographic plates which has altered certain letters of the text on various pages so that the facsimile is unreliable for scholarly purposes. But for pupils in schools and for most undergraduates, these defects are immaterial; the book can be examined and the plays read by them with profit.

A reference book constantly useful to those interested in the crystallization of experience into the common coin of men's speech—the proverbs used by Shakespeare and his contemporaries— is Morris Palmer Tilley's *A Dictionary of Proverbs in England in the Sixteenth and Seventeenth Centuries* (1950). More proverbs, and more variant forms, and more citations, can be found for Shakespeare's time in this book than in any of the other dictionaries of proverbs.

Many good and helpful books about Shakespeare and his times have perforce been omitted from a short survey like this. If the list is used to save a little time for busy and conscientious teachers, it will have served its purpose.

5

The Seventeenth Century

MERRITT Y. HUGHES

OF ALL THE CENTURIES IN ENG-
lish history the seventeenth is by common consent the most seminal
of principles and institutions, of ideas and of the sensibility which
we most value today. What political wisdom we have in our laws
and in our hearts we owe to the movement which Milton defended
and criticized in *Areopagitica*. What true sensitivity and strength
we may have as readers and writers of poetry we seem to be pretty
well convinced that we owe to John Donne and a few other
contemporary poets like George Herbert, Henry Vaughan, and
Andrew Marvell—to the "Monarch of Wit" and the princes of his
blood who shared his art of thinking with the heart and feeling
with the head.

In politics and poetry alike we have come to feel that our greatest debt is to the century of Milton and Donne. We know, of
course, that we are the political debtors of Pericles and Plato,
Demonsthenes and Cicero, but we feel much closer to their
disciples in the seventeenth century, the champions of liberty,
limited monarchy, and republicanism whose story is told by Z. S.
Fink in *The Classical Republicans: An Essay in the Recovery of a
Pattern of Thought in Seventeenth Century England* (1945). We
should be vividly aware that, without the incarnation of that
pattern of thought in Milton and men of his political convictions,
the settlement of this continent could hardly have taken either the
physical or the spiritual shape that it did. And in recent years we
seem to have agreed that without the example of John Donne and
the best of the other "metaphysical" poets it is possible, if not
likely, that the best poetry of our century could hardly have been
written. So William Van O'Connor thinks in *Sense and Sensibility
in Modern Poetry* (1948), and so Margaret Willy thinks in her

study of "The Poetry of Donne: Its Interest and Influence Today" in *Essays and Studies*, edited for the English Association by Guy Boas (1954). Indeed, it seems to her that Yeats's hope to

> . . . dine at journey's end
> With Landor and with Donne,

might be attributed to "the majority of English poets writing between 1918 and the present day."

Aside from Shakespeare, Milton and Donne dominate their century for us. In a survey as short as this one must be, there is no room even for their greatest rival, John Dryden. We ignore him with regret, for we agree with T. S. Eliot who in his *John Dryden* (1932) says that "it is hardly too much to say that Dryden found the English speechless, and he gave them speech"—the language which, "even in the nineteenth century, was still the language of Dryden, as it is today." We have time only for Milton and Donne though we may suspect that George Herbert was a better religious poet than either of them. For lack of time we cannot even glance at J. H. Summers's *George Herbert: His Religion and His Art* (1954) or at Rosemund Tuve's crushing corrections of some ingenious misreadings of him in her *A Reading of George Herbert* (1952). Nor are we to be lured away from Milton and Donne by the charm and glory which Marvell has assumed in studies like those by Muriel C. Bradbrook and M. G. Thomas in their *Andrew Marvel* (1940) and by Ruth Wallerstein in her *Studies in Seventeenth-Century Poetic* (1950), or by the prestige which Abraham Cowley assumes in R. B. Hinman's treatment of him in "Truth Is Purest Poesy," *ELH* (1956) as the first poet to understand the proper role of the imagination in interpreting Thomas Hobbes's "picture of an orderly and knowable universe whose system of correspondences could be discovered by observation of phenomena and whose reflection of a divine order could be arrived at rationally." We shall pause only long enough to agree with Mr. Hinman that "the influence of the New Philosophy on Abraham Cowley" was very different from its influence on Milton or Donne.

Our interest in Milton and Donne rests, of course, upon our really well assured faith in them as the two greatest poets of their century and upon our experience with them as writers who can be effectively "taught" in colleges and more or less in secondary schools. The invidious comparisons which T. S. Eliot began the fashion of drawing between them, let us agree, have long since served their purpose of stimulating interest in both men so that both now rightfully have no small place in every respectable English "major." Individually, we all reserve the right to have our preferences between them, but not—I hope—to the point of advising students to neglect either. This does not mean that we should hide our preferences from our students, but it does mean that we should check our thinking about Eliot's criterion of "dissociated sensibility" by Frank Kermode's thorough and penetrating analysis of the history of that cultural problem in *KR* (1957).

I

Let me begin by frankly confessing my preference for Milton and doing it even a bit invidiously by quoting the closing words of E. M. W. Tillyard's new book on *The Metaphysicals and Milton* (1956). After paying a final tribute which is short of idolatry to Milton, Mr. Tillyard says of Donne that he "was a great innovator, but with a narrower, more personal talent. He made people heed him, he stirred them up, he contributed to the age's vitality. But he remains the exception, and his admirers will do him no good in the long run if they pretend he was anything else." And lest I seem to rely too much on the judgment of a professional "Miltonist," let me remind you of the challenge of the most recent book-length analysis of Donne's poetry—that by Clay Hunt—to T. S. Eliot's famous assertion of a "unification of sensibility" in his poetry. Denying that this "evaluation of Donne is true, even if one allows for the rather special meaning which Eliot assigns to 'sensibility,' " Mr. Hunt rates Marlowe, Sidney, Spenser, Shakespeare, Jonson, Browne, and Milton above Donne in range of sensibility and mastery even of "the kinds of experience which his poetry could master."[1] The most recent deliverance on the point is by R. G. Cox in a new Pelican book, *From Donne to Marvel*, edited by Boris Ford (1956), and it denies "mastery of experience" to most of Donne's poems with the possible exceptions of *The Goodmorrow*, *The Extasie*, *The Valediction forbidding mourning*, and

[1] Clay Hunt, *Donne's Poetry: Essays in Literary Analysis* (1954). A generally comparable study is Doniphan Louthan's *The Poetry of John Donne: An Essay in Explication* (1951).

the *Nocturnall*. Only in K. W. Gransden's *John Donne* (1954), among recent books, is a more favorable opinion of the poet's powers implied, but in that popular little essay the main interest is in the analysis of the metaphysical wit of his secular poems in contrast with the "wit as the agent of the high good" in his religious lyrics.

This is not the place to attempt more than the briefest sketch of the recent redefinition of metaphysical poetry as seen in the light of the problem of the relation of Donne's images to the structure of his poems. The debate on that subject which began in 1928 with Pierre Legouis's *Donne, The Craftsman*, was shifted to new ground in 1939 by Cleanth Brooks's insistence in *Modern Poetry and the Tradition* on "the poet's ultimate attitude" as more basic in Donne's work than his wit and his wittiest conceits, even though they might give outward shape and inner unity to some of his poems. Brooks staked his case on a series of elaborate analyses of many of the *Songs and Sonnets*, and thereby exposed himself to much dissent from his interpretations of individual poems. The most recent dissenting opinion is William J. Rooney's reconsideration of Brooks's treatment of paradox in *The Canonization*, in *ELH* (1956). The most extensive and systematic and sympathetically critical anatomization of Brooks's interpretations is that by Leonard Unger in *Donne's Poetry and Modern Criticism* (1950), a book which seems once for all to have "demonstrated that, though metaphor is frequent in Donne's poetry, there is no special use of metaphor by which structure generally develops."

Carrying Brooks's analysis further, Unger emerged believing that the "distinguishing feature of Donne's poetry" is the poet's "complexity of attitudes," as we see them in poems like *Twicknam Garden* and *A Valediction: Of My Name*. His efforts to describe and label Donne's evolving moods and points of view in a number of poems have set a pattern for a game of explication which is becoming only too popular. It should be played only by critics who are thoroughly familiar with the commentaries of Sir Herbert Grierson and their supplements by later editors and contributors to the journals (George Williamson, Don Cameron Allen, and others), with Hunt's *Essays in Literary Analysis*, which has just been mentioned, and Milton A. Rugoff's book on *Donne's Imagery: A Study in Creative Sources* (1939). The final result will certainly not be a denial of Donne's complexity, but it may more happily be a confirmation of J. B. Leishman's conclusion on the last page of our most substantial appraisal of Donne—*The Monarch of Wit* (1951)—that "the dramatic element in his life and genius and poetry" was the root of Donne's character and work.

Those of us who teach undergraduates may find their interest veering away from the problems which attract most of his professional explicators, and towards concern over the "New Philosophy" which he declared "calls all in doubt." William Van O'Connor in *Sense and Sensibility in Modern Poetry* (1948) spoke for many readers when he described Donne as having caught "the sense of intricacy, the interrelatedness and dissonances of experience as they flow through the mind," and added that, "Through his ability to put down a whole of tangled feelings, Donne appeals to the modern mind." There was a time when the knowledge and interest behind Donne's countless scientific images seemed to add up at least to an enlightened curiosity about the physical world. His admirers were implying claims for him as sweeping as that made for Cowley in Mr. Hinman's article. The picture was that of a man "intensely interested in the great scientific movement of thought which was initiated by Copernicus, Kepler, and Galileo," a man "reared in the medieval climate of thought" and "chilled" by "the fresh winds of scientific discovery," but strong in "the courage to go on reading and studying." So Evelyn Simpson described him in her fine *A Study of the Prose Works of John Donne* (second edition, 1948). No one made claims for him as a spokesman or initiate in contemporary scientific movements quite as confident as the claims which Marjorie Nicolson made for Milton in "Milton and the Telescope," *ELH* (1935), but it was generally agreed that "Donne's was a dawning scientific mind," although, as Evelyn Hardy said in *Donne: A Spirit in Conflict* (1942), it was "clogged with medievalism." Writing in 1937 in *John Donne and the New Philosophy*, C. M. Coffin dared assert that he had cut loose from medieval trammels and caught a glimpse of the modern scientific attitude towards "the irreducible and stubborn facts of nature"; but at the same time Coffin described Donne's nature as fundamentally skeptical and inclined to envisage "the world in a state of perplexing lawlessness."

By the time Victor Harris wrote his *All Coherence Gone* in 1949, however, Donne's early interest in the "recent discoveries in science" had become evidence of only the most amateurish kind of study, and his concern about Copernican astronomy as it emerged in many of his works from the early *Ignatius his Conclave* to his latest sermons could be treated simply as proof of a life-long obsession with "the old belief" in the inevitable decay of nature. If we turn to a Catholic scholar like Michael Francis Moloney in his *John Donne: His Flight from Medievalism* (1944) for light on Donne's attitude toward natural science, we find him frankly agreeing with the view which Mary P. Ramsay stated back in 1917 in her study of the medieval element in Donne's thought: "the new science was a negligible factor in shaping his mind." It seems that the most that can be claimed for him as an amateur of the sciences can be packed into Helen White's comparison of his curiosity about astronomy, physics, and anatomy to his exhilaration by reports of the new discoveries of the explorers. And she adds the sage remark in her book on *The Metaphysical Poets* (1936, reprinted 1956) that "it should not be forgotten that he was quite as actively interested in the theories of pseudo-science and quasi-science" as he was in the real thing.

There cannot be any doubt of the accuracy of Moloney's position at the close of *John Donne: His Flight from Mediaevalism* when he declares that the poet's "interest in the 'new science' of his day was rather a popular and poetic interest whereby he caught up new ideas, toyed with them, wove them into the fabric of his poetry, but at no time saw in them a challenge to the stability of traditional Christianity." In a brilliant study of "Donne, Montaigne, and Natural Law," *JEGP* (1956) Robert Ornstein came to the parallel conclusion that Donne "looks back upon a medieval Christian heritage out of which he fashions a satisfactory moral framework." But this conclusion is based upon a study of *Biathanatos* and Donne's *Essays in Divinity*. It does not invalidate Moloney's challenge to the still prevailing view of Grierson, Miss Ramsey, George Williamson, and Louis I. Bredvold "that Donne achieved a synthesis between the warring worlds of flesh and spirit," and that in his poetry we find that union of the intellect and sensibility whose loss in the later seventeenth and succeeding centuries has been so much deplored by T. S. Eliot, Allen Tate, and Cleanth Brooks. Because the medieval synthesis of flesh and spirit had lost its validity for Donne, his "only alternative" seems to Moloney to have been "to rely on the intellect as the sole contributor to the work of poetic creation." The inevitable conclusion seems to be that, "The rationalization of the poetic process" began with Donne and "continued with his followers."

For readers sharing Moloney's faith in the partnership of the emotions with the mind in the writing of poetry before Donne corrupted the art, it may seem possible to regard him as the great mischief-maker in the history of English poetry. He may even come to look as guilty as T. S. Eliot once taught us to think that Milton was of dividing the minds of English poets from their emotions and their sensuous perceptions. But it does seem clear that we have ceased to look for the key to Donne's mind in his scientific interests. It may be true—as William Empson brilliantly pleads in "Donne the Space Man," *KR* (1957)—that he gloried in visions of multiple worlds, but prevailing opinion is better indicated by the silence about his scientific enthusiasms which Theodore Redpath preserves in his discriminating Introduction to *The Songs and Sonnets of John Donne* (1957).

There can be no doubt that even among Donne's friendliest critics in recent years there has been a growing perception that (to use Douglas Bush's words in *English Literature in the Earlier Seventeenth Century*) whereas "the greatest artists dominate and unify experience. . . . Donne's fragments of experience remain fragments," and "his sensibility is not unified but multiple." The changing attitude towards him emerges in Robert L. Hickey's opening remark in a study of "Donne's Art of Preaching" in *Tennessee Studies in Literature* (1956), that he was "a great poet, almost as great as his modern admirers say he was; but it is in 'the other harmony of prose' that his genius achieved its fulfillment." It is no accident that editorial work on Donne is now culminating in the great edition of his Sermons in eight volumes (six of which we already have) by Evelyn Simpson and George R. Potter, and that the way to them has been blazed by John Sparrow's edition of the *Devotions upon Emergent Occasions* (1923), Herbert H. Umbach's edition of his *Prayers* (1951), and Evelyn Simpson's edition of his *Essays in Divinity* (1952). Interest in his Sermons, Devotions, and Prayers inevitably focusses attention on the man and his character, even though we have a wealth of intelligent discussion of his art in Mrs. Simpson's *A Study of the Prose Works of John Donne* (second edition, 1948). As we follow her analysis of Donne's thought and art in the Introductions to the successive volumes of the *Sermons*, his biography and psychology become more and more interesting. His greatness is alloyed and at the same time enriched by many human weaknesses. We see him learning the unaccustomed art of preaching and finding that its essence is its own concealment. Most frequently we see him struggling with himself and revealing amazing power as well as weakness. *The Man in the Name*—Leonard Unger's title for a book in which he studied Donne's personality together with several others last year—is becoming a profile which is not entirely elusive. And the emerging personality commands sympathy. It may be that we see it most clearly in what Helen White calls Donne's "devastatingly thorough arraignment of himself," but it is impossible not to agree with her that in his "self-contempt there is a certain strength, the strength of a resolute if not always consistent spirit, able to face itself."[2]

II

Turning now to Milton and to the current flux of theories about his personality, it is interesting to find a wholesome stress being laid upon the principle that his major poems can and should be judged with more respect for their intrinsic elements rather than for their supposed or actual reflection of the man. Meanwhile, our immense knowledge of Milton's biography through Masson's *Life* and through James Holly Hanford's researches into his reading at Horton, has been supplemented by J. Milton French's study of *Milton in Chancery* (1939) and his first four volumes of *Life Records of John Milton* (1949–1956), which are soon to be supplemented by a fifth and final volume. We really know a great deal about the outward life of the man, and as Don Wolfe and his colleagues give us the later volumes of their generously annotated *Complete Prose Works of John Milton*, the first volume of

[2] Helen C. White. "John Donne and the Psychology of Spiritual Effort," in *The Seventeenth Century: Studies in the History of English Thought and Literature from Bacon to Pope,* by Richard Foster Jones and others writing in his honor (1951).

which appeared in 1953, we shall know more and more about both the man and the poet. A clear picture seems to be emerging, yet it is edifying to watch the changes in it as we have had it given to us by one of the most devoted and competent of living Miltonists, E. M. W. Tillyard, in his succession of books from his *Milton* in 1930 (second edition, 1949), to his *The Miltonic Setting* (1938), and his *Studies in Milton* (1951). Even the grand features of the poet are in some dispute. The bold theological speculator whom Denis Saurat gave us in *Milton: Man and Thinker* in 1925 has been built up into an unqualified believer in human perfectibility by Ruth Mohl in *Studies in Spenser, Milton, and the Theory of Monarchy* (1949) and into a Christian humanist believing that man might enjoy a state of grace at least foreshadowing human "Ominiscience, all-might, and perfection" by Gordon W. O'Brien in *Renaissance Poetics and the Problem of Power* (1956). Miss Mohl rests her case upon a rapid survey of the idea of Christian perfectibility in the Church Fathers and in the more enthusiastic writings of Milton's Puritan contemporaries, whose influence upon him has been much more thoroughly studied by William Haller in *The Rise of Puritanism* (1938)—see also the sections on Milton in his *Liberty and Reformation in the Puritan Revolution* (1955). Mr. O'Brien's case rests upon an assumption of Milton's complete acceptance of the optimistic theology of Marsilio Ficino, Pico della Mirandola, and the Italian Neoplatonists. It is pushed to the point of rash challenge of the more traditional and soberly rational Christian humanism which is admirably described in the chapter on Milton in Douglas Bush's *English Literature in the Earlier Seventeenth Century* and in his *Paradise Lost in Our Time* (1945). Before breathing the rarefied and intoxicating atmosphere of *Renaissance Poetics*, or even the clearer air of Maurice Kelley's study of Milton's theological treatise *De Doctrina Christiana* in *This Great Argument* (1941) however, most readers with philosophical curiosity will prefer to look into Milton's outlook upon the natural science of his century.

If we compare the changing ideas of scholars about Milton's scientific information and attitudes with their changing ideas about Donne, we find a fundamental resemblance and difference. At this moment the last word on this aspect of Milton has been said by Kester Svendsen in *Milton and Science* (1956). Building on studies of Milton's cosmology by W. C. Curry, W. B. Hunter, and Grant McColley (whose *Paradise Lost: An Account of its Growth and Major Origins, with a Discussion of Milton's Use of Sources and Literary Patterns*, 1940, he severely criticizes), Svendsen tones down the picture of the young Milton preaching a Baconian faith in the advancement of science which is often seen in some of his Academic Exercises at Cambridge. Very similar praises of the study of all the sciences, Svendsen reminds us, were to be found in contemporary encyclopedias, and Milton and the encyclopaedists were alike in finding that all "problems in natural philosophy reached their last solution only in divine philosophy." Instead of reading a passionate delight in astronomical studies and a veiled purpose of opening readers' minds to the Copernican theory of the solar system into *Paradise Lost*, Svendsen sees the science in all of Milton's works as "mainly classical in origin, medieval in implication, literary in function. To one who sees the progress of science as a cultural index," he adds, "Milton's practice seems old-fashioned and intellectual." Though Milton was a generation younger than Donne and was young enough to stand within the threshold of the movement which led up to the founding of the Royal Society, he emerges from Svendsen's study almost as medieval in his outlook as Donne has been made to appear by his recent critics.

Almost, but not quite. For Svendsen goes on to point out that the science in *Paradise Lost*—particularly that in Raphael's conversation with Adam about the creation and the order of the heavenly bodies—is a main pillar in the design of the poem and by no means a digression. The ambivalent treatment of the still undetermined choice to be made among the Ptolemaic and the Copernican theories and that of Tycho Brahe only emphasizes the fact that the real center of the universe was man and the choice which lay before him. God and man are the two centers of Milton's universe. The sincerity and depth of Milton's Christian humanism are affirmed on evidence which has been no less interestingly treated in another recent study of an aspect of Milton's attitude towards natural science, Howard Schultz's *Milton and Forbidden Knowledge* (1955). Superficially, the two books give the impression that Milton and most of his contemporaries were as "Medieval" as Donne in their thinking about scientific matters, but the steadier and philosophically better grounded character of Milton's thought is obvious. For Milton earth was, in a Platonic sense, the shadow of heaven; but he had no trace of the melancholy of the "deep sense of the vanity and shadowiness of things" which Leishman in *The Monarch of Wit* finds everywhere in Donne. Nor is there a trace in any of Milton's poems of a conflict between the poet's will and his temperament which Helen Gardner sees in her edition of Donne's religious poetry—*The Divine Poems* (1952)— as the main source of the divine poems. In examining Milton's attitude towards science both Svendsen and Schultz open windows upon such various and vital currents in his thought and imagination as are studied in seminal essays like Irene Samuel's *Plato and Milton* (1947), Don Cameron Allen's *The Harmonious Vision* (1954), and Arnold Stein's *Answerable Style* (1953). Some of Svendsen's windows also look out on problems of Milton's imagery which are handled in very different ways by three recent books dealing with *Paradise Lost*: Theodore Banks' *Milton's Imagery*, (1950), Malcolm M. Ross's *Milton's Royalism* (1943), and his more recent *Poetry and Dogma*, (1954).

III

A good single piece of interpretation of Milton's imagery in terms of the structure, tone, and symbolism of two of his shorter poems seems to me to be that of *L'Allegro* and *Il Penseroso* by Cleanth Brooks and John Edward Hardy in their edition (1951) of his 1645 volume, *Poems of Mr. John Milton*. It stems from Dr. Johnson's observations on the poems but comes closer to the heart of the matter than he did—closer even than did Tillyard in his famous essay, reprinted in *The Miltonic Setting* (1938), on the resemblances of *L'Allegro* to Milton's first Academic Exercise. The essays by Brooks and Hardy, however, are shrewdly criticized in Rosemund Tuve's *Images and Themes in Five Poems by Milton* (1957). Her book combines enthusiastic reading of the poems with skillful analysis of their subjects and imagery as both are controlled by the traditions of their respective literary genres.

Our best exposition of the visual imagery in *Paradise Lost* seems to me to be the essay entitled "Description as Cosmos" in Allen's *The Harmonious Vision;* it encircles and overwhelms T. S. Eliot's

contention that Milton was as blind imaginatively as he was physically. Tillyard has also made a telling reply to Eliot on critical
grounds rather different from Allen's by challenging the now
almost conventional modern doctrine that precise visual imagery
is right, while all else is wrong. And on interesting scientific
grounds Eleanor G. Brown showed in her dissertation on *Milton's
Blindness* (1934) that it did not impair his visual imagination. The
nonsense which was written about Milton's character on the basis
of his alleged "photophobia" in Germany in the 1920's has been
forgotten, but some amusing attacks on the artistic integrity of
Paradise Lost and on Milton's own integrity as a Christian humanist
are to be found in Ross's books[3] on the "royalism" which is latent
in the imagery of the poem and on the theological tendencies of
Milton's poetry in general. Ross's reasoning may convince
readers who are moved by the case which Liljegren and Phelps-
Morand have made against Milton as a supreme egotist and as one
of the early, and very culpable contributors to British imperialism,
both political and spiritual.[4] The case is still being grimly prosecuted abroad by scholars like Theodor Seibert, who has devoted
a monograph to the subject of the *Egozentrisches in Miltons
Schreibweise, in Anglia* (1930), and is convinced that in *Samson
Agonistes* Milton naïvely identified himself with the hero and in-
dulged in an imaginary holocaust of the Cavaliers at the court
of Charles II.

For those of us who are in danger of being unduly influenced
by the schools either of Ross or Phelps-Morand there are some
spiritual exercises to prescribe. The first of them is to read some of
Milton's prose tracts like *The Tenure of Kings and Magistrates*,
Eikonoklastes, some appropriate passages from the *History of
Britain*, and—above all—*Areopagitica*, with its famous assumption
that God always reveals new truth "first to his Englishmen." The
second step in the cure is to consider what *Areopagitica* actually
and effectively stands for in the world today as it is reflected in

[3] Malcolm MacKenzie Ross, *Milton's Royalism: A Study of the Conflict of
Symbol and Idea in the Poems* (1943) and *Poetry and Dogma: The Transfiguration of Eucharistic Symbols in Seventeenth Century English Poetry*
(1954).

[4] S. B. Liljegren, *Studies in Milton* (1919). Liljegren's evidence is largely
repeated by Paul Phelps-Morand in *The Effects of his Political Life upon
John Milton* (1939).

the symposium on *Freedom of Expression* which was held by the International P. E. N. in London on the tercentenary of its publication. The papers then read—on August 22–26, 1944, while the last of the German attacks by guided missiles was rocking London—are available in a volume[5] edited by Herman Ould. The cure may also be supplemented by reading W. R. Parker's very scholarly and conservative study of *Milton's Contemporary Reputation* (1940)—"contemporary" meaning in his own century—and G. F. Sensabaugh's enthusiastic collection of the evidence tending to prove that *That Grand Whig Milton* (1952) had a voice in the Revolutionary Settlement of 1688 and in the subsequent triumph of Whig theory in the reign of William and Mary. The cure consists, of course, in getting a proper perspective on Milton's political thinking and activity, subjects to which Sir Herbert Grierson has devoted his attention in some chapters of *Milton and Wordsworth* (1937), as Tillyard has in the chapter on "Milton and Prophetic Poetry" in *The Miltonic Setting*. If still more critical medicine is needed to give the right perspective, the prescription should be the *Study of the Imagery of John Donne* (1953) in which the author, Kaichi Matsura, makes a plausible attempt to convict Donne of a guilty share in the launching of British imperialism on the strength of his royalist imagery and his "vision of an imperialistic mission" for his country.

For readers who may be looking for antidotes to Seibert's theory that Milton's Samson was created simply as an outlet for the poet's spleen against his enemies it will be worth while to read W. R. Parker's study of the drama in terms of the hero's spiritual development, *Milton's Debt to Greek Tragedy in Samson Agonistes* (1937), and F. Michael Krouse's study of it in the light of its correspondences to the medieval conception of Samson as a Christian saint, *Milton's Samson and the Christian Tradition* (1949). And for those who are worried by Liljegren's contention that the Christ of *Paradise Regained* is a monstrous reflection of Milton's own harsh Stoicism there is very large encouragement to be found alike in the recent exploration of the imaginative and spiritual riches of the poem by Northrop Frye in "The Typology

[5] This volume is trenchantly criticized by George Orwell in "The Prevention of Literature," which was first published in *Shooting an Elephant* (1950) and is also available in *The Orwell Reader*.

of *Paradise Regained*," *MP* (1956), by A. S. P. Woodhouse in
"Theme and Pattern in *Paradise Regained*," *UTQ* (1956), and by
Arnold Stein in "The Kingdoms of the World: *Paradise Re-
gained*," *ELH* (1956).[6] Or if scholarly evidence of the impersonal-
ity of Milton's Christ is needed, it is to be had in Elizabeth M.
Pope's *Paradise Regained: The Tradition and the Poem* (1947).

There is enlightening reading too for those who regard *Comus*
as a stark and barren betrayal of Milton's Puritanism or as the
dramatic failure which is implied in an objection by Tillyard in
his *Milton* (1934), and which has been approved by later critics:
the objection that (in Allen's summary of it in *The Harmonious
Vision*) "the poetic texture of the masque is mixed in a fashion
that suggests confusion rather than the more desirable quality of
variety." The first objection has been more or less encouraged
by critics who, like A. S. P. Woodhouse in "The Argument of
Milton's *Comus*," *UTQ* (1941) and John Arthos in *A Mask Presented at Ludlow Castle* (1954), have tried to penetrate its Christian
and Platonic idealism. Instead of trying to summarize or arbitrate
the still unending debate, let me refer you to R. M. Adams' witty
survey of it in the opening chapter on "Reading *Comus*" in his
Ikon: John Milton and the Modern Critics (1955). And for students who fall in love with the mask and are ashamed of their
naïveté in doing so, let me recommend the confort to be found
in J. C. Maxwell's "The Pseudo-Problem of *Comus*" in *The Cambridge Journal* (1948).

If—all the way from *Comus* and *Lycidas* to *Samson Agonistes*—
students are appalled by Milton's uncompromising ethic and biblical theology, there may be no royal road through criticism to
understanding him or pentrating his poetic secret. But for a few
there may be a hard though exhilarating road to that goal through
such direct confrontation of his ethic as can be found in Douglas
Bush's *Paradise Lost in Our Time* (1945), or in John Diekhoff's
Commentary on the Argument of Milton's Paradise Lost (1946,
and now being reprinted), or through a study of his theology
such as Maurice Kelley's *This Great Argument* (1941). For
perhaps too many students Milton proves most attractive in the
guise of the heretic that Martin A. Larson enthusiastically pro-

[6] This essay is reprinted in Stein's new book on *Paradise Regained* and
Samson Agonistes, Heroic Knowledge (1957).

claimed in *The Modernity of Milton* (1927), but that picture is very much modified in George N. Conklin's *Biblical Criticism and Heresy in Milton* (1949), and it all but disappears in Sister Miriam Joseph's "Orthodoxy in *Paradise Lost*," *Centenary Publications of Saint Mary's College* (1954). For other students the road may run through translations of some of the famous Neo-Latin, Italian, or French analogues of parts of *Paradise Lost* as they are judiciously sampled by Watson Kirkconnell in *The Celestial Cycle* (1952). Or it may run through some of the parallels to his handling of the creation story among the commentators on Genesis as they are gathered in Sister Mary Corcoran's *Milton's Paradise with reference to the Hexameral Background* (1945) and in Arnold Williams' *The Common Expositor* (1948). Or the way may go through such tracing of the classical epic backgrounds as they are shown to have contributed to the Christian epic in C. M. Bowra's *From Virgil to Milton* (1948) or in C. S. Lewis's *A Preface to Paradise Lost* (1942).

IV

Books on a variety of more technical interests are too numerous for any justice to be done them here. Milton's versification has recently been studied in a book by S. Ernest Sprott, *Milton's Art of Prosody* (1952), along lines essentially like those followed by the poet Bridges in his little essay called *Milton's Prosody* in 1901, but even more recently the whole problem was thrown wide open by an analysis of the rhythms of the verse paragraphs of *Paradise Lost* in James Whaler's *Counterpoint and Symbol* (1956). Some of the best recent theorizing about this whole problem is to be found in F. T. Prince's *The Italian Element in Milton's Verse* (1954).

A pleasant non-technical study of a very different kind of technical subject is Robert H. West's *Milton and the Angels* (1955). Still another technical subject, Milton's education, is treated with solid knowledge and real humanity in Donald L. Clark's *John Milton at St. Paul's School* (1948), and with exhaustive thoroughness in the first volume of Harris Fletcher's *The Intellectual Development of John Milton* (1956). And for those who wish to go into the more absorbing problems of Milton's development in his mature years there are two good books: James H. Hanford's *John Milton, Englishman* (1949) and Arthur Barker's *Milton and the Puritan Dilemma* (1942, reprinted 1956). And finally, for those who are trying to avoid the technical and the biographical jungles and find their way to the pure poetry in the major poems we have W. B. C. Watkins' rather misleadingly entitled *An Anatomy of Milton's Verse* (Baton Rouge, 1955), Kenneth Muir's superb *John Milton* (1955), and David Daiches' *Milton* (1957).

This survey ought not to end without recognition of the great editions of *Paradise Lost* which have recently been completed after years of loving labor by Helen Darbishire, by Harris Fletcher, and by B. A. Wright,[7] as well as of the first volume of Don Wolfe's complete edition of Milton's *Prose Works* through the Yale University Press.

[7] *The Poetical Works of John Milton*, edited by Helen Darbishire. Vol. I. *Paradise Lost* (1952). Vol. II. *Paradise Regain'd, Samson Agonistes, Poems Upon Several Occasions, Both English and Latin* (1955); *John Milton, Complete Poetical Works, Reproduced in Photographic Facsimile*, by Harris Fletcher. Vol. I (1943), Vol. II (1945); and *Milton: Paradise Lost*, edited by B. A. Wright (1956). Recent (1957) annotated editions for more general use are *Milton: Shorter English Poems and Samson Agonistes*, edited by Arthur Barker; *John Milton: Complete Poems and Major Prose*, edited by M. Y. Hughes; *Milton: Samson Agonistes*, edited by F. T. Prince; and *Paradise Lost: Books I and II*, edited by E. M. W. Tillyard with notes by Phyllis B. Tillyard.

6

The Eighteenth Century

JAMES L. CLIFFORD

IT IS A TRUISM THAT EACH AGE disdains that which has gone before. Nineteenth-century critics looked down on the literary productions of the eighteenth century (Dryden and Pope, said Matthew Arnold, were masters of English prose, not true poets at all), just as the Augustans had found fault with most of what had been written in the sixteenth and early seventeenth centuries. Time is always necessary for perspective. Thus only recently has it been possible to achieve any balanced estimate of the work of the so-called neoclassic period.

At the risk of oversimplification, it might be said that three considerations have stood in the way of this new appreciation. First, there has been the undeniable fact that most of the important creative artists of the period were politically conservative, sometimes apparently even reactionary. The best poets—Dryden, Pope, Johnson—the greatest satirist—Swift—and the clearest thinker—Hume—were all Tories. For young people imbued with romantic idealism this fact alone has made them unattractive. Moreover, the striving of these writers for classical objectivity, with its stress on the general rather than the specific, has proved uncongenial to those who are steeped in the complexities of modern personal analysis. And third, there has been a feeling that poetry is inevitably shackled and congealed when restricted to any such narrow verse form as the couplet.

Nevertheless, during the past thirty years there has been a determined onslaught on these basic assumptions, so that by the mid-twentieth century we are in a better position to examine their validity. It must be admitted that the new approach has not usually found its way into high school or college texts, or into the standard reference works, though there are a few surveys which

can be heartily recommended. The best is that by George Sherburn in *A Literary History of England*, edited by A. C. Baugh
(1948). Also excellent, but shorter, is that by Louis I. Bredvold
in *A History of English Literature*, edited by Hardin Craig
(1950). Superseding all earlier handbooks is A. D. McKillop, *English Literature from Dryden to Burns* (1948); and there are compact summaries by John Butt in *The Augustan Age* (1950) and by
Roger P. McCutcheon in *Eighteenth-Century English Literature*
(1949).

For the most part, the most stimulating discussions must be
sought in out-of-the-way volumes of research and in the little
magazines and quarterlies. If many of the scholarly works are
slighted in what follows, the reason is that emphasis is placed on
critical reappraisals immediately applicable to classroom presentation. Those who so desire may find everything which is important
listed in the annual bibliography sponsored by the periodical
Philological Quarterly (a convenient reprint for the years 1926–
1950 was prepared by Louis A. Landa in two volumes, 1950, 1952).
Concentration here must be on authors and works normally included in school courses.

I

As suggested, one of the chief difficulties in the appreciation
of the early eighteenth-century satirists has been that they were
politically so conservative. We call them "Tory satirists." But
for Americans the term *Tory* carries reflections of our own Revolution. To be a Tory is to be a heartless reactionary, out of tune
with the liberal aspirations of the common man.

The trouble, perhaps, is largely semantic. A Tory in the Age
of Queen Anne had different ideals and different assumptions
from those of the Tories of the nineteenth and early twentieth
centuries. It is necessary to recover the earlier state of mind before
judgment can be passed. Happily through the exhaustive investigations of the English historian Sir Lewis Namier and his co-workers
we can now see what it was to have been a Tory in the time of
Swift and Johnson. Namier's classic volume *Structure of Politics
at the Accession of George III* (1929), Richard Pares's *King
George III and the Politicians* (1953), Herbert Butterfield's *George*

III, Lord North, and the People (1949), and Robert Walcott's *English Politics in the Early Eighteenth Century* (1956), while strictly devoted to political realities, are of immense importance for any understanding of the literature of the period.

For one thing, there were then no active party organizations, as we know them today, and no clear-cut divisions between capital and labor, or between "right" and "left." Instead, there were merely small splinter groups, held together by family loyalties, court connections, or economic alliances. Most modern students have assumed that the workers, the poor and the destitute, were always on the side of the Whigs, that liberalism and philanthropy were always Whig attributes. So we have been told repeatedly by the most famous nineteenth-century historians—see Herbert Butterfield, *The Whig Interpretation of History* (1931). But J. H. Plumb in the first volume of his fascinating life of Sir Robert Walpole (1956) insists that in the age of Queen Anne and the early Hanoverians the workers were largely on the Tory side. It was the rich and ambitious, those involved in the rise of the new industrialism, who were chiefly Whigs. The financial interests saw clearly that they could control Parliament more easily than they could the King. The bulk of the laborers, on the other hand, found working conditions deteriorating, for the business men, who were eager for expanding production, insisted on longer hours and tried to destroy what remained of the protective legislation and guild organization of the time of the Tudors and Stuarts. As a result, the journeymen, like the country gentry, looked back to a world in which their place had been more secure.

With all this in mind, we can find a more radical tinge in many of the protests of the Tory satirists. Of course, the Tories did not look forward for a solution. They were basically aristocratic and monarchial, for they placed their reliance on a strong central government which could restrain the rampant exploitation of workers by the new capitalists. But what they feared and what they fought was essentially what many modern liberals are still attacking. When placed in the proper political setting the pessimistic satires of Pope, Swift, and Johnson should have greater relevance for modern students.

Besides, the despair of these men, as L. I. Bredvold has pointed out so well in his essay "The Gloom of the Tory Satirists" in

Pope and His Contemporaries: Essays Presented to George Sher-burn, edited by J. L. Clifford and Louis A. Landa (1949), is tough-minded and virile. Deeply serious and realistic, it is scornful of utopias and dubious of easy solutions. Naturally such pessimism was unacceptable to many in the nineteenth century, with their deep faith in progress. But today, when the belief in man's steady advance through the discoveries of science and through the expansion of industrialism is beginning to fade, what the satirists have to say is clearly more acceptable. Indeed, nowhere in literature is there a more horrifying prophecy of what has happened to Europe during the past two decades than the majestic conclusion of Pope's *Dunciad.* The fact that the savage predictions of what man would make of man which were uttered by the Tory satirists did not immediately come true does not mean that these men were merely jaundiced misfits motivated by personal spite and frustrated ambition. Today their world view may appear only too tragically apposite (see, for example, Aubrey Williams' admirable study of the *Dunciad* and other discussions of the work of Pope and Swift and their group mentioned later in this essay).

From a literary point of view also the assumptions of the English Augustan writers, which seemed so utterly absurd to the Romantics, have been objectively examined. Though the mid-twentieth-century sensibility is still not wholly in tune with that of the eighteenth century, we can at least approach these earlier writers with a clearer insight into their aims and accomplishments. Valuable are a number of brilliant surveys: Ronald S. Crane, "English Neoclassical Criticism: an Outline Sketch," reprinted in *Critics and Criticism* (1952); René Wellek, *A History of Modern Criticism* (1955); and W. K. Wimsatt, Jr., and Cleanth Brooks, *Literary Critcism: A Short History* (1957). Other books which illumine special problems are: W. J. Bate, *From Classic to Romantic* (1946); F. A. Pottle, *The Idiom of Poetry* (second edition, 1946); James R. Sutherland, *A Preface to Eighteenth Century Poetry* (1948); Ian Jack, *Augustan Satire: Intention and Idiom in English Poetry, 1660–1750* (1952); and Meyer H. Abrams, *The Mirror and the Lamp* (1953).

Although not emphasizing literary values, what we call the History of Ideas school of research is basic for much of our new understanding of the concepts of the age. This is not the place to analyze the whole movement, but a few major accomplishments may be mentioned: A. O. Lovejoy, *The Great Chain of Being* (1936) and his *Essays in the History of Ideas* (1948); Samuel Monk, *The Sublime* (1935); Marjorie H. Nicolson, *Newton Demands the Muse* (1946) and her *Science and Imagination* (1956); Ernest L. Tuveson, *Millennium and Utopia* (1949); and R. F. Jones, *The Seventeenth Century: Studies in the History of English Thought and Literature from Bacon to Pope* (1951). These works concentrate on ideas and intellectual history, not aesthetic concerns. Yet if much of the material used as evidence comes from long-forgotten third-rate authors, the conclusions reached are essential also for any comprehension of the shifting currents of thought in which the major writers moved.

A few other special studies may be mentioned here—useful for explaining various shifts of taste during the period: Elizabeth W. Manwaring, *Italian Landscape in Eighteenth Century England* (1925); Christopher Hussey, *The Picturesque* (1927); Hoxie N. Fairchild, *The Noble Savage* (1928); John W. Draper, *The Funeral Elegy and the Rise of English Romanticism* (1929); B. Sprague Allen, *Tides in English Taste* (1937); William Appleton, *A Cycle of Cathay* (1951); and Samuel Kliger, *The Goths in England* (1952).

Recently much significant work has been done in examining the verbal and prosodic difficulties which have stood in the way of our full appreciation of eighteenth-century poetry. Too long we have accepted Wordsworth's attack on the stock diction of his predecessors without understanding completely why this type of writing came into use or what it professed to do. Pioneer work in background has been done by Geoffrey Tillotson in "Eighteenth-century Poetic Diction," *Essays in Criticism and Research* (1942); W. K. Wimsatt, Jr., *Philosophic Words: A Study of Style and Meaning in the Rambler and Dictionary of Samuel Johnson* (1948); and John Arthos, *The Language of Natural Description in Eighteenth-Century Poetry* (1949). Other stimulating discussions may be found in Donald Davie, *Purity of Diction in English Verse* (1952) and F. R. Leavis, "The Augustan Tradition" in *Revaluation* (1936).

A stumbling block for many modern readers is the constant use of the personified abstraction by eighteenth-century poets. But a number of critics have of late come to its defense. The first was Bertrand H. Bronson in "Personification Reconsidered," *ELH* (1947). He was followed by Earl R. Wasserman in "The Inherent Values of Eighteenth-Century Personification," *PMLA* (1950); and finally by Chester F. Chapin in *Personification in Eighteenth-Century English Poetry* (1955). Chapin shows that there were two basic types of personification used in the period, one largely pictorial, related to the image and allegorical in effect (it was this kind which led to such works as those of Erasmus Darwin and the sort of writing which Wordsworth so detested); and a second type which in poets like Pope and Johnson achieved deep metaphorical meaning through passionate personal experience.

For a technical study of the shift in prosodic theory from neoclassic syllabism and stress regularity to romantic accentualism, Paul Fussell, Jr., *Theory of Prosody in Eighteenth-Century England* (1954) may be recommended.

II

As part of the reviving interest in the art of the couplet, the poetry of Alexander Pope is central. From the pioneer volumes of R. K. Root, *The Poetical Career of Alexander Pope*, and Geoffrey Tillotson, *On the Poetry of Pope*, which appeared in the same year (1938), to the recent penetrating studies by Maynard Mack and W. K. Wimsatt, Jr., there has been a steady attack on the old, entrenched illusion that the heroic couplet is a confining, jogtrot form. Wimsatt, in two articles reprinted in *The Verbal Icon* (1954) and in the Introduction to his useful paper-back Rinehart edition of Pope (1951), points to the rhetorical techniques through which variety and tension are obtained. What seems to me to be the best single analysis of Pope's art is Maynard Mack's " 'Wit and Poetry and Pope': Some Observations on His Imagery" in *Pope and His Contemporaries* (1949). Also valuable are his "On Reading Pope," *CE* (1946) and "The Muse of Satire," *Yale Review* (1951). Rebecca Price Parkin, *The Poetic Workmanship of Alexander Pope* (1955) is, for the most part, a summation of the new approaches.

What all this inescapably shows is the complexity of Pope's art. Lines which so many have assumed to be merely highly polished epigrams carry under their smooth surface a multitude of tensions and many layers of meaning. Beneath what often appears to be almost the language of prose lie depths of metaphor, which students need to have shown to them. Indeed, the poetry of Pope is difficult in a way in which romantic poetry is not. The richness is not open to every sensitive reader. To understand him fully requires work, just as Donne demands hard study. But the rewards, too, are great, once the keys to his deeper meaning are provided.

Renewed interest in Pope has shown itself in more ways than an awareness of the richness of his prosodic art. George Sherburn, in his *Early Career of Alexander Pope* (1934) and in his recent superb edition of Pope's correspondence (see later), has set straight many false impressions concerning the poet's career. Norman Ault in *New Light on Pope* (1949), Robert W. Rogers in *The Major Satires of Alexander Pope* (1955), and others have continued the process of bringing light to many dark corners of Pope's tangled relationships.

Six volumes have so far been published of the long-awaited new edition of the poetical works—the Twickenham Edition—under the general supervision of John Butt, and with the aid of James R. Sutherland, Geoffrey Tillotson, Maynard Mack, Frederick W. Bateson, and Norman Ault. Only the early poems and the Homeric translations have yet to appear. This edition has now become standard. In addition, it is expected that the late Norman Ault's edition of Pope's prose works (Vol. I appeared in 1936) will be completed by Maynard Mack. The *Peri Bathous* has been reproduced in facsimile, with full annotation, by Edna Leake Steeves (1952); and Pope's part in the Scriblerian projects is examined by Charles Kerby-Miller in his edition of the *Memoirs of Scriblerus* (1950).

The new sympathetic approach to Pope as a creative artist is evidenced by a number of stimulating shorter estimates, notably in F. R. Leavis, "Pope" in *Revaluation* (1936), D. Nichol Smith, "Pope: Poetic Diction" in *Some Observations on Eighteenth Century Poetry* (1937), G. Wilson Knight, "The Vital Flame: An Essay on Pope" in *The Burning Oracle* (1939), Gilbert Bagnini, "The Classical Technique: Virgil, Dante, and Pope" in *The*

Phoenix, (1947), and Austin Warren, "The Mask of Pope" in
Rage for Order (1948).

But of even more immediate value to the teacher in the classroom are various searching studies bearing on particular poems.
Explaining much about the background and form of the early
verses are: J. E. Congleton, *Theories of Pastoral Poetry in England,
1684–1798* (1952); *Pope's Windsor Forest, 1712: A Study of the
Washington University Holograph*, edited by Robert M. Schmitz
(1952); and Ann Winslow, "Re-evaluation of Pope's Treatment
of Nature," *University of Wyoming Publications* (1938).

To those who have been repeating the venerable generalization
that the *Essay on Criticism* is a bundle of trite but facile epigrams,
two recent essays, the first by William Empson, "Wit in the *Essay on Criticism*," *Hudson Review* (1950) and the second by
Edward N. Hooker, "Pope on Wit: the *Essay on Criticism*" in
R. F. Jones's *The Seventeenth Century* (1951), may come as something of a shock. Empson demonstrates the carefully planned
ambiguities involved in Pope's shifting use of the term *wit*,
while Hooker goes even further in showing the consummate skill
with which Pope in this poem was defending poetry in an original
way against the various Philistine attacks of his day.

Two stimulating approaches to "The Rape of the Lock," one
partly Freudian and the other social, may be found in Cleanth
Brooks, "The Case of Miss Arabella Fermor: A Re-examination,"
reprinted in *The Well Wrought Urn* (1947), and Hugo M.
Reichard, "The Love Affair in Pope's *Rape of the Lock*," *PMLA*
(1954). Possibly the last word concerning the puzzling game of
cards is said by W. K. Wimsatt, Jr., in "The Game of Ombre in
The Rape of the Lock," *RES* (1950). Another interesting point
is made by William Frost in "*The Rape of the Lock* and Pope's
Homer," *MLQ* (1947). By all odds the best appraisal of the
Homeric translations is contained in Douglas Knight's *Pope and
the Heroic Tradition* (1951).

Maynard Mack's Introduction to his edition of the *Essay on
Man* in the Twickenham series (1950) should be required reading
for any who still consider it a shallow, optimistic poem, which
merely repeats in memorable lines the glib precepts of Boling-
broke. Perhaps no phrase in literature is more often used with an

implied false interpretation than Pope's "Whatever is, is right." Rather than a Leibnitzian statement that this is the best of all possible worlds, it may be understood more accurately as a simple, orthodox reaffirmation of the goodness of God. That Pope was fundamentally a pessimist about human existence on this earth the whole body of his work makes plain.

Finally, the key work for any true understanding of Pope's position is the *Dunciad*. All the standard objections to the poem have been vigorously marshalled by Gilbert Highet in "The *Dunciad*," *MLR* (1941). On the other hand, the ablest defense comes in Aubrey L. Williams, *Pope's Dunciad: A Study of Its Meaning* (1955). Further excellent points are made by Austin Warren, "The Mask of Pope," *Rage for Order* (1948), Ian Jack, *Augustan Satire* (1952), George Sherburn, "The *Dunciad*, Book IV" *University of Texas Studies in English 1944*, and Hugo M. Reichard, "Pope's Social Satire: Belles-Lettres and Business," *PMLA* (1952).

Pope has been discussed at some length because from a literary point of view he is the most central, as well as the most controversial, figure of the period. Dryden is his closest rival as a poet, some would say his superior. Yet since Dryden died in 1700 he can scarcely be put into the eighteenth century. Nevertheless, something must be said here about the widespread revival of interest in his life and work. Significantly, a great new edition of his poetry and prose has been started at the University of California, with the late Edward N. Hooker and H. T. Swedenberg, Jr., as general editors. The first volume of the poetry, scrupulously reproduced and voluminously annotated, appeared in 1956. Meanwhile G. R. Noyes's one-volume edition of the poetry has been thoroughly revised and reissued (1950). It is the best single source of information about Dryden's life and major poems. Samuel Monk has provided a valuable reference tool in *John Dryden: A List of Critical Studies Published from 1895 to 1948* (1950), and J. M. Osborn, in *John Dryden: Some Biographical Facts and Problems* (1940) a mine of miscellaneous information.

Since the pioneering work of A. W. Verrall, Mark Van Doren, and T. S. Eliot, much has been done to rehabilitate Dryden's reputation. Of chief importance for teachers are L. I. Bredvold, *The Intellectual Milieu of John Dryden* (1934), conveniently re-

issued as a paperback; D. Nichol Smith, *John Dryden* (1950); and
several chapters in Ian Jack, *Augustan Satire* (1952). That Dryden
has been sadly neglected as a lyricist because his short poems are
usually too indecent to be included in popular anthologies is apparent from Cyrus L. Day's edition, *The Songs of John Dryden*
(1932), and J. H. Wilson, *The Court Wits of the Restoration*
(1948).

There is opportunity to glance at only a few significant analyses
of individual works: E. N. Hooker, "The Purpose of Dryden's
Annus Mirabilis," *HLQ* (1946); George Williamson, "The Occasion of *An Essay of Dramatic Poesy*," *MP* (1946); Frank L.
Huntley, *On Dryden's Essay of Dramatic Poesy* (1951); Ruth C.
Wallerstein, "To Madness Near Allied: Shaftesbury and His Place
in the Design and Thought of *Absalom and Achitophel*," *HLQ*
(1943) and her " 'On the Death of Mrs. Killigrew': The Perfect-
ing of a Genre," *SP* (1947); Godfrey Davies, "The Conclusion of
Dryden's *Absalom and Achitophel*," *HLQ* (1946); and Hoyt
Trowbridge, "The Place of Rules in Dryden's Criticism," *MP*
(1946). Useful estimates of the value of Dryden's criticism may
be found in J. W. H. Atkins, *English Literary Criticism 17th and
18th Centuries* (1951), though his approach is generally traditional and uninspired, and in W. K. Wimsatt, Jr., and Cleanth
Brooks, *Literary Criticism: A Short History*.

If Dryden and Pope are the major poets of the period, Jonathan
Swift is without doubt the greatest genius. Though the fact has
long been recognized, it has only been within recent years
that we have been able to take all of his writing without revulsion.
Fortunately, the prudery and sensitive taste which for so long
banished many of his more savage pieces to the scholar's shelves
have now for the most part been put aside, and with this shift
there has come a reawakening of interest in Swift's poetry, which
Sir Harold Williams's three volume edition (1937) now makes
easily available. The most cogent defense even of the so-called
unprintable verses may be found in Maurice Johnson, *The Sin of
Wit: Jonathan Swift as a Poet* (1950).

Now that the Shakespeare Head Edition of Swift's prose works
is nearing completion under the indefatigable editorship of
Herbert Davis, there will be easy access to everything of importance which Swift wrote. The *Journal to Stella*, omitted from this

set of volumes, has been admirably edited by Sir Harold Williams for the Clarendon series (1948). Indispensable for keeping up with earlier research is *Jonathan Swift: A List of Critical Studies Published from 1895–1945*, compiled by Louis A. Landa and James E. Tobin (1945).

For beginning students, an excellent book to recommend is Ricardo Quintana, *Swift: An Introduction* (1955), more up-to-date, though in less detail, than his *Mind and Art of Jonathan Swift* (1936, reissued 1953). There have been numerous popular biographies, the latest being John Middleton Murry's intriguing, though not always completely balanced, *Jonathan Swift* (1954). Irvin Ehrenpreis is completing what should be an exhaustive, scholarly account. Of the many attempts at psychoanalysis, Phyllis Greenacre, *Swift and Carroll* (1955) is perhaps the most rewarding. A prerequisite to any evaluation of Swift's professional career is Louis A. Landa, *Swift and the Church of Ireland* (1954).

The most notable development in Swift scholarship is the recent stress on his rhetorical techniques. Three books published within two years take this approach: John M. Bullitt, *Jonathan Swift and the Anatomy of Satire* (1953), Martin Price, *Swift's Rhetorical Art: A Study in Structure and Meaning* (1953), and W. B. Ewald Jr., *The Masks of Jonathan Swift* (1954). A more general approach may be found in Herbert Davis, *The Satire of Jonathan Swift* (1947).

Necessary for any full appreciation of Swift's first published volume are R. F. Jones, *Ancients and Moderns: A Study of the Background of the Battle of the Books* (1936); Miriam K. Starkman, *Swift's Satire on Learning in A Tale of a Tub* (1950); and also, for two differing approaches, Robert C. Elliott, "Swift's *Tale of a Tub*: An Essay in Problems of Structure," *PMLA* (1951), and Harold D. Kelling, "Reason in Madness: *A Tale of a Tub*," *PMLA* (1954). The standard edition by Guthkelch and Nichol Smith has just been completely revised and reissued.

By common agreement Swift's universal masterpiece is *Gulliver's Travels*. For continuing controversies concerning the text, see Sir Harold Williams, *The Text of Gulliver's Travels* (1952). Chiefly, however, concentration in recent years has centered on explication of Swift's complex political allegory, his special use of symbols, and his often well-hidden general meaning. The best single volume of commentary is Arthur E. Case, *Four Essays on Gulliver's Travels* (1945), but there has been a wealth of supplementary discussion since 1945. Only a few stimulating overall commentaries may be listed: Z. S. Fink, "Political Theory in *Gulliver's Travels*," *ELH* (1947), Robert C. Elliott, "Gulliver as Literary Artist," *ELH* (1952), Harold D. Kelling, "*Gulliver's Travels*: A Comedy of Humors," *UTQ* (1952), Samuel H. Monk, "The Pride of Lemuel Gulliver," *SR* (1955), and Ellen D. Leyburn, *Satiric Allegory: Mirror of Man* (1956).

Linguists, as well as those interested in Joycean coinage of words, may find some minor interest in a series of very controversial arguments concerning Swift's manufacture of proper names and various word plays. A few which will be useful in teaching *Gulliver's Travels* might be mentioned: H. D. Kelling, "Some Significant Names in *Gulliver's Travels*," *SP* (1951), Paul Odell Clark, "A *Gulliver* Dictionary," *SP* (1953), and Roland M. Smith, "Swift's Little Language and Nonsense Names," *JEGP* (1954, 1957).

Of the three earlier voyages the third undoubtedly requires the most scholarly explication, and for this purpose articles by Marjorie H. Nicolson collected in her *Science and Imagination* (1956) will be invaluable. See also John H. Sutherland, "A Reconsideration of Gulliver's Third Voyage," *SP* (1957).

Teachers and students alike inevitably find the fourth voyage the most provocative, for it has always been an obstacle to any easy interpretation of Swift's meaning. A survey of past attitudes may be found in Merrel D. Clubb, "The Criticism of Gulliver's 'Voyage to the Houyhnhnms,' 1726–1914," *Stanford Studies in Language and Literature*, edited by Hardin Craig (1941). For stress on the theological background there are Louis A. Landa, "Jonathan Swift," *English Institute Essays 1946*, Ernest Tuveson, "Swift: The Dean as Satirist," *UTQ* (1953), and Roland M. Frye, "Swift's Yahoo and the Christian Symbols for Sin," *JHI* (1954). Kathleen M. Williams uses the sermons as evidence of Swift's intentions in "Gulliver's Voyage to the Houyhnhnms," *ELH* (1951). For a debatable theory that the end of the voyage was meant to be comic, see John F. Ross, "The Final Comedy of Lemuel Gulliver," *Studies in the Comic* (*University of California*

Studies, 1941), and Edward Stone, "Swift and the Horses: Misanthropy or Comedy?" *MLQ* (1949).

A few valuable articles having to do with other important works by Swift should be listed: Irvin Ehrenpreis, "Swift's 'Little Language' in the *Journal to Stella*," *SP* (1948), Louis A. Landa, "*A Modest Proposal* and Populousness," *MP* (1942), George Wittkowsky, "Swift's *Modest Proposal*: The Biography of an Early Georgian Pamphlet," *JHI* (1943), Carl R. Woodring, "The Aims, Audience, and Structure of the Drapier's Fourth Letter," *MLQ* (1956), and Mackie L. Jarrell, "The Proverbs in Swift's *Polite Conversation*," *HLQ* (1956).

The fascination of Swift is so great that one might be tempted to continue with the many complicated problems connected with his satiric intentions, but it is necessary to move on to other notable authors of the period. There have been excellent collections of the letters of Addison and Steele (listed later), and a sound, factual biography of Addison by Peter Smithers (1954). For a discriminating shorter study see C. S. Lewis, "Addison" in *Essays on the Eighteenth Century Presented to David Nichol Smith* (1945). Rae Blanchard progresses steadily with her editing of the lesser works of Steele, and John Loftis has provided a study of his connection with the theater in *Steele at Drury Lane* (1952).

For the most part, discussion of the *Spectator* has centered on Addison's critical papers. Active in claiming Addison as a precursor of romantic theory is Clarence Thorpe. See, for example, his "Addison's Contribution to Criticism," in R. F. Jones's *The Seventeenth Century*, and various earlier studies in *ELH* (1935), *Papers of the Michigan Academy* (1936), and *PMLA* (1937). Not everyone, it might be added, will agree with all of Thorpe's contentions. Further interesting approaches appear in E. F. Carritt, "Addison, Kant, and Wordsworth," *Essays and Studies by Members of the English Association* (1937), Martin Kallich, "The Association of Ideas and Critical Theory: Hobbes, Locke, and Addison," *ELH* (1945), and Edward and Lillian Bloom, "Joseph Addison and Eighteenth-Century 'Liberalism,'" *JHI* (1951).

Still the best life of Defoe is that by James R. Sutherland (1937), though John Robert Moore is now completing an exhaustive biographical account which should be in print soon. To name all the recent contributions of Moore to Defoe scholarship would require almost a volume itself, for he has been untiring in widening the canon and in discovering every fact that can be turned up about one of the most enigmatic personalities of the period. There has been a flurry of interest concerning the background of the "Apparition of Mrs. Veal," the latest discovery being a newspaper version which appeared some months before Defoe's. For a summary of the latest evidence, see Arthur H. Scouten, "An Early Printed Report on the Apparition of Mrs. Veal," *RES* (1955), and Arthur W. Secord, "A September Day in Canterbury: the Veal-Bargrave Story," *JEGP* (1955). A few discerning approaches to the novels may be found in A. D. McKillop, *The Early Masters of English Fiction* (1956), Ian Watt, *The Rise of the Novel* (1957), E. B. Benjamin, "Symbolic Elements in *Robinson Crusoe*," *PQ* (1951), Benjamin Boyce, "The Question of Emotion in Defoe," *SP* (1953), and Spiro Peterson, "The Matrimonial Theme of Defoe's *Roxana*," *PMLA* (1955).

The standard life of Gay is by W. H. Irving (1940), and there is a delightful appreciation of his art by James R. Sutherland in *Pope and His Contemporaries*. Sven M. Armens in *John Gay, Social Critic* (1954) stresses the serious side of his work. Bertrand H. Bronson has provided the best discussion of *The Beggar's Opera* in *Studies in the Comic* (*University of California Studies*, 1941).

C. K. Eves has written the most complete life of Prior (1939), but for criticism of the ideas in his poems one should go to a series of articles by Monroe K. Spears in *ELH* (1946), *SP* (1948), *PMLA* (1948), and *PQ* (1948). In the Rede Lecture at Cambridge in 1957, R. W. Ketton-Cremer provides a charming summary of the poet's career. A new scholarly edition of Prior's poems in the Clarendon series is being prepared by Spears and H. Bunker Wright.

For James Thomson there are the recent biography by Douglas Grant (1951), and the thorough discussions of his ideas by A. D. McKillop in *The Background of Thomson's Seasons* (1942) and "The Background of Thomson's *Liberty*," *Rice Institute Pamphlet* (1951). See also C. A. Moore, *Backgrounds of English Literature, 1700–1760* (1953).

Excellent biographies of other figures should be pointed out: David Hume by Ernest Mossner (1954), Lady Mary Wortley Montagu by Robert Halsband (1956), Richard Savage by C. R. Tracy (1953), Allan Ramsay the Younger by Alastair Smart

(1952), and Tom Brown by Benjamin Boyce (1939), to name only a few. And also significant are special studies such as those of Bishop Joseph Butler by Ernest Mossner (1936), Sir Joshua Reynolds by F. W. Hilles (1936), William Hogarth by Robert E. Moore (1948), and the Third Earl of Shaftesbury by R. L. Brett (1951). Concerned with the last named is a useful article by Ernest Tuveson, "The Importance of Shaftesbury," *ELH* (1953).

III

The mid-century has often been called "The Age of Johnson." Although Ernest Mossner may argue that David Hume has a better claim, as a more profound thinker, a better balanced personality, and as being closer to the chief currents of thought, Samuel Johnson has traditionally been considered the central figure of this colorful period. Paradoxically, he has held this pre-eminence despite long neglect of his own published works. See B. H. Bronson, "The Double Tradition of Dr. Johnson," *ELH* (1951). Indeed, some casual critics have gone so far as to claim that his fame rests solely on the brilliance of his biographer, James Boswell. It was Boswell's genius, they say, that made Johnson great. In scholarly circles and among the New Critics, however, there has recently been a determined effort to fasten attention again where it belongs, on Johnson's literary productions. As part of the campaign, a complete edition of his works is in progress at Yale, under the supervision of Allen T. Hazen and Herman W. Liebert, and the first volume will appear early in 1958.

Active in pushing the new appreciation of Johnson the thinker and literary artist have been D. Nichol Smith, editor with E. L. McAdam Jr. of the poems; T. S. Eliot, who in an introduction to an edition of the poems (1930), has called *London* and *The Vanity of Human Wishes* "among the greatest verse Satires of the English or any other language"; F. R. Leavis in *Scrutiny* (1944); Joseph Wood Krutch, who has written the best modern biography (1944); and Walter Jackson Bate, whose *The Achievement of Samuel Johnson* (1955) represents one of the most cogent and persuasive arguments for the Great Cham's claim to fame. These, together with a number of admirable special studies—Bertrand H. Bronson, *Johnson Agonistes* (1946), W. K. Wimsatt, Jr., *The*

Prose Style of Samuel Johnson (1941), E. L. McAdam, Jr., *Dr. Johnson and the English Law* (1951), and Jean H. Hagstrum, *Samuel Johnson's Literary Criticism* (1952), to name only some of the more obvious—have fastened attention again on Johnson's powerful mind and genuine literary gifts.

Since my *Johnsonian Studies 1887–1950: A Survey and Bibliography* (1951) lists all recent studies of Johnson in every category; and since in the Introduction I have described the various shifts of Johnson's reputation, there would appear to be no need to repeat that discussion here. But a few other works which have been published since 1950 may well be mentioned. My *Young Sam Johnson* (1955) attempts to gather together all that is known about the great man's early life. There have been two excellent critical analyses of the major poems: Macdonald Emslie, "Johnson's Satires and the 'Proper Wit of Poetry,' " *Cambridge Journal* (1954), and Henry Gifford, "*The Vanity of Human Wishes*," *RES* (1955).

The touchstone of Johnsonian taste is *Rasselas*. If anyone wishes to know whether he can be a true Johnsonian, in addition to being a Boswellian, a reading of this philosophical tale will provide the answer. Gwin J. Kolb has provided an analysis in "The Structure of *Rasselas*," *PMLA* (1951), and Mary Lascelles a critical appraisal in "*Rasselas* Reconsidered," *Essays and Studies by Members of the English Association* (1951). Three volumes about other works of Johnson bring together much that is new and important: Benjamin B. Hoover, *Samuel Johnson's Parliamentary Reporting* (1953), James H. Sledd and Gwin J. Kolb, *Dr. Johnson's Dictionary: Essays in the Biography of a Book* (1955), and Arthur Sherbo, *Samuel Johnson, Editor of Shakespeare* (1956). Donald J. Greene has completed an impressive study of his political beliefs (University Microfilms, 1954).

But it is as a critic that Johnson's reputation has taken the most pronounced turn. Whereas the Romantics and Victorians thought his pronouncements completely insensitive and wrong-headed, many twentieth-century critics are finding much to praise, even in some of his notorious comments. "Johnson is a better critic of eighteenth-century poetry than Matthew Arnold," says F. R. Leavis. His treatment of Gray, Leavis insists, actually shows his excellence in sensing a basic "weakness of taste in his age." Krutch,

Hagstrum, and Bate, as well as Wellek and Wimsatt show clearly the strength and basic validity, yet at the same time certain self-imposed limitations, of many of Johnson's literary judgments. For an admirable short summing up there is W. R. Keast, "The Theoretical Foundations of Johnson's Criticism," *Critics and Criticism*, edited by R. S. Crane (1952). An interesting analysis of one of the *Lives of the Poets* appears in Benjamin Boyce, "Samuel Johnson's Criticism of Pope in the *Life of Pope*," *RES* (1954).

Increasing emphasis on Johnson as a writer has not meant any depreciation of Boswell. Indeed, Boswell's stature as a creative artist has also been mounting, for with the fabulous discovery of his lost journals and letters we can see that besides being one of the world's great biographers he ranks with Pepys and Rousseau as one of the most fascinating and revealing diarists. His *London Journal* (1950) has already taken its place as a classic of its kind. Under the able direction of Frederick A. Pottle and his group of assistants, other volumes in the Yale-McGraw-Hill series of the journals are appearing regularly. The first volume of Pottle's authoritative life of Boswell is expected shortly. Meanwhile, L. F. Powell has completed (1950) his re-editing of the G. B. Hill standard edition of the *Life of Johnson* and the *Tour to the Hebrides*. For an important analysis of Boswell's method of recording conversations, see F. A. Pottle, "The Power of Memory in Boswell and Scott," *Essays on the Eighteenth Century Presented to David Nichol Smith* (1945).

There has been no such reawakening of interest in Oliver Goldsmith, though T. S. Eliot has led the way in giving high praise to *The Deserted Village* in "What is Minor Poetry?" *SR* (1946). Perhaps any full reassessment must await the appearance of the complete edition of his works begun years ago by R. S. Crane and now nearing completion under the editorship of Arthur Friedman. In the meantime F. W. Hilles has provided an excellent selection for the Modern Library (1955). Very effective for reading aloud in class is a character sketch of Goldsmith by Sir Joshua Reynolds, hitherto unknown, and printed for the first time in Hilles' *Portraits by Sir Joshua Reynolds* (1952). Also useful for stimulating student discussion are W. F. Gallaway, Jr., "The Sentimentalism of Goldsmith," *PMLA* (1933), and Howard J. Bell, Jr., "*The Deserted Village* and Goldsmith's Social Doctrines," *PMLA* (1944).

Because it is impossible in this short survey to include discussions of all major figures, such writers as Burke, Gibbon, John Wilkes, and Tom Paine, whose place is pre-eminently political or historical, have regretfully been omitted. There is no space for the philosophers and theologians. The dramatists are included in other chapters of this book.

IV

As everyone knows, the art of letter writing reached a high point in the eighteenth century, but the rigorous censorship and careless methods of the early editors had so mangled the original documents that new editions were badly needed. To list all the scholarly collections of complete correspondences which have appeared in recent years is outside the province of this essay. Yet because of the remarkable sweep of the endeavors some quick survey should be made.

Famous for its completeness, accuracy, and beautiful format, the Yale Walpole Edition, being produced under the benevolent guidance of W. S. Lewis, will finally run to over fifty volumes. A similar long series of volumes devoted to the correspondence of James Boswell is in the planning stage at Yale, while another concerned with that of Edmund Burke is being produced by the University of Chicago Press, with Thomas Copeland as general editor. *The Percy Letters*, under the supervision of D. Nichol Smith and Cleanth Brooks, is being issued by the Louisana State University Press.

Gradually the Clarendon Press in Oxford has been supplying admirable annotated editions of the letters of other important writers of the period. The following have appeared so far: Robert Burns, edited by De Lancey Ferguson (1931); David Hume, by J. Y. T. Greig (1932); Thomas Gray, by Paget Toynbee and Leonard Whibley (1935); Laurence Sterne, by L. P. Curtis (1935); Joseph Addison, by Walter Graham (1941); Richard Steele, by Rae Blanchard (1941); Samuel Johnson, by R. W. Chapman (1952); Daniel Defoe, by G. H. Healey (1955); and Alexander Pope, by George Sherburn (1956). In preparation for this series are Jonathan Swift, edited by Sir Harold Williams;

Matthew Prior, by H. B. Wright and Monroe K. Spears; Lady Mary Wortley Montagu, by Robert Halsband; and John Locke, by Esmond de Beer.

Volumes from other publishers include: Oliver Goldsmith, edited by K. C. Balderston (1928); Sir Joshua Reynolds, by F. W. Hilles (1929); Lord Chesterfield, by Bonamy Dobrée (1932); William Shenstone, by Duncan Mallam (1939); John Dryden, by Charles E. Ward (1942); Wilkes and Churchill, by E. H. Weatherly (1954); and Edward Gibbon, by J. E. Norton (1956). Others expected in the next few years are: David Garrick, edited by George M. Kahrl; William Cowper by Neilson C. Hannay; and Richard B. Sheridan, by Cecil Price. A comprehensive survey of the genre may be found in W. H. Irving, *The Providence of Wit in the English Letter Writers* (1955).

Outstanding editions, not correspondences, useful for students of aesthetics and criticism should also be mentioned: Mandeville's *Fable of the Bees*, edited F. B. Kaye (1924); *The Critical Works of John Dennis*, by E. N. Hooker (1939, 1943); *The Critical Works of Thomas Rymer*, by Curt Zimansky (1956); and Hogarth's *Analysis of Beauty*, by J. Burke (1956).

The brilliant recent work of the bibliographers—Allen T. Hazen on Horace Walpole and the Strawberry Hill Press, J. E. Norton on Gibbon, William M. Sale on Richardson, and William B. Todd on a variety of topics, may be only mentioned in passing, since it is largely directed to specialists. Occasionally, however, the detailed work of the bibliographical and textual scholar provides exciting new evidence immediately useful for the teacher of literature. Witness Donald F. Bond's "The First Printing of the *Spectator*," *MP* (1950), and W. H. Bond's "Christopher Smart's *Jubilate Agno*," *Harvard Library Bulletin* (1950), where the antiphonal structure of this strange work is ably demonstrated.

V

Although consideration of the rise of fiction properly belongs in another chapter, some few remarks may be included about the major novelists, since they easily rank among the principal writers of the eighteenth century. For over-all commentary the most stimulating books are those by McKillop and Watt listed earlier in the section on Defoe. There have been a number of recent issues of the Augustan Reprint Society (Clark Library, University of California at Los Angeles) devoted to little-known original prefaces and criticism of the novel form. These will be found most rewarding.

Possibly because of our own preoccupation with psychological problems, there has been a startling renaissance of interest in Samuel Richardson. Already mentioned are the notable bibliographical researches of W. M. Sale. There is much that is new in A. D. McKillop's *Samuel Richardson: Printer and Novelist* (1936), and in his "Epistolary Technique in Richardson's Novels," *Rice Institute Pamphlet* (1951). Perceptive comments may be found in Arnold Kettle, *An Introduction to the English Novel* (1951). Significant in the new evaluation of Richardson's place in literature is A. E. Carter, "The Greatest English Novelist," *UTQ* (1948). Teachers will find acute critical analyses in Christopher Hill, "Clarissa Harlowe and Her Times," *Essays in Criticism* (1955), and Norman Rabkin, "*Clarissa*: A Study in the Nature of Convention," *ELH* (1956). *Pamela* has found a vigorous champion in B. L. Reid, "Justice to *Pamela*," *Hudson Review* (1956–57).

The most recent life of Henry Fielding by F. Homes Dudden (1952) adds little, but is a convenient gathering together of the known facts. Valuable for general discussion are Wolfgang Iser, *Die Weltanschauung Henry Fieldings* (1952) and George Sherburn, "Fielding's Social Outlook," *PQ* (1956). There are two convenient reprintings of *Shamela* now available: edited by Sheridan W. Baker, Jr. (1953), and in facsimile by the Augustan Reprint Society (1956). All doubts of Fielding's authorship have been removed by Charles B. Woods in an article in *PQ* (1946). Unhappily there is insufficient space to do justice to the wealth of interesting commentary on Fielding's art which has appeared in recent years. Only a very few having to do with the major novels may be mentioned: Mark Spilka, "Comic Resolution in Fielding's *Joseph Andrews*," *CE* (1953), I. B. Cauthen, Jr., "Fielding's Digressions in *Joseph Andrews*," *CE* (1956), W. R. Irwin, *The Making of Jonathan Wild* (1941), Bernard Shea, "Machiavelli and

Fielding's *Jonathan Wild*," *PMLA* (1957), R. S. Crane, "The Concept of Plot and the Plot of *Tom Jones*," reprinted in *Critics and Criticism* (1952), George Sherburn, "Fielding's *Amelia*: An Interpretation," *ELH* (1936), and A. R. Towers, *"Amelia* and the State of Matrimony," *RES* (1954).

Various aspects of the life and work of Tobias Smollett are well covered by Lewis M. Knapp, *Tobias Smollett: Doctor of Men and Manners* (1949), Louis L. Martz, *The Later Career of Tobias Smollett* (1942), Claude E. Jones, *Smollett Studies* (1942), George M. Kahrl, *Tobias Smollett: Traveler-Novelist* (1945), and in two persuasive articles by Rufus Putney, "The Plan of *Peregrine Pickle*," *PMLA* (1945), and "Smollett and Lady Vane's Memoirs," *PQ* (1946).

Excellent general studies of Laurence Sterne may be found in A. D. McKillop, *The Early Masters of English Fiction* (1956), D. W. Jefferson, *Laurence Sterne* (1945), and Alice G. Fredman, *Diderot and Sterne* (1955). Ernest N. Dilworth, *The Unsentimental Journey of Laurence Sterne* (1948) is perceptive and amusing, but highly controversial. For comparison see also Rufus Putney, "Laurence Sterne, Apostle of Laughter" in *The Age of Johnson*. L. V. Hammond, *Laurence Sterne's Sermons of Mr. Yorick*, (1948), although not specifically concerned with the novels, should not be overlooked. By all odds the best edition of *Tristram Shandy* is that by James A. Work (second edition, 1953). The novel's past reputation is surveyed by John H. Hicks in *Boston University Studies in English* (1956). Special studies which will be found rewarding are: Wayne Booth, "Did Sterne Complete *Tristram Shandy?*" *MP* (1951), D. W. Jefferson, *"Tristram Shandy* and the Tradition of Learned Wit," *Essays in Criticism* (1951), John Traugott, *Tristram Shandy's World* (1954), and A. R. Towers, "Sterne's Cock and Bull Story," *ELH* (1957). And for Sterne's later work, there is Rufus Putney, "The Evolution of *A Sentimental Journey*," *PQ* (1940).

To return now to the poets—there has been an excellent edition of the poems of Charles Churchill, prepared by Douglas Grant (1956), and a critical analysis of his art by W. C. Brown in *The Triumph of Form: A Study of the Later Masters of the Heroic Couplet* (1948).

VI

It has been customary to give special treatment to a number of the mid-century writers, chiefly as precursors of romanticism. Their productions have been eagerly sifted for every evidence of a new rebellious spirit. That there should have been a revulsion to this approach is natural, and one modern critic has acidly remarked that the nineteenth century's over-praise of the second-rate poets of the eighteenth century was its way of saying that it disliked the literature of that period altogether: see R. C. Churchill, "Gray and Matthew Arnold," *Criterion* (1938). Yet any attempt to call these poets "post Augustans" and to search their work for continuing strains of the strong neoclassic tradition also runs into trouble. For some amusing remarks on the problem see Bertrand H. Bronson, "The Pre-Romantic or Post-Augustan Mode," *ELH* (1953). There can be no doubt that a major shift of sensibility was in progress. After all, Pope begins and Blake ends the century.

Perhaps the most valid approach is to examine each writer separately, with appreciation of his individual struggle to adjust in a period of unusual uncertainty of aesthetic taste. In an age when a husband and wife could disagree about the proper architecture for their new home, and solve the problem by making one side Palladian and the other Gothic, it is not to be wondered at that creative artists were often in a quandary: see Curtis B. Bradford and Stuart G. Brown, "On Teaching the Age of Johnson," *CE* (1942).

A key figure is Thomas Gray, whose life has been fully and delightfully described by R. W. Ketton-Cremer (1955). In recent years there has been a decided reaction critically to the "Arnoldian transfiguration" of Gray: see F. R. Leavis in *Scrutiny* (1936, 1944), and there have been a number of vigorous attacks. As samples, in addition to Leavis there might be mentioned: Hilary Steuert, "Two Augustan Studies," *Dublin Review* (1945), and Geoffrey Tillotson, "Matthew Arnold and Eighteenth-Century Poetry" in *Essays on the Eighteenth Century Presented to David Nichol Smith* (1945).

More and more emphasis is now being placed on Gray's classical background and his scholarship. Witness W. Powell Jones, *Thomas Gray, Scholar* (1937), A. R. Humphreys, "A Classical

Education and Eighteenth-Century Poetry," *Scrutiny* (1939),
M. H. Griffin, "Thomas Gray, Classical Augustan," *Classical
Journal* (1941), and Geoffrey Tillotson, "Gray, the Scholar-Poet,"
Essays in Criticism and Research (1942).

For teachers, what is happening to the "Elegy" should also be
instructive. So long as we were content to accept the "Elegy" as a
"mood" poem, expressing the meditative-melancholic theme in
perfectly chiseled phrases, there appeared to be little difficulty
about interpretation. But with the modern zeal for specific explication of form and meaning, the "Elegy" surprisingly turns out to be
one of the most puzzling poems in the language. It is not at all clear
just what Gray means, or to whom the epitaph at the end refers.
Is it Gray himself, as many in the past have assumed? Or is it his
friend Richard West as Odell Shepard suggests in "A Youth to
Fortune and to Fame Unknown," *MP* (1923)? Yet see H. W.
Starr in *JEGP* (1949). Or a persona representing a typical unknown country poet? Or is it the stonecutter? For this startling
theory see an amazing article by Frank H. Ellis, "Gray's *Elegy*:
The Biographical Problem in Literary Criticism," *PMLA* (1951).
Morse Peckham in "Gray's 'Epitaph' Revisited," *MLN* (1956),
though disagreeing in part, reinforces Ellis's main thesis, but J.
H. Sutherland in "The Stonecutter in Gray's *Elegy*," *MP* (1957)
disagrees. See also A. E. Dyson, "The Ambivalence of Gray's
Elegy," *Essays in Criticism* (1957). One thing is certain: the
"Elegy" can provide a fertile topic for student attempts at critical
interpretation.

Concerning others of the so-called preromantic group, only
a few special studies may be listed. So little has hitherto been
known about William Collins that the discovery of even a few
manuscript versions of his verses among the papers of Thomas
Warton is very exciting. These are described by J. S. Cunningham
in *William Collins: Drafts and Fragments of Verse* (1956). For
an analysis of Collins as a representative of the rococo in art, see
Wylie Sypher, "The *Morceau de Fantaisie* in Verse: A New Approach to Collins," *UTQ* (1945). For the author of the *Night
Thoughts* there is C. V. Wicker, *Edward Young and the Fear of
Death* (1952). The latest authoritative analysis of the background
of the poems of "Ossian" is contained in Derick S. Thomson, *The*

Gaelic Sources of Macpherson's Ossian (1952). Two valuable approaches to the *Reliques of Ancient English Poetry* may be found in Leah Dennis, "Thomas Percy: Antiquarian vs. Man of Taste," *PMLA* (1942), and W. J. Bate, "Percy's Use of His Folio-Manuscript," *JEGP* (1944).

Still the standard biography of Chatterton is that by E. H. W. Meyerstein (1930), but some doubt is now cast on his suicide by Donald S. Taylor in *PQ* (1952). A critical estimate is contained in Frances S. Miller, "The Historic Sense of Thomas Chatterton," *ELH* (1944). For an earlier parallel study see her "The Historic Sense of Thomas Warton, Jr.," *ELH* (1938). Of major significance for any understanding of Warton and of the beginnings of interest in the Middle Ages there is René Wellek, *The Rise of English Literary History* (1941). An excellent example of a modern re-examination of traditional older generalizations may be found in Hoyt Trowbridge, "Bishop Hurd: A Reinterpretation," *PMLA* (1943).

Christopher Smart is in a class by himself. Long considered merely as a second-rate poet who in a fit of madness had scribbled a fascinating outburst of religious exaltation, "A Song to David," Smart in our day is steadily achieving a position as one of the major creative artists of the period. It is not the remarkable discovery of a strange piece, *Jubilate Agno*, actually written while he was in a madhouse (first published by W. F. Stead in 1939, and more accurately re-edited by W. H. Bond in 1954) that has been responsible for the change, but an increased emphasis on Smart's metrical paraphrases of the Psalms and his charming Blake-like *Hymns for the Amusement of Children* (reprinted by the Luttrell Society in 1948). Indeed, Robert Brittain, in his admirable selected edition of the *Poems by Christopher Smart* (1950), claims that Smart is one of the greatest English religious poets.

What is substantially a complete edition of Smart's poems may be found in the Muses' Library, edited by Norman Callan (2 vols., 1949). Arthur Sherbo is at work on a biography, and during recent years has been issuing various specialized studies. For an important explication, useful for classroom presentation, see R. D. Havens, "The Structure of Smart's *Song to David*," *RES* (1938). But for the moment the most perceptive discussion of the poems is to be found in Brittain's selected edition mentioned above. Brittain insists in his Introduction that Smart is not inherently romantic, but that the transcendent spiritual quality of his best work was the result of a strange fusion of Hebraic splendor and the unique verbal style of Horace. Whatever the source, the religious verses of Smart deserve a special place in our affections.

If Blake and Burns are excluded from this discussion as being essentially in the romantic tradition, then the major poet of the late eighteenth century is William Cowper. As may be seen from Lodwick C. Hartley's list of critical studies of Cowper published from 1895 to 1949 (*North Carolina State College Record*, 1950), much has been written about his life and work. The most authoritative biography so far is that by Maurice J. Quinlan (1953). Lord David Cecil's *The Stricken Deer* (1929), though charmingly written, is not up-to-date in facts. Other volumes containing valuable comments include: Gilbert Thomas, *William Cowper and the Eighteenth Century* (1935; reissued 1949), Lodwick C. Hartley, *William Cowper, Humanitarian* (1938), and Norman Nicholson, *William Cowper* (1951). Mark Van Doren has provided a selection from Cowper's letters in the Great Letters Series (1951). Charles Van Doren is planning a critical study of Cowper's art as a poet. Also important are two special articles: Lodwick Hartley, "The Worm and the Thorn: A Study of Cowper's *Olney Hymns*," *Journal of Religion* (1949), and Maurice J. Quinlan, "Cowper's Imagery," *JEGP* (1948). For a provocative claim that Cowper is essentially neoclassic in his approach to poetry, see Donald A. Davie, "The Critical Principles of William Cowper," *Cambridge Journal* (1953).

In conclusion, it might be added that teachers will find very useful a portfolio of prints called *Life in Eighteenth-Century England*, selected by R. J. Allen, and issued by the Boston Museum of Fine Arts in 1941. Among the many volumes devoted to background material there are *Johnson's England*, edited by A. S. Turberville (1933), Rosamond Bayne-Powell, *English Country Life in the Eighteenth Century* (1935) and her *Eighteenth-Century London Life* (1937), Dorothy Marshall, *English People in the Eighteenth Century* (1956), and W. B. Ewald, Jr., *Newsmen of Queen Anne* (in the U.S. entitled *Rogues, Royalty, and Reporters*, 1956).

In order fully to appreciate the neoclassic position, perhaps even more than the romantic, it is necessary to be conversant with every human activity of the period—social, political, philosophic, and aesthetic. "The proper study of mankind is man," so Alexander Pope insisted, and it is on the broad human level that eighteenth-century writing must be studied.

7

The Romantic Movement

RICHARD HARTER FOGLE

THE EXPANSIVE SPIRIT OF ROMAN-
ticism was dominant in English literature from 1800 to the beginning of World War I. It is quite possible that it still rules, though
concealed under various disguises. Romanticism was dangerously
divided by the Victorians, diminished by the pre-Raphaelites and
fin-de-siecle aesthetes, and then in the twentieth century deni-
grated by neo-Humanists, imagists, symbolists, "metaphysicists,"
and reactionary classicists, but its essence, which is life itself, is
indestructible. It has been under attack continuously for the last
fifty years by vigorous and skillful opponents—a fact in itself
significant of its continuing vitality.

I

The attacks upon Romanticism have come from many directions, but they concentrate upon the same objective. Highly interesting in themselves, they are also useful in revealing the nature
of the thing they oppose. The American neo-Humanists condemned Romanticism as an all-embracing naturalism which confused nature, man, and God in one indiscriminate, inchoate mass.
Romanticism, said Paul Elmer More in "The Drift of Romanticism," *Shelburne Essays*, VIII (1913), is "the illusion of behold-
ing the infinite within the stream of nature itself, instead of apart
from that stream." This is the central indictment, which Irving
Babbitt repeated in his influential *Rousseau and Romanticism*
(1919). The book contains an interesting although biased account
of Romantic synesthesia, the doctrine of the unity of sense impressions.

The neo-Humanists were formidable and acute, but their ethical prepossessions led them away from literature as such. The Englishman T. E. Hulme was a better critic, though with assumptions much like theirs, in his posthumous "Classicism and Romanticism," *Speculations* (1924), and *Notes on Language and Style* (1930). Hulme forcefully opposed an imagist theory of language, a classicist staticism, and an absolute dualism of the natural and supernatural to Romantic rhetoric, dynamism, and idealist monism. What happens in Romanticism, he thought, is that "You don't believe in Heaven, so you begin to believe in a Heaven on earth. . . . The concepts that are right and proper in their own sphere are spread over, and so mess up, falsify, and blur the clear outlines of human experience. It is like pouring a pot of treacle over the dinner table. Romanticism then . . . is spilt religion" (*Speculations*). Hulme, like T. S. Eliot whom he influenced, was thinking of French at least as much as of English Romanticism in his condemnation of it, and Victor Hugo shares a bad eminence with Shelley as his target. Also like Eliot, he identified Romanticism with political liberalism and false optimism about human nature. He associated it with the French Revolution, the end of the old order, and the beginning of a modern world for which he felt a profound distaste. Murray Krieger has recently pointed out, however, certain Romantic tendencies in Hulme in *The New Apologists for Poetry* (1956).

T. S. Eliot was like Hulme a reactionary. (The word is not pejoratively intended: see its use by Allen Tate in *Reactionary Essays on Poetry and Ideas*, 1936.) His taste for the seventeenth-century metaphysical poets precluded respect for the Romantics, particularly for Shelley. In such works as *The Sacred Wood* (1920), *Homage to John Dryden* (1927), *The Use of Poetry and the Use of Criticism* (1933), "The Function of Criticism," and "The Metaphysical Poets" (*Selected Essays*, 1932, 1950), he found in metaphysical poetry a union of intellect and feeling which was absent in Romanticism. Eliot's Anglicanism in religion, which he adopted about 1930, also led him to distrust Romantic poetry as an artistic expression of Protestant noncomformity, a foolish reliance upon an "Inner Voice." As did Hulme, however, Eliot distinguished between the Romanticism of the Romantics and their greatness, and his attack upon them was in part a strategic feint to clear the way for the modern poetry that was to come. Influ-

enced by the French Symbolists, as Edmund Wilson has shown in
Axel's Castle (1931), he reacted against what seemed to him the
confusion, imprecision, and rhetorical vagueness of some Romantic
verse. The language of poetry, as he memorably said in his essay on
"Hamlet" (*Selected Essays*), should precisely convey the subtlest
nuances of feeling by their equivalents in concrete, sensuous imagery, which were to be their "objective correlative."

Eliot's attitude toward Romanticism is shared by the American
Southern Agrarians, especially John Crowe Ransom and Allen
Tate. Along with their political and religious conservatism, their
hatred of scientism and abstract utilitarianism has led them to think
of Romanticism as a compromise between poetry and science that
satisfies the requirements of neither. Thus in *The World's Body*
(1938), Ransom condemned Romantic poetry as a "Platonic"
poetry which pretended to be solid and sensuous, but was actually
an allegory of abstract ideas presented in images. Tate's argument
in *Reason in Madness* (1939) closely resembles Ransom's. Such
critics as the early I. A. Richards (*The Principles of Literary
Criticism*, 1924) and Cleanth Brooks (*Modern Poetry and the
Tradition*, 1939, *The Well Wrought Urn*, 1947), although themselves Romantic in many of their tastes and employing the Romantic criterion of "wholeness" as their standard of judgment, found
much Romantic poetry sentimental and excessively "pure" or
"exclusive," and adopted metaphysical poetry as their norm of
value. Richards, Brooks, and Richards' student William Empson
in his book *Seven Types of Ambiguity* (1930; second edition,
1947), used such terms as "irony," "paradox," and "ambiguity" to
convey their sense of the complexity of language and the complex
unity of poetry. For their critical theories and methods they drew
upon modern semantic explorations of meaning, from modern
(though basically Romantic) distinctions between poetry and
science, and from the imponderable of modern taste itself. In the
case of Brooks there is an ethical and metaphysical kinship with
the Southern Agrarians of which he himself has not taken full
account. Richards, Empson, and Brooks have all as close and expert readers furnished excellent accounts of Romantic poems:
"explications" unprecedented in their skill, complexity, and in
the main their literary tact. Richards in *Coleridge on Imagination*
(1934, 1950) illuminated a number of Coleridge's poems; in his

Seven Types of Ambiguity Empson produced an original though excessive interpretation of Keats's "Ode on Melancholy"; and Brooks in *The Well Wrought Urn* contributed to the understanding of Keats and Wordsworth.

Almost alone among scholarly specialists in Romanticism, as distinguished from general critics of English poetry, Hoxie N. Fairchild has consistently viewed Romanticism with alarm. He blames its expansive individualism for many of our current difficulties, in *The Noble Savage* (1938), *The Romantic Quest* (1931), and his monumental *Religious Trends in English Poetry* (1939–), the fourth volume of which has at this writing just been published. From his high-Anglican position Fairchild has consistently dealt with Romanticism as a puerility to be scorned or a temptation to be shunned. In a current volume of revaluations, *The Major English Romantic Poets* (1957), edited by C. D. Thorpe, Bennett Weaver, and Carlos Baker, his essay, "Romanticism: Devil's Advocate," finds "the taproot of romanticism in man's desire to feel independently good, strong, wise, and creative, his thirst for boundless expansion of being in a universe which echoes back to him his assertion of self-sufficient power." "To be romantic," he continues, "is to reject that finitude which is inherent in all pattern." While there is much good in the great Romantic poets, "They represent the climactic phase in that rise and fall of human pride which constitutes the main theme of modern history." Professor Fairchild is among the most learned of Romantic scholars, and he is both acute and deeply serious. His word is to be carefully regarded. One may question, however, whether he has sufficiently considered the complex nature of the relationships between theology and imaginative literature, whether he has solved the problem of "poetry and belief" that has exercised many of the sharpest critical minds of our time. For criticism the religious standard has particular dangers, since it can so easily be argued that religious considerations include or supersede all others.

More, Babbitt, Hulme, Eliot, and Fairchild have all seen Romanticism as the same thing, and they have seen it in about the same way, as a confusion or illusion of infinitude within the finite, an excessive confidence in the individual and the human. The term is usually regarded, however, as extremely hard to define, as is emphasized by the list of formulas given by Ernest Bernbaum in his excellent *Guide through the Romantic Movement* (second edition, 1949). Among modern students A. O. Lovejoy has notably emphasized the number and the heterogeneity of the attributes generally called Romantic, in "On the Discriminations of Romanticisms," *PMLA* (1924), and in his epoch-making *The Great Chain of Being* (1936).

The issue involved here needs some consideration. The present essay is of course concerned with the manifestations of Romanticism at a particular period, roughly from 1798 to 1832, in a particular country, England, and in a limited group of poets and critics: Robert Burns, William Blake, William Wordsworth, Samuel Taylor Coleridge, Lord Byron, Percy Bysshe Shelley, John Keats, Robert Southey, William Hazlitt, Charles Lamb, Sir Walter Scott, Thomas De Quincey, and Leigh Hunt. These men seldom thought of themselves as parts of a single movement, and, to put it mildly, they had their disagreements. Byron detested the theory and frequently the practice of his great contemporaries—his opinion of Keats's poetry was obscene—and his feelings were reciprocated. Blake where he was known at all was regarded as a gifted eccentric at best; Shelley and Keats were not really congenial, despite Shelley's *Adonais*; Scott's poetry struck Wordsworth and Coleridge as popular trash; and Hazlitt, Byron, and Shelley looked down upon Wordsworth, Coleridge, and Southey as timeserving apostates from liberalism, subsidized by a reactionary government.

These differences, however, are minor when compared with the likenesses of the Romantics, and Romanticism is an intelligible concept, as René Wellek effectively argued in "The Concept of 'Romanticism' in Literary History," *CL* (1949). Doubtless no single verbal formula can be completely satisfactory, but it is nevertheless a single idea, difficult of definition because the idea of Romanticism is the idea of life itself. It is the principle of vital growth, manifested in poetry by organic unity, or a oneness of form and content not superimposed from outside by mechanical rules but organically proceeding from the interaction of the poet's mind with his materials. In England this doctrine was most fully articulated by Coleridge, the best of Romantic theorists. Morse Peckham has recently restated it in an influential article, "Towards a Theory of Romanticism," *PMLA* (1951); and M. H. Abrams examined it more elaborately in *The Mirror and the Lamp* (1953). Like any other concept it is, as Coleridge would have said, a principle rather than a rule; to serve as a theory of literature it needs explanations and modifications. Properly handled, it is complex: the life which is the source of organic or Romantic unity comes from above it as well as within it. This life is in spirit as it is in matter, or it is a spirit in matter; it is at once ideal and real, natural and supernatural, as I have maintained in several essays ("A Note on Romantic Oppositions and Reconciliations," in *The Major English Romantic Poets*, edited by Thorpe, Weaver, and Baker, 1957; and "Organic Form in American Criticism, 1840–1870," in *The Development of American Literary Criticism*, edited by Floyd Stovall, 1955).

The central principle of Romanticism, as was remarked, requires amplification to serve as a literary theory. Naïvely interpreted, organic growth would imply mere automatism, and to do justice to poetic form and creation one must add and reconcile the elements of conscious intellect and will. Romantic aesthetics, in fact, ✳strive to be all-inclusive—which is what thinkers like Hulme and Fairchild from their point of view object to. It may be argued that Romanticism is the only adequate theory of artistic creation, and further noted that any basic idea is liable to be used foolishly by the foolish, and wisely by the wise.

Authoritative interpreters of English Romanticism have often used other terms and approaches, but they are generally reconcilable with the ideas presented above. C. M. Bowra, for example, focusses upon *The Romantic Imagination* (1949); the poet and critic W. H. Auden locates Romanticism in consciousness itself, and the value for consciousness as an end (*The Enchaféd Flood*, 1950); and Albert Gérard has recently considered it in terms of subject and object as a reconciliation of the mind and nature (*L'idée romantique de la poésie en Angleterre*, 1955). Growth and organic unity, however, are central to all these theories, which view the same phenomenon from different directions and in various lights. Indeed, after a period during which a single conception of it was almost despaired of, there is now a growing confidence that general agreement can be achieved about the nature of Romanticism.

Modern defenders of Romanticism have been less spectacular than its attackers. This is in the nature of things, since the position adopted is in criticism generally dictated by the aggressor. Controversy over Romanticism has been valuable in causing both sides to re-examine their critical assumptions, but it is doubtful that the issues have been entirely clarified. John Crowe Ransom, commenting in *The World's Body* upon the scholarly essays of Fairchild, Elizabeth Nitchie, and others in "Romanticism: A Symposium," *PMLA* (1940), found that the scholars were too much "inside" their subject to take an objective view of it; a specialist in Romanticism, on the other hand, will probably find Mr. Ransom too far outside it. The attacker writes about Romantic poetry usually to define and dramatize his preference for another kind, so that the two perspectives are hard to unite in a single focus.

C. S. Lewis, whose literary preferences are not Romantic, nevertheless defended Romanticism in *Rehabilitations* (1939) against F. R. Leavis's provocative but prejudiced *Revaluation* (1936). Lewis made excellent use of common sense and historical perspective, as he pointed out that Shelley's idealism was at least as respectable as the ironic skepticism of the 1930's. In *Skepticism and Poetry* (1937) D. G. James reasserted the power, the scope, and the dignity of the Romantic imagination. J. W. Beach's *A Romantic View of Poetry* (1944) was a sympathetic exposition, as its title indicates, and a profitable one. Donald Stauffer, like C. S. Lewis, invoked common sense, orthodox poetics, and historical perspective in favor of the romantic poets in *The Nature of Poetry* (1946). In "Romantic Bards and Metaphysical Reviewers," *The Imagery of Keats and Shelley* (1949) the present writer took on T. E. Hulme, T. S. Eliot, F. R. Leavis, John Crowe Ransom, Allen Tate, and Cleanth Brooks *en bloc* in defense of Romanticism and of Shelley, with results entirely gratifying to himself. Most recently Elizabeth Nitchie has vindicated Romantic craftsmanship in a substantial essay, "Form in Romantic Poetry," in *The Major English Romantic Poets* (1957). Ernest Bernbaum has vigorously supported the values of Romanticism in several directions, in his *Guide through the Romantic Movement* (second edition, 1949), and *The English Romantic Poets: A Review of Research*, edited by T. M. Raysor (1950; second edition, 1957). Bernbaum points out that Romanticism is verified by contemporary science, though it was repudiated by the materialism of the latter nineteenth century.

A considerable number of substantial studies of English Romanticism have appeared in the last thirty years, which have not been mentioned in this essay. There is room here to speak only of a selection of the outstanding books. Annie E. Powell (Mrs. A. E. Dodds) cast new light upon the theories of Blake, Coleridge, Wordsworth, Shelley, and De Quincey in *The Romantic Theory of Poetry: An Examination in the Light of Croce's Aesthetic* (1926). Croce makes a good point of departure, as has Bergson for some other students of Romanticism. S. F. Gingerich skillfully investigated Romantic doctrines of Nature, pantheism, transcendence, necessity, and free will in his *Essays in the Romantic Poets* (1929), which is particularly valuable upon Coleridge and Wordsworth. Joseph Warren Beach treated the same themes more extensively in his learned and influential *The Concept of Nature in Nineteenth-Century English Poetry* (1936). Perhaps because of the lesser scope of his work, Gingerich is more successful than Beach with individual poets. *The Romantic Agony*, by Mario Praz (English translation by Angus Davidson, 1933) is a study of aberrations in English and Continental Romanticism. It is a book of absorbing interest, but it deals only with unfortunate by-products of Romantic emotionalism. The shadow of the divine Marquis lies heavily upon *The Romantic Agony*.

Douglas Bush's *Mythology and the Romantic Tradition* (1949) is an excellent fusion of broad historical scholarship with critical taste. It is so solid and so comprehensive that its goodness in detail may be overlooked, and it is likely to be a little neglected today because our understanding of mythology has changed since its publication. Bush deals exclusively with *classical* myth, but his study of the Romantic use of it is highly significant. D. G. James considers the same problem in *The Romantic Comedy* (1948). James, unusually well-equipped in philosophy, provides fresh and penetrating studies of the thought of the major Romantics. G. Wilson Knight's *The Starlight Dome* (1943) contains a series of eloquent appreciative interpretations of English Romantic poetry. Knight, an intensely suggestive critic, has in this and other books proposed an astounding number of valuable ideas, which his incessant and indiscriminate enthusiasm unfortunately cheapens.

Walter Jackson Bate, proceeding from the eighteenth century shift from neoclassical premises to associationism and feeling, portrayed English Romanticism in *From Classic to Romantic* (1946) as a "loose and compromising empiricism" that "avoided both excessive relativism and mere emotionalism." Bate found Romanticism to be closely connected with the "eighteenth-century transition in conceptions of art and taste." Sir Herbert Read looked in the opposite direction in *The True Voice of Feeling* (1953), toward Romantic influence upon modern Freudianism, surrealism, and the like. Read, for many years a faithful adherent of Romanticism in his books and articles, has always been a radical exponent of pure dynamism and progression, divested of checks and balances.

M. H. Abrams' *The Mirror and the Lamp: Romantic Theory and the Critical Tradition* (1953) sets the theory of Romanticism against the background of the entire tradition of criticism in Western civilization, though the emphasis is ultimately upon the English tradition. The method, avowedly indebted to the modern Aristotelian Ronald Salmon Crane of the University of Chicago, distinguishes four main critical approaches, or as Abrams says, four different orientations of critical theory: the mimetic, the pragmatic, the expressive, and the objective. The mimetic considers literature as an imitation of reality; the pragmatic approach is concerned with the effect of literature upon its audience; the expressive treats it as the embodiment of the author's mind, especially of his feelings; while the objective approach focusses upon the literary work in itself as an object, without reference to external reality, or to its audience, or to the author's mind.

This fourfold method implies critical relativism. Abrams expounds these four possible orientations of criticism without choosing between them, unless his emphasis itself is to be understood as a preference for the expressive or Romantic approach. He distinguishes, however, between judicious and injudicious applications of theory, particularly between simple and radical and complex and balanced critical systems. He finds, however, the most characteristic Romanticism in such theorists as John Stuart Mill, Carlyle, and Keble, who are generally thought of as Victorians. These are extremist critics, who by emphasizing the Romantic doctrines of feeling, sincerity, and spontaneity make art an inferior substitute for life itself. One is tempted to wonder whether Abrams praises Coleridge, whom he justly gives more attention than any other critic, because he is Romantic or because he incorporates the largest number of non-Romantic elements in his system.

The Mirror and the Lamp is a full, fair, and magnificently acute analysis of literary ideas and critics. It is excellent in detail, as it is admirable in its ordered perspective of the entire panorama of European criticism from its beginnings. The main figures of English Romanticism are all profitably discussed. Wordsworth and Coleridge are placed at the center of the English Romantic movement, with Blake and Shelley toward the periphery. Abrams is basically Aristotelian, so that the Platonism of Blake and Shelley is for him outside the main current.

II

Wordsworth, Coleridge, Byron, Shelley, and Keats have traditionally been thought of as the major English Romantic poets. The most recent co-operative scholarship of Romanticism still confines itself to these five, relegating William Blake to a minor position, but he is too important to remain thus in the rear. As a radical extremist Blake is rather hard to bring into line with his peers, and this fact may account for scholarly reluctance to accept him. He refused to accept Nature, and called Wordsworth an atheist for doing so, whereas the most widely accepted Romantic doctrine maintains the unity of Nature and the poetic mind. Nevertheless, Blake's organicism and his reliance upon the poetic imagination, along with our increasing recognition of his literary stature, should permit him within the pale.

Interest in Blake as both poet and artist has steadily increased during the twentieth century. In some respects he is more modern than the other Romantics: his radicalism of the imagination, his violence against materialism, his esotericism and use of myth all strike a responsive chord within the twentieth-century "outsider," and the alienated modern poet who feels that he must create his own metaphysics, his own myth, and even his own language. Mark Schorer's *William Blake: The Politics of Vision* (1946) is most revealing upon this aspect of Blake, especially in the chapters on

"The Mask of William Blake" and "The Necessity of Myth."
Milton O. Percival has written the most systematic and illuminating account, *William Blake's Circle of Destiny* (1938), of the age-
old esoteric tradition from which Blake sprung, along with his
use of it. The matter of tradition is of decided importance, since
modern poetry has spent much effort trying to find one, and since
such influential critics as T. S. Eliot have placed Blake on the outside of all tradition.

The greatness of Blake's lyric poetry in *Songs of Innocence and
Experience* has been adequately noted and explained in the last few
years, which have been able to utilize the pioneering work of
commentators like S. Foster Damon, *William Blake, His Philosophy and Symbols* (1924). Alfred Kazin, for example, writes brilliantly on "The Tiger" in the introduction to *The Portable Blake*
(1946), and such textbooks as Brooks, Purser, and Warren's
Approach to Literature are likely to contain remarkably good
criticism of Blake's lyrics.

The aesthetic status of his longer poems, the "Prophetic Books,"
remains unsettled. As Margaret Rudd said in her *Divided Image:
A Study of William Blake and W. B. Yeats* (1953), "It is vision,
mystical vision, that Yeats longed to win in imitating Blake, and it
is vision that we are examining in this study. Too often this leaves
me talking about what a poem *says* rather than what it *is*." More
recently the same writer has remarked in her *Organiz'd Innocence:
The Story of Blake's Prophetic Books* (1956) that "The long poems
known as the prophetic books tell, like all epics and myths, a very
wonderful story about universal human events of the spirit. I
believe that the primary value of the poems lies in this story." A
cynical reader might question whether the prophetic books do not
tell this wonderful story over and over again, up to and somewhat
beyond the point of monotony; at all events, the difficulty in dealing with these astonishing works as poems has been felt by every
Blake scholar. Blake was a poet-seer in theory and in fact, and the
simple, common-sense verdict is that the seer increasingly dis-
lodged the poet in him. One wishes for a study which comprehends
the entire body of his poetry, yet confines itself to the problem of
his poetics. It may be, however, that such a book is not possible.

The authoritative text is *The Writings of William Blake*, edited
in three volumes by Geoffrey Keynes (1925), and more accessible

in shorter form in *Poetry and Prose of William Blake* (1948). The prophetic books by themselves, with commentary, are given in *The Prophetic Writings of William Blake*, edited by D. J. Sloss and J. P. R. Wallis (1926). The most noteworthy books on Blake of recent years are Schorer, previously mentioned; Northrop Frye's *Fearful Symmetry* (1947); and David V. Erdman's *Blake, Prophet Against Empire: A Poet's Interpretation of the History of his own Times* (1954). (Percival's somewhat earlier work deserves mention in this class as well.) Schorer is especially good in relating Blake to contemporary poetic theory, and his conclusion is highly judicious:

> William Blake provides the inspiring spectacle of a man who absolutely triumphed over his world; but as a poet, in the length and breadth of his career, the world was too much for him, his poetic genius could not beat it into forms that would not burst their seams. . . . His work continues to challenge our attention largely for this reason, that as the monument to one of the great casualties in the history of poetry, perhaps the greatest, its hieroglyphs unlock the contradiction of his success and failure.

Northrop Frye was less reserved than Schorer in his much-admired *Fearful Symmetry*, which is a sympathetic and perceptive exposition of Blake's creation and use of myth. Frye needed no reservations, since he accepted myth as the copula of art and life, without distinguishing a separate aesthetic dimension. Erdman, like Kenneth Cameron with Shelley, painstakingly revealed Blake's relation to the political and social problems of his time and country, reacting against the esoteric tradition in Blake studies. "What I have attempted," he says, "is a bold survey of the history of Blake's time as it swirls about and enters into the texture of his emblematic painting and poetry."

Most books on Blake are interesting, and at least several others should be noted even in this brief survey. Biographies are scarce: Mona Wilson, *The Life of William Blake* (1927, 1932), and a 1942 revision of Alexander Gilchrist's earlier *Life* by Ruthven Todd. Helen C. White wrote in 1927 a valuable study of *The Mysticism of William Blake*. (Critics have questioned whether Blake can be called a true mystic.) Bernard Blackstone and Stanley Gardner have contributed to Blake scholarship within this decade

(*English Blake*, 1949; and *Infinity on the Anvil*, 1954); and most recently Hazard Adams in *Blake and Yeats; the Contrary Vision* (1956) has definitely furthered knowledge of Blake's aesthetics.

III

The Wordsworth studies of the last few decades have been steady rather than spectacular. Wordsworth's poetry and thought have not had the vital relations to twentieth-century literature of Blake, Coleridge, and Keats. His mode of poetic expression is too literal and too generalized to have direct influence today, in a period of radical metaphor, symbol, and intense concreteness in poetry, as Blake influenced William Butler Yeats. The young of recent years have no doubt received Wordsworth as has been their wont, with a calm indistinguishable from lethargy. His virtues require reflection to appreciate; it takes experience to discern his originality, since we have assimilated so many of his ideas and feelings in the last hundred years. By good general critics Wordsworth has nevertheless been treated with consistent respect, and by professional scholars with something akin to reverence. We shall see that there are those who have dismissed him as heretical, outmoded, and soft-headed; and doubtless his work will continue to cause controversy, since it is simple only on the surface. But Wordsworth's fortunes have not on the whole undergone the vicissitudes that beset Byron and Shelley.

Modern Wordsworth scholarship commenced with George McLean Harper's *William Wordsworth, His Life, Works, and Influence* (1916; second edition, 1923; third edition, 1929). (Priority should perhaps be given to Emile Legouis for his *La jeunesse de Wordsworth*, 1896.) Harper enlivened the scholarly world in 1921 by revealing the existence of *Wordsworth's French Daughter*, born of Annette Vallon before Wordsworth's marriage to Mary Hutchinson. This discovery decidedly altered the priestly Victorian image of the poet which was prevalent. For later scholarship Harper set a pattern of emphasis upon Wordsworth's liberal youth; it came to be a habit to divide his career sharply in two, between an early period of daring, liberal politics, and inspiration, and a late period of cautious conservatism and respectable dullness. This conception of Wordsworth's development, which has only a general relationship to fact, has been gradually refined and corrected. Edith C. Batho notably helped to redress the balance in *The Later Wordsworth* (1933), in which she attempted to discover from Wordsworth's writing "what were his real opinions in the latter half of his life: how far they were in agreement with or in contradiction to those of the earlier half: the impression which he made upon his contemporaries: and his attitude towards them."

The neo-Humanists, enemies of Romanticism in general, attacked Wordsworth as the Romantic archpriest of "naturalism." Melvin Rader, however, stressed the influence of transcendentalism in *Presiding Ideas in Wordsworth's Poetry* (1931). Joseph Warren Beach, in *The Concept of Nature in Nineteenth-Century English Poetry* (1936), respected Wordsworth's idea of nature, but regarded it as a noble fallacy, untenable in the harsh light of modern science. The philosopher-scientist A. N. Whitehead, however, reversed this imputation of poetic falsity. Especially in *Science and the Modern World* (1925) he paid tribute to the "instinctive convictions" and "imaginative backgrounds" upon which both science and philosophy depend. He and others demonstrated that Wordsworth and the English Romantics in general were more in tune with modern scientific theory than was post-Darwinian nineteenth-century materialism, from which most of Wordsworth's detractors drew their knowledge of science. Newton P. Stallknecht in *Strange Seas of Thought* (1945) and individual essays, most recently in "The Quality of Man," *The Major English Romantic Poets* (1957), showed systematically that Wordsworth's vitalist vision of nature in many ways corresponds to the modern theories of Bergson, Santayana, Whitehead, Collingwood, Albert Schweitzer, and other philosophers of science. Ernest Bernbaum vigorously defended Wordsworth in his *Guide through the Romantic Movement* and *The English Romantic Poets: A Review of Research*, as well as in articles in the scholarly journals. Bennett Weaver took the same positive view of Wordsworth in a substantial series of essays, which have not been collected. Hoxie N. Fairchild, however, treated Wordsworth in *Religious Trends in English Poetry* with other Romantics as a sentimental egotist seeking satisfaction in a vision of nature which is merely a projection of himself. Fairchild does not care to accept the protestations of Coleridge and Wordsworth themselves on this subject.

There have been many fine studies of Wordsworth with no ulterior motives except to pay tribute to a well-loved poet and a pillar of the English tradition of common sense and cautious idealism. Among these are H. W. Garrod's *Wordsworth* (1923; second edition, 1927), Sir Herbert Read's *Wordsworth* (1931), and Helen Darbishire's *The Poet Wordsworth* (1950). Ernest de Sélincourt's services as modern editor of Wordsworth have been outstanding, as well as Miss Darbishire's. De Sélincourt has edited *The Prelude* (1926), which prints parallel 1805 and 1850 versions of the poem and interprets their differences, with a history of the various intervenient texts; *The Early Letters of William and Dorothy Wordsworth, 1787–1805* (1935); *The Letters of William and Dorothy Wordsworth* (1939); the important *Journals of Dorothy Wordsworth* (1941); and *The Poetical Works of William Wordsworth*, in five volumes (1940–1949), with Helen Darbishire.

Among Wordsworth's longer poems *The Prelude* has excited most interest and discussion, as is unquestionably proper. Raymond D. Havens has written the classic commentary in *The Mind of a Poet: A Study of Wordsworth's Thought with Particular Reference to The Prelude* (1941). Havens provides an intensive interpretation and an analysis of the major themes, with special emphasis upon the theme of imagination. George W. Meyer was iconoclastic in *Wordsworth's Formative Years* (1943) and "The Early History of *The Prelude*," *Tulane Studies in English* (1949), as he emphasized the gap between Wordsworth's actual experience and the poem's idealized account of it. More recently Abbie Findlay Potts has written a book-length commentary in *Wordsworth's Prelude: A Study of its Literary Form* (1953), which focusses upon the poet's indebtedness to eighteenth-century poetry. Much remains to be said about *The Prelude* as a *poem*, and doubtless much more will be said. *The Excursion*, less attended than *The Prelude*, has nevertheless had its chronicler in Judson S. Lyon, *The Excursion: A Study* (1950), who deals with the poem's reputation and history, its sources, and its content and style.

Shorter individual poems have also maintained their hold upon critical interest. *The Ode on Intimations of Immortality* occasioned Lionel Trilling's good Freudian interpretation in the

English Institute Annual for 1952; Cleanth Brooks's acute analysis of its theme and imagery in *The Well Wrought Urn;* and T. M. Raysor's soberer "The Themes of Immortality and Natural Piety in Wordsworth's Immortality Ode," *PMLA* (1954). In "A Note on the Sources and Symbolism of the Intimations Ode," *Tulane Studies in English* (1952), George W. Meyer offered a provocative argument for the influence of the Christian Platonist Thomas Burnet upon the Ode. Short lyrics, eminently "A Slumber Did My Spirit Seal" from the Lucy Poems, have in keeping with modern critical methods and interests been intensively explicated for irony and paradox (Brooks and Warren, *Understanding Poetry*), or, as the case may be, condemned for lack of these qualities ("London, 1802" sonnet, in Brooks, Purser, and Warren, *An Approach to Literature*). James Benziger's " 'Tintern Abbey' Revisited," *PMLA* (1950), is the most satisfying appreciation of this poem's art, and F. A. Pottle is thoroughly illuminating upon "The Daffodils" in "The Eye and the Object in the Poetry of Wordsworth" in *Wordsworth: Centenary Studies*, edited by G. T. Dunklin (1951). Among more general studies of poetic technique are Josephine Miles, *Wordsworth and the Vocabulary of Emotion* and "Wordsworth: The Mind's Excursive Power" in *The Major English Romantic Poets* (1957); Florence Marsh's *Wordsworth's Imagery, A Study in Poetic Vision* (1952); and John Crowe Ransom's interesting analysis of Wordsworth's poetic devices in *Wordsworth: Centenary Studies*.

IV

Samuel Taylor Coleridge's reputation stands very high today, and his literary criticism in particular has been almost incalculably influential. Stanley Edgar Hyman has remarked in *The Armed Vision* (1948)—the title is a quotation from Coleridge's *Biographia Literaria*—that "The *Biographia Literaria*, published in 1817, is almost the bible of modern criticism," and that with the exception of Aristotle Coleridge is contemporary criticism's most important progenitor. His proclamation in *Biographia Literaria* that "Poetry, even that of the loftiest and, seemingly, that of the wildest odes, had a logic of its own, as severe as that of science," has been the rallying-cry of a critical generation, the "new apologists for poetry" of whom Murray Krieger has written.

Modern scholarship in Coleridge commenced with Alice D. Snyder's pioneering monograph in 1918 on the principle of the reconciliation of opposites in his criticism. This work was instrumental in reviving interest in and respect for Coleridge's thought, and Miss Snyder carried on her studies in *Coleridge on Logic and Learning* (1929), and Coleridge's *Treatise on Method* (1934). Her arguments for the significance of Coleridge's thought were supported by J. H. Muirhead's notable *Coleridge as Philosopher* (1930), Gordon McKenzie, *Organic Unity in Coleridge* (1939), and I. A. Richards' *Coleridge on Imagination* (1934). Richards' book was controversial, since he fathered his own logical positivism upon his subject, but full of exciting perceptions. D. G. James's attack upon it in *Skepticism and Poetry* placed Coleridge as high as had Richards, which was very high indeed. Among other appreciative estimates C. D. Thorpe's "Coleridge as Aesthetician and Critic," *JHI* (1944), and Basil Willey's *Nineteenth Century Studies: Coleridge to Matthew Arnold* (1949) may be mentioned.

Since his own days Coleridge has been regarded as perhaps the greatest of all critics of Shakespeare, but he has recently suffered in some degree from the general reaction against the Romantic approach to drama, with its emphasis upon psychological elaboration of Shakespeare's characters. T. M. Raysor's edition of *Coleridge's Shakespearean Criticism* (1930), with a full and judicious introduction, was nevertheless an event of the first magnitude. Raysor also edited *Coleridge's Miscellaneous Criticism* (1936). Coleridge's criticism of Shakespeare has been widely misunderstood and distorted, and the time is ripe for a revaluation of it.

Coleridge's poetry, always thought of as consisting almost exclusively of *The Ancient Mariner*, *Kubla Khan*, and *Christabel*, has received rather less attention than his criticism and philosophy, although scholarly specialists have worked upon it steadily. J. L. Lowes's *The Road to Xanadu* (1929), the most famous of all source-studies and perhaps the best-known book by an American scholar, has inhibited criticism of Coleridge's poems by its emphasis upon the role of the unconscious in them. As did Lowes for *The Ancient Mariner* and *Kubla Khan*, Arthur H. Nethercot studied the history and the sources of *Christabel* in *The Road to Tryermaine* (1929). Robert Penn Warren in "A Poem of Pure Imagination," *The Rime of the Ancient Mariner* (1946) emphasized Coleridge's conscious artistry and his active thought as Lowes had failed to do. His essay is a classic of contemporary appreciation.

Like *The Ancient Mariner, Kubla Khan,* with its added problem of incompleteness, has crucially raised the issue of spontaneity versus conscious art. Is *Kubla Khan* simply a fascinating specimen of automatic writing, and if so is it to be condemned? T. S. Eliot has felt that it is; Elisabeth Schneider took a middle position in *Coleridge, Opium, and Kubla Khan* (1953); and Humphry House defended the poem in his fine *Coleridge* (1953), as I have in "The Romantic Unity of 'Kubla Khan,' " *CE* (1951).

Recent scholarship has taken great interest in *Dejection: an Ode.* In 1937 Ernest de Sélincourt published the original text of the poem for the first time in *Essays and Studies of the English Association,* a version much longer and more explicitly autobiographical than the one that most of us know from the standard editions and anthologies. Humphry House asserted the superior poetic value of the original in his *Coleridge,* while a careful comparison of the two versions by Stephen F. Fogle led to the opposite conclusion in "The Design of Coleridge's 'Dejection,' " *SP* (1951). Most readers will probably agree with Fogle. *Dejection* represents a crux in Coleridge's philosophy of nature, since it raises the question of the truth of imagination and the possibility of knowing external reality. J. W. Beach treated it in *The Concept of Nature in Nineteenth Century English Poetry* as a denial of Coleridge's usual creed; I. A. Richards in *Coleridge on Imagination* found the problem itself unreal; while Newton P. Stallknecht took an opposite view to Beach in *Strange Seas of Thought.* M. H. Abrams, who dealt briefly but well with the poem in *The Mirror and the Lamp,* has projected a critical and historical full examination of *Dejection* in collaboration with R. C. Bald, but the book has not yet appeared. *Dejection* has not the distilled intensity of *The Ancient Mariner* and *Kubla Khan,* and for that very reason is more representative than they of the body of Coleridge's poetry: for example, his "conversation" poems, like *Frost at Midnight.* As such its artistry has commanded a gradually increasing respect.

The study of Coleridge's criticism and philosophy presents two related problems, the relative originality and value of his thought, and the reliability of many of his texts. René Wellek has consistently argued, in *Immanuel Kant in England* (1931), *The English Romantic Poets* (1950), and *A History of Modern Criticism* (1955), that Coleridge is largely derivative from German Romantic philosophy and criticism. This verdict is opposed by most English and American scholarship. On such a question a final decision is difficult, but it may safely be said that Coleridge partook of a vital body of ideas and assimilated them with his own discoveries in a coherent and vital system.

The problem of texts in Coleridge, the "great master of the fragment" who left so much unpublished, has made the work of his editors peculiarly important. Miss Snyder, Muirhead, and Raysor have done valuable service in the 1920's and '30's, and E. L. Griggs in 1933 added to previous collections *Unpublished Letters of Samuel Taylor Coleridge*. Griggs is now preparing the definitive edition of the letters, the first installment of which is *Collected Letters of Samuel Taylor Coleridge, 1795–1806* (1956). Kathleen Coburn, Coleridge's most recent editor, has published *The Philosophical Lectures* (1949), and *Inquiring Spirit* (1951), a combination of old and of new material. Her most important enterprise, an edition in many volumes of Coleridge's hitherto inaccessible notebooks, has been announced as in the press.

V

Modern treatment of Lord Byron has been strongly biographical, in keeping with his spectacular career. His poetry has solid worth, and it is no doubt widely read still. It does not fit our approved patterns, however, so that it is difficult for a critic to say much about it. Byron's language and metaphor are not distinguished enough to demand the intensive analysis which modern criticism has learned to do, and he is best in his long "guidebook" and narrative poems, of which we have little to say. Even in continental Europe, where his influence has been perhaps greater than in England, there seems for the moment to be little occasion for his poetry. The implications of Albert Gérard's refusal in his valuable *L'idée romantique de la poésie en Angleterre to* treat

Byron as a Romantic poet at all are very interesting, when one recalls the great Taine's glorification of him in his nineteenth-century history of English literature.

Byron *is* a Romantic poet of great scope and power, but as both man and poet he is a riddle; and riddles are more alluring to biographers than to critics. It might be said that Byron possessed the maximum variety with the minimum of unity, or that his very center was eccentricity. He was a fatalist free spirit, a Calvinistic deist, a neoclassicist Romantic, a vulgar gentleman, a limping Apollo, a self-despising egotist, a popular recluse, a snobbish democrat, a Philistine poet—his contradictions are endless. No doubt they come down to the single fact that, knowing many things, he never knew himself. In his poetry the solution is probably to be found in the contradiction itself, which is not merely willful or affected. If one takes the Byronism of *Childe Harold* and *Manfred* seriously it reveals much, as does the exquisite gloom of A. E. Housman, from its persistent paradox of the fire and the clay, of the soaring spirit with its clog of matter. It would take no great change to reconcile Byron's dualism with neo-orthodox Christian theology, with the important reservation that Byron would never have believed in any God he could imagine.

Modern biography of Byron begins darkly with Lord Lovelace's *Astarte, a Fragment of Truth* (1905; new edition, 1921), which made the charge of incest against him. The book, by a descendant of the poet, arose from the long-lasting Byron-Lady Byron controversy, in which Harriet Beecher Stowe and even Mark Twain had once participated. Ethel Colburne Mayne accepted the charge in her *Byron* (in two volumes, 1912; volume one revised, 1924), still the standard life. The poet and dramatist John Drinkwater attempted to refute it in his for the most part excellent *The Pilgrim of Eternity* (1925), but for almost all scholars Sir John Fox settled the question against Byron by a lucid and dispassionate review of the evidence in *The Byron Mystery* (1924). Among further biographies of Byron, covering all or in many instances a single phase of his life, are Andre Maurois' witty and urbane *Byron* (English translation by Hamish Miles, 1930); Peter Quennell, *Byron: The Years of Fame* (1935), and *Byron in Italy* (1941); and the Marchesa Iris Origo's *The Last Attachment; the Story of Byron and Teresa Guiccioli* (1949). Quennell, a graceful writer, is entertaining and at times penetrating; he is especially good on the background of high society. *The Last Attachment*, drawn from new sources, is indispensable for information upon Byron's most famous love affair, and for its account of Byron's political activities in Italy. Leslie A. Marchand's forthcoming biography of Byron is anticipated as the definitive synthesis of all previous attempts in the field. It is expected to substantiate still another accusation against Byron, long hinted at. Marchand presumably will add most notably to knowledge of the poet's days in Italy and Greece.

Among partly biographical studies Samuel C. Chew's *Byron in England: His Fame and After-Fame* (1924) is outstanding as a rich source of fact and an absorbing narrative. Richard A. Rice's briefer *Lord Byron's British Reputation* (1924) is also valuable. Peter Quennell's *Byron, a Self-Portrait* (1950), is an interesting selection of Byron's letters and his journals; and more recently Ernest J. Lovell has recorded Byron as talker in *His Very Self and Voice; Collected Conversations of Lord Byron* (1954). Byron stands very well both as conversationalist and as letter-writer. Aspects of his career are examined in Willis Pratt's *Byron at Southwell: The Making of a Poet* (1948), which publishes new poems and letters from the collection of the University of Texas; William A. Borsts's *Lord Byron's First Pilgrimage* (1948), on the travel background of the first two cantos of *Childe Harold;* and E. R. P. Vincent's *Byron, Hobhouse, and Foscolo* (1949), which is concerned with a double collaboration on *Childe Harold*, Canto IV.

In non-biographical studies William J. Calvert's *Byron: Romantic Paradox* (1935) found an essential dichotomy between Byron's classicism and his Romanticism, his obedience to tradition and his emotional spontaneity. Wayne Marjorum set forth a corresponding paradox in his *Byron as Skeptic and Believer* (1938) in the contrast between Byron's heritage from the Calvinism of his Scottish childhood and his relations to eighteenth-century rationalism. Specifically critical works on Byron's poetry are few, but *Don Juan* has been distinguished by two book-length commentaries, Elizabeth Boyd's *Byron's Don Juan: A Critical Study* (1945), and Paul G. Trueblood, *The Flowering of Byron's Genius* (1945), and is this year to be further honored in a variorum edition furnished by Guy Steffan and Willis Pratt.

The standard edition of Byron is the John Murray *Works of Lord Byron*, edited in thirteen volumes by E. H. Coleridge and R. E. Prothero (1898–1903; reissue, 1922). Among single-volume editions the American "Cambridge Poets" Byron is noteworthy for Paul Elmer More's introduction, and the Oxford University Press volume is good. Three excellent college texts ought also to receive notice among selections from Byron: *The Best of Byron*, edited by Richard A. Rice (1933); *Don Juan and Other Satiric Poems*, edited by Louis I. Bredvold (1935); and *Childe Harold's Pilgrimage and Other Romantic Poems* (1936), edited by Samuel C. Chew, who is undoubtedly the most eminent Byron specialist of our time.

VI

The poetic reputation of Percy Bysshe Shelley has undergone startling changes. Relatively little known in his own lifetime, and when known often feared and hated as an infidel and revolutionary, as Newman Ivey White has shown in *The Unextinguished Hearth: Shelley and his Contemporary Critics* (1938), by the 1830's he had become, as the young Browning thought him, the very archetype of the Romantic poet. He held this place in England and America throughout the nineteenth century (see Julia Power, *Shelley in America in the Nineteenth Century*, 1940). Probably he exercised less influence on poetry than did Keats in the same period, but he was closely studied by such men as W. M. Rossetti, Swinburne, Henry Sweet, Edward Dowden, and Harry Buxton Forman. His posthumous reputation in England, together with the fortunes of his surviving family, is entertainingly chronicled by Sylva Norman in *The Flight of the Skylark* (1954). Shelley's poetry, especially *Queen Mab*, was persistently popular with radical thinkers and labor groups, and Bernard Shaw always revered him as a great poet and seminal mind. Marchbanks in *Candida* seems to be a mixture of Shelley and Swinburne, with Shaw himself to keep the chill on.

A thorough study of the vicissitudes of Shelley's reputation in the twentieth century is greatly needed, for it would explain much about contemporary shifts in tastes and beliefs. His expansive affirmations and his belief in social progress, distorted by cursory reading of him, repelled such critics as T. E. Hulme, Ezra Pound, T. S. Eliot, F. R. Leavis, and W. H. Auden, and in America John Crowe Ransom, Allen Tate, and Cleanth Brooks, who have taxed him with sentimentality, insensibility to evil (a terrible charge this, but shown by Ellsworth Barnard in *Shelley's Religion*, 1936, to be mainly unfounded), confusion of mind, and unpoetic abstraction in his language and imagery. Most of these charges have been previously mentioned in the first section of this essay, and need not be further discussed. The charge against Shelley of poor artistry is based upon a particular doctrine of poetic imagery which its proponents have wrongly supposed to be universal in application. Some very acute modern critics seem completely blind to the essential Shelley as he was many years ago revealed by A. C. Bradley, *Oxford Lectures on Poetry* (1917), and by W. B. Yeats in his memorable "The Philosophy of Shelley's Poetry," *Ideas of Good and Evil* (1914).

Professional scholarship and "new" critical opinion have on Shelley been almost completely separate. For many years Shelley has commanded the devotion of learned academic specialists. These scholars, assuming Shelley's poetic greatness proven, have dealt chiefly with his biography and with his place in the history of ideas. The late Newman Ivey White was the dean of Shelleyans, whose studies were climaxed by his definitive and monumental critical biography, in two volumes *Shelley* (1940; abridged as *Portrait of Shelley*, 1945). The work of Kenneth Neill Cameron in *The Young Shelley: Genesis of a Radical* (1950) and Frederick L. Jones in *Mary Shelley's Journal* (1947) is incisive and authoritative. Edmund Blunden's *Shelley: A Life Story* (1947) is less thorough and meticulous than the books of the leading American Shelley scholars, but it is very strong in criticism and interpretation of Shelley's poetry. Carlos Baker's *Shelley's Major Poetry* (1948) is a learned and careful consideration of the poems by way of their sources, their themes, and the conventions of their genres. Baker's interpretations, unlike Kenneth Cameron's, avoid biography. Carl Grabo expounded Shelley's scientific and philosophic thought with much originality and learning in *A Newton among Poets: Shelley's Use of Science in Prometheus Unbound* (1930); *The Meaning of the Witch of Atlas* (1935); and his culminating *The Magic Plant: The Growth of Shelley's Thought* (1936).

For some years students have been questioning the precise nature of Shelley's intellectual development. It has been increasingly maintained that Shelley owed more to British empiricist philosophy than had been supposed. A. M. D. Hughes, *The Nascent Mind of Shelley* (1947), Joseph Barrell, *Shelley and the Thought of his Time: A Study in the History of Ideas* (1947), and Kenneth Cameron's *The Young Shelley* have given close attention to the differences in Shelley's ideas at various times and under various influences. David Lee Clark has emphasized the empiricist strain in Shelley in his articles and in his recent edition, *Shelley's Prose; or, The Trumpet of a Prophecy* (1954), which makes the body of Shelley's prose writing more accessible than it has been hitherto. James A. Notopoulos demonstrated the case for Platonic influence in his voluminous and thorough *The Platonism of Shelley: A Study of Platonism and the Poetic Mind* (1949).

The tendency of scholars to treat Shelley's poems purely as philosophical arguments has often produced interesting results, as in the work of Grabo, but it has its limitations. The early *Alastor* really does not contain all the difficulties and contradictions that scholars have found in it, if one assumes that Shelley was representing rather than arguing his way out of the problems of the Poet in his relations to nature. Indeed, the method of the history of ideas, which analyzes into ultimate components, is hostile to poetry as poetry. Scholars like Newman Ivey White have paid due heed to Shelley's aesthetic dimension, but to right the balance of content and form one should go to Melvin T. Solve's *Shelley: His Theory of Poetry* (1927). Bennett Weaver gave attention to Shelley's art in *Toward the Understanding of Shelley* (1932), and his forthcoming book on *Prometheus Unbound* should prove extremely illuminating. Floyd Stovall's *Desire and Restraint in Shelley* (1931) caught the integral quality of the poet's thinking, and Oscar W. Firkins achieved the same result with more concentration upon the poetic texts in his *Power and Elusiveness in Shelley* (1937). My book, *The Imagery of Keats and Shelley* (1949) attempted to establish Shelley's poetic characteristics as objectively as possible. Since this volume has now been referred to twice, it will not be mentioned in connection with Keats studies. Frederick A. Pottle also tried to define Shelley's art against the background of twentieth-century critical opinion in "The Case of Shelley,"

PMLA (1952). As Bennett Weaver has said in his essay in *The English Romantic Poets,* much remains to be done in specifically literary criticism of Shelley. His poetry needs to be fully and fairly aligned with twentieth-century criticism: a task that is difficult because of existing prejudices and prepossessions. Four thoughtful essays of revaluation in *The Major Romantic Poets* move in this direction: "Shelley the Artist" by Raymond D. Havens, "The Bottom of the Night" by Carlos Baker, "Present Values in Shelley's Art" by Stewart C. Wilcox; and "Shelley's Philosophy" by Sir Herbert Read. Opposition to Shelley, although settled in some quarters, has at any rate lost its original impact; and it should be mentioned that the Keats-Shelley Memorial Association of England and the Keats-Shelley Association of America both publish scholarly journals devoted primarily to the works of the two poets.

The most complete edition of Shelley is the "Julian," *The Complete Works of Percy Bysshe Shelley,* edited by Roger Ingpen and Walter E. Peck, in ten volumes (1926–30), but it is scarce and expensive, and most students have gotten along very well with the older editions of H. B. Forman, in eight volumes (1880) or G. E. Woodberry, in four volumes (1892). The best one-volume edition of the poems is the Oxford, though Woodberry's American "Cambridge Poets" Shelley has many virtues. Neville Rogers is now preparing a new edition for Oxford which should supplant all earlier texts. Among selections for school and college use N. I. White's *The Best of Shelley* (1932) and Ellsworth Barnard's *Selected Poems, Essays, and Letters* (1944) are especially good.

VII

Keats biography and criticism flourished so richly during the 1920's and the early 1930's that more recent scholarship has had the duty of refining upon it rather than creating anew. The centenary year of Keats's death, 1921, brought forth *The John Keats Memorial Volume,* edited by G. C. Williamson, an excellent collection of essays by various hands, including the unexpected one of Bernard Shaw. That veteran Socialist fastened unerringly upon the most socially-conscious passage in Keats's poetry, four rather undistinguished stanzas from *Isabella.* In 1925 appeared Amy

Lowell's two-volume *John Keats*, an ambitious critical biography based upon an unprecedented amount of new material. It had a mixed reception, but it stands out as a genuine portrait of Keats, with an original conception of his poetry. There are occasions in the book when the large Miss Lowell seems about to tuck the diminutive Keats under one arm and crack the line of opposing scholars for a touchdown; and this proprietary attitude helps to explain the irritation felt by some of her reviewers. Despite the great merits of her biography, Sidney Colvin's *John Keats: His Life and Poetry, His Friends, Critics, and After-Fame* (1917) is considered a sounder book. H. W. Garrod, who was among Miss Lowell's most caustic critics, published his small but good *Keats* in 1926. His *Poetical Works of John Keats* (1939; revised 1956) is the most accurate and scholarly text of the poems. Garrod was among the skeptics about Keats's qualities of intellect, which were now emphasized in two epoch-making studies: C. D. Thorpe's *The Mind of John Keats* (1926), and J. M. Murry's *Keats and Shakespeare: A Study of Keats's Poetic Life from 1816 to 1820* (1926).

Both of these books treat Keats as a wise man and a serious thinker. Hoxie N. Fairchild in *The Romantic Quest* and *Religious Trends in English Poetry* thought these claims exaggerated, and put the poet back in about the same spot where Matthew Arnold had deposited him in the 1880's. Indeed, Arnold was somewhat kinder than Fairchild. The new, exciting Keats of Thorpe and Murry aroused a lively critical debate, in which Romantics took the affirmative and Anglicans and neo-humanists the negative. Thorpe's interesting Platonic account of the *Ode on a Grecian Urn* led to a series of explications which still continues, until in 1957 one is tempted to appeal for a moratorium.

Newell F. Ford adopted a later version of Garrod's and Fairchild's position as he emphasized the sensuous Keats in a number of vigorous articles and a book, *The Prefigurative Imagination of John Keats* (1951). Werner Beyer on the other hand saw a substantial amount of Platonic and neo-Platonic idealism in Keats's poetry in *Keats and the Daemon King* (1947), a study of the influence of Wieland's *Oberon*. Earl Wasserman has endeavored to reconcile the two positions in *The Finer Tone: Keats' Major Poems* (1953), by discerning a "mystic oxymoron" or merging of sense with idea at the core of Keats's poetry. Wasserman's book contains the most searching dialectical explications in Keats scholarship, but he has perhaps lost sight of Keats's immediate poetic purposes.

J. M. Murry, who died in 1957 one of the great Keatsians of his time, maintained his exciting and enthusiastic point of view in a number of books, revisions, and additions to his *Studies in Keats* (1930). C. D. Thorpe in addition to many substantial articles has published a fine students' text, *John Keats: Complete Poems and Selected Letters* (1935), with excellent critical commentary and annotations. His treatment of *Endymion, Lamia,* and *Hyperion* is particularly noteworthy.

Keats lends himself to studies of poetic development, and there are several works that use this method. Of these Claude L. Finney's *The Evolution of Keats's Poetry* (1936) is the most ambitious and elaborate, weaving together Keats's life, ideas, literary sources, and techniques. Every student of Keats should be acquainted with it, but it has the weakness of rigidity. It divides the brief career of the poet too definitely into separate periods, without providing adequate connections between one period and another. Ernest de Sélincourt's appendices to the various editions of his *The Poems of John Keats* (fifth edition, 1926) contain much valuable analysis of Keats's style and vocabulary. M. R. Ridley's *Keats' Craftsmanship: A Study in Poetic Development* (1933) is highly illuminating and Ridley's love of Keats in infectious. W. J. Bate's *The Stylistic Development of Keats* (1945) is more ambitious than Ridley's study and even more thorough. Bate's brilliant monograph *Negative Capability* (1939) paved the way for his later volume, which he has recently supplemented with "Keats's Style: Evolution toward Qualities of Permanent Value," in *The Major Romantic Poets.*

Among letters and records of Keats, M. B. Forman's *The Letters of John Keats* is outstanding (third edition, 1947), although Hyder E. Rollins has pointed out various errors of omission. Keats's letters are among the finest in literature, and Forman's is an attractive, authoritative, and generally well-annotated rendering of them. One might wish for a fuller index, with more relation to recent studies of Keats. Professor Rollins has made accessible much valuable material upon Keats's environment, his family, friends, and posthumous reputation, in *Keats' Reputation in America to 1848*

(1946), *The Keats Circle: Letters and Papers, 1816–1878* (1948), *Keats and the Bostonians* (1951), with S. M. Parrish, an absorbing account of Amy Lowell's unsuccessful struggle to get access to Fanny Brawne's letters, and *More Letters and Poems of the Keats Circle* (1955). The fullest edition of Keats is *The Poetical Works and Other Writings of John Keats*, edited by H. B. Forman, revised by M. B. Forman, in five volumes (1938–39). This is the "Hampstead Edition."

Keats has fared well with the New Critics, that uncompromising group of painstaking analysts whose norms are generally drawn from metaphysical poetry. Cleanth Brooks, whose interpretations were earlier mentioned, and Allen Tate have given brilliant readings of Keats's odes, although Tate cannot grant more than a qualified approval to any Romantic poet (" A Reading of Keats," *On the Limits of Poetry*, 1948). Brooks has recently contributed "The Artistry of Keats: A Modern Tribute," to *The Major English Romantic Poets*.

VIII

The lesser Romantics are (doubtfully) Robert Burns, Sir Walter Scott, Robert Southey, Charles Lamb, Leigh Hunt, Thomas De Quincey, William Hazlitt, and Walter Savage Landor. One might question whether Burns is either "lesser" or a Romantic. On the one hand he is a fine and durable poet, while on the other he falls outside the chronological period, and does not share the Romantic world-view. The label given him above, however, can be justified briefly by remarking that he is minor in the sense that his poetry has not in the recent past aroused significant critical interest, and Romantic as a potential organicist in assimilating and recreating Scottish literary tradition. What we have learned about Burns in the twentieth century is to respect the breadth and depth of his literary and cultural heritage. Burns did not properly belong among the thresher and waterman and washerwoman poets of whom the later eighteenth century was fond, although he may have owed his popularity to being mistaken for the plough-boy poet. De Lancey Ferguson has been the leading Burns scholar of our time, with *The Letters of Robert Burns* (1931), *Pride and Passion: Robert Burns, 1759–1796* (1939), and *Selected Letters*

(1953). David Daiches published a solid critical study in *Robert Burns* (1950). It may be remarked for what it is worth that all recent Burns scholars have Scottish names, and that this observation also holds true for Sir Walter Scott, with few exceptions. Contemporary work on Scott includes John Buchan (Lord Tweedsmuir), *Sir Walter Scott* (1932); Sir Herbert J. C. Grierson, *Sir Walter Scott, Bart.* (1938), Dame Una Pope-Hennessy, *Sir Walter Scott* (1949), and the indefatigable Hesketh Pearson's *Walter Scott: His Life and Personality* (1954).

Robert Southey, one of the greatest names of his era and known in ours as the supreme example of the pure self-supporting man of letters, has interested us today mainly for his relations with his greater contemporaries Coleridge and Wordsworth, and his controversy with Byron. Jack Simmons devoted a book to him, *Southey* (1945), and Malcolm Elwin an interesting chapter in *The First Romantics* (1947). The much-loved Charles Lamb has had the services of E. V. Lucas in *The Letters of Charles Lamb*, including letters of Mary Lamb (1935) and Edmund Blunden in *Charles Lamb: His Life Recorded by his Contemporaries* (1934). As a Romantic critic Lamb has been little discussed of late, but M. H. Abrams in *The Mirror and the Lamp* and René Wellek in *A History of Modern Criticism* gave consideration to his critical principles.

Interest in the literary and dramatic criticism of Leigh Hunt has been stimulated by the editorial work of L. H. and C. W. Houtchens in *Leigh Hunt's Dramatic Criticism, 1803–31* (1949), and *Leigh Hunt's Literary Criticism* (1956). C. D. Thorpe has contributed a memorable essay of evaluation to the second of these volumes. Edmund Blunden's *Leigh Hunt and his Circle* (1930) is the standard biography, and Louis Landré established a new peak of scholarship in Hunt with *Leigh Hunt (1784–1859): Contribution à l'histoire du romantisme anglais* (1936). Evaluation of Hunt has been beclouded since his own earlier days by personal feeling: versatile, charming, sociable, opinionated, generous, shiftless, and vain, he aroused strong reactions and does so still. William Hazlitt, a greater critic whom few have ever accused of charm, has had somewhat the same fortune. Hazlitt's quarrels with his great contemporaries have according to his leading student in our time, Elisabeth Schneider, prejudiced the case against his criticism, which has yet to receive full justice. Professor Schneider's *The Aesthetics of William Hazlitt* (1933) is the outstanding evaluation. Hazlitt's criticism has been more briefly treated by Abrams in *The Mirror and the Lamp*, and by Wellek in *A History of Modern Criticism*. The definitive edition is *The Complete Works of William Hazlitt*, edited by P. P. Howe (1930–34).

Thomas De Quincey's famous *Opium-Eater* has been re-edited within the last decade, and his literary criticism has received steady though not pronounced notice. Horace A. Eaton wrote the standard biography in 1936, and Edward Sackville-West's notable *A Flame in Sunlight: The Life and Work of De Quincey* appeared in the same year. Sigmund K. Procter's *De Quincey's Theory of Literature* (1943) is to my knowledge the only full-scale modern discussion of his criticism. Walter Savage Landor, a good but not an influential poet, was honored in 1954 by R. H. Super's definitive biography. A review of research upon the lesser Romantics, *The English Romantic Poets and Essayists*, edited by L. H. and C. W. Houtchens, has already appeared or will be published shortly.

In summarizing modern studies in English Romanticism, it may be said that in England and the United States Romantic poetry was implicitly accepted as the standard to follow up until the First World War. About 1920 it was vigorously attacked, not only as art but also as ethics and philosophy, for a dangerous naturalism which allied itself with scientism and the idea of material progress to hasten the ill effects of the industrial revolution upon modern society. Among critics and poets Romanticism was a barrier to be cleared from the way of a new generation. Regarding Romanticism simply as an obstacle, its critics distorted both its nature and its products. Now, past the turn of the century, there is hope that the great Romantic poets may be seen more clearly.

8

The Victorian Period

LIONEL STEVENSON

THERE CAN BE LITTLE DOUBT THAT
the Victorian period is the area of English literature that has grown
most rapidly in prestige during the past twenty-five years. It is
now probably the field in which the greatest amount of important
and original research is being conducted. Two principal reasons
for this development can be adduced. For one thing, many of the
essential materials, in the form of letters, diaries, and other documents, could not become available until the original authors and
the first generation of their descendants had died, so that personal
data could be published without causing embarrassment or ill-
feeling. The second reason is that a perspective of time was necessary before Victorian literature could be discussed dispassionately
and with a due sense of proportion. During the first quarter of the
twentieth century the inevitable revolt against the immediate past
was in full force, and few scholars were willing to risk the scorn
of their colleagues by devoting themselves to a serious and respectful investigation of the despised Victorians.

Until about 1930, therefore, the large output of books and
articles about Victorian literature was mainly supplied by amateurs
who were motivated by their personal enthusiasm for the works
and ideas of certain authors, particularly Carlyle, Ruskin, Browning, and Dickens. Even the relatively small number of genuinely
scholarly and thorough studies produced in that era are now
partially invalidated by the factual information more recently
disclosed.

I

The increasing significance of the Victorian period is illustrated
by the development of specialized scholarly aids. Beginning in

1932, an annual Victorian Bibliography was published in *Modern Philology*, under the sponsorship of the Victorian Literature group of the Modern Language Association of America. This invaluable reference guide covers background works on the history, social conditions, and other general aspects of the period, in addition to all books and articles that made any significant contribution to literary study. It has been conveniently reprinted in two volumes, one (edited by W. D. Templeman) covering the years 1932–44, the second (edited by Austin Wright) covering 1945–54.

For the past five years this has been supplemented by the *Victorian Newsletter*, issued twice a year by the same group of the MLA. It gives a selected list of the most recent publications in the field, thus providing the latest references before they have time to be included in the annual bibliography. It also lists dissertations in progress and other research projects, and it has recently been expanded to include short scholarly articles, reviews of important books, and reports on the Victorian materials available in various libraries. It is currently edited by W. H. Buckler of New York University.

The latest development is the establishment of a quarterly, *Victorian Studies*, conducted at Indiana University, beginning in 1957. This has been planned as an interdisciplinary journal, including any aspect of the social and physical sciences and the humanities that may have relevance to the Victorian age, but the preponderance of the contents will probably always lean toward literature. The annual bibliography is being transferred to this journal from *MP*.

Yet another project of the Victorian group of the MLA was a volume of essays, *The Reinterpretation of Victorian Literature*, edited by J. E. Baker (1950). Eleven contributors wrote on various aspects of the subject; and while it is open to some objection on the grounds of selection and proportion (giving too much attention to the trend of ideas and not enough to aesthetic considerations) it is full of stimulating insights and is further noteworthy as a symbol of the new self-confidence with which Victorian specialists claim that their era has something vital to say to the present day. It includes many suggestions of topics that still await further research.

Two convenient handbooks are *English Literature of the*

Victorian Period, by J. D. Cooke and Lionel Stevenson (1949), and *A Companion to Victorian Literature*, by T. M. Parrott and R. B. Martin (1955). Both can be recommended as giving the essential information in concise form, with reading lists for fuller inquiry.

The period was far too crowded and complex to be compressed into a single critical analysis; but a remarkable gesture in that direction was achieved by Jerome H. Buckley in *The Victorian Temper* (1951). This fairly short book traces some of the main currents and eddies of ideas through seventy years, and is especially valuable for reminding us that a literary atmosphere is not determined wholly by the dozen major figures but also by scores of others whose reputation does not survive beyond their own time. By citing many apt examples from the secondary authors, Buckley adds a necessary dimension to his discussion of Tennyson, Ruskin, Rossetti, and the other giants.

Most of the books on the period, however, defer to the difficulty of giving a general survey, and confine themselves either to disconnected chapters on selected authors or else to the isolating of a single theme from the intertangled mass. Apparently English scholars tend toward the former type of book, American scholars toward the latter. Some of the best recent English discussions of the Victorian age can be found in *Towards the Twentieth Century*, by H. V. Routh (1937), and in two volumes by Basil Willey, *Nineteenth-Century Studies* (1949) and *More Nineteenth-Century Studies* (1955). Other English books of the same sort, confined to authors in particular genres, are *Ten Victorian Poets*, by F. L. Lucas (1940), *Early Victorian Novelists*, by Lord David Cecil (1935), and *Novels of the 1840's*, by Kathleen Tillotson (1954). In general, the English writers are more inclined to write critical studies, while their American confreres usually restrict themselves to the safer activity of marshaling factual evidence. Hence the American reader may feel a faint shock when he encounters an occasional touch of asperity in the English works in place of the impartial tone usually maintained in American scholarship.

The Victorian age seethed with discussion of social, political, and religious ideas, and so a number of recent studies have been devoted to significant segments of those discussions. By contrast, only one book has dealt with the major prose writers as literary artists rather than as idea-mongers. This is *The Victorian Sage: Studies in Argument*, by John Holloway (1953), which examines the rhetorical methods of Carlyle, Newman, Disraeli, Arnold, Eliot, and Hardy, emphasizing the emotional and imaginative qualities of their work.

Among the books dealing with the ideological currents of the time, one of the most helpful is *Victorian Critics of Democracy*, by B. E. Lippincott (1938), a political scientist who analyzed the objections to the democratic concept that were expressed by Carlyle, Ruskin, Arnold, and several others. Another good study, discussing those three authors and also Kingsley and Morris, is *Human Dignity and the Great Victorians*, by B. N. Schilling (1946), which surveys the warnings against the dehumanizing effects of industrialism and machinery. More restricted in scope than the title indicates, *The Victorian Conscience*, by Clarence R. Decker (1952), concerns itself chiefly with the opposition of English critics to the new realistic literature infiltrating from abroad, and in doing so the book throws some light on the problem of Victorian prudery. Geoffrey Tillotson's *Criticism and the Nineteenth Century* (1951) has good chapters on Newman, Arnold, and Pater.

One of the most explosive crises of the century was precipitated by the publication of Darwin's theory of evolution and its subsequent popularization by Huxley. A full and lively account of this controversy is given in *Apes, Angels, and Victorians*, by William Irvine (1955). The impact of the new scientific theories upon the thinking of the poets has been surveyed by Ralph B. Crum in *Scientific Thought in Poetry* (1931) and by Lionel Stevenson in *Darwin Among the Poets* (1932). A parallel study of the novelists is Leo J. Henkin's *Darwinism in the English Novel, 1860–1910* (1940). This problem is linked to wider philosophical attitudes in *The Concept of Nature in Nineteenth Century English Poetry*, by Joseph Warren Beach (1936). Along with these should be mentioned *Matthew Arnold, The Ethnologist*, by F. E. Faverty (1951), which presents the controversial concepts of races and cultures held not only by Arnold but also by Carlyle and other authors. The various responses of Victorian poets to "the ferment of attraction and repulsion between Christianity and romanticism in an increasingly secularistic age" are analyzed fully by Hoxie N. Fairchild in the fourth volume of his *Religious Trends in English Poetry* (1957).

Even with regard to the poets, more has been written about their ideas than about their art. The only recent study that attempts an intensive inquiry into the poetry as a creative process is *The Alien Vision of Victorian Poetry*, by E. D. H. Johnson (1952), which is confined to the three major figures, Tennyson, Browning, and Arnold; but although the subtitle states that it deals with "Sources of the Poetic Imagination," the book is actually concerned as much with their social thinking as with the aesthetic element, as it is dominated by a rather rigid hypothesis that their poetry reveals a constant conflict between their innate artistic intuitions and their unwilling conformity to the rationalistic and practical demands of the public. An article by Lionel Stevenson in *UTQ* (1952), "The Pertinacious Victorian Poets," suggests possible lines of approach to the creative aspects of the poetry.

Indispensable to anyone who intends to investigate the poetry of the period is *The Victorian Poets: A Guide to Research*, edited by F. E. Faverty (1956). The nine contributors provide full discussion of all the significant books and articles in the field, with special attention to the more recent publications.

There is no equivalent volume for the Victorian novelists, though the need for one is equally great. Only in the past quarter-century has the fiction of the period been deemed worthy of accurate and exhaustive study. Indeed, the necessary criteria for evaluating it became available only with the publication of such basic treatises as *The Craft of Fiction*, by Percy Lubbock (1921); *Aspects of the Novel*, by E. M. Forster (1927); *The Structure of the Novel*, by Edwin Muir (1928); *Technique of the Novel*, by Carl H. Grabo (1928); and *Aesthetics of the Novel*, by Van Meter Ames (1928).

As long as fiction was judged strictly by the doctrine of realism laid down by Henry James in the eighties, few of the Victorian novelists were granted much stature as major artists. The latest exponent of the dogma is F. R. Leavis in *The Great Tradition* (1949), which asserts that George Eliot and Henry James were the only significant novelists of the Victorian era. But various forces have been at work to displace this uncompromising view.

Most critics now recognize that the novel shares in the emotional and imaginative objectives of poetry and hence that distortions of reality are justifiable for symbolic or "mythopoeic" purposes. Hence acclamation of Dickens as the greatest English novelist has become almost unanimous.

The only detailed survey of Victorian fiction as a whole is to be found in Volumes VII–X of Ernest A. Baker's monumental *History of the English Novel* (1936–39). Nor is there a bibliography of the gigantic total output. The works of most of the representative novelists are listed in the sumptuous compilation by Michael Sadleir, *XIX Century Fiction* (1951); but as this is merely a catalogue of his own collection (now in the library of the University of California at Los Angeles) it is limited to the books that interested him. As a basis for investigating specific topics, a valuable classified bibliography of "Problems and Digressions in the Victorian Novel, 1860–1900," by Leo J. Henkin, came out serially in the *Bulletin of Bibliography* (1946–47).

Perhaps the best evidence of the current interest in the novelists is the success of the quarterly journal, *Nineteenth-Century Fiction*, which was established by Bradford A. Booth in 1945 as *The Trollopian*, but which was extended in scope four years later when the editor became aware of the need for a medium of publication for articles dealing with the whole field. A file of this journal provides a good record of trends in research and criticism.

The most stimulating general book on the subject, though its conclusions cannot be accepted without serious qualification, is *The Hero in Eclipse in Victorian Fiction*, by Mario Praz (English translation by Angus Davidson, 1956). Praz makes many perceptive comments in his long chapters on Dickens, Thackeray, Trollope, and Eliot; but his material is forced to conform with a theory about the pressure of Victorian bourgeois complacency as the cause for the disappearance of romantic intensity from the novel.

II

An essential source of information about any author is an accurate edition of his correspondence and diaries. This apparatus has already been provided for several major Victorian figures, and others will soon be available. *The Letters and Private Papers of W. M. Thackeray*, edited by Gordon N. Ray (1945–46), is a model of completeness and thorough annotation, and it is rivaled by *The George Eliot Letters*, edited by Gordon S. Haight (1954–55). On a smaller scale there is *The Letters of Anthony Trollope*, edited by Bradford A. Booth (1951). Joan Evans and J. H. Whitehouse are editing *The Diaries of John Ruskin*, the first volume of which came out in 1957. The correspondence of Gerard Manley Hopkins was collected by Claude Colleer Abbott in a series of volumes between 1935 and 1957, and *The Notebooks and Papers of Gerard Manley Hopkins* were edited by Humphry House in 1937. *The Note-Books of Matthew Arnold*, annotated with scrupulous thoroughness by Howard F. Lowry, Karl Young, and Waldo H. Dunn (1952), form an essential source for any discussion of Arnold's literary background. The rapid expansion of this type of material is well illustrated by the case of Dickens. As recently as 1938 an imposing three-volume collection of his letters was edited by Walter Dexter, and was accepted as authoritative; but in less than twenty years it has proved to be so inaccurate and incomplete that a new edition, at least twice as large, is in preparation.

As soon as such documentary material is completely accessible, full and impartial biographies can be written. Thus Professor Ray has followed his edition of the letters with a life of Thackeray in two massive volumes, covering every aspect of his career and personality and also including perceptive analysis of his books and discussion of his place in English fiction. The first volume, subtitled *The Uses of Adversity, 1811–1846*, appeared in 1955; and the second, *The Age of Wisdom, 1847–1863*, in 1958.

Equally thorough and authoritative is the two-volume biography by Edgar Johnson, *Charles Dickens: His Tragedy and Triumph* (1952). This brings together all the known information about Dickens, including many facts only recently brought to light. Its critical chapters on Dickens's novels and other writings provide a good view of the current evaluation.

Even more extensive will be a biography of Ruskin now being written by Helen Gill Viljoen. The first volume, published in 1956, is *Ruskin's Scottish Heritage*, which deals entirely with his ancestry, and which justifies Professor Viljoen's undertaking by demonstrating that almost all the supposed facts given in the previous biographies of Ruskin and in his own autobiography are seriously inaccurate. The only other Victorian author whose life has been covered in such detail is Carlyle, in D. A. Wilson's six-volume work (1923–1934); but this is an amateurish, laborious compilation, and is in many respects now out of date.

Such intensive biographies will always be basic sources of information for students pursuing specialized investigation of the respective authors; but for a general knowledge of the subject it will usually be sufficient to read a one-volume biography if a recent and responsible one is in existence. Most of the important Victorian authors have been thus dealt with in the past few years.

Considering the poets first, one finds that there is a good life of Tennyson by his grandson, Sir Charles Tennyson (1949), which uses family documents and traditions but avoids the adulation and excessive discretion that in the past have been the bane of biographies written by descendants of the subject.

An utterly different sort of book is Betty Miller's *Robert Browning: A Portrait* (1952). This employs the methods of psychoanalysis to establish an interpretation of Browning's personality which is almost diametrically opposite to the sentimental conception of him that has prevailed ever since his lifetime. In a vigorous and rather spasmodic manner Mrs. Miller makes a convincing case for her particular hypothesis as to Browning's lack of self-confidence and his dependence on women for guidance. The book is therefore a necessary corrective to the older portrayal of him as a virile activist. But it cannot be accepted as a complete biography, as it ignores every element in his life that does not directly support the author's theory. Part of this theory being that Browning suffered from recurrent spells when his creativity was paralyzed, these are recorded in such detail as to convey an impression that he seldom wrote any poetry at all.

Browning's relationship with his wife is so essential to the argument that Mrs. Miller's book is almost equally important as a revision of Elizabeth Barrett's biography, and should be read in conjunction with *The Life of Elizabeth Barrett Browning*, by Gardner B. Taplin (1957), the most thorough account of her life. A remarkable piece of special investigation is *The Family of the Barrett*, by Jeannette Marks (1938), which reconstructs the life

of Mrs. Browning's ancestors in the West Indies and does something toward humanizing the behavior of her father.

There is no full-scale biography of Matthew Arnold. Louis
Bonnerot's *Matthew Arnold: poète* (1947) is subtitled an "essai de
biographie psychologique," and tries to account for his emotional
and intellectual attitudes in terms of neurosis. A short book by E.
K. Chambers, *Matthew Arnold: A Study* (1947), is a convenient
synopsis of his uneventful career and attempts little further.

Dante Gabriel Rossetti: A Victorian Romantic, by Oswald
Doughty (1949), is a full and scholarly biography, which provides
also a good many incidental details about the other Pre-Raphaelite
poets, for whom there are no equally recent or complete studies.
The most useful biography of Swinburne is still the one by
Georges Lafourcade (1932), though it and virtually all other writ-
ings on the subject have been ferociously condemned by Randolph
Hughes in his long introductions to two of Swinburne's previously
unpublished works, *Lucretia Borgia* (1942) and *Lesbia Brandon*
(1952). Hughes is unfortunately both fanatical and inaccurate.
Humphrey Hare's *Swinburne: A Biographical Approach* (1949)
suffers from a doctrinaire psychoanalytic emphasis. On William
Morris, probably the most satisfactory book is *William Morris,
Medievalist and Revolutionary*, by Margaret B. Grennan (1945).
It should be pointed out that *William Morris: Prophet of England's New Order*, by Lloyd Eric Grey (1949), is simply a re-
printing of a book entitled *A Victorian Rebel* which was published
in 1940 by the same author under the name of Lloyd Wendell
Eshleman. E. P. Thompson's *William Morris: Romantic to Revolu-
tionary* (1955) is a detailed interpretation of his career from the
Marxist standpoint. For a graceful general view of the whole
movement one can read *The Pre-Raphaelite Tragedy*, by William
Gaunt (1942).

Several of the less eminent poets have been treated in extensive
biographies. *The Life of Edward FitzGerald*, by A. McKinlay
Terhune (1947) is based on much new material. *The Life and
Times of Coventry Patmore*, by Derek Patmore (1949), is written
by the poet's great-grandson and uses documents in the possession
of the family. A more meticulous scholarly work is *Coventry
Patmore*, by E. J. Oliver (1956). James Pope-Hennessy is the

author of a two-volume biography of Monckton Milnes (1950–52).

Among the major writers of expository prose, the most adequate recent biography is *The Life of John Stuart Mill*, by M. St. John Packe (1954). Joan Evans's *John Ruskin* (1954) is a good presentation of the existing data, taking a moderate position in the midst of various extreme psychological interpretations of his character that have been advanced in the past few years. As Carlyle's ideology has fallen into general disfavor, few modern scholars have written about him. The only recent book that has undertaken to cover the whole subject is *Thomas Carlyle: The Life and Ideas of a Prophet*, by Julian Symons (1952). By contrast, a great deal has been written about Cardinal Newman, but much of it lacks objectivity. The best balanced of the critical biographies is C. F. Harrold's *John Henry Newman* (1945). Readable but undependable books are John Moody's *John Henry Newman* (1945), Eleanor Ruggles's *Journey into Faith* (1948), and Seán O'Faoláin's *Newman's Way* (1952). The only modern biography of Macaulay is *Lord Macaulay: A Victorian Liberal*, by R. C. Beatty (1938).

The current vogue of the Victorian novelists is well demonstrated by the spate of good biographies of them. On Dickens there is no wholly trustworthy one-volume work, Hesketh Pearson's *Dickens: His Character, Comedy and Career* (1949) being lively but superficial. An example of brilliant research on a limited and controversial subject is Ada B. Nisbet's *Dickens and Ellen Ternan* (1952), which provides documentary evidence to replace a tissue of hearsay, guesswork, and willful prejudice. The career of Thackeray is covered in *The Showman of Vanity Fair*, by Lionel Stevenson (1947). For Trollope the best biography is still Michael Sadleir's *Trollope: A Commentary* in the revised edition of 1947. Lawrence and Elizabeth Hanson have produced an efficient book in *Marian Evans and George Eliot* (1952), and these collaborators are responsible also for what is probably the best account of the Brontë family, *The Four Brontës* (1949), welcome for its sanity and balance after many emotional orgies on the subject. Annette B. Hopkins's *Elizabeth Gaskell: Her Life and Work* (1952) is a thorough and sympathetic treatment of an unexciting subject. Wilkie Collins had never been the subject of a biography until five years ago, and since then one has been published by an Englishman, Kenneth Robinson (1952), and another by an American, Nuel Pharr Davis (1956). The first full-scale biography of another once-popular novelist is *R. D. Blackmore,* by Waldo H. Dunn (1956). Lives of novelists who were flourishing nearer the end of the century include *The Ordeal of George Meredith,* by Lionel Stevenson (1953); *Hardy of Wessex,* by Carl J. Weber (1940); and *Voyage to Windward: The Life of Robert Louis Stevenson,* by J. C. Furnas (1951).

III

Biographical information, interesting though it often is, cannot be justified as an end in itself. The record of an author's life is important insofar as it sheds more light on the sources of his knowledge, the reasons for his opinions, and the process by which he created his works. For most of the Victorian authors, it can be argued, the output of critical interpretation has not caught up with the biographical, either in quantity or in quality; but the total of significant criticism is steadily increasing.

Granting the traditional precedence again to the poets, we find that Tennyson is beginning to receive close attention as a master of poetic technique. This has been facilitated by the publication of the original drafts and successive revisions of some of his poems. See the "Tennyson Papers," II–IV, by Sir Charles Tennyson, *Cornhill Magazine* (1936), an article by Joyce Green in *PMLA* (1951), and others by Mary J. Donahue (Ellmann) in *PMLA* (1949), *PQ* (1949), and *MLN* (1950). The psychological basis for the imagery in his early poems is analysed by W. D. Paden in *Tennyson in Egypt* (1942). A balanced critical judgment of his poetry, pointing out his merits but acknowledging his defects, can be found in *Tennyson Sixty Years After,* by Paull F. Baum (1948). *Tennyson and the Reviewers,* by Edgar F. Shannon, Jr. (1952), is an exhaustive "study of his literary reputation and of the influence of the critics upon his poetry" up to 1852. Two of the most influential modern poets have expressed their opinions of Tennyson in introductions to selections of his poetry: T. S. Eliot (1936)[1] and W. H. Auden (1944). A remarkable attempt to com-

---

[1] Reprinted as "In Memoriam" in Eliot's *Essays Ancient and Modern* (1936).

mend his work in Freudian terms, depicting him as a forerunner of Yeats, Eliot, Joyce, and other twentieth-century giants, is "Tennyson as a Modern Poet," by Arthur J. Carr, in *UTQ* (1950). H. M. McLuhan's "Tennyson and Picturesque Poetry," *Essays in Criticism* (1951), makes a strong claim for the modern element in some of his early and late poems, when he was free of pressure to expound ideas. Dealing specifically with *Maud*, Roy P. Basler in "Tennyson the Psychologist," *South Atlantic Quarterly* (1944), [2] asserts that he showed a remarkable prevision of Freud's theories of psychopathic states. A Freudian interpretation is also given to his portrayal of Guinevere by Betty Miller in "Tennyson and the Sinful Queen," *Twentieth Century* (1955). Milton Millhauser analyses his imagery by current methods in "Tennyson: Artifice and Image," *Journal of Aesthetics and Art Criticism* (1956). His most ambitious work, *The Idylls of the King*, often a major target of scorn, receives intelligent vindication in articles by F. E. L. Priestley (*UTQ*, 1949) and S. C. Burchell (*PMLA*, 1953).

The vast mass of published material about Robert Browning is so largely subjective and indiscriminate that a great part of it need not occupy the attention of modern students. The study of his poetry has therefore been immensely facilitated by two recent publications. *Robert Browning: A Bibliography, 1830–1950*, compiled by C. S. Northup, L. N. Broughton, and Robert Pearsall (1953), includes an accurate listing of all secondary material, which helps in picking out what is of any value; and the second edition of W. C. DeVane's *Browning Handbook* (1955) supplies the essential information about each poem and often summarizes the principal critical opinions. The best book about his poetry is *The Infinite Moment and Other Essays in Robert Browning*, by W. O. Raymond (1950). Discussion of his imagery began with "Touch Images in the Poetry of Robert Browning," *PMLA* (1922), by J. K. Bonnell. A very intensive study of this sort is *Browning's Star Imagery*, by C. Willard Smith (1941). The latest such inquiry is " 'The Jewelled Bow': A Study in Browning's Imagery and Humanism," *PMLA* (1955), by W. O. Raymond. S. W. Holmes sought to apply psychoanalytic methods in two articles, "Browning's Sordello and Jung," *PMLA* (1941), and "Browning: Semantic Stutterer," *PMLA* (1945).

[2] Reprinted in *Sex, Symbolism, and Psychology in Literature* (1948).

The Ring and the Book naturally has received a good deal of attention ever since its source, *The Old Yellow Book*, was first published by C. W. Hodell in 1908. John M. Gest made a legal study of the use of the evidence, in *The Old Yellow Book* (1925). Recently Beatrice M. Corrigan has discovered and edited another report of the original trial, under the title *Curious Annals* (1956). Helpful in reading the poem is "The Narrative Structure of Browning's *The Ring and the Book*," *Research Studies, State College of Washington* (1943), by B. R. McElderry, Jr. The best brief analysis of the poem's purpose and method is "*The Ring and the Book:* A Relativist Poem," *PMLA* (1956), by Robert Langbaum.

Browning's Parleyings: The Autobiography of a Mind, by W. C. DeVane (1927), was the first application of modern scholarly methods to one of Browning's long poems and remains of prime importance. Earl Hilton comes to grips with a notoriously difficult poem in "Browning's *Sordello* as a Study of the Will," *PMLA* (1955). Margaret E. Glenn deals with "The Meaning and Structure of *Pippa Passes*" in *UTQ* (1955), and F. E. L. Priestley elucidates the ideas in another of the difficult poems in "A Reading of *La Saisiaz*," *UTQ* (1956). The most interesting recent discovery was made by Donald Smalley and published as *Browning's Essay on Chatterton* (1948) with a long introduction discussing the significance of this prose essay in relation to Browning's poetry.

For Matthew Arnold as poet the basic general work of reference is *The Poetry of Matthew Arnold: A Commentary*, by C. B. Tinker and H. F. Lowry (1950), which provides accurate and complete information about each poem. A brilliant critical study is Lionel Trilling's *Matthew Arnold* (second edition, 1949), though like most of the works on Arnold's writing it pays more attention to his prose then to his poetry. Valuable discussions of particular poems are "Arnold's Marguerite," by Paull F. Baum in the *Booker Memorial Studies* (1950), and "The Scholar Gypsy: A Reinterpretation," *RES* (1955), by G. Wilson Knight.

Swinburne has received relatively little critical discussion in recent years. The best general analysis is still to be found in the book by S. C. Chew (1929). A survey of earlier opinions of his work can be found in *Swinburne's Literary Career and Fame*, by C. K. Hyder (1933). As a brief statement of his significance the best article is E. K. Brown's "Swinburne: A Centenary Estimate," *UTQ* (1937). During the past twenty years most of the commentary on Swinburne has been psychological rather than literary.

Critical study of Dante Gabriel Rossetti has centered mainly in the close examination of his text conducted by P. F. Baum in his editions of *The House of Life* (1928) and *The Blessed Damozel* (1937) and by Janet C. Troxell in her edition of *Sister Helen* (1939). His relationships with earlier poets are discussed in "The Influence of Keats upon Rossetti," by Hill Shine in *Englische Studien* (1927), and in two articles in the same journal by B. J. Morse, one on Rossetti and Blake (1932) and the other on Rossetti and Dante (1933). K. J. Knickerbocker has a good article on "Sister Helen" in *SP* (1932).

On the poetry of his sister, the only valid general work is *Christina Rossetti: A Study*, by Fredegond Shove (1931). Margaret Sawtell's *Christina Rossetti: Her Life and Religion* (1955) attempts to correlate her poems with her emotional experiences. Her longest poem has been treated in "The Sources of Christina Rossetti's 'Goblin Market,' " *MLR* (1933), by B. I. Evans.

The best general criticism of Coventry Patmore is to be found in *Patmore: A Study in Poetry*, by Frederick Page (1933), and in *The Mind and Art of Coventry Patmore*, by J. C. Reid (1957). Also useful is "Prophet Without Responsibility: A Study of Coventry Patmore," by J. M. Cohen, *Essays in Criticism* (1951).

The only book dealing extensively with Hardy's shorter poems is *The Poetry of Thomas Hardy*, by James G. Southworth (1947). This is supplemented by two books on his epic-drama: *The Dynasts and the Post-War Age in Poetry*, by A. C. Chakravarty (1938), and *Thomas Hardy and the Cosmic Mind*, by J. O. Bailey (1956). Some of the best discussion of his poetry is in books which deal also with his fiction, and which will be mentioned later.

The most amazing phenomenon connected with Victorian poetry is the belated fame of Gerard Manley Hopkins. His poems were not made available until 1918; but their appeal to the modern temperament, combined with their experimental techniques and their highly concentrated expression, evoked a torrent of interpretation during the past thirty years. It is possible to mention here only a few of the chief critical works. The most authoritative one is *Gerard Manley Hopkins: A Study of Poetic Idiosyn-*

cracy in Relation to Poetic Tradition, by W. H. Gardner (1944–49). John Pick's *Gerard Manley Hopkins: Priest and Poet* (1942) examines the relationship between his poetry and his religious principles. An exhaustive study of Hopkin's theory of "inscape" is made in *Gerard Manley Hopkins: A Critical Essay Towards the Understanding of His Poetry*, by W. A. M. Peters (1948). There are two volumes made up of separate articles by various writers: *Gerard Manley Hopkins by the Kenyon Critics* (1945) and *Immortal Diamond*, edited by Norman Weyand (1949).

On the major writers of non-fictional prose there is space here for naming only a few items of critical interpretation that are outstanding for one reason or another. Since C. F. Harrold's *Carlyle and German Thought* (1932) there has been no significant book on any general aspect of Carlyle's work. Knowledge of his intellectual background has been immeasurably aided by *Carlyle's Early Reading to 1834*, by Hill Shine (1953), which lists over 3000 works that he had read by the time he was forty, prefaced with a thorough essay on the development of his mind. His actual methods of work are illustrated in *The Writing of Past and Present*, by Grace J. Calder (1949), dealing with his sources, style, and revisions. Carlisle Moore's article, "*Sartor Resartus* and the Problem of Carlyle's Conversion," *PMLA* (1955), deals convincingly with the autobiographic element in his first important book.

Regarding Newman, critical discussion has centered on the literary technique of his best-known book. *The Art of Newman's Apologia*, by W. E. Houghton (1945), has been followed by articles on the same subject by Martin J. Svaglic, *PMLA* (1951) and *MP* (1952), and by Robert A. Colby, *Journal of Religion* (1953) and *Dublin Review* (1953). On another aspect of his work a thorough book is *The Imperial Intellect: A Study of Newman's Educational Ideal*, by A. Dwight Culler (1955).

There are some indications of a tendency to credit John Ruskin with a modicum of value to contemporary readers, particularly in his opinions about art. *The Victorian Morality of Art: An Analysis of Ruskin's Aesthetic*, by Henry Ladd (1932), is a useful survey of his ideas. Francis G. Townsend's *Ruskin and the Landscape Feeling* (1951) traces the development of his theories during the crucial years 1843–56. "Ruskin's Views on Non-representational Art" are examined by Charles Dougherty in the *College Art Journal* (1955).

On Matthew Arnold's prose the most stimulating book is E. K. Brown's *Matthew Arnold: A Study in Conflict* (1948), which in seven short chapters provides a wide range of insights into the workings of his mind. One of his most notorious literary doctrines has been studied by J. S. Eels, Jr., in *The Touchstones of Matthew Arnold* (1955).

The new scholarly respectability of the novel during the past quarter century is demonstrated by the increased output of critical work on the subject, both in books and in periodical articles. One notices, however, that the specialized studies are apt to concentrate repeatedly on certain novels—*Bleak House, Great Expectations, Wuthering Heights, Adam Bede, Middlemarch, Jude the Obscure*—while scores of other interesting examples remain unexplored. The files of *Nineteenth-Century Fiction* naturally contain the greatest accumulation of articles in this field, and also there are two periodicals confined to minute investigation of particular novelists—the *Dickensian* and the *Transactions of the Brontë Society*.

The significant discussions of Dickens during the past twenty years are conveniently summarized by Fred W. Boege in "Recent Criticism of Dickens," *Nineteenth-Century Fiction* (1953). In the work of so prolific an author it is possible to select evidence in support of almost any ideology. Thus T. A. Jackson's book, *Charles Dickens: The Progress of a Radical* (1937), undertook a Marxist interpretation of Dickens's social outlook, and this has been repeated in Jack Lindsay's *Charles Dickens* (1950). To offset these doctrinaire critiques, George Orwell's essay on Dickens in *Inside the Whale* (1940)[3] insists that Dickens had very little perception of social forces, and on the whole tended to be reactionary. A more dependable point of view is taken in *The Dickens World*, by Humphry House (1941), which emphasizes the creativeness and variety of his work and its truth to actual conditions rather than to ideologies. The strongest influence upon the modern attitude toward Dickens, however, has been Edmund Wilson's essay, "Dickens: The Two Scrooges" in *The Wound and the Bow* (1941), from which descend numerous psychological studies both of the author and of his fictional characters. Equally important

[3] Reprinted in *Dickens, Dali, and Others* (1946).

are many recent articles dealing with the structure and style of his novels. Finally, high commendation is due to *Dickens and His Readers*, by George H. Ford (1955), which combines a history of his reputation with a good deal of acute criticism of his novels and of the whole development of Victorian fiction.

On Thackeray the first of the modern studies, *Thackeray: A Critical Portrait*, by John W. Dodds (1941), is still perhaps the best balanced survey of his work. In contrast, a prejudiced though often stimulating book is *Thackeray: A Reconsideration*, by J. Y. T. Greig (1951), which denies him the stature of a major novelist. Lambert Ennis's *Thackeray: The Sentimental Cynic* (1952) tries to achieve a psychological analysis that recognizes both his defects and his merits. *The Buried Life*, by Gordon N. Ray (1952), is chiefly concerned with identifying the originals of some of his characters. The balance swings to enthusiastic admiration in Geoffrey Tillotson's *Thackeray the Novelist* (1954), which points out particularly his achievement of creating a coherent "world" in his novels. There is a good article by John A. Lester, Jr., on "Thackeray's Narrative Technique" in *PMLA* (1954).

For help in exploring the huge mass of Trollope's fiction, it is advisable for the student to consult *A Guide to Trollope*, by W. A. and J. T. Gerould (1948), which contains, among other information, a good summary of critical opinions. The most thorough recent book on his novels is *Anthony Trollope: A Critical Study*, by A. O. J. Cockshutt (1955).

Most of the earlier criticism of the novels of the Brontë sisters was rendered obsolete in 1933 when the tales they invented in their childhood were published as *Legends of Angria*, edited by Fannie E. Ratchford and W. C. DeVane. By proving that many of the themes and episodes of their mature work descended from these fantasies, the book offered a unique demonstration of how the creative imagination works, and this topic was effectively developed by Miss Ratchford in *The Brontës' Web of Childhood* (1941). Her latest book on the question is *Gondal's Queen: A Novel in Verse* (1955), which contains a fascinating account of how she used Emily Brontë's poems to reconstruct her missing contribution to the juvenile cycle.

The total difference between the creative processes of the

Brontës and those of George Eliot can be seen by comparing these studies with *Quarry for Middlemarch* (1950), in which Anna T. Kitchel has edited a notebook containing details methodically collected by the author for her longest novel. The greater part of Joan Bennett's *George Eliot* (1948) is devoted to perceptive criticism of her novels. The biographical part is not so dependable. In addition to numerous recent articles treating single works of hers, three with more general topics may be mentioned: "Social Analysis in the Novels of George Eliot," *ELH* (1951), by Claude T. Bissell; "The Moment of Disenchantment in George Eliot's Novels," *RES* (1954), by Barbara Hardy; and "Religion in the Novels of George Eliot," *JEGP* (1954), by M. J. Svaglic.

George Meredith's novels, strangely enough, have not attracted so much critical attention, though their lavish use of symbolism and their idiosyncracies of style and structure would seem to render them peculiarly appropriate for the current kind of inquiry. The only recent book on his techniques is Walter F. Wright's *Art and Substance in George Meredith: A Study in Narrative* (1953).

By contrast, there have been a number of good books on Thomas Hardy, and only the outstanding ones can be mentioned here. Richard L. Purdy's *Thomas Hardy: A Bibliographical Study* (1954) is a model work, containing much information about the genesis and publication of the novels. Three valuable general discussions are *Hardy the Novelist*, by Lord David Cecil (1943), *On a Darkling Plain*, by H. C. Webster (1947), and *Thomas Hardy: The Novels and Stories*, by Albert J. Guérard (1949). The relationship of his novels and poems with his personal life is traced in detail in *Thomas Hardy: A Critical Biography*, by Evelyn Hardy (1953).

Within the limits of this chapter it has proved impossible to mention the research (much of it highly commendable) which has been devoted to secondary and minor authors, since even to list such work by title would occupy too much space. The foregoing survey, though confined to the outstanding figures, may serve to indicate the vigor and variety of the investigation that has been going on, and to justify the claim that the Victorian age offers much to interest the contemporary student.

9

American Literature

LESLIE A. FIEDLER

THE LAST THIRTY YEARS HAVE been a time of triumph for American literature. Throughout the world, our classic books have come to seem more and more not merely excellent or interesting but central to the development of contemporary literature everywhere—a challenge to other long accepted traditions and an example for the writer in a mass culture. Such world-wide acceptance has given American critics and commentators greater confidence in their own judgment, assurance that their enthusiasm for Whitman and Melville, for example, is more than provincial pride. Boastful chauvinism and self-deprecation before European art have tended to disappear together, while the deliberate choosing of exile by our young writers has seemed since the close of the twenties an outmoded gesture.

On the other hand, we have come to realize that most of our people do not read, in some cases do not even know of, the writers who represent them and their country. More than half of all Americans, despite a rising literacy rate, read no books at all—and of the remainder the larger part surely devotes most of its time to ephemeral entertainments. Moreover, there has been a profound revision in the current evaluation of our authors. The reputation of those bearded and genteel patriarchs from New England who still preside over our elementary school classrooms, has steadily gone down. Longfellow and even Lowell seem these days not merely limited but irrelevant to our concerns. During 1955, the centenary of *Leaves of Grass* was celebrated everywhere with speeches, articles, and symposia, but the hundreth anniversary of *Hiawatha* was scarcely noticed. Meanwhile, the estimate of Melville continues to soar fantastically, threatening to make of him *the* typical American writer or even the great epic poet of the nineteenth century. Certainly, the prevailing view has come to be that our literature is marked by two great periods: a first renaissance in the mid-nineteenth-century, involving Melville and Whitman, Hawthorne and Emerson, and a second flowering which begins about 1912 and moves from Eliot and Pound to Faulkner, Hemingway, and so forth. Most writers outside of these two periods, however extravagantly admired once, tend now to seem to us of minor consequence.

This shift in evaluation has not occurred without creating a good deal of confusion. On the popular level, there persists still, in some quarters at least, a longing for the kind of middle-brow poetry created by Longfellow and for a new poetry clearly derived from that strain. To make matters worse, the revolution in taste which de-throned the Brahmins and elevated Twain, Whitman, and Melville, was led in the earliest stages by people outside of the universities, literary journalists like Van Wyck Brooks, Lewis Mumford, H. L. Mencken, and Randolph Bourne, who thought of the "professors" (was not Longfellow himself a professor?) as the enemies of what was most vital in contemporary art and a re-examined past. It is salutory for academics to remember that for thirty years they have been consolidating reputations made first of all in their despite.

A good deal of the excitement which accompanied the pre-World War I redefinition of American literature had begun to fade as the universities took over the movement begun outside of them and made of American literature another subject in the standard curriculum. The appearance of the *Cambridge History of American Literature* between 1917 and 1921, the founding of the American Literature Group in the Modern Language Association in 1921, and the initiation of the quarterly *American Literature* in 1928 as an official organ for scholarly work on our literature mark important stages in the process. An earlier resistance on the part of English departments to courses on American authors had begun to give way, as it became apparent that the growth of our university population and the decline of classical studies made it more and more necessary to *teach* the kind of book one once assumed would be read for pleasure outside of the classroom. It is in part the spread of mass culture and the consequent decline in the average reading ability of those who enter college which have helped make way for a proliferation of courses in recent and modern literature by which the study of American literature has profited.

As late as fifteen years ago, the graduate student who devoted himself primarily to American literature instead of, say, Renaissance drama or Medieval epic was looked on as not quite "serious." Indeed, in an attempt to placate the germanically oriented scholars, to whom the only totally satisfactory approach was historical and philological, some teachers of American literature began to introduce into their own classroom procedures the "scientific" rigor of their colleagues, putting "research" in place of the "impressionism" of their non-academic predecessors.

Since 1928, however, the battle has been really won; and it becomes clear now that the continuing resistance of the thirties and the forties was only a desperate rear-guard action. For better or for worse, the criticism of American literature has been captured by the university departments of English; and conversely, those departments seem on the verge of being captured by the study of American literature. There are in some colleges separate departments for that exclusive study and almost everywhere a growth in the number of people within each English department whose primary interest is American. Articles increase bewilderingly; the number of these on Whitman and Melville and James approaches the appalling level of studies of Shakespeare. Despite the paucity of truly great American works and the scarcely more than one hundred and fifty years during which we have had anything like a real literature, course offerings in the field multiply by fission: examinations of third-rate local color fictionists, studies of political documents from the earliest period and later of no literary value, and so forth. There has been in recent years an attempt to make more substantial offerings possible by defining an area called variously "American Studies" and "American Civilization," which sets our books not in the context of world literature but rather at the center of ideas, ideals, and cultural impulses otherwise considered the subject matter of classes in American philosophy, history, religion and political science. Since the spring of 1949, there has been a magazine, *The American Quarterly*, devoted to publishing articles in this field.

Since World War II, new strength has been added to the mass

academic migration into American literature by the demand from abroad (sustained and subsidized by Fulbright Awards, State Department grants, and so forth) for American professors prepared to teach courses in our literature in fòreign universities. It must finally be said that many of our best talents, young men with the highest of literary and scholarly ambitions are being attracted to teaching and writing about American books—and that the number of studies in the area continues therefore to increase bewilderingly. The implications of such a mushrooming of interest in a fairly limited subject has produced, as one would expect, results of widely varying value. Beginning with the establishment of texts for consequential writers and the recovery of their fugitive and forgotten pieces, the hunt moves on to less and less interesting authors and does not stop at thoroughly worthless ones. Beginning with exegesis and comment on complex and rewarding texts, the process moves on to more and more minute and futile analyses. Indeed, one of the chief problems in surveying recent critical and scholarly work on our classic literature is the distinguishing of significant contributions in the welter of textbooks, demi-textbooks and academic exercises: the mechanical sort of publication aimed at getting and holding jobs or insuring promotion.

I

It is no longer possible, as it once was (or as it was once possible to believe), to solve the problem by stepping outside the universities; for almost all the critics concerned with American literature, whether they have come up along conventional Ph.D. channels or not, have moved into the universities. Indeed, the period of the triumph of studies in this field has coincided almost exactly with a major movement of professional writers from free lance careers to academic ones. To understand, therefore, the shifting of attitudes and critical estimates of our literature, one must understand the rise and fall of various aesthetic and moral points of view inside the literature departments of our colleges.

At the beginning of the modern period of studies in American literature stands an unfinished monument to an approach, very limited, very natively American and not yet exhausted, V. L. Parrington's *Main Currents in American Thought*. The first two volumes, covering the years 1620–1860, appeared in 1927; the third volume, dealing with our writing up through 1920, was published only posthumously, patched together out of notes and fragments by one of Parrington's colleagues at the University of Washington. It seems improbable at first glance that a critical survey of American literature should devote one-third of its total bulk to an analysis of texts written before 1800. The clue is contained in the title, however, in the phrase "American Thought" where one might have looked for "American Letters" or "American Literature." Parrington was, indeed, resolved not to permit his view of our writing to be influenced by what he called disdainfully "an exaggerated regard for aesthetic values," which he equated with the "genteel tradition" and to which he opposed "a world of masculine intellects and material struggles." Parringtons' teaching at the University of Washington has certain symbolic weight; he represents, as it were, the voice of the West and of the state university, self-consciously masculine, raised against the too-long persuasive tones of gentility sent forth by the private colleges of the East. It is a pity Parrington did not love literature (which he had an unfortunate way of condescending to as "belles-lettres") except as it subserved the development of the liberal ideal. He is a lively, polemical writer with a courageous synthesizing mind and a style which only occasionally betrays him into hortatory rhetoric; but he goes to pieces before "illiberal" figures like Poe and Henry James, aristocrats of the spirit who seemed to him "outside of the main current of American thought" and therefore the sources of problems "which may be left with the psychologist and belletrist."

Nevertheless, *Main Currents* is an impressive book in scope and ambition, an unparalleled attempt to see through a single mind and state in a single continuous essay the essential shape of our literature. There is something attractive in the sheer nerve of Parrington's undertaking, especially when one sets it beside more recent attempts to make composite or collective literary histories. His disciples carry on to this day, though they are more likely to be frankly historians rather than quasi-critics or literary scholars, and so their work falls outside the range of this essay. Nevertheless, the essential mythic drama Parrington imagined: the struggle to adapt ideas derived from the Enlightenment and Puritanism to an expanding west and the triumph of capitalism; the battle between realism and liberalism on the one hand and genteel "idealism" on the other; the emphasis on such essentially American figures as Whitman and Twain—all these continue to haunt classroom lectures and textbooks, to confuse sociology and criticism. Indeed, the seed of the concept of "American Civilization" as a mode of study preferable to "pure literary" scholarship is essentially Parrington's. Some later writers sympathetic to his view have managed to mitigate his blatant use of works of art as mere documents and his tendency to simplify the conflicts of our moral and intellectual lives into melodrama. In the process, however, they have lost what is most appealing in Parrington—his naïveté. It was the quality that he himself appreciated in Whitman, that hero of his legend of American thought; and when one feels kindliest toward Parrington, he can almost say of him what Parrington said of Whitman: " a great figure. . . yet perhaps only a great child. . . ."

Parrington's sociological bias made him attractive to certain Marxist critics both in and out of the universities; and one strain derived from him is developed in such works as V. F. Calverton's *The Liberation of American Literature* (1932), Granville Hick's *The Great Tradition* (1933), and Bernard Smith's *Forces in American Criticism* (1939); though, indeed, these authors are more likely to cite Marx himself than their American prototype. All such studies have tended to rigidify further Parrington's none too subtle sense of the interplay between social forces and ideas into Marxian or Stalinist orthodoxy, and none seems finally a distinguished work or even an illuminating one.

Perhaps the most eminent of writers to follow up the lead of Parrington, and certainly the most ambitious among them, is Van Wyck Brooks. Actually, Brooks's earliest and most effective work precedes *Main Currents* and predates the period this essay treats. His vision of the American artist in conflict with his genteel society, set forth polemically in *The Ordeal of Mark Twain* (1920), belongs to a period in which the academy was treated as necessarily the enemy of art. Between 1936 and 1952, however, Brooks completed a Parringtonian series of books (*The World of Washington Irving, The Flowering of New England, The Times of Melville and Whitman, New England: Indian Summer, The Confident Years: 1885–1915*) finally called by an over-all title derived from Whitman, *Makers and Finders: A History of the Writer in America, 1800–1915.* More "belletristic" than Parrington, as his beginning with the nineteenth century indicates, Brooks nonetheless subscribes to the notion that the essential grandeur of our literature resides in its embodying the liberal ideal.

In immensity of range and sheer bulk, his five-volume project yields not even to *Main Currents;* but though much admired in some quarters for its richness of texture and grace of style, it seems finally a nostalgic and sentimental evocation of our past, more decorative than insightful, more commemorative than analytic. Brooks has yielded, on the one hand, to a temptation to make the "interesting" his chief category of value, so that trivial writers are often treated more fully and lovingly than better ones. On the other hand, he has allowed his own conviction that contemporary literature is "negative" and consequently second-rate to impose a pattern on his account of our literary history, which becomes finally an unconvincing portrayal of the fall from Jeffersonian virtue to modern despair. There is an unintended pathos in the development of Brooks which gives to his work an exemplary value. It is, indeed, the prime instance of a protest against the academic and genteel becoming, amid the complexities of American life, itself academic (though Brooks has remained outside the university) and genteel.

The victory of Parrington and his point of view was by no means immediate in official university circles. Though he contributed an essay on "The Development of Realism" to a symposium called *The Reinterpretation of American Literature,* issued in 1928 as the first official publication of the American Literature Group of the Modern Language Association, he does not at all represent the organizing view of that volume. This arises rather out of the approach of its editor, Norman Foerster, who already identified himself with the "New Humanist" movement, a basically conservative position which considered itself descended from Lowell and Charles Eliot Norton via Paul Elmer More, Irving Babbitt, and such other favorite academic butts of the new Americanists as Professor G. E. Woodberry. There seems something disconcerting at first in the notion of an alliance between the "Jeffersonians" and the followers of Babbitt and More; but whatever differences, aesthetic and political, separated Foerster and

Parrington, their historical and ideological frameworks for understanding American Literature had much in common. The four
factors which, according to Foerster, shape our letters are the
Puritan tradition, the frontier spirit, romanticism, and realism—
all of which fit easily enough into the scheme of *Main Currents*.
Noticeably absent from the approach of both are such concepts as
myth and symbol, which would have undercut the moralistic
attitudes each in his own way held.

The methods of Freudian analytic psychology had already provided clues for a way into our literature which might bypass the
historical-moral approach of the New Humanists and Parrington-
ians; but such a tack had, as we have seen, been discredited in
advance by Parrington to whom the psychologist seemed no more
admirable than the belletrist. The few pioneers of psychoanalytic
criticism remained outside the universities and compounded the
original academic mistrust of their methods by affecting a contempt for bibliographical apparatus and an offhand, unbuttoned
style. Unfortunately, the chief mouthpiece for a psychoanalytic
approach in the early thirties was Ludwig Lewisohn, whose insights were often lost in rhetoric and who seemed sometimes more
eager to save the world than to understand literature. His *Expression in America* (1932) is somewhat misleadingly titled; the French
version which is called *Psychologie de la littérature americaine*
more properly reminds the reader of Freud rather than Croce.
Lewisohn deserves a certain amount of credit for having raised
openly such hitherto hushed-up pertinent questions as Whitman's
homosexuality, without understanding of which it is difficult to
judge his work; but Lewisohn seldom pursues a perception far or
deep, since he is pledged to treating literature as "scripture," the
projection of "a vision which was to . . . save the world."

D. H. Lawrence was also largely psychological in approach,
though his psychology was rather improvised and at odds in some
respects with orthodox Freudianism; and Lawrence, too, was a
salvationist, less disciplined, more deliberately and joyously dissociated, more maddeningly prophetic than Lewisohn himself.
But Lawrence was also an artist of first rank, capable of utterly
dazzling revelations, which make of his *Studies in Classic American
Literature* (begun in 1915 and published in 1922) one of the most
illuminating books on our literature. He was able as a foreigner to

approach our classic works with a freshness of vision and a seriousness uncontaminated by piety or parochial pride. His criticism is
uneven in the extreme, ranging from the irrelevancies of his essay
on Melville to the uncanny acuteness of his piece on Cooper, but
it does not lack unity. He has a clear perception of the myth of
America and of American Man which underlies the apparent
differences of our writers from Franklin through Cooper and Poe
to Hawthorne and Dana and Whitman. As the conviction has
grown among our more recent critics and scholars that the center
of a literature is to be sought in its obsessive and recurring themes
with their symbolic overtones, this long-neglected book by a
Englishman, which antedated Parrington but is in every sense
more contemporary, has come to seem essential to an understanding of our culture and our great books.

Rather improbably, Lawrence was celebrated in the first essay
in the *Reinterpretation of American Literature* by F. L. Pattee,
who calls for a new American literary history "as detached from
classroom thinking as D. H. Lawrence's amazing volume." But
certainly the New Humanists did not, in their period of the dom-
ination of university courses, succeed in fostering a history even
remotely comparable to the example proffered them by Pattee.
For a long time, students of Foerster and of his follower, Harry
Hayden Clark played a leading role in the training of teachers of
American literature and in the long campaign to gain recognition
for them in departments of English; but there is no first-rate large
critical or literary historical work produced under their aegis. As
late as 1953, they were issuing under the editorship of Professor
Clark another co-operative volume *Transitions in American
Literature;* and the same Professor Clark had presided since its
beginning over the American Writers Series, which, though it
published Longfellow four years before Melville, has by now
provided excellent classroom selections, complete with bibliographies and biographical notes, of all our major writers.

When a long enough period of biographical study and the
editing of texts had gone by to justify for the academic community
the appearance of a new full-length treatment of American letters,
the influence of the New Humanists had waned; and the dream
of a single, unified survey of the field had been surrendered to the
notion of a work by many hands, given some superficial semblance

of unity by editorial revision. This work is the *Literary History of the United States* (1948), of which one of the most persistent criticisms has been what its detractors have described as the editorial counterfeiting of transitions and agreements where none really exists. The names of none of Foerster's chief followers appeared on the editorial panel which presided over the *Literary History* and which was head by Robert E. Spiller, Willard Thorp, Thomas H. Johnson, and Henry Seidel Canby. The spirit which unites contributors and editors, journalists, historians, professors, and anti-academic survivors of the twenties is largely extra-literary: the spirit of liberalism, no longer asserted in the name of Western vigor as in Parrington, but redefined to suit a world bounded on one side by the Ivy League colleges and on the other by such a middlebrow magazine of enlightened politics and limited literary taste as the *Saturday Review of Literature*.

The words *humanitarian*, *bouyancy*, *virile*, and *optimistic* recur in the preface and declaration of aims of the *Literary History;* and though the Parringtonian contempt for the belletrist has been tempered, there is a tendency to define literary movements in terms of *isolationism* and *internationalism*, the political metaphors uppermost in men's minds at the time the book was compiled. The study as a whole sets itself squarely against the notion variously defined by Brooks and Lawrence of an "ordeal" of the American writer, or, indeed, of any conception of a conflict between the writer and his culture. It is the handbook of an age of enlightened and civilized conformity. Its most disturbing distortions come in its treatment of contemporary literature; but even in the period with which we are immediately concerned (treated chiefly in Volume II) there is some tendency to follow recent trends by considering a mythopoeic writer like J. F. Cooper as primarily a "social critic" or even by emphasizing the "adjusted" and democratic aspects of a melancholic like Hawthorne.

The *Literary History* is finally thick and inclusive, moderate and dependable in terms of fact and reference, and it will doubtless outlast its generation as a useful guide for beginning students. It is really impressive, however, only occasionally in single essays; there is really no comprehensive view on a level higher than tautology or platitude; and a sort of compulsory cheerfulness keeps breaking in everywhere, hopelessly disguising the tragic meaning of our classic books. Yet one of the contributors to the *Literary History*, F. O. Matthiessen, had elsewhere set himself the task of defining precisely that tragic significance of our greatest writers. In *The American Renaissance* (1941), Matthiessen had not only attempted to identify a central moment of our literature in terms of the work of Thoreau, Emerson, Hawthorne, Melville, and Whitman; but he had tried further, in dealing with these five, to shift the traditional emphasis, displacing it from the "optimistic" Emerson to the dark Hawthorne—following, in this regard, the lead of T. S. Eliot. His work does not attempt to deal with the whole of our literature even in the nineteenth century except in an exemplary way, that is to say, by dealing deeply with its heart; and in this sense his study represents the nearest thing we have to a large scale counter-statement to *Main Currents*. Referring to Parrington's distrust of the aesthetic, Matthiessen writes. "My concern has been the opposite . . . to evaluate . . . in accordance with the enduring requirements of great art." Yet Matthiessen's mind is double. If, on the one hand, he has learned from T. S. Eliot to seek for meaning in symbol and form rather than in explicit statement—and to search, in a way that approaches the religious, for the tragic vision at the greatest moments of art; on the other, he is pledged to look everywhere for "the myth of the common man," to consider the literature of the nineteenth century as "literature for our democracy." He sets down for us the challenge he hears in his inner ear as he writes, the words of Louis Sullivan: "Are you using the gifts you possess for or against the people?"

It is at a point where his own democratic and Marxian commitments verge on sentimentality that Matthiessen is attracted to the sociologizing liberalism of the *Literary History* despite his resolve to treat works of art according to aesthetic criteria. But he shows, in a way that scarcely any of the other contributors do, the impact of twenty years of the New Criticism: that long attempt to isolate essential artistic values by close attention to the text and to reassess all literature in terms of a tradition which makes metaphysical poetry and French *symboliste* art the touchstones of merit. The primary dedication of the chief New Critics to the analysis of poetry, combined with their distrust of both Poe and Whitman, and their reluctance to leave the British seventeenth century except for the French nineteenth, has meant that some of the liveliest critical minds of our time have dealt only peripherally, when at all, with American literature. Obiter dicta by Eliot on Hawthorne and Whitman and Poe, brief treatments by R. P. Blackmur of Melville and Whitman, and an essay or two by Allen Tate on Poe represent typically the small proportion of their attention allotted by such critics to our own writers. Henry James, it is true, is a notable exception; indeed, for some New Critics, he becomes the official counterweight to Walt Whitman, an American witness against the prevailing American confusion of art with raw experience. In general, however, major books by New Critics on American authors have a tendency to remain unfulfilled promises like Tate's projected full-scale study of Poe or Blackmur's proposed book on Henry Adams. The nearest approach to an inclusive volume on American writing by such a critic is Yvor Winter's *In Defense of Reason* (1947), which includes *Maule's Curse*, a discussion of our nineteenth-century literature, originally published in 1938. Winters is placed at a disadvantage in confronting a literature primarily Romantic, since he opposes, on moral and religious as well as aesthetic grounds, Romanticism itself. Moreover, *Maule's Curse* is a polemical book, written backward, as it were, to make clear the roots of the "obscurantism" which Winters had earlier persuaded himself was everywhere ruinously present in recent American poetry. The insights available to hostility are doggedly and devastatingly presented by Winters and his attack in Poe represents the case against that poet in classic form. Occasionally he finds a writer (the poet Jones Very, for instance) or a work (*The Scarlet Letter*) congenial to his own morality and responds with something like sympathy; but on the whole his book is too rigidly dedicated to making its case to do justice to the complexity of our classic works.

One turns with some relief from the hard polemical stance of Winter's essay to the softer focus of Matthiessen's approach: the constant tendency to blur implicit in his often approximate prose and in the conflict of views that underlies it. It is difficult to recognize in any single passage of Matthiessen's book a definitive treatment of a writer or a work; yet the whole study gives us the sense of a passionate involvement with American letters and life and of a point of view complex enough to achieve those critical insights available to inclusiveness and reasonableness. The success of *The American Renaissance* has been immense; it has given a name and shape to new courses in American literature, and has had an impact outside of our own country unequalled by any other single study, except, perhaps, D. H. Lawrence's. Especially where in recent years a drift toward Marxism and an interest in our literature have emerged together, the *American Renaissance* has encouraged other studies, attempts to assimilate our major works to the needs of contemporary literature in other countries. A particularly notable example is the *La letteratura americani e altri saggi* (1953) of Cesare Pavese, the young Italian novelist, poet, and critic, whose insights into American literature were confirmed by Matthiessen's and whose influence continues to be felt in Italy to the present moment.

Perhaps, the New Criticism cannot come to terms with our literature without abandoning its own orthodoxy; and therefore must typically approach it in such hybrid forms as Matthiessen's socially oriented semi-formalism. Among the younger critics in this country, those primarily interested in American literature tend to approach it outside of the Eliotic-textual-traditional school. The English-trained Marius Bewley, however, has recently published a group of essays rather loosely connected in theme and commonly entitled *The Complex Fate* (1952). One hundred and fifty pages of his book are made up of essays dealing with Henry James, particularly as James represents the developments of themes and conventions in Hawthrone; this central core is eked out by fewer than one hundred pages of miscellaneous studies of other authors. F. R. Leavis of Downing College, Cambridge, who was Bewley's teacher and who leads one English wing of the New Criticism, compounded of Eliotic anti-Romanticism and British Puritanism, contributes an introduction and two short rejoinders to certain emphases of Mr. Bewley.

Leavis's notes help define further *the* tradition in the American novel in the spirit in which Leavis himself had already defined such a tradition in British fiction and Martin Turnell had defined one for the French. At any rate, Bewley, seconded by Leavis, proposes as candidates for his version of the American tradition, a "mature" strain whose theme is the "nature of the American writer's separateness, and . . . his connection with European culture": Cooper, Hawthorne, Melville, and James. He sets these

writers against the "insidious magnification of the frontier colloquial tradition," with which Mr. Leavis specifically connects
Whitman, Dreiser, Scott Fitzgerald, and Hemingway, but from
which he exempts Mark Twain, preferring to kidnap him for the
Hawthorne-James camp. It is all quite solemn and improbable,
though it leads by the way into certain illuminations of James and
Hawthorne, besides indicating another possible unified view of our
literature which escapes the Humanist-Parringtonian dilemma.

In quite recent years, there have been other synthesizing
attempts by younger critics, influenced to a degree by new critical
methods though unwilling to accept the orthodox New Critics'
exclusive willingness to deal with single works of art as discrete
objects. R. W. B. Lewis, whose shorter work typically appeared
in such journals as *Kenyon Review* and *Hudson Review*, quarterlies whose tone is set by writers like Ransom, Blackmur, and Allen
Tate, attempted in *The American Adam: Innocence, Tragedy,
and Tradition in the Nineteenth Century* (1955) to resurvey the
literature and history of our nineteenth century in terms of an
original vision of innocence and its qualification in the direction
of tragedy. The quotation from Lawrence which serves as one of
the book's epigraphs and begins "This is the true myth of
America . . ." indicates how radically *Studies in Classic American
Literature* has influenced at least one recent commentator on our
culture.

Richard Chase and Leslie Fiedler each reflects in his own way a
similar preoccupation with myth: a sense that the deepest meanings, meanings which extend beyond the single work to a whole
body of books, are to be sought in the archetypal symbols to which
succeeding writers compulsively turn. Both Chase and Fiedler have
begun in the literary quarterlies rather than the official scholarly
journals, both of them appearing often in the *Partisan Review*, a
more truculent and political journal than the *Hudson* or *Kenyon
Review* and one still involved in the "ordealist" tradition, which
sees the artist as enemy and victim of the society for which he
speaks. Indeed, the rise of such critics is one symptom of the
academization of formerly non-academic journals, and of the complementary acceptance of articles written in them as academic
credentials. Neither Chase nor Fiedler has yet written a large survey of our literature, but both have laid the foundations for it:

the former by his political-mythic reading of Melville (marked often by more energy than tact), the latter by an attempt to define a central American *mythos* of love in which the lover is an outcast or orphan and the beloved a dark-skinned primitive male.

The widely shared concern with symbol and symbolism has led naturally enough to an effort to define the essence of American letters in terms of symbolic method itself rather than in any particular symbol. Charles Feidelson's *Symbolism and American Literature* (1953), which starts out to redress what Feidelson feels to be Matthiessen's excessive sociological and political emphasis, ends by demonstrating, through examinations of Hawthorne, Whitman, Melville, and Poe, that symbolism is, indeed, the very center of our art. Though there is in Feidelson's work a certain doctrinaire narrowness, a tendency to make of the term symbolism an all-sufficient honorific and the single criterion of poetic excellence, his book provides a long overdue counterbalance to the never-satisfactory view of our literary history as a slow struggle upward from darkness toward realism. Certainly in Feidelson as in many other recent attempts to see our literature whole, there is everywhere apparent a concern with the mythic and the tragic which brings them oddly enough back through Parrington to D. H. Lawrence, the improbable ancestor of an approach to our literature which seems most fruitful at this moment.

II

Despite differences in method, approach, and underlying values, most scholarly and critical commentators on American literature have come to a somewhat unexpected agreement on the key figures of our tradition. Certain reputations have died hard, Longfellow, for instance, and Lowell; and regionalists of one brand or another have continued to tout their special favorites, James Whitcomb Riley or William Gilmore Simms, for example. There have been, moreover, various attempts in recent years to redeem certain authors from obscurity: to reinstitute Charles Brockden Brown as a leading novelist or to rescue from neglect poets like Jones Very or the hitherto scarcely noticed seventeenth-century figure, Edward Taylor. None of these, however, has come to seem a major writer or seriously to challenge the pre-eminence of the eight authors recently selected for discussion in a review of research and criticism published by the Modern Language Association under the editorship of Floyd Stovall as *Eight American Authors* (1956).[1] The eight authors included were Poe, Emerson, Hawthorne, Thoreau, Melville, Whitman, Mark Twain, and Henry James. William Dean Howells and Emily Dickinson were also considered but finally excluded from the list; and with this decision one is driven to concur, with some regret in the case of Dickinson and with some relief in that of Howells. Emily Dickinson has continued throughout recent years to move poets and scholars alike and our period has seen the establishment of a critical text of her poems (edited by T. H. Johnson, 1955) as a kind of monument to her acceptance as one of our leading poets. Howells, on the other hand, though he remains still a considerable figure, seems not so much relevant to our present concerns as representative of past ones.

The status of the chosen eight writers is, then, reasonably secure; but they have been regarded with varying degrees of affection and suspicion by different segments of the intellectual community, thus providing, in an exemplary way, a history of taste in the recent period. We have had occasion to notice some of these differences in emphasis in our comments on synthesizing studies from Parrington to Matthiessen. It is worth pausing a little, in addition, over recent specific studies of these authors, and especially interesting to note in what areas nothing of real consequence has been produced.

On Edgar Allan Poe the present period has brought forth no full-length critical work. In this, to be sure, it has merely continued a long, unhappy tradition; there is no full scale critical study of Poe which seems now of first rank. A. H. Quinn's study of his life is called *Edgar Allan Poe: A Critical Biography* (1941); but, whatever its value as a repository of fact, it provides nothing currently recognized as critical perception. Poe occupies a peculiar place in the self-consciousness of modern poets, many of whom think of themselves as indebted to the French Symbolists, who

[1] The reader is referred to the Stovall volume for complete bibliographies of the writers concerned. This essay attempts only a summary of the main trends in critical response to our major authors over the last thirty years.

in turn recognized deep obligations to Poe. Yet Poe has seemed to many of these Symbolist-oriented poets himself vulgar, obvious, and mechanical. T. S. Eliot attempts to come to terms with this vexing dilemma in his essay *From Poe to Valery* (1948); and Allen Tate, who has long promised a book on Poe, has wrestled with it even harder in two pieces reprinted in *The Forlorn Demon* (1951), both of which reflect the influence of certain comments of D. H. Lawrence. The case against Poe is stated most unqualifiedly in Yvor Winter's *Maule's Curse*, to which we have already referred; and a rather gallant defense is attempted by William Carlos Williams in his polemical book on our culture, *In the American Grain* (1925). A further indignity of Poe's position is his capacity for stirring up extra-literary responses. In Europe he has remained what he seemed to Baudelaire, the very symbol of the artist's inability to survive in bourgeois society in general and in America in particular; while for our critics, to minds as diverse as Matthiessen's and Parrington's, he has seemed in his "dandyism" and aristocratic pretensions something distressingly outside the mainstream of American life. On the other hand, he has been especially attractive to the psychologically-oriented as a pathological case; beginning with Ludwig Lewisohn (who attempted to join him with Hawthorne and Melville in the general category of "Troubled Romancers") commentators have analyzed with endless satisfaction his mother-centeredness, his quasi-impotence, his fantasies of death, castration, and incest. A full scale psychoanalytic approach to his life and work (only obliquely useful for critical understanding) is Marie Bonaparte's *Edgar Poe, Étude psychanalytique* (1933).

Emerson in recent years has had to survive almost as drastic a series of attacks as Poe, though without stirring up quite the bafflement induced by Poe's odd relationship to modern poetry. D. H. Lawrence did not even think of including him among his handful of American classics, whereas Matthiessen obviously found Thoreau (once considered only a somewhat embarrassing follower of Emerson) more sympathetic, and Yvor Winters has produced the expected virulent rejection of him and his point of view. In a strange way, Melville, the age's great favorite, seemed to anticipate the contemporary attitude toward Emerson in his bitter caricature of the latter as Mark Winsome in *The Con-*

fidence Man; Melville's view of the man's essential iciness under his pretended enthusiasm, and of the connections between his Cosmic Optimism and the pragmatic philosophy of the American business man continue to haunt us.

Emerson has not lacked defenders, to be sure, but they have represented in most cases academic opinion at the point where it is most distant from the values of the practicing writer. Two leading defenses of him occur, for instance, in a recent handbook for classroom use and in Robert E. Spiller's article in the *Literary History of the United States*. Emerson is also, of course, attractive to Van Wyck Brook, faithful still to Parringtonian literary liberalism and therefore pledged to celebrating one who seems to him to speak for a pristine American optimism now presumably abandoned by the young. As we have seen, however, there is a growing tendency to look for the clue to American character and literary excellence in the problematical and the tragic, areas in which Emerson is likely to strike a younger critic as inadequate. Oddest of all, have been certain recent essays attempting to redeem Emerson for the fashion by demonstrating that he was not optimistic, after all. In general, current opinion finds him a writer of considerable though not often sympathetic interest, who erected a notable monument to an insufficient view of life. Occasionally, he is portrayed (by F. R. Leavis, for example) as the founding father of a line of writers who, via Whitman, lead into a populist tradition variously represented by Dreiser or Sandburg. There is a pedestrian though careful and thorough biography by Ralph Leslie Rusk, *The Life of Ralph Waldo Emerson* (1949).

Most recent work on Hawthorne, whether avowedly biographical or critical, has centered around a debate over whether Hawthorne was in fact "the solitary brooder upon life." The phrase quoted is by G. E. Woodberry, but the point of view from which it speaks was originally formulated by Henry James in *Hawthorne* (1879), a work which still possesses considerable weight as the direct response of one great American writer to another who was his cultural father. It is, of course, Hawthorne himself, who, for his own literary and psychological ends, found it necessary to invent the legend, contrive the mask, or confess the fact (all of these are surely blended in the act) of being alienated from his society and from life. Many sensitive critics and literary historians up to the present moment have continued to use the notion of isolation as a key to Hawthorne's work; and in Newton Arvin's *Hawthorne* (1929), there is an attempt to refine and analyze that concept in terms of contemporary psychology.

The liberal academic mind, however, has found the concept of Hawthorne's unhappiness and alienation incompatible with its own view of the artist in our society; and there have been several studies aimed at showing that Hawthorne really *was*, after all, an involved and participating "critic of society" (it is the highest accolade for the writer in certain socially oriented quarters—a reassurance that his work is really useful rather than merely pathological protest or lonely play) Randall Stewart in *Nathaniel Hawthorne: A Biography* (1948), a study which is the culmination of the whole "normalcy" counter-attack, assures us that Hawthorne was a believer in "the Christian doctrine of charity" as well as "the social doctrine of the democratic way." One amateur scholar, eager to clear away the last obstacle to thinking of Hawthorne as perfectly "normal", explains his twelve years of apparent self-exile in Salem as being only a cover-up for his activities as a government secret agent! A more complex approach aimed at displaying Hawthorne as *both* participant in society and withdrawn recluse, as essentially double in nature, is Mark Van Doren's *Hawthorne* (1949).

Hawthorne, with his explicit dedication to allegory and symbol, has seemed especially viable for symbolic analysis. Recent approaches along this line include W. B. Stein's *Hawthorne's Faust: A Study of the Devil Archetype* (1953), a rather rigid over-application of a good initial insight, as well as R. H. Fogle's *Hawthorne's Fiction: The Light and the Dark* (1953), and H. H. Waggoner's *Hawthorne, A Critical Study* (1955). In the light of such approaches, the reputation of the *Scarlet Letter* has remained firm (though, following the lead of D. H. Lawrence, some critics have suggested that the book has a concealed bias quite different from its avowed morality), but the evaluation of *The House of Seven Gables* has tended to decline while interest has grown in *The Marble Faun*. Among Hawthorne's short stories such school anthology favorites as "The Great Stone Face" and even "The Minister's Black Veil" have come to seem less subtle and rewarding than "Young Goodman Brown" and "My Kinsman, Major

Molineux," the latter of which has provided special opportunities for Freudian analysis. In the developing over-all view of our literature, Hawthorne has been coupled with Melville as defining a tragic and mythic center for our achievement in the novel; and there has consequently been little dissent from his high ranking and no flagging in analytical and critical studies of him and his work.

Thoreau, on the other hand, though accepted everywhere and more highly rated as the years go by, has not really attracted the critical mind of our time. Quite oppositely from the case of Hawthorne, the discussion of his life and personality (was he humorless? a prig? desexed? what were his relations with Emerson's wife?) has led away from not toward the center of his work as an artist. Recent biographies of some utility are H. S. Canby's *Thoreau* (1939) and J. W. Krutch's *Thoreau* (1948), neither of which enable us to penetrate very deeply into Thoreau's writing. Not only the biographical hurdle stands between us and real analysis and evaluation of Thoreau, but his social theories and his role as a naturalist become formidable obstacles, too. There is something in *Walden* which appeals alike to the amateur sociologist and the amateur botanist, leading, once Thoreau's precise observation and fanatically exact style have been lost from sight, to impassioned adolescent discussions of Society and Nature. Only a few writers on him have found their way out of the bull-session-*National Geographic* trap. Picking up certain clues from Mark Van Doren's *Thoreau* (1916), Matthiessen in the *American Renaissance* moved deep into the center of Thoreau's world, touching the level where myth and morality are one; and suggesting an approach later carried on (if not always forward) in essays by Stanley Edgar Hyman and Sherman Paul, as well as in Feidelson's *Symbolism and American Literature*. The passages in Matthiessen dealing with Thoreau are perhaps the most acute and moving, certainly the most original in the book; but they do not seem to have made the difficult and masked figure of Thoreau as appealing to the contemporary imagination as Hawthorne or Melville. We are, certainly, an age predominantly attracted to fiction and the essay form seems not to provide us with major satisfaction.

Before Melville, the bibliographer retreats in confusion, waiting for the wave of commentary, explication, and documentation to recede before combing the beach to see what of value the flood has cast up. In as summary a sketch as this, it is impossible to do more than suggest the astonishing richness, the maddening prolixity, the contradictory and confused nature of the literature on Melville in general and *Moby Dick* in particular. The essential fact to be recorded is that this nineteenth-century novelist, especially in his difficult and unorthodox masterwork, has come to seem not only for America but for the Western world of eminent importance. He is our age's darling; and this has meant not only a revision of the earlier estimates of him and his work, but a redefinition of the writers around him (Hawthorne attracted to his pole, Emerson thought of as opposite to him in temper and theme), indeed, of our literature as a whole.

It must be added next that Melville has come to be regarded as essentially a symbolist writer; the few protests which continue to be raised against the prevailing view seem oddly old-fashioned, betrayals of the limitations of those who raise them rather than valid comments on Melville. Such a reading of Melville has led to a continuing revaluation of the books around *Moby Dick*, an elevation in importance of works especially amenable to symbolic analysis (the stories "Benito Cereno" and "Bartleby, the Scrivener"—almost extravagantly *Billy Budd*, even, in some cases, *The Confidence Man*) with the consequent deflation of the early romances like *Typee* and *Omoo*, still excessively admired by D. H. Lawrence.

Even into the biographies, the symbolic approach has steadily intruded, both because Herman Melville himself has become a symbol, almost the mythical American Writer, and because his life lacks final interest and meaning, so deeply was he committed to his art, without deep analysis of his books. The early biographies by R. M. Weaver (1921), John Freeman (1926), and Lewis Mumford (1929), were unembarrassed by the masses of trivial biographical data since dredged up by industrious scholars; and thus they could devote themselves frankly and unreservedly to the job of deriving an Olympian or a Titanic figure from the books. This tradition (based ultimately on the conviction that the truth about Melville resides in the imagination rather than in historical fact— and that his books and his life must be apprehended in a single act) has led to the continuing production of critical books organized on a more or less obtrusive biographical frame. Among these two interesting and eccentric examples are Richard Chase's *Herman Melville, A Critical Study* (1949) and Lawrence Thompson's *Melville's Quarrel with God* (1952). Both books are lively and provocative: Chase's in a more fashionable way dependent on recent theories of the psyche and of myth, Thompson's in a more old-fashioned, anti-clerical, bourgeois-baiting style; but both seem to be betrayed into special pleading. Mr. Chase reads into Melville his own quarrel with our anti-tragic tradition of liberalism and Mr. Thompson his personal quarrel with a Presbyterian God. More rewarding than either (though chiefly on *Moby Dick* and not at all on the work after *Pierre*) is Newton Arvin's *Herman Melville* (1950); for he is willing with balance and good sense but without fear of those who cry "Freud!" to penetrate such ticklish questions as that of Melville's uncertain sexuality and his consequent feelings of guilt; which means that he arrives finally at those deep places that more orthodox scholars excuse themselves from entering on the grounds that all there is "surmise."

Certainly, compared to Arvin (compared even to occasional comments like W. H. Auden's in the *Enchafèd Flood*, 1950, of Charles Olson's frantic but illuminating little essay *Call Me Ishmael*, 1947), the recent reaction from "surmise" to "facts" led by Leon Howard and Jay Leyda seems dull and unilluminating. However secure their work may make us feel, however superior to the earlier critics who confused dates and places, they leave us with the sense that the art of Melville and its meanings have been lost from sight. Leyda's collection of documents organized only by chronology (plus his editing) seems somehow more valuable than Howard's careful, remote biography (1951). At least in Leyda's *Melville Log* (1951), we have the sense of being presented with the materials with which one properly *begins;* but Howard's biography claims to take us where we want to go, and this (critically speaking) proves a delusion.

Commentaries on individual works besides *Moby Dick* are plentiful but not ordinarily acute or useful. Some of the introductions in the new Hendricks House edition of Melville's works provide insight and critical guidance, especially H. A. Murray's rather orthodox psychoanalytical notes on *Pierre* (1949) and Elizabeth

Foster's introduction to the immensely difficult and ambiguous (perhaps finally incoherent) *The Confidence Man*. On the poems, Robert Penn Warren's essay which appeared in the *Kenyon Review* in 1953 is thorough and illuminating; but Melville's long poem *Clarel* still awaits a satisfactory analysis.

Walt Whitman is a figure who himself assumed so many masks and poses, and who has had for succeeding generations so many meanings that the commentary on his work has all the polemical confusion of the literature on a prophet or the founder of a new religion rather than a poet. He has, indeed, been considered by one or another group of admirers precisely such a prophet: the Mental Healer, the Great Apostle of the New Democracy, the Revealer of Cosmic Consciousness, the Sexual Emancipator. To Parrington he seemed, of course, the greatest figure of our literature—his poem the very gospel of democratic self-consciousness and a faith in humanity which Parrington felt to be slipping away from America at the beginning of the thirties. Van Wyck Brooks embroiders a similar view in *The Times of Melville and Whitman* (1947); and Matthiessen, though he stresses Whitman's execution rather than his themes, treats him with special tact and sympathy because he finds Whitman's hopes for America so similar to his own. It is D. H. Lawrence (who in this regard as in so many others anticipated the most recent trends), who saw in *Leaves of Grass*, beneath the official enthusiasm and Fourth-of-July Americanism that wear out only too soon, a profound and complex involvement with death. It is this Whitman of the "dusky demon," whom Lawrence first clearly perceived, that seems least equivocally attractive to the recent reader.

Little sense can be made of the latest studies of Whitman without an awareness that many of the best practising poets of the twentieth century, beginning with Ezra Pound, felt it necessary to turn for a while at least against Whitman—to disavow what they felt to be his posturing, his overstuffed rhetoric, and his romantic lack of focus. The clearest statement of this reaction (though perhaps also the most extreme) is to be found in Yvor Winter's essay "The Significance of *The Bridge* by Hart Crane," available now in his volume *In Defense of Reason* (1947). Small awareness of this critical questioning of Whitman's reputation, which sharply divided practicing writers from Whitmanian professors, can be obtained from Gay Wilson Allen's otherwise very useful *Walt Whitman Handbook* (1946) which should be supplemented in this regard by L. A. Fiedler's article in the symposium edited by Milton Hindus, *Leaves of Grass One Hundred Years After* (1955). Indeed, the essays in this collection, plus Randall Jarrell's piece on Whitman in *Poetry and the Age* (1953), give the best indication of where Whitman criticism is going at the moment, a moment when a whole new approach seems in the making.

It will, of course, take a book which is at once full-scale biography and textual analysis to do the job; for there is no absolute boundary between Whitman's life as he lived it and as he wrote it. Our period has seen a series of lives, by Emory Hollowey (1926), Jean Catel (1929), Frederick Schyberg (1933, translated into English in 1951), Newton Arvin (1938); and most recently there has been an autobiographical study by Richard Chase (*Walt Whitman, Reconsidered*, 1955) which attempts to apply certain new critical insights to the old problems. All of these, however, have been overshadowed in scope and depth of documentation by Roger Asselineau's *L'Evolution de Walt Whitman* (1954) and G. W. Allen's *The Solitary Singer* (1955). The former, psychologically oriented, begins only with 1855; and the latter disappointingly evades the more ticklish issues of Whitman's life and is scant on the truly critical side. Allen's book possesses all the charm and value of a balanced and genial account; but one remembers that it was two eccentric, unbalanced, and unfriendly books which managed to ask the sort of question about Whitman's relationship to his mask and poses which have opened the way to a new understanding of the man and his poem. These are Harvey O' Higgins' *Alias Walt Whitman* (1930) and *Walt Whitman's Pose* (1938) by Esther Shepard.

The case of Henry James is almost precisely opposite to that of Whitman. Not only have they been conventionally paired off against each other as polar exponents of "raw experience" and "aesthetic form"; but the history of critical approaches to them provides neat and illustrative contrasts all along the line. In the case of Whitman, the question has been unceasingly posed: does not the attempt to embrace all of America turn art into patriotic editorial? In the case of James, the opposite problem is typically raised: does not the rejection of one's country lead to an attenuation of the basic stuff of art, leaving room only for elaborations of nothingness? Did not, to refurbish the old quip, one bite off more than he could chew, the other chew more than he had bitten off? To arrive at the essential James it is not necessary to pass through a welter of expositions of his ideas, themes, doctrines, and messages. No one has ever been tempted to find him an apostle of anything but art; and, indeed, as staunch an admirer of his work as T. S. Eliot has described his mind, in a notorious passage, as being so "fine that no idea could violate it." It is perhaps for this very reason that James has become a culture hero to some of the best writers of our time, writers uncomfortable and unsympathetic before Whitman. Even poets have found his scrupulous, self-conscious prose a more useful example than the unbuttoned verse of Whitman.

James' critical expositors, at least the earliest ones, were typically nonacademic. They were not, of course, adherents of the Van Wyck Brooks Americanist school, who fused readily into the Parringtonian academic tradition with its distrust of the man who loved his art more than his country; even Lawrence failed to discover in James, beneath his drawing room manners, the essential American touch and the perceptions of a great novelist. It was rather certain twentieth-century expatriates like Pound and Eliot whose early advocacy of James made the advance of his reputation simultaneous with the establishment of the New Poetry and the New Criticism. The history of the redemption of James from the temporary neglect into which he had fallen just before the first world war and of his subsequent near apotheosis can be traced through the special James numbers of various "little magazines": *The Little Review* 1918 issue containing two short pieces by Eliot; the *Hound and Horn* symposium in 1934; the *Kenyon Review* centennial number in 1943.

Not only the formalist New Critics and their fellow-travellers, but also sociological-psychological critics like Edmund Wilson and Philip Rahv quickly joined the chorus of approval and explication, disavowing the orthodox Marxist view which coincided with Parrington's contemptuous dismissal of James as "the last refinement of the genteel tradition." The first academics who came one by one to sanction James and extend the interest in his work tended to be independents and mavericks: writers like Francis Fergusson, William Troy, and R. P. Blackmur without the conventional Ph.D. training, or academically prepared professors like Joseph Warren Beach, F. O. Matthiessen, and Lionel Trilling, committed to formalist or symbolist approaches rather than historical and philological ones.

There has been some tendency recently among the youngest scholars to produce on James the kind of formal scholarship visited for good academic ends upon those much longer dead and less vital to practising authors in establishing their own styles; but on the whole the work on him has developed so untypically that in 1956 a scholarly spokesman could complain: "Although Henry James has been the subject of perhaps more critical essays than any other American novelist . . . basic research on him has lagged . . . there has been little documentation of the . . . debt he owed to English or European fiction . . . or his influence on . . . the whole company of moderns. . . ." To some this would seem small cause for complaint; it is at any rate a fact. To the newer critics, mythic, analytic, or psychological, James has seemed endlessly attractive; to the hunters of sources and expounders of influences he has appeared somehow a poor prospect.

There is not even an authoritative biography, though Leon Edel seems in the process of repairing this lack, the first volume of a proposed three volume life having appeared in 1953 under the title of *Henry James: The Untried Years: 1843–70*. Among existing volumes, most usually sketchy glances at the life used as a framework for an analysis or estimate of the work, the more interesting are: Van Wyck Brooks, *The Pilgrimage of Henry James* (1925) and an answering study by Pelham Edgar, *Henry James, Man and Author* (1927), which between them provide a classic instance of the debate over whether James did not fatally injure himself as an artist when he exiled himself from his homeland. Matthiessen's *The James Family* (1947) read in conjunction with his *Henry James, the Major Phase* (1944) and his edition of the *Notebooks* (with Kenneth Murdock, 1947) develops what might be called the new standard version of his work: the high evaluation of his general achievement, the preference for the later novels, and the sense of his dedicated aesthetic approach as more truly moral than more obvious brands of didacticism. The most recent biographical study is *Henry James* by F. W. Dupee (1952), a relatively unexciting book with few new insights; while the newest attempt at a full-scale analysis is Quentin Anderson's *The American Henry James* (1957). Anderson's thesis that Henry James is best understood in terms of his father's Swendenborgianism, and his effort to extract a coherent metaphysics from the novels has stirred up more protest than assent. A reader desiring some sense of the variety and temper of recent critical exegesis of James can find a representative selection of essays in F. W. Dupee, *The Question of Henry James: A Collection of Essays* (1945).

Mark Twain has received less truly critical attention than any of our major authors. What has baffled commentators is not a lack of sympathy with Twain or an uncertainty about the value of his work (*Huckleberry Finn* is almost universally regarded as one of the greatest of our novels, and, indeed, is challenged for first place only by *Moby Dick*); they are put off rather by Twain's own pretense that he was a non-artist or even an anti-artist. Walt Whitman adopts a similar mask, but he is so obviously a great experimental writer and depends so clearly on anti-literary literary sources that he challenges rather than discourages critical commentary. Whitman, moreover, whatever his theoretical program, has never been in fact a *popular* writer like Twain, taken in by the simple as an unpretentious "phunny phellow"; and certainly *Leaves of Grass* has never seemed to anyone just a boys' book. Between every aspiring critic and Twain stands the author's warning posted before the beginning of this greatest book: "Persons attempting to fiind a motive in this narrative will be prosecuted; persons attempting to find a moral in it will be banished. . . ."

The real problem has been to find a context in which to place Twain and his work: to decide in what sense he represents a continuation of the European tradition of the picaresque, in what sense he is an exponent of the tall tale and the crude humor of the frontier newspaper and the popular lecture platform. Beyond this there is the deeper question of how far he can be taken as a spokeman for the baffled American dream of innocence and how far he must be understood as a literary manifestation of status-striving: a desire to get rich and genteel quick. Biographical studies not content merely to get the facts straight or piously to add anecdote to anecdote, have had to face up to these crucial issues. The best book still, in so far as it attempts to present a coherent theory of Mark Twain's life and work, is Van Wyck Brooks', *The Ordeal of Mark Twain* (1920, revised 1933), which contends that Twain remained an incomplete artist, baffled on the one side by aspirations to gentility and on the other by the dream of big money and the spiritual poverty of the world out of which he came.

The most profitable critical discussion of Twain up to the most recent period was triggered by the appearance of this book; among the responses to Brooks was De Voto's defense in *Mark Twain's America* of the fronter and of the concept of a Twain "devoted . . . to the production of laughter." Lives by Wagenknecht (1935) and DeLancy Ferguson (1943) do not develop fruitful new literary insights. Dixon Wecter's *Sam Clemens of Hannibal* (1952) is the only part of an intended many volume biography to have been printed since Mr. Wecter's untimely death; and it contributes to the growing mass of recent material aimed at creating, though not quite in Brooks' sense, the image of Twain as a tragic figure rather than inspired satirist and buffoon, or even the "pure American" enemy of all "medievalism" and sham envisaged by Parrington.

There is still no full-length critical study of Twain's work, though one has been promised by Lionel Trilling, whose introduction to a 1952 edition of *Huckleberry Finn* ranks with one by T. S. Eliot (1950) and a B.B.C. interview by W. H. Auden (in the *Listener*, 1953) as one of the best "non-scholarly" discussions of the book. Other illuminating, if controversial, approaches have been suggested almost by the way in occasional essays here and there. Leslie Fiedler's "Come Back to the Raft Agin, Huck, Honey," which appeared in *Partisan Review* in 1948 set *Huckleberry Finn* in a new context along with other key American books (*Moby Dick, Last of the Mohicans, Two Years Before the Mast*, and so forth) which isolate at sea or in the wilderness two male lovers, colored and white, whose alliance symbolizes an escape from "civilization" and woman. This affirmation of a characteristic American "myth of love" was greeted in some orthodox academic quarters with scepticism and dismay, but was extended and particularized by James Cox in *Sewanee Review* in 1954, and finds certain parallels in remarks on Twain by Philip Young in a book on Ernest Hemingway published in 1952.

Indeed, it is *Huckleberry Finn* which has almost pre-empted critical attention recently, leading into a full-scale debate which has raged in the quarterlies during the past five or six years, involving such questions as: is the structure of *Hucklebury Finn* aesthetically defensible? is the impact of the book finally joyous or tragic? There is a growing consensus that except in *Huckleberry Finn* and parts of *Life on the Mississippi*, Twain is not a writer of first rank; though attempts have been made on occasion, by those who do not find Twain's *express* philosophy provincial and shallow, to rescue "The Mysterious Stranger" as a minor masterpiece. More recently there has emerged what appears the beginning of a movement to establish *Pudd'nhead Wilson* as Twain's second book; 1955 saw the publication of analyses by Leslie Fiedler and F. R. Leavis, which attempted, in quite different ways, to assert the moral and symbolic impressiveness of that imperfect but haunting book. One has the sense, however, that critical writing about Twain is only on the verge of getting under way. Certain facts have been established; certain approaches have been tentatively proposed; full scale analysis and authoritative evaluation are still to come.

10

Contemporary British Literature

FRED B. MILLETT

BEFORE ONE ATTEMPTS TO DISCUSS scholarship in the field of contemporary English literature, one would do well to define the terms involved in the discussion. Teachers of twentieth-century literature frequently fall into absurd errors by assuming that what is contemporary to them is similarly contemporary to their students. A teacher whose reading life coincides with the first fifty years of the twentieth century may find it difficult to face the fact that his youngest students have only the vaguest memories of the second world war! With respect to literary scholarship, the general editor has wisely suggested that these surveys should focus on works that have appeared since 1930, with only occasional reference to works published earlier. With respect to English literature, however, the term *contemporary* will be given a somewhat wider meaning here. I feel that it is historically legitimate to define *contemporary* as identical with the twentieth century, and, therefore, I shall emphasize the major authors who have reached the peak of their productivity or their reputation during the last fifty years or more but also take into account the spectacular changes in critical taste and judgment that have occurred since 1900. In this particular essay, the term *scholarship* also requires clarification. If it has any meaning in relation to contemporary English literature, it is a very different meaning from that it has in relation to the Renaissance, the eighteenth century, or even the Victorian period. The term *scholarship*, in the sense of a careful scientific manipulation of literary documents, is only rarely applicable here, although it may be exhibited by the best biographies of twentieth-century literary figures. What this survey, therefore, will be concerned with is those *critical* works that, in the writer's judgment, might be of the greatest use to teachers and students of twentieth-century literature.

One further preliminary observation seems advisable. The study of twentieth-century English literature raises problems that the study of earlier periods in English literature does not involve. The literary hierarchy of authors of earlier periods has been gradually determined by the interaction of a number of forces: the popular and critical reputation of authors in their own time, the consequent esteem in which certain—but not all—these authors have continued to be held by anthologists, critics, and writers of literary history, and the acceptance or rejection of these estimates by modern teachers and students. In this connection, the alleged popularity of authors of earlier periods with the general, or even the cultivated, reader is so illusory as to be negligible. Aside from the reading of teachers and students, contemporary reading is so nearly current that authors of earlier periods figure in it only in very rare instances. Most authors of earlier periods survive—if at all—only in classrooms and textbooks, in libraries, and in the publications of scholars.

For both teachers and students of twentieth-century literature, no less than for the historian of this literature, the problem of selection is extremely acute. The quantitative popularity of contemporary authors is of no assistance here; if it were, Mickey Spillane and Frances Parkinson Keyes—strange bedfellows, to be sure—would occupy prominent positions in any survey of contemporary American literature! Nor can the individual teacher's taste be relied on heavily, even if that teacher reads widely and discriminately. The authors whose works are seductively advertised and enthusiastically reviewed in such influential media as the *New York Times Book Review* and the *New York Herald-Tribune Books* would overwhelm the questing reader if he were to attempt to give them serious attention. Probably the most reliable and objective guide to the contemporary authors most worth reading is the amount of attention given them by serious critics and students of the period. In this consideration lies perhaps the justification for writing this particular survey. Even here, an important caveat must be entered. Within the narrow limits of the first half of the twentieth century, as I have said, striking changes in critical taste have already occurred. On the eve of the first world war, it would not have been absurd to say that the leading contemporary English novelists were H. G. Wells, Arnold Bennett, John Galsworthy, and Joseph Conrad. Oblivion has almost covered the once lively figure of Wells; Bennett survives dubiously outside the pages of literary history, only in *The Old Wives Tale*; Galsworthy's *The Forsyte Saga* is read occasionally by students in the better high schools and private schools, and his short story "The Apple Tree," to the regret of this particular writer, has found a conspicuous niche in the mausoleum of short-story anthologies. Of the four novelists who in 1914 ran neck to neck, only Joseph Conrad is now the object of serious biographical and critical attention. But we are too intimately enmeshed in our own times to permit us to be certain that such a change in taste and judgment as this fact indicates will be accepted by teachers, students, and literary historians of the twenty-first century or later.

I

In the light of these observations, it is inevitable that literary histories of twentieth-century English literature will not bulk large in the frame of reference that I have attempted to establish. And yet, the urge to order and to systematize the literary events of our own time is so strong that it has, fortunately, proved irresistible, since teachers and advanced readers clamor for the most reliable guides they can find. Oddly enough, it was two distinguished American medievalists, John Matthews Manly and Edith M. Rickert, who made the first serious attempt to provide a bibliographical guide to the authors of the period. Their *Contemporary British Literature*, first published in 1921, appeared in a revised edition in 1928. In 1935, the present writer brought out an amplified edition of the work under the title, *Contemporary British Literature, a Critical Survey with 232 Author-bibliographies*. Although the book is now hopelessly out of date bibliographically, the Critical Survey will give at least an impression of what "contemporary" literature looked like two decades ago. Slightly later than the first edition of Manly and Rickert's book came Carl and Mark Van Doren's *American and British Literature since 1890*

(1925, revised 1939), the first significant attempt to treat discursively the major writers of the first quarter of the century. A more narrowly selective and still interesting index to the taste of the time is John W. Cunliffe's *English Literature of the Twentieth Century* (1933). An English work, Edwin Muir's *The Present Age from 1914* (1939), strikingly similar in design to my edition of Manly and Rickert's *Contemporary British Literature*, contains a more extensive survey but far less inclusive bibliographies; this work, Volume V of the series *Introductions to English Literature*, is now (1957) in process of modernization by David Daiches. The only subsequent attempt to deal inclusively with twentieth-century literature is Mark Longaker and Edwin C. Bolles' *Contemporary English Literature* (1953). It includes brief critical comments on the works of a great number of authors of the period, with excellent select bibliographies of their works and of critical books and articles about them. Less inclusive but more critically discriminating is William Y. Tindall's *Forces in Modern British Literature, 1880–1946* (1947). It differs from the Longaker-Bolles handbook in that it relates particular writers to what Tindall regards as the most significant movements in the period. Although some of its judgments verge on the idiosyncratic, it is an intimately informed and witty series of critical essays. Narrower in range but useful for its observations on the activities of major and minor writers of three decades is B. Ifor Evans's *English Literature Between the Wars* (1948). H. V. Routh's *English Literature and Ideas in the Twentieth Century* (1948) is valuable for a stress unusual among English critics on contemporary currents of thought and their expression in literary forms. More popular in tone and less sophisticated in manner is A. C. Ward's *Twentieth Century Literature* (1940), which has undergone repeated revisions to keep pace with the significant literary events of the period.

II

The student of contemporary English fiction might well be staggered by the problem of selecting from the floods of works published every year the writers most deserving of serious attention, were it not for the guidance offered him by the critics whose responsibility it is to separate the literary wheat from the chaff. Even here, there is no very recent work—aside from the surveys mentioned above—that attempts to point up the novelists of greatest importance to the student. But David Daiches's *The Novel and the Modern World* (1939) by its highlighting of Joseph Conrad, James Joyce, Virginia Woolf, and Aldous Huxley, and Dorothy M. Hoare's *Some Studies in the Modern Novel* (1938) by focussing on Virginia Woolf, E. M. Forster, D. H. Lawrence, Conrad, and Joyce assist in directing attention to the writers who —at least in quantitative terms—have received the most absorbed treatment from the largest number of critics. We shall probably not go far wrong then if we emphasize here the major studies devoted to the lives and fiction of Conrad, Joyce, and Lawrence, and give less space to the criticism of E. M. Forster, Virginia Woolf, Aldous Huxley, and one or two of the younger novelists.

For a study of Joseph Conrad, the basic biographical documents are *Joseph Conrad: Life and Letters* (1927) by G. Jean-Aubrey and the same author's *The Sea Dreamer: A Definitive Biography of Joseph Conrad* (1957). Jessie Conrad's reminiscences, *Joseph Conrad as I Knew Him* (1926) and her *Joseph Conrad and his Circle* (1935), and Richard Curle's *The Last Twelve Years of Joseph Conrad* (1928) are also biographically indispensable. The best avenue of first approach to Conrad perhaps is Morton Dauwen Zabel's *Portable Conrad* (1947), a tastefully chosen anthology with a masterly introduction. An illuminating study of the development of Conrad's artistry is John D. Gordan's *Joseph Conrad: The Making of a Novelist* (1940). Gordon concerns himself particularly with the influence of Conrad's Polish heritage and his early maritime experiences on the first steps in his literary career. Other recent studies are M. C. Bradbrook's *Joseph Conrad: England's Polish Genius* (1941), Walter F. Wright's *Romance & Tragedy in Joseph Conrad* (1949), Douglas Hewitt's *Conrad: A Reassessment* (1952), and Paul L. Wiley's *Conrad's Measure of Man* (1954). The student would also do well to consult the four short essays on Conrad in Morton Dauwen Zabel's *Craft and Character in Modern Fiction* (1957). These critical studies seem sufficient to substantiate the contemporary view that Conrad is the novelist of the generation of Wells, Bennett, and Galsworthy who most deserves study in the mid-twentieth century for his technical skill, his symbolic subtlety, and his profound reading of life.

To James Joyce, perhaps the best introduction for the un-acquainted reader is Harry Levin's *Portable Joyce* (1947), which reprints four of Joyce's six books complete, contains selected passages from *Ulysses* and *Finnegans Wake*, and has an admirably perceptive introduction. Two brief surveys of Joyce's complete work are Levin's *James Joyce: A Critical Introduction* (1941) and L. A. G. Strong's *The Sacred River* (1949). Joyce's works, rather than his life, have been the focus of attention on the grounds that the man's life was relatively unspectacular while certain of his works are among the most problematical productions in twentieth-century fiction. For the life, however, the *Letters of James Joyce,* edited by Stuart Gilbert (1957) are indispensable, if somewhat unrevealing, documents. A brilliant light is thrown on the development of the technique of Joyce's first novel, *Portrait of the Artist as a Young Man,* by Theodore Spencer's edition of the manuscript of *Stephen Hero* (1944), the first—and drastically different—version of the *Portrait.* Of Joyce's six books, however, *Ulysses* and *Finnegans Wake* have challenged and stimulated more numerous interpreters. Frank Budgen's *James Joyce and the Making of Ulysses* (1934) gives many of the facts essential to an understanding of the genesis of the novel. The first extensive interpretation of this epoch-making novel is Stuart Gilbert's *James Joyce's Ulysses, a Study* (1930, revised edition 1952). A later important study is Richard M. Kain's *Fabulous Voyager* (1947). The first serious attempt to decipher *Finnegans Wake,* the most difficult, if not quite unintelligible, novel ever written, was made by Edmund Wilson in an essay that in its final form appeared in *Axel's Castle* (1936). Joseph Campbell and Henry Morton Robinson offered a more intensive and elaborate analysis of the book in *A Skelton Key to Finnegans Wake* (1944). For the advanced student of Joyce, Hugh Kenner's comprehensive analysis of all the works in his *James Joyce* (1956) and the history of Joyce's reputation and of the interpretation of his works in Richard M. Kain and Marvin Magalaner's *Joyce: The Man, the Work, the Reputation* (1956) bring up to date the story of the most learned and technically complex of modern English novelists, a writer whom T. S. Eliot sees as the destroyer of the conventional realistic novel and the initiator of a more meaningful type of fiction, the mythic.

No major novelist of the twentieth-century has attracted so much attention and inspired so much biographical and critical commentary as D. H. Lawrence. He has been the occasion of more lively controversy than any other novelist of the century. For the reader who has not encountered Lawrence or who is only vaguely aware of the "scandalous" reputation of *Lady Chatterley's Lover*, the best introduction is Diana Trilling's *Portable Lawrence* (1947), which begins with a spirited defense of the author and his works. The "literature" inspired by Lawrence is already so extensive that only the most significant works can be mentioned here. Since almost every one who knew Lawrence intimately was moved to write a memoir of him, the number of such works is almost portentous. Of these, the most valuable are the *Early Life of D. H. Lawrence* by Ada Lawrence and G. Stuart Gelder (1932), Catherine R. Carswell's *The Savage Pilgrimage* (1932), Dorothy Brett's *Lawrence and Brett* (1933), Mable Dodge Luhan's *Lorenzo in Taos* (1933), and Frieda Lawrence's *Not I but the Wind* (1934). Lawrence, as these works make abundantly evident, was extraordinarily attractive to women, but since his wife, Frieda, achieved perhaps the most wise and balanced attitude towards him, her book is by all odds the one most worth consulting. For an understanding of the man, *The Letters of D. H. Lawrence*, edited with a superb introduction by Aldous Huxley (1932) is indispensable.

Of the numerous biographies of Lawrence, unquestionably the best is Harry T. Moore's *The Intelligent Heart* (1954). Although Moore is a great admirer of Lawrence, he did not have the advantage (or the disadvantage) of knowing him personally; his book is, therefore, perhaps the more judicious. Of the more recent critical works devoted to Lawrence, only a few can be mentioned. The most considerable is F. R. Leavis's brilliant, if opinionated, *D. H. Lawrence, Novelist* (1955). Leavis is convinced that Lawrence is indubitably not only the greatest novelist of his generation but the only major English novelist of the twentieth-century. A suggestive, if basically hostile, investigation of the sources of Lawrence's ideas is William Y. Tindall's *D. H. Lawrence and*

Susan his Cow (1939). Among other more recent studies are Father William Tiverton's *D. H. Lawrence and Human Existence* (1951) and Mark Spilka's *The Love Ethic of D. H. Lawrence* (1955).

Although no other English novelists of the twentieth century have received so much critical attention as Joseph Conrad, James Joyce, and D. H. Lawrence, other older and younger novelists have not gone unnoticed, and for the student who wishes to venture farther afield, the following biographies or critical studies may be recommended: Reginald Pound's *Arnold Bennett: A Biography* (1952), Rose Macauley's *The Writings of E. M. Forster* (1938), Lionel Trilling's *E. M. Forster* (1945), Kenneth Allott's *The Art of Graham Greene* (1951), Antonina Vallentin's *H. G. Wells, Prophet of Our Day* (1950), and Vincent Brome's *H. G. Wells, a Biography* (1951); David Daiches's *Virginia Woolf* (1942), Joan M. Bennett's *Virginia Woolf: Her Art as a Novelist* (1954), R. L. Chambers's *The Novels of Virginia Woolf* (1947), Bernard Blackstone's *Virginia Woolf, a Commentary* (1949), and James Hafley's *The Glass Roof: Virginia Woolf as Novelist* (1954). J. K. Johnstone's *The Bloomsbury Group* (1954) gives a lively account of the personal and literary lives of the brilliant circle that included Mrs. Woolf, E. M. Forster, Lytton Strachey, and Roger Fry. An extremely diverting picture of English literary life between the two wars is presented by Rupert Hart-Davis's *Hugh Walpole, a Biography* (1952), a quietly sardonic study of a once popular novelist and his famous literary friends.

III

English dramatists of the twentieth century have received far less serious attention than the novelists of the same period, for the simple reason that productivity in the drama has been nowhere nearly so consequential as that in the novel. In the decade or more preceding the first world war, the English drama, under the influence of Henrik Ibsen and other major European playwrights, showed a vitality and a brilliance that seemed to promise a renascence unequalled perhaps since the Restoration. The widespread success won in the theater by such English playwrights as Bernard Shaw, James M. Barrie, John Galsworthy, and Harley Granville-

Barker and by such Irish playwrights as William Butler Yeats and J. M. Synge seemed to augur the continuation of a vigorous and exciting movement. But for reasons beyond the ken of the literary historian the movement petered out rapidly. Barrie's skillful admixture of sentimentality and cynicism (except in the perennial *Peter Pan*) lost its appeal to the disillusioned post-war audience, Galsworthy's social dramas seemed tepid and parochial, and only Bernard Shaw succeeded in maintaining his conspicuous position in the esteem of England, America, and the Continent. It has been the easily available and always compelling plays of Shakespeare and Shaw, no less than the contributions of minor, if adroit, professional dramatic craftsmen and a fine tradition of skillful, if conventional, production that has kept the English theater flourishing since the creativity of the first decade of the century began to languish. Under the circumstances, it is inevitable that there was little incentive to critics and literary historians to work intensively in this field, and, since the outburst of literary-historical writing that accompanied the abortive dramatic renascence, there has been little or no significant critical activity.

Inevitably, also, the towering figure of Bernard Shaw has inspired the widest critical activity, but, although the quantity of commentary on Shaw is abundant, if not overpowering, the quality is not impressive. Shaw's "official" biographer, Archibald Henderson, an American mathematician, had the advantage of easy access to the ample biographical materials that association with Shaw supplied, but his philosophical and aesthetic equipment made him relatively insignificant as a critic. His first attempt at biography, *George Bernard Shaw, His Life and Works* (1911), was brought out in a revised and amplified edition as *George Bernard Shaw, Man of the Century* (1956). Shaw's ninetieth birthday in 1946 and his death in 1950 precipitated a number of useful memoirs: Blanch Patch, *Thirty Years with Bernard Shaw* (1951), Robert F. Rattray, *Bernard Shaw, a Chronicle* (1951), Stephen Winsten, *Days with Bernard Shaw* (1948) and *Shaw's Corner* (1952). Hesketh Pearson's *Bernard Shaw* (1942), is supplemented usefully by his *G. B. S., a Postscript* (1950). The best biography to date, however, is St. John Ervine's *Bernard Shaw: His Life, Work and Friends* (1956). It may safely be said that no really searching study of Shaw's complex and sometimes contradictory ideas and their origins has yet been made, and the task of placing Shaw as both thinker and critic, therefore, is still to be done. For the student of Shaw, the best guides are still the dramatist's discursive *Prefaces* (1934). But there are useful attempts at an over-all view of this astonishing man in Eric Bentley's *Bernard Shaw* (1947), William Irvine's *The Universe of Bernard Shaw* (1949), the philosopher C. E. D. Joads' *Shaw* (1949), and Arthur H. Nethercot's *Man and Superman* (1954).

In the last twenty-five years, other twentieth-century playwrights have received a minimal amount of critical attention, but the student who is curious about the secondary figures of the period would do well to consult Una Ellis-Fermor's *The Irish Dramatic Movement* (1939), W. A. Darlington's *J. M. Barrie* (1938), Denis Mackails' *The Story of J.M.B., a Biography* (1941), Cynthia Asquith's *Portrait of Barrie* (1955), Mark Longaker's *Lord Dunsany* (1944), H. C. Marrot's *Life and Letters of John Galsworthy* (1935), Charles B. Purdom's *Harley Granville-Barker, Man of the Theatre, Dramatist, and Scholar* (1956), Richard A. Cordell's *Henry Arthur Jones and the Modern Drama* (1932), Robert Greecen's *The Art of Noel Coward* (1953), Derek Stanford's *Christopher Fry* (1951), C. S. McIver's *William Somerset Maugham, a Study of Technique and Literary Sources* (1936), Pierre Dottin's *Le Théâtre de W. Somerset Maugham* (1937), R. H. Ward's *William Somerset Maugham* (1937), K. W. Jonas's *The Maugham Enigma* (1954), and Sean O'Casey's two-volume *Mirror in My House, Autobiographies* (1956).

IV

If the English drama has been disappointingly uncreative since the end of the first world war, English poetry has manifested a vitality that makes it comparable to that of the most productive periods in English literature. Its vitality may be suggested simply by recalling the changes in style and taste apparent in the work of such successive contemporaries as Yeats, Eliot, Auden, and Dylan Thomas, changes so striking as to justify the notion of their constituting a series of brief poetic "generations." Poetic activity has, moreover, been so multifarious as to force on both critics and literary historians a difficult and perhaps misleading selectivity.

Thus, the most ambitious attempts to survey contemporary twentieth-century poetry are bound to be limited and exclusive, and most literary critics and literary historians have simplified their tasks by limiting severely the number of poets on whom they comment. Stephen Spender, on the other hand, in his pamphlet, *English Poetry since 1939* (1946) lists and comments on the works of fifty-nine poets; such inclusiveness, however, may well be considered self-defeating. More extended surveys have their utility in suggesting that the works of the major writers should not be considered in isolation from their followers and companions; of this sort are such early works as R. L. Mégroz's *Modern English Poetry* (1933) and David Morton's *The Renaissance of Irish Poetry* (1929). More recent surveys are Vivian de S. Pinto's *Crisis in English Poetry, 1880–1940* (1951) and Raymond Tschumi's *Thought in Twentieth-Century English Poetry* (1951). More useful by reasons of their selectivity and consequent concentration are Elizabeth Drew and Joseph L. Sweeney's *Directions in Modern Poetry* (1940), David Daiches's *Poetry and the Modern World* (1940), James G. Southworth's *Sowing the Wind, Studies in British Poets from Hopkins to MacNiece* (1940), and Francis Scarfe's *Auden and After* (1942). The first of these books might well serve as a guide to the student who finds modern poetry strange and difficult, since it devotes itself to a discussion of the characteristics of modern poetry generally rather than to an extended consideration of particular writers. Daiches's book, to be sure, studies certain of the post-Victorians, but focusses especially on Yeats, Eliot, Auden, Spender, and C. Day Lewis. Scarfe's collection of short studies of individual poets, although somewhat opinionated and tendentious, is a handy introduction to a number of poets who made their reputations in the 1930's. We would do well to limit our consideration to the most important critical commentaries on the four most conspicuous English poets of the twentieth century: Yeats, Eliot, Auden, and Dylan Thomas.

William Butler Yeats has been the subject of a number of biographical and critical studies. A basic source for the study of Yeats is his *Autobiography* (1953). His indispensable *Letters* have been edited by Allan Wade (1954). The poet's "official" biography *W. B. Yeats, 1865–1939* (1943) was written by J. M. Hone. *The Permanence of Yeats*, edited by James Hall and Martin Steinmann (1950), is a convenient selection from the countless articles and essays on the poet and his work. Thomas B. Parkinson's *W. B. Yeats, Self-Critic* (1951) is a subtle and illuminating study of the development of his art as made manifest by his repeated revisions of his poems. Ingenious and detailed attempts to relate the man and his work have been made by Richard Ellman, *Yeats, the Man & the Masks* (1949) and Alexander N. Jeffares, *W. B. Yeats, Man & Poet* (1949). More specialized studies that deserve attention are Thomas R. Henn's *The Lonely Tower* (1950), Vivienne Koch's *W. B. Yeats, the Tragic Phase* (1951), and Donald A. Stauffer's *The Golden Nightingale* (1949). Henn addresses himself to some of the most difficult problems raised by Yeats's poetry: his use of the mask, his conception of symbols, his preoccupation with magic, and the cyclic theory of culture as set forth in *A Vision*. Miss Koch limits herself sternly to a very close analysis of thirteen of the *Last Poems*.

Although T. S. Eliot's poetic career up to the present has been much shorter than that of William Butler Yeats, his writings have attracted almost as much comment and analysis as those of the older poet, since they seemed to present to readers unaccustomed to a novel poetic style problems that demanded interpretation. Although his personal history invites speculation, as yet there has been no attempt to write a full-length biography of the poet; the most convenient collection of biographical data is that made by Richard March and Tambimutti under the title *T. S. Eliot: A Symposium* (1948). A judicious selection of the innumerable articles devoted to the interpretation of Eliot's poetry may be found in *T. S. Eliot: A Selected Critique*, edited by Leonard Unger (1948); a less extended collection of critical articles is *T. S. Eliot, A Study of his Writings by Several Hands*, edited by B. Rajan (1947). The first major extended critical discussion of Eliot's work was F. O. Matthiessen's *The Achievement of T. S. Eliot* (1935, revised 1947). Two books have been devoted to a poem-by-poem, play-by-play analysis of Eliot's works: George Williamson's *A Reader's Guide to T. S. Eliot* (1953) and Grover Smith, Jr.'s *T. S. Eliot's Poetry and Plays: A Study of Sources and Meaning* (1956). Of the considerable number of studies of special aspects of Eliot's work, the student would do well to consult Helen Gardner's *The Art of T. S. Eliot* (1949) for its subtle analysis of the later poems.

The serious reader who does not succumb completely to the beauty and power of Eliot's complex poetry may find some comfort in Rossell Hope Robbins's *The Eliot Myth* (1951).

For the study of such poets as W. H. Auden and Dylan Thomas, who may be taken as representative of the two most recent poetic "generations," there are naturally few guides to interpretation and evaluation. Auden, however, has been the subject of two studies, by Francis Scarfe (1949) and Richard Hoggart (1951). The darker phases of the meteoric rise and the tragic fall of Dylan Thomas have been grimly recorded by John Malcolm Brinnen in his *Dylan Thomas in America* (1955). This relentless account of the self-destruction of a young genius should, however, be supplemented by the more sympathetic memoir by his wife, Caitlin Thomas, now (1957) in process of preparation. There are two important critical studies: Henry Treece's *Dylan Thomas* (1949) and Elder Olson's *The Poetry of Dylan Thomas* (1954).

V

As the preceding pages clearly show, both English and American critics have been remarkably active in their consideration of at least the major figures in twentieth-century English literature. They have not been so active in their exposition and discussion of English works on the theory of literature and criticism or of the large body of practical or applied criticism produced by English writers. Stanley Edgar Hyman's *The Armed Vision* (1948) is the most elaborate study yet made of both English and American literary criticism of the twentieth-century. Among the English critics to whom he gives considerable attention are I. A. Richards, his disciple William Empson, T. S. Eliot, and Christopher Caudwell. Hyman is widely read and extremely well informed; his judgments sometimes tend to be extravagant or idiosyncratic. Murray Krieger's *The New Apologists for Poetry* (1956) necessarily gives considerable attention to the major influences on contemporary English criticism—Richards and Eliot, writers who are likewise treated, though more briefly, in a far more widely inclusive work, *Literary Criticism: A Short History* by William K. Wimsatt, Jr. and Cleanth Brooks (1957). Some of the best, if over-aggressive, critical writing of the period has come from F. R. Leavis, his disciples, and associates; selections from their work may be found in Eric Bentley's *The Importance of "Scrutiny"* (1948). No attempt, however, has yet been made to discuss searchingly either the critical principles or the practices of this influential group. For an over-all consideration of twentieth-century criticism, within a European frame of reference, the student will have to wait for the publication of the third and fourth volumes of René Wellek's *A History of Modern Criticism, 1750–1950.*

11

Contemporary American Literature

R. W. B. LEWIS

THE FORMALISED STUDY OF CON-
temporary—that is, roughly, twentieth-century—literature in
America is itself a cultural phenomenon of the first order. Every
generation of uncommon artistic vitality has, I suppose, been
curious about its own impulses and achievements; and indeed, a
tense preoccupation with the present moment has long been a
familiar American habit. Lectures on "the times" have been inor-
dinately popular in this country for more than a century; and
Emerson, who delivered a number of them, was wittily scornful
of the persistent American nose for news. But it is hard to imagine
in any other century what has taken place in this American
century—the institutionalising of interest in the very recent and the
immediate. Courses have been introduced in colleges all across the
continent, and they have proliferated to the degree that "contemporary literature" has become a formal and extremely popular
field of academic study. It has earned the ultimate acknowledgement, bestowed by educationists, of requiring seminars and symposia in the methods of teaching it. I understand that something of
the kind has occurred in the fields of music and the fine arts; so that
perhaps the first thing to notice about contemporary American
culture is its fascination with its own form and pressure.

One reason, no doubt, is that the contemporary arts are incarnate
within our universities and schools, in the person of teaching poets
and novelists and critics and painters and composers; though that
is probably a symptom rather than a cause. There has been a good
deal of talk about this development, and here I note only the fact
that, whatever the effect upon the academic world, the effect upon

the world of literature is the paradoxical rebirth of something very traditional and European: truly home-grown men of letters—cultivated artists. We are not yet so French that we can look up "men of letters" in the classified sections of our telephone-books, as one can in Paris; but that privilege may not be long delayed. There are at least two other larger reasons for the increasing academic stress upon contemporary literature. It represents, for one thing, a phenomenon reflected in the literature itself—namely, a very serious and honorable apprehension over the enigmatic, the perhaps destructive force of contemporary history; and this is not a fad, but an alert response to the bruising facts of our time. About several of our most esteemed novelists—about Faulkner and Dos Passos, for example (as about Malraux in France and Silone in Italy)—it has been argued in high places that they don't really write *novels*. It is an acute critical observation, if it is not intended as a scolding. Much of the most impressive fiction in the past three or four decades has been written out of a special and as it were extra-literary urgency. The contemporary novel has often been less a direct and unprejudiced impression of life (as Henry James said the novel ought to be) than an act of defiance, or a passionate inquiry, or of expiation. It has sought not to describe but to penetrate or challenge the present age: to resist it or transcend it. The novelistic relation to the immediate scene has infected students of literature in turn, and they have begun to go at the literature with the same intensity, the same personal involvement, that the literature has gone at the scene.

As a corollary to the immersion in history, the study of contemporary literature is also a part of America's repeated effort to identify itself. We not only stand tiptoe to detect new trends; we are constantly taking stock. And we not only appraise our past, we are regularly changing our minds about its durable content. The rather tangled story I have to tell in this article is in fact the story of progressive determinations of the very substance of contemporary literature; the story not only of scholarly and critical opinion about poetry and fiction, but the establishment of the poetry and the fiction about which opinion is required. What Melville called the shock of recognition (that is, of some writer or group of writers of unmistakeable talent) has been so frequent and contradictory an occurrence that of late it has declined into a succession of slight nervous shudders. The start of the second half of the century was the obvious occasion for quite a few of them—most notably, perhaps, the series on "twentieth-century literature in America," published by Henry Regnery Company in Chicago, and including such items as *Achievement in American Poetry, 1900–1950* by Louise Bogan, *The Modern Novel in America, 1900–1950* by Frederick J. Hoffman, *Fifty Years of American Drama, 1900–1950* by Alan S. Downer (all published in 1951), and *An Age of Criticism, 1900–1950* by William Van O'Connor (1952), co-editor with Mr. Hoffman of the entire list. None of these books is—or, one judges, was intended to be—a document for the ages; but they all have their uses in sorting out the major figures and the connecting lines since 1900.

I

The fact is, of course, that contemporary literature is not really a subject for scholarship. It can be a subject for criticism, though only of a provisional kind; I shall refer mostly to critical rather than scholarly work. For in a deep and insuperable sense, contemporary literature must always be unfinished business, even if the writer studied has been dead for forty years. We are only just beginning to calculate—how could we have done it sooner?—the uncanny *prophetic* power in the later novels of Henry James, even as we are just catching up with the fearful accuracy of Henry Adams.[1] Both men felt, in very different ways, the approach of some immense cultural disaster; and only now that we know more about the disaster as it has happened—after two wars and the shaking of almost all spiritual foundations—can we start to assess the imagery thereof in James's fiction and Adams's history.

Because contemporary literature is by nature incomplete it is not easy to point with assurance to any clearly successful study of it: general, special, or particular. Alfred Kazin's *On Native Grounds* (1942) remains, I think, the most stimulating and in-

---

[1] R. P. Blackmur has considered this aspect of Adams in essays published over the years in *Sewanee Review, Kenyon Review* and elsewhere; his full-length book on Adams has yet to make its appearance. A recent and excellent contribution is J. R. Levenson's *The Mind and Art of Henry Adams* (1957). On James's only semi-conscious prophecies, too little has been said. Quentin Anderson's *The American Henry James* (1957) discusses the matter within a somewhat perverse context.

formative general account of literature of all kinds since 1900. *Contemporary American Authors* by Fred B. Millett (1940) has a long (two-hundred page) introductory survey, followed by an extensive bibliography of those authors. It is a helpful check-list, but it is now rather out of date; its inclusions and exclusions seem a bit quaint, like the styles in hats of the year it was published; and the introduction is on the conventional and undiscriminating side. The chapters on the twentieth century, by various scholars, in the second volume of the *Literary History of the United States* (1948), should be consulted also. They tend to be summaries or even abstracts of findings recorded elsewhere, and the effort to fit them together required taking the edge off all of them. The bibliography in the third volume, however, is genuinely indispensable. I emphasise its value here, since I do not propose, for some of the reasons given, to offer a detailed list of secondary writings. Students seeking such a list will find it, valid up to 1948, in the *Literary History*, topic by topic and writer by writer.

If Kazin's book, *On Native Grounds*, is so much more exciting, more illuminating, and more *living* than the other general studies, it is not because either his method or his judgment is impeccable. Kazin is temperamentally more interested in writers as personalities than as authors of books; his method is biographical impressionism. And his own book is ridden by a thesis about what constitutes authentically native grounds which is so dubious that it forces him to deal unfairly, even ineptly, with many of the key figures, especially with Henry James, T. S. Eliot, William Faulkner, and the so-called new critics. But the attractive energy of *On Native Grounds* derives not only from a vigorous rush of style and a host of vivid and suggestive portraits. It derives, oddly, from just that method and that bias: they are so impulsively American. A preference for the lives of writers rather than for their writings and a hostility to the delicacies of James, the traditionalism of Eliot, the horrors of Faulkner, and the scientific precision of the critics: this is the very stuff of a recognizably American point of view. Kazin's book is an example of its subject. His enthusiasm and his skepticism are themselves part of the expansive, romantic, innocent but aggressive, non-(if not anti-)European, native tradition which he celebrates. His thesis is that it is *that* tradition which is authentically American: the tradition which begins with Emer-

son and Thoreau, rather than with Hawthorne; continues through
Mark Twain and Dreiser, rather than Henry James; flourishes
in the work of Sandburg and Frost, rather than in Eliot and Ezra
Pound; and is understood best in free-wheeling lyrical criticism
like his own, rather than in the highly civilized analyses of critics
like R. P. Blackmur and Allen Tate.

Kazin's book thus belongs to the drama of American literature.
It participates in the old inspiriting conflict, discoverable in both
imaginative and in scholarly or critical writing, between the
"romantic" tradition and a tradition we may cautiously call "neoclassical".[2] It is the proper book to consider at such relative length
at the start of our survey. If there is a trend to be spotted in the
developing study of twentieth-century American literature, it is a
sort of crab-like shift of attention from the lofty estimate of the
neoclassical towards a restoration to prominence of the romantic.
Such a shift carries with it a gradual displacement of persons; and
perhaps the most succinct symbol is the recent emergence of Walt
Whitman as America's greatest poet. Readers unfamiliar with
literary criticism in America may be surprised to learn that he
has not always been so considered; but now, in any case, the wind
is shifting in his direction. I do not mean to exaggerate the development, and I cannot tell how wise and culturally fruitful the change
will be. I must inevitably oversimplify; but something is happening, I believe, and it may be of the utmost significance.[3]

II

What *is* happening is more evident in the discussion of poetry
than in that of fiction; and I might say in advance that the change
can be measured by comparing the essays in Cleanth Brooks's
volume, *Modern Poetry and the Tradition* (1939) with those in
the book by Randall Jarrell, *Poetry and the Age* (1952). The very
outlines of contemporary American poetry as a distinguished body
of work with definable attributes, a mixed but specific ancestry,
and an observable momentum were most firmly established by the

2 Or between what Philip Rahv in *Image and Idea* (1949) shrewdly calls
"the redskins" and "the palefaces."

3 The change of taste I am referring to is probably more apparent in reassessment of nineteenth-century American literature, which is the major
scholarly and critical task of this decade.

late F. O. Matthiessen, in the latter part of his introduction to the
Oxford Book of American Verse (1950). Matthiessen was a scholar
of solid and communicable taste; and his essay is especially sound
not only because he was alert to the achievement of the then
youngest poets of talent—Karl Shapiro and Delmore Schwartz,
for example—but because he saw the history of American poetry
as a coherent story. Identifying the native idiom and impulse as
they expressed themselves from the eighteenth century onwards,
he did not fail to recognise their continuation in twentieth-century poets like Robinson and Frost. He was one of the first to grasp
the achievement of Eliot, but that did not make him blind to Sandburg; and he could discriminate to a nicety the mingling in Hart
Crane of the "native" and the "imported." But his essay is something of an exception. Much more characteristic of the prevailing
taste and knowledge are books like Louise Bogan's *Achievement
in American Poetry*, Brooks's *Modern Poetry and the Tradition*,
William Van O'Connor's *Sense and Sensibility in Modern Poetry*
(1948), and *Modern Poetry* (1951), an anthology with comment,
edited by Kimon Friar and John Malcolm Brinnin.

It is in the latter that we read: "The modern idiom in poetry
depends primarily on two traditions—the metaphysical, stemming
from John Donne and his period, and the symbolist, stemming
from Mallarmé." Miss Bogan's uniformly intelligent little book
demonstrates the latter part of that statement, by relating the felt
nourishing influence of Mallarmé and his fellows to the "break-
through" of American poetry from the "imitative, sentimental
and 'genteel' verse" so fashionable around 1900 to the first performances by Pound and Eliot.[4] And O'Connor demonstrates the
other part of it by emphasizing the usable appeal to the modern
poetic imagination of John Donne's "sense of intricacy, the interrelatedness and dissonances of experience as they flow through the
mind." That appeal is the very heart of Cleanth Brooks's thesis.
Donne with his intensive paradoxes—

> Nor ever chaste except you ravish me

and his extreme tensions—virtually *is* the tradition to which Brooks
accommodates modern poetry. "Our age rejoices in having re-

[4] Two highly seminal books may be mentioned as background for this aspect: Edmund Wilson's *Axel's Castle* (1931, reprinted twice), and Marcel
Raymond's *From Baudelaire to Surrealism* (1933, reprinted 1950).

covered Donne," says Brooks; "but in doing so we have recovered not just Donne's poetry, but poetry."[5] This is the principle behind the extraordinarily influential textbook, *Understanding Poetry* (1944), on which Brooks collaborated with Robert Penn Warren; and it has been the idea disseminated by the more effective literary quarterlies.

Such convictions, in short, have been the basis of both the theory and the practice of what is called modernist poetry: poetry which, in America, as Miss Bogan demonstrates, was begotten mainly by the remarkably varied and tireless activities of Ezra Pound. It is a poetry which found its greatest practitioner in T. S. Eliot and its motto in Eliot's famous essay on the seventeenth-century metaphysical poets: "Our civilization comprehends great variety and complexity, and this variety and complexity, playing upon a refined sensibility, must produce various and complex results. The poet must become more and more comprehensive, more allusive, more indirect, in order to force, to dislocate if necessary, language into his meaning." The validity of those statements and of the principles they helped establish are reflected in the astonishing fertility of American poetry from (say) Eliot's "The Love Song of J. Alfred Prufrock," published in the magazine *Poetry* in June, 1915, onwards for a quarter of a century: a period as rich in its way as the early seventeenth century in England.

They are reflected, too, in the brilliant series of critical analyses which attempted to grasp and to explain the poetry itself—the story of poetry and the story of criticism in twentieth-century America are inseparable.[6] *Poetry* had published one of Vachel Lindsay's best poems, "General Booth Enters Heaven" just two years before "Prufrock," in January, 1913; but after Eliot's appearance, the new school of criticism would have nothing to do with Lindsay, or with Robinson or Sandburg or Frost. They were too native, too direct, too conventional in syntax and in rhythm; too evangelical or too jazzy; too Yankee or too midwestern. They were not, as Pound and Eliot were, *in*direct, metaphysical, symbolistic, culturally allusive; they were not various and complex

[5] Actually a quotation from an essay, "Milton and the New Criticism," *SR* (1951).

[6] Compare the essay in this volume by William Van O'Connor.

enough. Criticism turned to other voices: to those listened to so intently, for example, by R. P. Blackmur.

I select Blackmur for special mention, because his essays—begun in the late twenties and collected later in *Language as Gesture* (1952)—served as much as the critical work of any one man can serve to settle the canon of modern poets. Blackmur's attention descends chiefly on Eliot (two essays), Pound (two essays), Wallace Stevens (three essays), Hart Crane, Marianne Moore, and E. E. Cummings (one essay each), along with a fresh evaluation of Emily Dickinson, who may be said to be one the most admired "living" poets; and several discussions of Yeats. If to Blackmur's list we add the English names of W. H. Auden and Dylan Thomas, we are in possession of the acceptable galaxy of modern poets—acceptable, at least, until recently. How almost tyrannically acceptable they became is indicated in the anthology cited above by Friar and Brinnin: which gives us twenty-two pages of Eliot, but only five of Frost;[7] eleven poems by Wallace Stevens, as against three by Edwin Arlington Robinson; twenty-eight pages of Pound, but only two (one poem) of Sandburg; ten poems by W. H. Auden, and one by Vachel Lindsay. A similar emphasis, or (if you prefer) disproportion, is shown in the book-length studies of individual poets which have found the warmest response—those on Eliot,[8] on Pound (*The Poetry of Ezra Pound* by Hugh Kenner, 1951), on Stevens (*The Shaping Spirit* by William Van O'Connor, 1950), and on Hart Crane (*Hart Crane* by Philip Horton, 1937; and *Hart Crane* by Brom Weber, 1948). An exception to the fashions was Yvor Winters' sturdy little volume of *Edwin Arlington Robinson* (1946).

Blackmur seems to me one of the best critics of poetry who has ever lived. In America he has no rival: except possibly, in a rather different context, Edgar Allan Poe. To find a critic in England as competent to get inside the actual language of poems and to detect its unique activity (not merely its color and flavor), one

[7] And, incidentally, fifty pages of notes on Eliot, whereas it is merely noted, in a single line about Frost, that he was born in California in 1875.

[8] Books on Eliot continue to accumulate. The most recent and thorough is *T. S. Eliot's Poems and Plays* by Grover Smith, Jr. (1956). Earlier and still valuable studies include *T. S. Eliot: A Selected Critique*, edited by Leonard Unger (1948) and *The Achievement of T. S. Eliot* by F. O. Matthiessen (1935).

probably has to go back to Coleridge. It is Blackmur's formidable ability to describe a poem as an event, a *happening*—an act of creation, of bringing into being not only a meaning but a reality—that has persuaded many readers of the rightness of his choices, that has or temporarily had established the list of representative modern poets. His method *works* with Eliot and Crane; it would not work with very many other poets—who were, consequently, excluded from the canon. But Blackmur was not alone; and I must at least mention the deft and elegant essays of Allan Tate (who writes much better than Blackmur and is, in fact, one of the handsomest stylists in America) which deserve much credit in domesticating for us the work of Pound, Eliot, and the others.[9] A more recent contribution, which seems to follow faithfully the judgment of the new critics, is *The Metamorphic Tradition in Modern Poetry* by Sister Bernetta Quinn (1955). Sister Bernetta considers the modern concern with metamorphosis—with a change observed or accomplished in the nature and reality of persons and objects—in the poetry of Pound, Eliot, Stevens, and Crane. But then, somewhat surprisingly, she goes on to consider the same effect in the work of William Carlos Williams and Randall Jarrell. And by doing so, her detailed and almost dogged study becomes a sign of changing times: for it is exactly Jarrell's excitement over Williams, in *Poetry and the Age*, that is a leading sign of the new taste.

Jarrell, a poet of winsome quality, has nothing to say about Donne or Mallarmé, the two alleged sources of this age's poetry, and very little about Eliot or Pound; but his book contains exuberant and witty "rediscoveries" of Walt Whitman and Robert Frost, and three of the best short articles yet written on William Carlos Williams. No one could say that those three poets are alike in all respects, or that a single line connects them: Williams is intricately experimental in the modern manner; Frost has become increasingly mystical and dark-spirited; and Whitman is Whitman. But all three write out of a decidedly native idiom, and seem to have been reared on native grounds. They write about the knowable American world around them: the Brooklyn ferry; the Vermont farmland; Paterson, New Jersey; and their intention is to

---

[9] *On the Limits of Poetry* (1948).

celebrate those scenes rather than to decry them as wastelands or infernos. Their cultural allusions are sparing; their syntax more often than not is normal; they seem natural, local, and muscular. As against the poetry of Eliot, theirs is a *public* poetry, and seems anxious to communicate urgent bardic messages to the multitude.

It is not possible as yet to estimate the depth and seriousness of the new critical interest. One feels, perhaps, that Jarrell is sometimes only stirring things up for the fun of it; and I should warn once more against the overly tidy schematism of any article like the present one. But Jarrell's book is only one of a number of suggestive symptoms; and another probably more significant piece of evidence is Karl Shapiro's forthcoming *In Defense of Ignorance* (to be published in 1958). Shapiro, like Jarrell, is a poet of ruefully celebrational tendencies; and as his title suggests, he hopes to restore the "ignorant" and even the "innocent" poets to the place long denied them by the learned poets with their tragic vision of the irremediable evils of the modern world. In the new pantheon, Whitman replaces Emily Dickinson as the most living of the nineteenth-century poets; Frost, Robinson, and possibly Sandburg receive positions of eminence; and another aspect of Hart Crane— his myth-making, Whitmanesque aspect—is honored above his symbolistic, Baudelairian strain.[10]

Two points should be stressed, both exemplified by Shapiro. First, the "revolution in taste"—if that is not too strong a word— has been initiated by the younger poets themselves, as every such revolution must be. It is a part of their effort to free themselves for the kind of poetry they want to write and for the popular reception they hope to achieve; so that the force behind their move can be no greater than the talents of the poets involved. Second, the reaction they represent is basically not against "modernist" poetry so much as against "neo-modernist" poetry— the poetry not of Eliot, but of his imitators, all the sad and learned and somewhat mannered young men who have derived a surface and a posture but not a poetic core from the modern masters.

---

[10] At the moment of writing, Hart Crane seems likely to emerge as the twentieth-century American poet of greatest repute. His experimental techniques and his explosive symbolism appeal to the Donne-Mallarmé cult; and his expansive, mythological, American subject-matter appeals to the Whitman cult.

Eliot's head will probably roll before the revolution is over[11] (though one also predicts a resurrection after a decent interval); but it will be the kind of tragic error to which such convulsions in politics or in culture are prone.[12]

III

No book or collection of essays has been as valuable for the understanding of fiction and the establishment of its ablest American practitioners in this century as Blackmur's *Language as Gesture* has been for poetry and the poets. Joseph Warren Beach's *The Twentieth-Century Novel* (1932) and his *American Fiction, 1920-1940* (1941) are instructive combinations of formal and substantive analyses. One hopes that splendid and scholarly commentator will bring his work on fiction up to date, for it is one of the dangers of contemporary studies that they do date so quickly— Longinus on Homer is far less dated than Beach on Faulkner. Kazin's *On Native Grounds* may be cited again here, for its suggestive, uneven introductions to our major modern novelists; and among more special studies, Frederick J. Hoffman's crowded discussion of *The Twenties* (1955) has a sort of foggy but genuine merit. Hoffman had the good idea of relating social experience in America to key literary passages wherein the experience is crystallised and given permanence; his account of the experience is excellent, but his comments on the literature is rather perfunctory.

Both scholarly and critical discussion of fiction seem to me to suffer from a certain cloudiness of view as to the nature—the genus and the species—of the object discussed. There has been the tendency to treat novels as though they were poems of the purer and more metaphysical variety; and there has been the tendency to treat them as though they were documents in social history or

[11] He has been practically decapitated already by Robert Graves, who slaughters the entire canon in *The Crowning Privilege* (1955), and by Kathleen Nott, in *The Emperor's Clothes* (1954).

[12] Another revolutionary symptom, not worth more than a footnote at this stage, is the so-called Pacific School of Poets—poets centered not in the academic campuses of San Francisco but precisely across the bay and beyond the academic pale. The leading voice of the school is Allen Ginsberg, whose little book of poems in 1956, called *Howl* (it was originally to be called *Yawp*) is introduced by W. C. Williams, and contains a free-verse tour through a grocery store in the ghostly presence of Walt Whitman.

even sociology. The former case represents the somewhat mis-guided effort, notable in the literary quarterlies, to apply to fic-tion the methods of analysis which produced some impressive results with poetry. But fiction manipulates different objects than poetry does and it uses language differently—it is concerned with flesh-and-blood individuals in action amidst the changing pres-sures of society, and words in a novel serve (or ought to serve) to illuminate character and behavior rather than to generate special-ised aesthetic effects. The sense and sensation of life and the nature of the human heart (banal as those phrases may be) remain the proper subject for the narrative artist; and poetic criticism, which is primarily directed towards diction, reveals at best only marginal aspects of the novel. The second tendency I have mentioned is perhaps even less satisfactory. The poetic approach leaves out too much of the felt life in a work of fiction; but the historical and sociological approach leaves out all the art which gives that life its real feeling. The latter approach depends upon conventional and often irrelevant categories. It looks for "schools" which do not exist and never really have existed in America (who could be more different in force and fiber than Hawthorne and Melville, than Mark Twain and Henry James, than Faulkner and Heming-way?). It directs attention to regions, from which the novelists have mostly long since removed; to decades, which are arbitrary and distracting boundaries; and to ideas, which American writers are not very interested in. It talks about "isms" (realism, regional-ism) which have in fact almost nothing to do with the way novels get written or the shape they finally assume. It has not yet been sharply enough seen that what relates American novelists to each other and so makes possible a comprehensive view of their ac-complishments is not a place or a moment or a textbook category: but the habit of response to the impact of experience whereby they do appear to communicate within the same world of nar-rative discourse. The scholar-critic who takes hold of that fact will have an incalculably significant subject; but he will have to be familiar with early as well as recent American writing.

It can be argued that the Europeans are ahead of us in arriving at a coherent view of our own fiction. The situation in fiction, in one respect, reverses the situation in poetry. Where American verse was liberated by the influence of French symbolism and

English metaphysical poetry, European fiction in the past few decades has been profoundly affected by the enormous vigor, the sometimes savage vision of life, and the narrative techniques of the Americans. In this field of literature, the important effects have moved eastward from our shores. Dreiser, no doubt, seems betimes to be translating Zola into American; and Faulkner reflects an absorption with Joyce's stream-of-consciousness method. But much more striking has been, for example, the value of Henry James for the English novelist, Graham Greene, who says about James that "he is as solitary in the history of fiction as Shakespeare in the history of poetry;" of Hemingway for Camus in France and Vittorini in Italy; of Faulkner for both Camus and Sartre and for any number of aspiring younger writers. The American novelistic influence had its rapid echo in scholarship and criticism abroad; and perhaps the best single book on recent American fiction is *L'Age du Roman Americain* (1948) by the very talented Frenchwoman, Claude-Edmonde Magny. Mme. Magny's work, a series of interrelated essays on novelists since the twenties, is not free of factual error; her geography is shaky, and her knowledge of secondary material limited. But she has an extraordinarily rich approach, combining the lucidity of a Descartes with the far-ranging considerations of the most experimental American critic; and she is at home in the whole tradition of western fiction. Her title means to suggest that she views the modern age as an age exactly represented in and by American fiction—as one says "the age of Pope"; and her book traces the form and features of this age as they have been depicted by Faulkner, Hemingway, and their contemporaries: who are thus seen, not as members of a school, but as sharing in a habitual response to life.

Mme. Magney's essay on Faulkner is one of the most brilliant yet written; but it was prepared for by nearly twenty years of acute and often philosophical European appreciation of him. The Faulkner story, which though rather extreme is not untypical, is worth rehearsing here briefly, as an index to the pace of our own native appreciation of our best novelists. The symbol of it is a distinguished social philosopher, a woman, who arrived in America in 1945 and wanted at once to buy all of Faulkner's novels in English. She had read him in translation and had read about him (had even written about him) in European journals. Now she had the perhaps bizarre notion of improving her English by reading him closely in his native language; but she could find no new copy of any of his novels in any New York bookstore, and only one or two battered second-hand copies. That was 1945; and it was, in fact, in the year following that the Viking Press published *The Portable Faulkner* with Malcolm Cowley's introduction: an epoch-making essay for the history of Faulkner's reputation, and even, I venture, for the history of the appreciation of American fiction. Cowley was the first English-writing critic to realize that Faulkner, over a number of novels, was unfolding a kind of mythological history of the South; that all his books illuminated each other, and his horrors and verbal acrobatics made sense only within the whole enormous context. In the same year, 1946, Robert Penn Warren published his long critique of Faulkner, saying with some vehemence that Faulkner was the most important immediate challenge to criticism in America; and the flood-gates were opened.[13] Cowley's and Warren's essays are permanent contributions and deserve to be gratefully mentioned. But what is to be stressed is the extent to which American scholarship and criticism have lagged behind the Europeans in the very identification of native talent. The Europeans referred to are not only the French—André Malraux, who celebrated the radical originality of *Sanctuary* in 1934, or Jean-Paul Sartre who tellingly applauded the metaphysical perspective of *The Sound and the Fury* in 1939, or André Gide, who praised all of Faulkner's books in many places. There were also Sigurd Hoel, Norway's first man of letters, who recognised Faulkner's genius as early as 1931; Emilio Cecchi, one of Italy's foremost critics, who acknowledged Faulkner as a master in a colorful and sorrowful comment of 1934; and Erik Lindegren, the greatest lyric poet of modern Sweden who announced two decades ago that it was Faulkner's prose-rhythms which "delivered" his own poetic style.

The critical lag in the field of fiction has meant the absence of a "canon" of novelists, as there has been of poets. This is by no means a bad thing in itself. Canons are congealing affairs—they really are un-American; and they are especially dangerous with

[13] Warren's essay and a number of other items may be found in *William Faulkner: Two Decades of Criticism*, edited by Frederick J. Hoffman and Olga Vickery (1951).

novelists, who practice the most unstable literary art that the west has invented. But it may be helpful if I list the following as the writers who *appear to be* most in esteem at this moment among scholars and critics of known competence; and if I list them, not chronologically, but in what I take to be the order of esteem: Henry James, William Faulkner, Ernest Hemingway, F. Scott Fitzgerald, Theodore Dreiser, Stephen Crane, Thomas Wolfe, Sherwood Anderson, Edith Wharton, Willa Cather, and John Dos Passos.

That is not my private list; indeed, there are several names I regret not finding on it—notably, James Gould Cozzins, the author of *The Just and the Unjust, Guard of Honor* and other novels which display a talent scarcely exceeded by Hemingway or Dreiser. Cozzins is the most neglected of our serious novelists in this century; the *Literary History* does not even mention him. Katharine Anne Porter, the author of *Flowering Judas* and *Pale Horse, Pale Rider* belongs there too; she is weaver of emotional textures unrivalled in the country, and perhaps her very uniqueness has made the commentators (with a few exceptions) stay away from her. An interest in Sinclair Lewis may be resuscitated when the study of him by Mark Schorer, a very able and scholarly critic, makes its appearance. But James T. Farrell (regrettably) and John Steinbeck (less so, as regards his actual achievement in fiction) seem to be gone forever—both are considered, rightly or wrongly, to be motivated by social or political impulses rather than by artistic ones; and John P. Marquand will, apparently, continue to appeal more to "the average reader" than to students of literature.

The list I have recorded is deceptive, in any case. It conceals, for example, the fertile quarrel between those who articulately prefer the subtle moral and artistic qualities, the intricate psychological webbing of Henry James; and those who prefer the head-on assaults on the raw American scene of Theodore Dreiser. Those who esteem James tend to be at home also with Fitzgerald and Edith Wharton; those who honor Dreiser tend to gravitate also towards Thomas Wolfe and John Dos Passos. This is the one controversy within the field of fiction which can compare to the poetic debate between the admirers of Eliot and the enthusiasts of

Whitman: and here again, it is a matter of the sophisticated, ironic, civilized, and quasi-European against the bald, rumbling, nakedly American, "liberal" and uncomplex. A quick view of this argument may be had by comparing Lionel Trilling's essay, which deprecates Dreiser and elevates James, in *The Liberal Imagination* (1950); and Alfred Kazin's introduction to *The Stature of Theodore Dreiser* (1955) which he edited in collaboration with Charles Shapiro. Kazin, not unexpectedly, wants to re-establish the native significance of Dreiser; and while the appeal of Dreiser's naturalistic humanism is strong and honest in him, Kazin's attitude towards James remains one of contrived courtesy. No less unexpectedly, it is F. O. Matthiessen who has known how to deal fairly with both James and Dreiser, by detecting in both of them themes and obsessions and literary accomplishments at once traditionally American and perennial.[14]

On balance, Matthiessen seems the most powerful of the scholar-critics in the field of contemporary American fiction; and exactly because he combined scholarship—he was learned in the whole history of American literature and in that of western culture generally—and a vigorous ability to make critical discriminations. Indeed, among all the very many individual studies which have established the reputations of the novelists and supply our current knowledge about them, the best have been those which aim either to identify their subject by relating it to some continuing American tradition; or those which aim at developing a vocabulary able to cope with modern fiction; or both. The first volume of Leon Edel's biography of Henry James, *Henry James: The Untried Years* (1953), for example, makes excellent use of the command of psychology as a critical instrument which Edel also demonstrated in his book *The Psychological Novel* (1955)—wherein he has many fascinating things to say about James and Faulkner. Philip Young's little book on *Ernest Hemingway* (1952) fuses the psychological perception with a conviction about an American mythology, and he relates Hemingway to Twain and traces the special qualities of the Hemingway hero in a way that makes his study more provocative than the solider, more detailed and author-

[14] In *Henry James: The Major Phase* (1944) and *Theodore Dreiser* (1951). Matthiessen also did a great deal of editing and anthologizing of James's work.

itative book by Carlos Baker, *Hemingway: The Writer as Artist* (1952).[15]

The defect of Irving Howe's book on Faulkner (*William Faulkner*, 1952)—in other respects a steady and sensible work—is that Howe neither demonstrates Faulkner's closeness to Hawthorne and Cooper, to the American "tall-tale" tradition, and to the congenital American concern with innocence and experience; nor does he break much ground in suggesting methods for appraising the art of the novel. But adequate full-length treatment of Faulkner must await the publications of the findings of Carvel Collins on Faulkner's *real* life, as distinguished from the legend he has promulgated and which Howe unfortunately repeats. The case of Scott Fitzgerald is a reasonably satisfactory one: Arthur Mizener made a good story out of Fitzgerald's life in *The Far Side of Paradise;* while students interested in more searching critical judgments can find them in Alfred Kazin's collection of essays on *F. Scott Fitzgerald: The Man and His Work* (1951). But it has been exactly the trouble with most of the commentary on Thomas Wolfe that it has been, as it were, neither broad nor narrow enough—not broad enough, in terms of the traditions of American fiction; not narrow enough to indicate the special manifestation of Wolfe's art. Wolfe has not been very well served by his small band of passionate and devoted admirers; and the result, as regards his most uneven reputation, is indicated in the title of a volume of essays about him—*The Enigma of Thomas Wolfe*, edited by Richard Walser (1953). There is something to be rescued and absorbed from the vast output of this strange, trapped giant of a man; and a useful beginning has been made in Louis Rubin's unpretentious study, *Thomas Wolfe: The Weather of His Youth* (1955).

The twentieth century has been a good age, possibly a great age in fiction, though scholarship and criticism have yet fully to show it. No one since James has rivalled his peculiar eminence,

[15] An interesting collection of essays on Hemingway by several hands has been edited by John McCaffrey, *Ernest Hemingway: The Man and His Work* (1950). One of the signs of a novelist's arrival at some kind of permanence of reputation is the publication of a book of critical essays about him; reference is made in these pages to such books honoring Faulkner, Hemingway, Dreiser, Fitzgerald, and Wolfe; and mention may here be made of *The Question of Henry James*, edited by F. W. Dupee (1945).

and we have had no Melville, no Twain, no Hawthorne. But we have had something almost as good: the continuing production of that art of the second level (*not* the second rate) on which the literature of any country deeply depends. And the rumor that fiction may be moribund in America is disproved by the growing power of writers like Robert Penn Warren, and in a slightly younger category, of Saul Bellow and J. D. Salinger.[16] I do not wish to make matters sound easy and effortless: elements still conspire to make the lot of the writer in America as near unendurable as possible. But creative energy is not lacking among either poets or novelists; and it is the crucial assignment of criticism and scholarship that they preserve that energy by making its results known and knowable to the Americans who read. Henry Adams said a good many years ago that America's problem was to make its intelligence catch up with its energy. In the field of literature, *hic opus, hic labor est:* for all the rest of us.

[16] On the youngest writers, see the two books by John W. Aldridge, *After the Lost Generation* (1951) and *In Search of Heresy* (1956) and Malcolm Cowley's *The Literary Situation* (1954).

THE GENRES

12

Modern Literary Criticism

WILLIAM VAN O'CONNOR

> ... each generation brings to the contemplation of art its own
> categories of appreciation, makes its own demands upon art,
> and has its own uses for art.
>
> T. S. ELIOT

AMONG THE THINGS THAT OUR
contemporary critical movement has brought to the study of
literature are enthusiasm and common sense evaluations of literary situations. As an example I want to refer to a recent article by
Yvor Winters, "Problems for the Modern Critic," in the *Hudson
Review* (1956). Mr. Winters is a man with a mind of his own, and
willing to pass judgment on any number of things. In this essay
he ranges over a great number of topics and up and down the
centuries. I want to single out two comments. The first of these
is concerned with the dragon in the first book of *The Fairy Queen*.
This is what Mr. Winters says about the dragon:

The gentle knight encounters the dragon, and after many Spenserian
stanzas he slays it. We eventually learn that the dragon represents Error. But the dragon in general and in all its details, and merely as
dragon, is a very dull affair; it is poorly described and poorly characterized. I do not, frankly, know what one might do to make a dragon
more interesting, but it seems to me that unless one can do better than
this one had better not use a dragon. In its capacity as Error, the dragon
spews up a number of books and papers (along with other items), and
of course the dragon is ugly, but little is done in this way to further our
understanding of error: there is no functional relationship between the
dragon, either in general or in detail, and that which it represents. The
relationship is arbitrary, and we have to be told explicitly what the relationship is. . . . The gentle knight himself suffers from the same defects as the dragon, and to understand him and his actions we have to
read him with a chart at our elbow, and even then the significance re-

mains on the chart and is never functional in the poem. The poem has other defects: the clumsy and tyrannical stanza, the primitive and unvaried use of the iambic pentameter line, and an habitual redundancy; but at present I am concerned only with the incurable flaws in the method.

If I may be autobiographical here, I'd like to say that this paragraph pleased me very much, largely I think because it recalled and scored off for me a very dull semester course I once took in Spenser. I still have Jones, *A Spenser Handbook*, which we used in that course, and I took it down to see what was said about the dragon. This is what it says:

The monster encountered by the Red Cross Knight and Una in the Wandering Wood is, for Ruskin, "Error in her universal form, the first enemy of Reverence and Holiness; and more especially Error as founded upon Learning; for when Holiness strangles her,

'Her vomit full of bookes and papers was,
With loathy frogs and toades, which eyes did lacke.'

Having vanquished this first open and palpable form of Error, as Reverence and Religion must always vanquish it, the knight encounters hypocrisy, or Archimagus." Unequal to the machinations of this new enemy, Holiness is separated from Truth, and then, first of all, quite naturally meets Infidelity and Falsehood.

And on the passage goes, with never a word about whether the dragon is successfully conceived or not. The Jones handbook belonged to a tradition which required the scholar or the student to explain what Spenser, or whoever, meant; one was not asked to say how successful or unsuccessful it was.

Mr. Winters also has a few things to say about Pound's *Cantos*:

The details, especially in the early *Cantos*, are frequently very lovely, but since there is neither structure nor very much in the way of meaning, the details are details and nothing more, and what we have is the ghost of poetry, though I am willing to admit that it is often the ghost of great poetry. . . . A number of young scholars at the University of California and at Northwestern University are now engaged in running these references down, and the voluminous notes which they have provided for a few of the *Cantos* are very helpful; but the notes are almost as voluminous as the *Cantos* and can scarcely be held in the head—in fact, when the work is completed, it may well be impossible to hold them in the hand—so that we shall eventually have to read the *Cantos* with a guide more awkward than anything required by Spenser or Dante.

It may well be true that the *Cantos* are a white elephant; certainly it is true that many parts of the *Cantos* are monumentally lacking in any real significance.

I

Modern critical writing has made great inroads in English departments. *Understanding Poetry* (1938) began a revolution—and now about half of our textbooks are in the analytical mode.[1] Dissertations are now written on the theories and critical practice of T. E. Hulme, T. S. Eliot, Allen Tate, or John Crowe Ransom, and professors lecture about the "dissociation of sensibility," the "objective correlative," "the intentional fallacy," or "form as achieved content." University professors also write critical essays of a sort that twenty years ago could have been found only in advance guard magazines, and rather frequently they collect their essays in book form. Notable recent examples of such books are William York Tindall's *Literary Symbol* (1956) and Leonard Unger's *The Man in the Name* (1956). Students and teachers alike keep an eye out for critical articles being published in *Kenyon Review*, *Sewanee Review*, *Hudson Review*, *Western Review*, *Accent*, *Partisan Review*, *Essays in Criticism* and the other "little magazines." It is no exaggeration then to say that criticism flourishes in English departments.

But modern literary criticism—at least the criticism of poetry—did not originate in English departments. It began with T. S. Eliot's *The Sacred Wood* (1920) and Ivor Richards' *Principles of Literary Criticism* (1924). Or perhaps it began with Ezra Pound and T. E. Hulme, both of whom influenced Eliot. Again, there may be no great point in identifying the original source or sources of the movement, for it is clear that many of the preoccupations found in modern criticism have their antecedents in Coleridge, in Henry James, in Remy de Gourmont, or in Benedetto Croce. An

[1] Texts of this sort are Caroline Gordon and Allen Tate, *The House of Fiction* (1950), Robert Heilman, *Modern Short Stories* (1950), Leonard Unger and William Van O'Connor, *Poems for Study* (1953).

easier matter is the listing of the critics who have written books that have proved seminal or in other ways significant.

The close critical examination of fiction did have academic beginnings, the first significant study being Joseph Warren Beach's *The Method of Henry James* (1918). Beach wrote a similar volume on George Meredith, but his major contribution came with *The Twentieth Century Novel: Studies in Technique* (1932). Percy Lubbock's *The Craft of Fiction* had appeared several years earlier (1929), and it is sometimes held to be a landmark in the criticism of the novel. Brilliant though it is, Lubbock's book lacks the catholicity of taste and the critical range of Beach's *The Twentieth Century Novel*.[2]

R. P. Blackmur's *The Double Agent* (1935) and *The Expense of Greatness* (1940) are fairly early examples of the close reading of poems and novels. Blackmur has not developed a literary theory, or at least he has not published a theoretical book. His value as a critic, despite occasional involuted sentences and awkward phrases, has been in the acuteness and subtlety of his explications. Cleanth Brooks is perhaps the most "academic" of the new critics. His *Modern Poetry and the Tradition* (1939) is indebted to Richards, Eliot, Ransom, Tate, Leavis, and probably to Robert Penn Warren. In this book Brooks helped to formulate the break with Victorian standards and to point up connections between 17th century poetry and modern poetry. In *The Well Wrought Urn* (1947) Brooks developed his theory of the structure of poetry. He holds that the nature of poetry is essentially the same generation after generation, and he develops in great detail the thesis that poetry employs a language of indirection.

Kenneth Burke in *Counter-statement* (1931), *The Philosophy of Literary Form* (1941), and *A Grammar of Motives* (1945) showed himself possessed of a wide-ranging mind. Perhaps his primary interest is in the rhetorical aspects of language and in the structural aspects of a literary work. William Empson, a student of Richards, published his influential *Seven Types of Ambiguity* in 1930. A more precise term than *ambiguity* is Wheelwright's

[2] *Forms of Modern Fiction: Essays Collected in Honor of Joseph Warren Beach* (1948) is a collection of essays on the technique of the novel. John W. Aldridge edited a similar volume entitled *Critiques and Essays on Modern Fiction, 1920–1951* (1952). Many of the essays in both volumes are indebted to the earlier work of Beach and Lubbock.

pluri-signification, meaning that a word in a given context may have two or more meanings and that these meanings in some way complement each other or one another. It is quite possible that Empson was indebted to Freud for such concepts as *latent* meaning and *over-determination*. He is explicit about his indebtedness to Robert Graves and Laura Riding's *A Survey of Modernist Poetry* (1929).

John Crowe Ransom's *The World's Body* (1938) is an admirable defense of the needs and requirements of the sentiments, of the life of feeling, against the encroachments and restriction of scientism. *The New Criticism* (1941) is Ransom's interpretation of what Richards, Eliot, Winters, and certain other critics are trying to say. Allen Tate, once Ransom's student, has been a vigorous defender of literature as knowledge. "It [poetry] is neither the world of verifiable science nor a projection of ourselves; yet it is *complete*. And because it is complete knowledge we may, I think, claim for it a unique kind of responsibility, and see in it at times an irresponsibility equally distinct." Tate's books include *Reactionary Essays* (1936), *Reason in Madness* (1941), and *On the Limits of Poetry* (1948).

Lionel Trilling's *The Liberal Imagination* (1950) may be said to occupy a unique position in modern criticism. It grew out of the liberal tradition, a tradition that tended to minimize the nature of the work of art and to emphasize its social uses. Trilling does not deny the social consequences of a work of art, but he shows that the liberal's sense of urgency in bringing about social reforms frequently made for a *simpliste* point of view. Having recognized this, he re-examined the writers whom liberals have glorified, and pointed to virtues in writers whom liberals were suspicious or disapproving of. Edmund Wilson has also been identified with the liberal tradition. His books from *Axel's Castle* (1931) on tend to mirror the interests of each decade. He is not so much an original critic as a highly intelligent interpreter of books and movements.

Yvor Winters on the other hand is original even though he is often wrong-headed. His *In Defense of Reason* (1947) collects two earlier books and an essay. Winters insists that each element in a poem should be under the rational control of the poet, and that a work of literature, whether poetry or fiction, is explicitly a presentation and evaluation of a subject in moral terms. F. R.

Leavis, the editor of *Scrutiny*, should be mentioned in conjunction with Winters. Leavis' theory of poetry, unlike Winters' theory, is indebted to Eliot, but the manner and tone of the two men are alike insofar as both are intensely moralistic.

Perhaps the major lines that have emerged from the work of all these critics can be called Eliotic preoccupations and Ricardian preoccupations. By this I mean Eliot's interest in tradition, in the impersonality of art, and in the "dissociation of sensibility," and Richards' interest in the poetry of synthesis (tension) and in myth. A large body of commentary has grown up around each subject, and much of it has been assimilated into contemporary critical consciousness.

On the jacket of René Wellek and Austin Warren's *Theory of Literature* (1950) one reads this:

> This book will mark an important mile-stone in the study of literature. It crystallizes a movement that has been under way for two decades in this country, to focus literary criticism and literary study in general on literature itself, rather than on historical backgrounds, the psychological mechanisms, the political and social currents that influence literary creation.

This statement certainly implies that we have reached a point of summing up, evaluation, and recapitulation.

A study which is essentially a recapitulation (it has not, I believe, received much attention) is Solomon Fishman's *The Disinherited of Art* (1953). One reads it with the sense of going over old ground: the modern writer is alienated, the importance of tradition to the writer, the regional element in literature, and so on. Another volume greatly indebted to modern criticism at the same time that it is a history of it is Frederick Hoffman's *The Twenties* (1955). What is new in Hoffman's method is that first he summarizes various movements, for example, Freudian theory, or the idea of a "useable past," and then demonstrates how each of them functioned or operated in a literary work of major importance; in other words, he writes literary history in the older way but adds to this closely written analytical studies of poems and novels. Another volume that falls into our recapitulation category is Murray Krieger's *The New Apologists for Poetry* (1956). Krieger, with a good knowledge of aesthetics and considerable training in philosophy, sets out to clarify the positions of a number of contemporary critics, ranging from T. E. Hulme to the Chicago Aristotelians.[3] He examines them in the light of the history of certain critical concepts as well as certain general principles of his own, and in the process he demonstrates inconsistencies in and the partialness of the systems of all of them.

One could point to a great many books that draw upon the concepts developed and the terminology coined by one or another of the new critics. There is, for instance, Charles Feidelson's *Symbolism and American Literature* (1953). Feidelson makes good use of the theory of the impersonal nature of art in his discussion of *Moby Dick*. What I am trying to say is that we may have reached a plateau. We now have a great many useful concepts and terms: patterns of imagery, analogous actions, epiphanies, key word, ambiguity, unified tone, tension, foreshortening, ficelles, reflectors, intentional fallacy, affective fallacy, and so on. There is God's plenty in the way of aids for getting inside a work of literature.[4] Judiciously employed, they help us to see what is going on in a novel or play or poem and to talk more easily about what we see there. Models of critical explication are R. P. Warren's essay on Hemingway's *A Farewell to Arms*, L. C. Knights's "Restoration Comedy: The Reality and the Myth," and Francis Fergusson's chapter on *Hamlet* in his *The Idea of a Theater*. In such works, the new criticism has made an important contribution to the humanistic study of literature.[5]

II

In reading through volumes of the *English Institute Annual*, a remarkably useful and intelligent series of essays, one may ob-

[3] Much of the work of the Chicago critics is collected in *Critics and Criticism*, edited by R. S. Crane (1952). Crane's own position is best found in *The Language of Criticism* (1953).

[4] William Elton's *A Glossary of the New Criticism, Poetry* (1950) and R. W. Stallman *The Critic's Notebook* (1950) are useful for running down such terms.

[5] Useful anthologies of modern criticism are Ray West's *Essays in Modern Literary Criticism* (1952) and Morton D. Zabel's *Literary Opinion in America* (1952). A history of modern criticism in England and America is S. E. Hyman's *The Armed Vision* (1948) and a history of twentieth-century American criticism is *An Age of Criticism* (1952) by William Van O'Connor.

serve a preoccupation with rhetoric[6] and myth. The study of rhetoric is certainly useful, but it seems merely a further extension of the interest we have had in the verbal aspects of literature, another tool. There have been many books and essays on myth too, but there are grounds for assuming that we have had very little in proportion to what is ahead for us.

To talk about myth, one needs at least a working definition. In *The Greek Myths* (1955) Robert Graves says this:

> True myth may be defined as the reduction to narrative shorthand of ritual mime performed on public festivals, and in many cases recorded pictorially on temple walls, vases, seals, mirrors, chests, shields, tapestries, and the like.

Mr. Graves seems to be saying that truly mythical stories dramatize, partially through the use of established rituals and partially through the appeal of iconography of various sorts, the beliefs held by a society. Presumably Spenser's *Epithalamium* and Shakespeare's *A Midsummer Night's Dream*—both of which have the ritual of blessing the marriage bed, hoping for fecundity, spiritual unity, and mutual happiness, and even invoking the aid of supernatural or preternatural creatures in this hope—are mythic in Mr. Graves' sense. The contemporary reader may feel uneasy with this definition because Mr. Graves apparently insists on the relationship between public festivals and myths. Also the Greek world is a long, long way behind us, and our trying to get at an understanding of myth through its literature has obvious hazards. A definition at once closer to home and a little looser can be found in Mark Schorer's *William Blake* (1946):

> Myths are the instruments by which we continually struggle to make our experience intelligible to ourselves. A myth is a large, controlling image that gives philosophical meaning to the facts of ordinary life. . . . Without such images, experience is chaotic, fragmentary and merely phenomenal. It is the chaos of experience that creates them, and they are intended to rectify it. All real convictions involve a mythology, either in its usual, broad sense or in a private sense. In the first case it is embodied in literature or in ritual or in both, in which it has application to the whole of society and tends to be religious. In the second, it

[6] A good example of this sort of study can be found in "Rhetoric and Poems: Alexander Pope," by W. K. Wimsatt, Jr., which has been included in Wimsatt's *The Verbal Icon* (1954).

remains in the realm of fantasy, in which it tends to be obsessive and fanatical. . . . [Myths] unify experience in a way that is satisfactory to the whole culture and to the whole personality.

Schorer makes other useful points: the term *myth* does not mean a falsehood, nor is an acceptance of myth necessarily a form of anti-intellectualism or obscurantism; myths in our time tend to be political in character; and we live in a period of multiple and conflicting myths. Again, there is the relationship of myth to literature: "Literature ceases to be perceptual and tends to degenerate into mere description without adequate myth . . . when we feel that we are no longer in a position to say what life means, we must be content with telling how it looks." In contrast we have the Shakespearean or Elizabethan myths: that of divine and earthly governance, with the accompanying belief in man's dignity and potential nobility, and that of the transcendant importance and power of love, with the accompanying belief in plenitude and ripeness. On the other hand, as all students of modern literature know, the modern writer has faced the necessity of trying to create a myth, the very substance necessary before he can discover, imagine, or give order to his images: Eliot made his excursions into anthropology and various religions, Joyce, with a comic glint in his eye, made his into the psychology of human organisms, whereas Yeats and Stevens made theirs into various realms of the aesthetic. As Schorer says, "The hunt for the essential image goes on everywhere today—but the problem is hardly new."[7]

A philosopher and critic who has been writing about poetic language and about myth for a number of years is Philip Wheelwright. In 1954 he published an extremely interesting book, *The Burning Fountain*. Wheelwright has a subtle and far-ranging mind. For example, there is a chapter entitled "Four Ways of Imagination" in which he complains, with justice, that the new criticism has overemphasized the esemplastic, the synthesizing power of the imagination. Wheelwright lists and elaborates upon four general ways in which the active mind responds to and integrates its sense of the world:

There is the Confrontative Imagination, which acts upon its object by particularizing and intensifying it. There is the Stylistic Imagina-

[7] R. P. Blackmur has discussed this problem in "A Burden for Critics," *Lectures in Criticism* (1949).

tion, which acts upon its object by stylizing and distancing it. There is the Archetypal Imagination, which sees the particular object as embodying and adumbrating suggestions of universality. And there is the Metaphoric Imagination, which fuses heterogeneous elements into some kind of unity.

In this first category Wheelwright is isolating what Joyce, following Aquinas, called *integritas*, one's awareness of radical individuality in an object or situation. Discussing the second category, Wheelwright says: "Imagination, even in its stylizing and distancing aspect, is more than a play of fancy; it is subtly but effectively a real contributor to the very nature and significance of our world." Oddly, this problem, which would seem to be the very center of the study of imaginative literature, has received little attention. Possibly there may be many attempts to characterize it in the next few years.[8] In his third category, Wheelwright discusses certain particulars which have "more of an archetypal content than others"—"they enclose in themselves a certain totality, arranged in a certain way, stirring in the soul something at once familiar and strange, and thus outwardly as well as inwardly they lay claim to a certain unity and generality." In his fourth class, Wheelwright discusses the esemplastic imagination.

It is present in all art that is anything more than purely formal or purely decorative; for an artist's characteristic attempt, in its semantic aspect, is to express and communicate an experience comprising some grouping of perceived and imaginative here-nows for which there is no publicly accepted word, formula, or other symbol already available.

In another place, he says, "metaphor is a medium of fuller, riper knowing; not merely a prettification of the already given." Among other chapters that could be useful to students of literature are "The Mythic World-View," "The Semantic of Ritual" and "Dramatic Action and Mythic Imagery."

A recent book that is a detailed examination of Wheelwright's third category, that on Archetypes, is James Baird's *Ishmael* (1956). Baird says he is dealing with primitivism, which he defines as follows:

In this study, the mode of feeling which exchanges for traditional Christian symbols a new symbolic idiom referring to Oriental cultures

[8] Harry Levin has published an essay, "Notes on Convention," *Perspectives of Criticism* (1950), that is an important contribution in this field.

of Oceania and Asia is admitted as genuine primitivism, even with the closer qualifications that most of the authors [he is primarily concerned with Melville] involved, certainly the major ones, should have travelled in the Orient and that they should have derived from direct physical experience a medium of feeling to inform the symbols which their art presents.

Baird believes that Melville captured in at least certain provinces of his imagination "the sentience of archaic man." Baird has written a lengthy book, and the correctness of his interpretations probably should be left to Melville scholars and to those who know a good deal about archetypes. Even the general reader, however, can observe that Melville, like so many other American writers, was in pursuit of innocence. For example, he was greatly taken by the nakedness of the Polynesians, or, more specifically, the Marquesans. He celebrates, as Baird says, "the nakedness of the Polynesian body and the innocence in which it was displayed." Baird also has a chapter entitled "Puer Aeternus: Eternal Innocence," which centers around the Polynesian word *tayo*, which means friendship on a high plane of idealism and selflessness, and around the ideal of acceptance. "As the archetype of the primordial whale becomes the avatar of God the unknowable in *Moby Dick*," Baird says, "so the archetype of *puer aeternus* becomes in *Billy Budd* the avatar of God the knowable through the communion of fraternal love, innocent, free of self-consciousness, carelessly enduring."

It seems fairly clear that the "American experience" has been such that as a nation we desire virtuous conduct, freedom from difficulty, and that many of us like to believe that our motives are purer than the motives of people in other countries. This is a big subject, and one can merely point at it. John Sisk wrote an article in *Thought* (1952) which he called "American Pastoral." The common characteristic of the literature he examines is a desire to escape from complexity. He shows how frequently pastoral heros turn up in our novels. Behind all this, he says, "is the whole business of a young, hearty, clean-blooded, freedom-seeking, wilderness-encircled band finding a physical and spiritual vigor in its primitive environment and asserting itself boldly and successfully against an effeter, oversophisticated father-land." Quite a full discussion of innocence in nineteenth-century American literature is to be found in *The American Adam* (1955) by R. W. B. Lewis. Lewis centers his study around the American as a new Adam.

It was not surprising, in a Bible reading generation, that the new hero (in praise or disapproval) was most easily identified with Adam before the Fall. His moral position was prior to experience, and in his very newness he was fundamentally innocent. The world and history lay all before him.

It is easy enough to see how Emerson, Thoreau, Whitman, and certain others properly fall inside Lewis' study. Other books that are related to this subject of innocence are Philip Young's *Ernest Hemingway* (1952), Leslie A. Fiedler's *An End of Innocence* (1955), and Frederick I. Carpenter's *American Literature and the American Dream* (1956). This desire for innocence is obviously a two-sided medal, and undoubtedly the investigation of it that is currently under way tells us something about our capacity for self-scrutiny.

A work-in-progress which seems to deserve attention here is being written by Philip Young of Kansas State College. Mr. Young who expects to call his book *Studies in Classic American Myth* describes his subject this way:

I propose to examine certain American traditions which have worked their way through our literature, particularly, and our culture generally, chiefly by having been used and re-used by several hands. For instance; the stories of Pocahontas, Rip Van Winkle, the Kentucky Tragedy, and the Angel of Hadley. The purpose is primarily an interpretation of these themes in the hope of appreciating the significance for our civilization of this sort of American "literary mythology." The idea is that the meaning of the themes, if known, might throw a good deal of light both on the myths themselves and on the audiences, the generations of people of the United States, which have repeatedly found them compelling.

A good many scholars and critics are undoubtedly thinking and writing about literature in similar ways, and it seems likely a large number of articles and books having to do with belief and myth will be published in the next few years.

III

A postscript: *Literary Criticism: A Short History* (1957) by William K. Wimsatt, Jr., and Cleanth Brooks may prove to be a volume that ended an era of literary criticism. The histories of literary criticism written by Saintsbury or Atkins, their usefulness aside, are dull, and the reason for this is that they provide summaries of critical theories and critical quarrels that in large part are dead. Whether the epic or tragedy, for example, is (or was) the ultimate in literary achievement no longer strikes us as being a very significant question. It was, however, a significant question in its own day. As scholars, students, or practising critics, we should know the history of Western criticism. We should also be able to distinguish between the questions that are dead and the questions that are of radical significance for our own period. Wimsatt and Brooks tell us the history of criticism, but they are selective, trying to emphasize the issues that are alive for us, or at least to recast the way in which ancient literary theories or arguments were put, to the end of making them more available for us. Nor does their volume suffer from a common characteristic of literary histories: opinions and evaluations seeming to come from on high, from some ineffable realm where the gods have established a hierarchy of received opinion. Wimsatt and Brooks argue from a position, *their* position, which emerges clearly as chapter follows chapter, and which is stated explicitly in the epilogue. Theirs is an *analytical* history.

And this is a good word with which to close our little survey. The study of literature during the past twenty years or so has been largely in the *analytical* mode.

III

In beginning Literary Criticism: A Short History (1957), by William K. Wimsatt, Jr., and Cleanth Brooks they appear to be a volume that ended an era of literary criticism. The histories of literary criticism written by Wimsatt or Arkins, their treatises, are dull, and the reason for this is that they provide summaries of critical theories and critical quarrels that in large part are dead. Whether the epic or tragedy, for example, is or was the ultimate in literary achievement no longer strikes us as a being a very significant question. It was, however, a significant question in its own day. As scholarly students or practicing critics, we should know the history of Wimsatt's criticism. We should also be able to distinguish between the questions that are dead and the ones that are of critical significance for our own period. Wimsatt and Brooks tell us the history of criticism, but they are derived trying to emphasize the issue that are alive for us, or at least to recast the way in which a such an easy literary theories or arguments were put to the end of making them more available for us. Nor does their volume suffer from a common characteristic of diverse histories: opinions and evaluations seeming to come from on high, from some inevitable realm where the gods have established a hierarchy of received opinion. Wimsatt and Brooks argue from a position, their position, which emerges clearly in chapter, follow chapter, and which is stated explicitly in the epilogue. There is an analyzed history.

And that is a good word with which to close but little answer.

The state of literature during the past twenty years or so has been largely in the main tical mode.

13

Poetry

GEORGE ARMS

WITH THE POETIC RENAISSANCE, the beginning of which may be conveniently dated in 1912 with the founding of *Poetry: A Magazine of Verse*, it is only natural to expect a new emphasis on the reading of poetry as well as on its writing. From its inception *Poetry* had made Whitman's observation widely known: "To have great poets there must be great audiences too." And in spite of the alienation from readers that modern poets have often sensed, the audience—if it has not become great in either number or soul—has developed a conscious acuteness that sets it apart from the audience of the nineteenth century as much as "The Love Song of J. Alfred Prufrock" stands apart from "The Lady of Shalott."

As we shall see in examining its history, a renaissance in the reading of poetry occurred some time after 1912. As late as 1940 in "Dover Beach Revisited: A New Fable for Critics" in *Harper's Magazine*, Theodore Morrison had demonstrated the confusions still current in the reading of poetry. But this "new fable for critics" also has value outside of its own time, putting a perennial critical problem with richness and even beauty. Briefly the story is this: Professor Chartly, an educationist unsympathetic with literature, asks several critics for evaluations of Arnold's "Dover Beach" in order to determine the basis, if any, for common understanding. The evaluations will be examined by a man of letters widely revered among the literary profession, and then returned to the statistical professor for his "more scientific analysis." But an Arnold scholar asks to be excused because he is busy investigating "a fresh clue to the identity of 'Marguerite' " (he has no time to make value judgments). An aesthetic critic sorrowfully concludes that the poem is not "a uniformly satisfactory example of poetic art." A moralist grieves that in this poem Arnold had seen life neither steadily nor whole. A psychological critic uses "up-to-date psychological aid" only to find a "fundamental sense of insecurity" in the poem; and a social critic finds Arnold "too much a child of his class to disown it and fight his way to a workable remedy for social injustice."

The fable closes when the "elder statesman," our man of letters who has sensibility if not sentimentality, receives the packaged comments. He thinks of the poem for the first time in some years "like a coat that one has worn many times with pleasure and accidentally neglected for a while." None, he muses, "could miss the human feeling, the cry from the heart, in 'Dover Beach.'" Or could they?—and he is brought up short. "Who could tell what any job-lot of academicians might be trusted to see or fail to see?" So he puts off the task to do "some long-needed editorial work on his dry-fly book," for he is a fisherman—we might almost say a "Compleat Angler."

I suppose that even a modern reader of poetry (nurtured by Empson, trained by Brooks, polished by Wimsatt) will like Peter Lee Prampton, the elder statesman, best as a man. But he will wonder a little about him as a critic, and while admitting his large wisdom will question whether his seeing the action of the poem as a universal experience of a kind like that which he had undergone fifty years before is quite enough. More bluntly, do the Peter Lee Pramptons give rise to the situation in which the Chartlys can be so devastating? "Gentlemen," we hear them say in our classrooms of thirty years ago, "this poem speaks clearly and eloquently in a form classically pure and simple." What they said was true, but it did not mean very much; and too often they said it of poems inferior to "Dover Beach" with just as much conviction and resonance.

The modern reader will not have much use for the Arnold expert, the moralist, or the psychological and social critics. But in all of them he may recognize a method which if it had only looked discerningly at the poem first of all might have a great deal of validity. Perhaps he will have least use of all for the aesthetic critic as a person, "handsome in a somewhat speciously virile style," whom the class mimic represents as typically saying: "After all, gentlemen, it is pure poetry that lasts." But Bradley Dewing also recalled "phrases rounded with distant professorial unction" from his college days and wished that "Dover Beach" had been a little more like a poem of John Donne's. Mainly he found it unsatisfactory because of the shift in image from the sea to the plain—a complaint that is shortsighted and based on haphazard reading: for the shift of image may be regarded as one of the singular felicities of the poem—the plain as created by the ebbing of the sea of faith, the relation to it of the earlier images of light and the later ones of darkness, the use of these "objective correlatives" as ironical delineations of Arnold's problem—see John P. Kirby on "Arnold's *Dover Beach*," *Explicator* (1943), and Frederick L. Gwynn *et al.*, *The Case for Poetry* (1954). Still, Bradley Dewing has seen the poem as poem in a way that the scholar, the moralist, the psychological and social critics, and even Peter Lee Prampton have not. A comprehensive reading of the poem as poem serves as its own corrective and keeps the aesthetic from being merely aesthetical.

Such a comprehensive sense of the poem as poem marks, it seems to me, the renaissance in the reading of poetry in our own time. It has been given various names—close reading, formal or textual analysis, the New Criticism (in which rather it functions without being identical)—but most generally the word *explication* has been used for it. This I would define as the examination of a work of literature for a knowledge of each part and for the relation of these parts to each other and to the whole, a contemplative and comprehensive reading of the poem for all its values in their relationship. Though on another occasion I have tried to distinguish certain assumptions and discoveries that explication has made in the reading of poetry,[1] I have doubted the utility of this division. Rather I would now suggest that explication sees poetry as characterized by three major qualities. These are self-sufficiency, unity, and complexity.

I

In most respects the first quality, though affirming much in regard to the poem as poem, represents a clearing away of readers'

[1] See my Introducton to George Arms and Joseph M. Kuntz, *Poetry Explication: A Checklist* (1950). Parts of the present essay draw from this introduction.

dispositions to confuse the poem with something else—in the case of "Dover Beach" with Arnold's relation to Marguerite, with Arnold's philosophy as expressed in his essays, with Arnold's unexpressed psychological compulsions, or with Arnold's place in Victorian culture. Rather our reading of the poem should primarily be of a complete and fully articulated work of art, a poem (not a document) that is entirely self-contained. At one end, to be concerned with what Arnold was trying to say is the intentional fallacy; and at the other end, to be concerned with our response to it is the affective fallacy. These fallacies are discussed at length by W. K. Wimsatt, Jr., and Monroe C. Beardsley in *The Verbal Icon* (1954).

First, then, explication isolates the poem from biographical considerations, not regarding it as a message from author to reader but rather as an object that once produced by the author has an existence of its own. Perhaps few are so doctrinaire as to refuse any identification with the poet; yet there have been one or two, at least early in the development of this approach, and the practice in some textbooks of not identifying authors (except in the appendix) implies this rigorous attitude. As Wimsatt and Beardsley have pointed out, we have available three kinds of knowledge of a poem: internal, or the poem itself; external, or journals, letters, and interviews that tell us why and how and to whom the poem was written; and intermediate, or the private and semiprivate meanings of the poet. The internal meanings are really the public ones, accessible through dictionaries and grammars, while the external meanings are really private, not a part of the work as linguistic fact. Though these meanings shade into each other, to read a poem mostly on the first level is to read it quite differently—and more successfully—than on the second.

Yet perhaps some qualification of these distinctions is in order. Ultimately biographical intention becomes just as public as do the meanings of words; and the private meanings become public ones, even finding their place in dictionaries and grammars. *The Explicator* has regularly carried the notice, "Material concerned with genesis, parallelism, or biography cannot, however, be considered unless it has a direct bearing upon the interpretation of the text." Though some people objected because the editors thus admitted the *possibility* of biography affecting the work (so intense had become the movement toward isolation of the text), the position seems reasonable enough. Biography may at least give an intermediate help in reading, even if the perfect reader needs no such crutch. And at best biography may serve to check the irresponsibilities of the reader who thinks he is perfect but falls short of the ideal. Still everyone—whether explicator or not—must admit that the value of the poem is found in the poem itself: if we go along with the widespread exaltation of Elizabeth Barrett Browning's love for her husband or if we take the wryly psychological view of Betty Miller in her *Robert Browning: A Portrait* (1952), we still judge the *Sonnets from the Portuguese* as great or poor poetry on the basis of what they do—see Robert B. Heilman and William T. Going on "E. B. Browning's *Sonnet from the Portuguese, XLIII,*" *Explicator* (1945 and 1953).

The detachment of a poem from history was never so clearly urged by explication as the isolation from biography. But since the concern was more with contemporary literature than with past literature and since there was a sharp reaction against traditional scholarship, opponents could charge that explication sought to cut off the poem completely from its historical context. Certainly some kind of rapprochement between the view of literature as chronological order and that of literature as simultaneous order is needed, as Frederick A. Pottle has advised in his essay on "The New Critics and the Historical Method" in the *Yale Review* (1953). More pointedly Lionel Trilling has remarked in discussing "The Sense of the Past" in his *The Liberal Imagination* (1950), "If, for example, we try to make Shakespeare literally contemporaneous, we make him monstrous. He is contemporaneous only if we know how much a man of his own age he was; he is relevant to us only if we see his distance from us."

At its wisest explication would assent to both these cautions, but would still maintain the vital importance of the poem now. The beginning point is the now-meaning, and as far as teaching on lower levels is concerned, it is not wrong to stop with that, as traditional scholarship has complained. On the other side, a work that has only historical interest is only historical, serving fully in this fashion but not to be confused with literature, which must have literary value for the reader today. If indeed one had to discard the then-meaning or the now-meaning, explication would retain the now-meaning. But no such alternative is presented, and so the best readers will know both—and the meanings of intervening periods, out of which a certain richness derives that in itself adds to the work. Yet whatever the achievements of historical scholarship, explication would counsel that the then-meaning is inevitably misrepresented in its own time—sometimes drastically when taste has been inadequate to cope with the poem—and that the now-meaning is the point of consideration that the reader cannot escape—much as he would like to.

Increasingly, however, explication has become aware of the logical difficulties involved in viewing poetry as absolute in its self-sufficiency. To the extent that its detachment from author and time cuts it off from the reader's general core of knowledge, the poem becomes that much more difficult to know in any way. If in addition one cuts it off from its effect upon the reader, the poem becomes unknowable and it is best not to talk about it or to read it at all. Partly because he has faced this impasse, F. W. Bateson in *English Poetry: A Critical Introduction* (1950) holds that the ultimate criterion in poetic interpretation is " 'what the poet meant to his contemporaries,' i.e. the way his poem would have been understood by the particular social group to whom it was primarily addressed." But to limit the poem in this way would seem as unsatisfactory as the limitations imposed upon it by an absolute self-containment, for though it no longer cuts the poem off from knowledge it just as drastically separates it from experience. More successfully Murray Krieger has dealt with the problem in his recent study of *The New Apologists for Poetry* (1956), even though his solution is a less simple one:

> While I may be defending the autonomy of the poem, I will claim that the advantage of this position is not that it divorces poetry from life but rather that it enables poetry to reveal life to me in a unique and fresh way, a revelation it could not manage were it not autonomous, were its relations to life as immediate as they are in more referential forms of discourse.

But in the realm of self-sufficiency we have been consciously dealing with the negations. While explication has discarded the biographical and the historical to some extent, it has given greater force to the speaker of the poem (as distinct from the author) and to the situation in the poem (as distinct from the situation of the time). With a constant concern for point of view in its simplest sense of who is speaking and to whom and under what circumstances and in its more complex sense of the tone or mood of the poem, explication has brought the poem more closely into the reader's experience by its very assertion of the autonomy of the poem. Of course with the dramatic monologue, as Browning's "My Last Duchess" and its duke and envoy and palace, we hardly needed a new technique in reading to be aware of the particular quality of the poem; yet even with this poem, rather a good deal more can be known about it through a specific observation of the principles of point of view—see B. R. Jerman's "Browning's Witless Duke," *PMLA* (1957). With a dramatic lyric the reading by both the layman and the scholar has all too frequently bogged down from a lack of concern with point of view; without the sense of person and scene as revealed in the poem, Frost's "Stopping by Woods on a Snowy Evening" loses almost as much as "My Last Duchess" would lose if we regarded it as spoken by the author. Even in a descriptive lyric not to characterize the poet as he speaks from the poem and not to characterize his audience as it is assumed by the poem leads us to a response that at best is banal and at worst foolish. I would propose that the celebrated difficulties of Eliot's "Sweeney Among the Nightingales" derive less from obscurities of the allusions than from the reader's failure to comprehend point of view and tone.

Though tone is borrowed from the field of music, it has a meaningful currency in our ordinary language. "I like the tone of his voice," we say; or "I resent your tone" when we are quarreling— "When you say that, smile!" Explication has taught us unforgettably that a poem has a speaking voice, and that the occasion, the personality, and the situation as expressed in the poem are important things to look for, perhaps the most important things of all. It may have much more to teach us about ourselves as readers; as Walker Gibson has cogently observed in "Authors, Speakers, Readers, and Mock Readers," *CE* (1950), to distinguish between oneself as the actual reader and the mock reader "whose mask and costume the individual takes on in order to experience the language" is the beginning of literary wisdom—see also M. L. Rosenthal and A. J. M. Smith, *Exploring Poetry* (1955) and T. S. Eliot,

The Three Voices of Poetry (1954). Though at times explication has imparted a dramatic character to a poem beyond what the poem would bear, excess of zeal is better than lack of enterprise. Though Cleanth Brooks's specific detailing in *The Well Wrought Urn* (1947) of the speaker and situation in Gray's "Elegy" errs in some of its details, as I believe, he is getting farther into the poem than a description of it as "an imitative lyric of moral choice rather than of action or of mood." Yet even R. S. Crane's brief description of the poem in *The Languages of Criticism and the Structure of Poetry* (1953), of which the quoted words are only a part, touches upon point of view in describing the young man and his dramatic problem, and, as so often, demonstrates a greater closeness of reading techniques between the New and Chicago Critics than their theories seem to allow. Finally, to visit "Dover Beach" again, when we read the poem not as a communication from Arnold to a theologically disturbed Victorian audience but as the speaking voice of a man to his beloved on a beach fully located and described, we read the poem truly. In so far as Peter Lee Prampton comprehends this dramatic occasion through his identification of himself and his betrothed, he makes a reading better than Bradley Dewing's and his feeling for the tone as clear and eloquent can be defended as meaningful.

II

About the second major quality of poetry as known by explication, that of unity, less needs to be said, for with unity we have a concept more commonly accepted in the critical tradition than self-sufficiency and complexity. We find the basic statement in Aristotle— "Tragedy is an imitation of an action that is complete, and whole, and of a certain magnitude." Also, Aristotle looks upon the work of art metaphorically as a living tissue, from which the concept of an organic unity arises. Yet in Aristotle unity never becomes arbitrary or static, for its severity is mitigated and made vital by diversity. In its total concern for unity, however, explication has deepened and extended the idea, no longer a unity of this or of that, of action and character or the older time and place, but a totality of effect that considers all the aspects of the poem.

Possibly the primary problem of unity is that of form and content in the constant (one might even say provoking) tendency of these two aspects of the poem to separate from each other in any consideration of the work of art. T. S. Eliot, though not himself a practicer of explication, has in many ways been a leading theorist —as well as in his creative work a leading subject and even victim. And while he has been attacked for his dualism, it seems to me that he has come as close as anyone to resolving the problem when in "The Social Function of Poetry" (reprinted in R. W. Stallman's collection of *Critiques and Essays in Criticism, 1920–1948,* 1949) he says, "If we can enjoy the form while indifferent to the content, that poetry is for us mere virtuosity; if we can attend to the ideas and be indifferent to the words in which they are expressed, what we are reading is for us merely bad prose." But this pressing concern for the unity of all the parts of the poem can be found in every critical group in our present time, often more specifically designated than in Eliot. Indeed, René Wellek and Austin Warren in their *Theory of Literature* (1949) see the terms *content* and *form* as simply dichotomizing the work of art, and rather insist that "a literary work of art is not a simple object but rather a highly complex organization of a stratified character with multiple meanings and relationships." And Crane enumerates the "material elements of whatever kind—words, images, symbols, thoughts, character-traits, incidents, devices of representation—[which] are made to function in relation to a formal whole." Yet as Wimsatt has suggested in "Explication as Criticism," *The Verbal Icon* (1954), we do not in practice wait until we reach the end of a work of art before we appraise its parts as brilliant or dull, and he cites Coleridge's definition of a poem as a composition that proposes "to itself such delight from the *whole,* as is compatible with a distinct gratification from each component part." Good poems may have dull parts and bad poems bright parts. "Yet the validity of partial value as a general principle in tension with holism seems obvious. The whole with which explication is concerned is something elastic and approximate."

Though in their emphasis upon unity the Chicago and New Critics are at one, they show considerable difference in the particular aspect of unity to which they pay most attention. In the listing of elements made by Crane, that of theme or central idea has been omitted, for the belief that all poems have themes is one that he specifically repudiates. The New Critics would agree with him on the presence of a definite structure in any poetic work, but that structure would be less distinguished by a beginning, middle, and end than by a delineation of theme or by a collocation of images. Instead of forms as a sequence of events, some would see irony (a concept that we shall recur to) as producing a metaphoric structure that determines the manifold form and fuses it with content.

In emphasizing the presence of a central idea or theme, explication has avoided the reproaches both of an art-for-art's sake aestheticism and of a moralizing didacticism; it recognizes the ethical force of literature, yet in seeing the idea as infusing pattern does not detach it from pattern. Furthermore, with theme not so much abstract statement but metaphoric statement, the idea inheres even more closely in the poem. Possibly this view requires a redefinition of Aristotelian plot as a progress of meanings rather than a sequence of events; but the tracing of thematic imagery in the *Oresteia*, the location of the theme of *Macbeth* in the phrase "to outrun the pauser, reason," and the assertion of "metamorphosis" as the key metaphor in *The Tempest* accomplish more in both an Aristotelian and explicational spirit than the refusal to go beyond the limited consideration of plot that is basic but undeveloped in the *Poetics*.[2]

Explication then not only admits but insists upon the presence of ideas in poetry, yet refuses to allow the "truth" of these ideas to displace the poem or to exist as independent of it. Rather, as it has been suggested, "Philosophical ideas in poetry should be like those sculptures of Rodin's where the unfinished human or animal figure is left continuous with the unhewn stone." Or, as Philip Wheelwright elsewhere says in *The Burning Fountain: A Study in the Language of Symbolism* (1954):

> Even though an individual statement in a poem would be false if taken out of context (as is surely the case with Eliot's "jewelled unicorn" line and with Keats's "all ye need to know"), the relevant question is, How true is it within that context? And let us not delude ourselves with the hope that there are truths independent of any context whatever.

In recent years explication has met its severest critics in the

---

[2] See the series of papers on Aristotle by Philip Wheelwright, Francis Fergusson, and Reuben A. Brower in *English Institute Essays, 1951* (1952).

proponents of a mythic view of literature, who value poetry to the extent that it reveals archetypal experiences and insights that through the Cambridge anthropologists and the psychologist Jung have seemed to reveal a basic and vital truth shared in common by humanity. They have held that "myth is only art" (Richard Chase), assigning to art a religious function, or that the archetype that makes literature possible is the archetype of the poet (Leslie A. Fiedler), thus affirming the fundamental need of biographical study.[3] They look with disfavor upon explication in as much as it prizes an impersonal and self-contained art. But from the beginning those who practice explication have seen the possibility of recognizing myth without diverting the poem into a religious or biographical document. Thus the early *Archetypal Patterns of Poetry* (1934), by Maud Bodkin, observed myth in the self-contained unity of the poem; and in Brooks's observation expressed in the "Foreword" to Stallman's collection of *Critiques and Essays in Criticism* (1949) that "Words open out into the larger symbolizations on all levels—for example, into archetypal symbol, ritual, and myth," and in the whole of Wheelwright's *Burning Fountain* (1954), we find that a recognition of the poem as poem may be fully consonant with its mythic substratum.

III

The relation of myth and poetry is thus recognized by explication as an aspect of its complexity, which I have proposed as the third major quality of poetry as seen in this kind of reading. In dismissing simplicity as a virtue explication goes against much traditional criticism, yet not quite so much against it as may at first seem to be the case. For the simplicity that explication does not discover in poetry is the simplicity of plainness rather than the simplicity of appropriately integrated functions. Explication would, I think, hold that a poem by Donne in this latter sense is just as simple as a poem by Herrick. Yet since obviously explication has shown a good deal more concern for Donne than Herrick, the belief in complexity cannot be too easily dismissed.

The definition of explication in itself suggests a strong drive

[3] See William K. Wimsatt, Jr., and Cleanth Brooks, *Literary Criticism: A Short History* (1957) for citations of Chase and Fiedler, and for other matter in this paragraph.

toward those poems which have complexity and toward finding complexity in poems which might at first not seem to have it. The more possible relationships, the more explication will have to say. It has thus concerned itself more with the difficult and obscure poem. Worse, it has upon occasion produced a kind of ingeniousness and obfuscation in approaching poems that have little difficulty, producing the kind of explication burlesqued in a treatment of "Thirty Days Hath September" by Theodore Spencer in "How to Criticize a Poem (In the Manner of Certain Contemporary Critics)," *The New Republic* (1943), where it is discovered that "February is 'alone,' is cut off from communication with his fellows . . . the solitary and maladjusted individual who is obviously the hero and the crucial figure of the poem." As Eliot in *The Frontiers of Criticism* (1956) has described a recent volume of interpretations: "The method is to take a well-known poem . . . analyze it stanza by stanza and line by line, and extract, squeeze, tease, press every drop of meaning out of it that one can. It might be called the lemon-squeezer school of criticism."

Yet whenever a poem widely regarded as great has been squeezed in the press of explication, its interrelationships have proved more complex than most readers have consciously thought. If poems have been as simple as we used to say they were, it is small wonder that they have been as uninteresting to some people as they proved. That explication would only operate with a certain kind of poem—the metaphysical or the modern—was for a long time the principal charge against the method. But through Brooks's *The Well Wrought Urn* and similar works it became apparent that though particular metaphysical standards may not be applied everywhere, the *discordia concors* of metaphysical poetry exists in all poetry. The volume referred to by Eliot contains an explication of Bryant's "To a Waterfowl." To one satisfied with the usual headnote in anthologies that tells the old—and probably false— story of a forlorn Bryant glimpsing the bird on a walk from Cummington to Plainfield, eight pages will seem an excessive report of one's experience in reading it. But though freely observing its complexity, the explicator—in this instance, Donald Davie, writing of "Bryant: *To a Waterfowl*" in John Wain's collection of *Interpretations* (1955)—is also conscious of the need of not "multiplying the meanings to be found, but rather of limiting the meanings to those which are really there, excluding those that come from reading it in the wrong way, expecting things that the poem (not the poet) tells us, by inplication, not to expect." On the composition of the poem, see William Cullen Bryant, II, "The Waterfowl in Retrospect," *NEQ* (1957).

Another reason for the stress placed upon the complexity of the poem derives from a particular view of literature. Brooks, extending the belief of I. A. Richards in a "poetry of inclusion," has made the most outspoken plea for complexity, even positing a scale of poems from a low (or excluding) end to a high (or including) end. "Thus," Murray Krieger in *The New Apologists for Poetry* (1956) remarks, "we are led to imply that the more complexity the better, so that this theory easily lends itself to the sanctioning of complexity for complexity's sake." But as this critic also shows, Brooks's theory serves to distinguish poetry from science: the former by its adherence to reality cannot be asked to achieve the abstracting observation that science finds its proper goal. Brooks only expresses openly what other critics of his group have had in mind when they recognized in poetry the presence of texture or tension or impurity. But with them he keeps poetry, even in its complexity, from becoming synonymous with life; for complexity offers pattern as well as chaos. Even so, Krieger's note of caution deserves heeding: "The degree of complexity to be required for successful poetry should vary with the special needs of each poem."

As part of the subject of complexity, we must consider irony; and again we observe the close relation of Brooks and Richards. Richards first set the meaning and significance in his *Principles of Literary Criticism* (1949): "Irony in this sense consists in the bringing in of the opposite, the complementary impulses; that is why poetry which is exposed to it is not of the highest order, and why irony itself is so constantly a characteristic of poetry which is." This definition and emphasis has been enlarged by Brooks until irony or paradox has become the central fact of poetry, spreading out into a theory of language, of structure, of image, and of theme. The belief has not only undergone attack—see R. S. Crane, "The Critical Monism of Cleanth Brooks" in *Critics and Criticism* (1952)—but even those siding with Brooks have felt that the word was unsatisfactory, for to the layman it can scarcely rid itself of the connotation of sarcasm and to the literary critic its derivation from its traditional use in drama seems forced and its tendency to expand into an all-embracing abstraction dangerous. Perhaps the term *countersuggestion* may be preferable as conveying more immediately the essential element of irony (the presence of qualification or even reversal) and as not giving rise to a kind of mystical monism. Other alternatives have been proposed, as Wheelwright's "plurisignation" or Wimsatt's "multiple implication."

Whatever the term, the quality controls the complexity of poetry and allows an additional discrimination between poetry and other forms of discourse. Though its presence has always been recognized in metaphysical poetry, readers have observed it in other kinds of poetry only since explication has been practiced. While countersuggestion itself may run the danger of turning the poem itself into something else, perhaps its primary value is to keep the poem from becoming identical with an uncomplicated sentiment, a moral pronouncement, or a solemn myth. Admitting the limitations of laughter, Wimsatt and Brooks in *Literary Criticism: A Short History* (1957) have added, "But bright feelings and the smile go with metaphor and wit, and when playing on serious topics, wit generates a certain mimicry of substance which is poetry." Not only criticism but poetry can be fun.

Both complexity and countersuggestion look then toward the uniqueness that explication holds is the quality of every poem. Indeed, if each poem is not unique, then explication cannot justify its task, since this kind of reading functions in the continuing perception of relations present in each poem among the parts and the whole. Yet as with the other qualities, we would foolishly insist on an absolute uniqueness, for the same difficulty then arises that we have considered before: if the poem is unique in every particular, the reader comes to it without any experience of how to read it and the work is impervious to his approach. Of necessity, poems have qualities in common—the major qualities of self-sufficiency, unity, and complexity that are in the process of discussion—and innumerable minor qualities of tone and structure and image. Yet no two tones, explication would hold, are precisely alike; no two iambic pentameter lines, even if the words are the same, are identical in their context. Each poem is a living voice and a living creature, made even more various by art than nature allows. If in the face of hard logic we must sacrifice the absolute of uniqueness, we cannot give up the everpresent sense of freshness and of wonder.

With this sense of freshness and wonder in mind, explication has been ready not only to detach the poem from an historical context (if that implies that a work of art belongs more to its period than to itself), but also to give little note to the concept of genres. Yet it would hardly wish to ignore genre altogether, as the Chicago Critics reproach it with doing. Still, as elsewhere, the difference of the Chicago and the New Critics need not here be made too large, for according to Crane, in *The Languages of Criticism*, though we need general concepts to guide us, in our reading of poems we ought to look for the possibility of something unparalleled in each poem "inasmuch as it is the mark of good poets that they try to avoid repeating too often the inventions of others." Indeed, Crane contends that the Brooksian explicators come to a poem too fully equipped with specifications of what the poem ought to do and that the recognition of genres assists in realizing the essential uniqueness of each work of literature. To the extent that awareness of genre will accomplish this and is not the obscuring by classifying pedagogues in the past, all schools of explication will readily assent to its usefulness. But they must regard genre as the means and not the end.

Our final approach to the complexity of the poem will deal with image. As we have already seen, theme as metaphoric statement recognizes the centrality of image in the poem, and in general explication has revealed that an image or a related group of images is close to inevitable. Furthermore, images are seen by explication as always being in some degree symbols, whether out of traditional association, or by open or oblique explanation of the poet, or by their natural force. "Whether simple or complex, then," observe Rosenthal and Smith in *Exploring Poetry*, "the poetic symbol that gives direction to a poem is at the same time organizing a conception of reality or of the approach to some problem concerning it."

No more than elsewhere would I claim the sense of symbol as a conclusion arrived at by explication without the literary and cultural interplay of many other forces. The creations of the French symbolists, the speculations of Freud and Jung, and the treatises of Whitehead, Cassirer, and Langer have all contributed to the sense of language as a symbolizing force. The symbolistic outlook has attempted to resolve the dichotomy of the real and ideal, and in its literary applications Charles Feidelson in *Symbolism and American Literature* (1953) observes that the image and the meaning merge: "If the two terms are seen under the aspect of each other, the *real* tenor is a meaning produced by the interaction of the two terms, which together form the vehicle [the 'image']." But William York Tindall in *The Literary Symbol* (1955) has pointed out that the reader as distinguished from the philosopher cannot talk about symbolism without some kind of working distinction. "By analysis of image and context he may reveal the shape of the image, the relation of part to part and to the whole, and the function of each part." Though the radiance of the poem cannot be reduced to discursive statement, it is thus through the practice of explication that some sense of that radiance may be communicated as well as comprehended.

IV

Well aware of the discomfort of explication in considering poetry as a part of the historical context, we may still find it proper to look at this movement in close reading as it has developed during the past thirty years. To do so is not to be inconsistent, but rather to recognize that criticism exists within time and depends on time in a way that poetry does not.

Though I would fix the beginning of explication with the appearance of Richards' *Practical Criticism* in 1929, it would be brash to propose explication as something altogether new. In back of Aristotles' *Poetics* we may presume explication, since the conclusions that he makes about tragedy derive from a study of the individual works. And of course in all literary criticism one has putatively this basis, though most critics between Aristotle and the present give less evidence of an inductive approach. Actually the first explication that we know is that of a poem by Sappho in Longinus's *On the Sublime;* these few lines also have considerable interest in that they anticipate the element of countersuggestion that later explicators have so frequently been concerned with. Probably Longinus was not doing an unusual thing, and in the annotations and introductions of Alexandrian scholiasts there is explication of a fashion, though its direction lies more toward an explanation of parts than in the contemplative study of relationships.

Something of this direction is also present in neoclassical criticism, though here the modern explicator has the greater reason to be disappointed in an inelastic and mechanical approach to the work of art. The "examen" had been practiced by French critics, and Dryden seems first to have introduced it into English. But his several pages on Jonson's *The Silent Woman* do not look upon the play as a work of dramatic art to the extent that we might suppose from the holistic tenor of his remarks elsewhere in *An Essay of Dramatic Poesy*. With greater success Johnson practices explication both in his *Lives of the Poets* and in his edition of Shakespeare. But for both poems and plays Johnson concerns himself with passages rather than the whole; and while the acuteness of his understanding cannot be questioned, it is instructive to compare his treatment of Gray's "Elegy" with those of Brooks or Crane already mentioned.

More certainly Coleridge brings us into the modern practice of explication, yet more through his theory, with its emphasis upon organic form and the reconciliation of opposites, than from his practice. Because of this, though Coleridge's actual reading of poetry is disappointing, one seldom feels the piecemeal or mechanistic shortcomings of the neoclassical critics.

Occasional explicational passages in critical writing appear throughout the nineteenth century, but a substantial gap exists between Coleridge and Richards. Perhaps the most important predisposing factor in creating a new interest in close reading was what René Wellek, writing of "Literary Scholarship," in Merle Curti's *American Scholarship in the Twentieth Century* (1953), has called "the useless antiquarianism, the dreary factualism, the pseudoscience combined with anarchical skepticism and lack of critical taste"[4] that characterized literary study toward the end of the period. Less negatively, the growing need for a defense of poetry against science by indicating what was the true province

---

[4] The fourth volume of René Wellek's *A History of Modern Criticism*, only the first two volumes of which are now published, may be expected to give a definitive account of the history of modern explication.

of poetry played a strong part. Also positively and more specifically, the new poets of the Renaissance of 1912 were baffling to even the well-intentioned reader, so that the critics' function became more to make sense and less to judge—a shift in activity that the Browning clubs in the late nineteenth century foreshadowed and that reached a culmination with such modern puzzlers as Eliot. But just when the demands for an alert reading of poetry became greater, the neoclassical tradition of reading had faded perceptibly. Bateson believes that the disappearance of annotation from anthologies and reprints is revealing. In *English Poetry: A Critical Introduction*, he says, "Apparently up to about 1900 or so readers of English poetry *expected* to have the obscure expressions and the literary and topical allusions explained to them. And then, apparently quite suddenly, the expectation ceased." Yet in France at least on the school level the practice of *explication de texte* flourished (though as paraphrase rather than examination of the whole as an art form), and on critical levels among the Russians, Czechs, and Poles in the early 1920's a school of formalists was active.

Probably Richards did not know the continental formalists. Certainly his method was pedagogical at its inception, but most of all his great respect for Coleridge appears to have led him to confront the text of poetry in a fashion more thorough and intelligible than was then known in England. Though his *Foundations of Aesthetics* (1922) contained no explication and his *Principles of Literary Criticism* (1924) contained only a little, both voice the basis of the program. In *Practical Criticism* (1929), the report of the experiment with classes at Cambridge in the reading of thirteen poems, we have the clear starting point. Perhaps the greater significance of the book is not in Richards' own reading of the poems, which is casual as judged by today's standards, but in the distressing inadequacies of the students' "protocols"—a more naïve and unsatisfactory collection of falsifications and stock responses than one could possibly have expected and a clear signal of the need for a new kind of reading technique. The fact that the majority of the students were candidates for an honors degree made their faults even more grievous.

A year later William Empson's *Seven Types of Ambiguity* appeared, a work undoubtedly owing greatly to Richards though directly showing the influence of *A Survey of Modernist Poetry* (1928), by Laura Riding and Robert Graves. The authors of the books were poets themselves, and they stressed the linguistic complexity (the ambiguities or countersuggestions) of the poems that were studied. In both books there are relatively few systematic explications, but especially Empson's volume proved a landmark in the development of explication for its complex sensitivity and at times nearly unending exhaustion of the potentialities of the poems that were read. Though Eliot himself has not practiced explication, his own critical essays, beginning with *The Sacred Wood* in 1920, and his editorship of *The Criterion* from 1922 to 1939 provided a favorable literary climate. In *Scrutiny*, founded by F. R. Leavis in 1932, a fuller practicing of analytical reading is present, as also in Leavis' book *New Bearings in English Poetry* of the same year.

In America explication has centered around the writings of Cleanth Brooks, who as a Rhodes Scholar attended Oxford from 1929 to 1932, thus studying in England as the books by Graves and Riding, Richards, and Empson were making their appearance. Though resisting Richards' focus on the effect upon the reader rather than on the poem itself, Brooks followed Richards closely in his organic approach and particularly drew from him the concept of irony, extending it in the fashion that we have already noted. Returning to this country to teach at Louisiana State University, he founded the *Southern Review* in 1935 with Robert Penn Warren, also a Rhodes Scholar, and in the following year published with Warren and John T. Purser *An Approach to Literature*, in which a number of explications appeared. Far more influential was his next anthology for classroom use, also a collaboration with Warren, *Understanding Poetry* in 1938, which with explications more thorough and numerous than the earlier textbook became the classic book of poetry reading in the next decade.

Without detracting from the singular place of Brooks in the new reading of poetry, the contributions of others must be mentioned both in respect to them and as indication of the breadth of the movement. Symptomatic of distaste for a limited historicism and also of the early activity of the Chicago group, an influential essay by R. S. Crane "History Versus Criticism in the University Study of Literature" appeared in *The English Journal* (College

edition) (1935). The critical volumes by Allen Tate and John
Crowe Ransom, both older members of the Fugitive group at
Vanderbilt, where Brooks and Warren had studied as undergraduates, began to be issued in the 1930's; and Ransom's founding
of *The Kenyon Review* in 1939 provided another periodical even
more replete with explication than the earlier *Southern Review*.
Three years after the appearance of *Understanding Poetry* two
similar volumes for classroom use appeared, *Reading Poems* by
Wright Thomas and Stuart G. Brown and *The Art of Reading
Poetry* by Earl Daniel. That both these critical anthologies were
less closely allied with the New Criticism perhaps signifies the
growth of explication on a more general literary scene. In this
connection it should also be noted that just before *An Approach
to Literature* was published, Richard R. Kirk's and Roger P. Mc-
Cutcheon's *Introduction to the Study of Poetry* (1934) and Walter
Blair's and W. K. Chandler's *Approaches to Poetry* (1935) set
true if less formal explicational patterns. Since Kirk and Mc-
Cutcheon were teaching at Tulane during the year that Brooks
studied there as a graduate student, they perhaps had influenced
the formation of Brooks' techniques as a reader of poetry.

The widespread use of the term *explication* for this new reading of poetry comes from *The Explicator*, founded by a group of
four teachers in 1942—see John P. Kirby, "The Last Verse . . . Is
Not Sufficiently Explicated," *Virgina Librarian* (1956). Consciously indebted for their interest in close reading to Brooks and
his associates, the editors planned the magazine as "a clearing-
house for *explication de texte*" that would not be limited to one
school of explication and would draw widely on the contributions
of traditional scholars as well as of critics of different schools. As
I have already indicated, the admission of readings that utilized
biographical and historical contexts seemed to some at the time of
the founding a betrayal of the true principles of the explicational
method. The editors insisted upon a brevity in explications partly
because the size of the magazine did not allow more generous
treatment, but in addition they sensed an unnecessary verbalization
of analysis that lent itself too easily to jargon and to a displacement of the poem by the commentary upon it.

Since the middle 1940's explication has become so widely
practiced that it is almost impossible to open a book of literary

criticism or a journal of literary history without finding some display of it. An annual checklist of explication in the June issues of *The Explicator* has grown from twelve pages (for 1944) to sixteen pages (for 1956) in spite of an increasing severity on the part of its compilers in limiting the entries to unmistakable explication. A checklist attempting to gather explications of British and American poems between 1925 and 1949, *Poetry Explication* (1950) cites about seventeen hundred explications, even while omitting those from books devoted to single authors and making other exclusions. Material since 1949 would easily double the size of a revised volume; and each year sees the publication of several books patterned to some extent upon the pioneering effort of *Understanding Poetry*.

V

The vast popularity of explication would in itself bring about a reaction, and as I have indicated in considering the characteristics there are a number of rational reasons for discounting if not discrediting the activities of this kind of reading. As early as 1942 Lionel Trilling had remarked in the *Partisan Review* that "the elucidation of poetic ambiguity" often becomes " a kind of intellectual calisthenic ritual." In 1950 we have Edmund Wilson's allusion in the *New Yorker* to the "expounding of texts" that "makes such very dull reading for anybody except another expounder and the key to which, I am afraid, is that proud realization of the man in Molière that he had been talking prose all his life." As we have already seen, the proponents of myth view explication with lacklustre or disdainful eye. Thus Leslie A. Fiedler in "In the Beginning Was the Word," *SR* (1955) opens his consideration of "*logos* or *mythos*" with these words: "When the callowest doctoral candidate shuns the heresy of the paraphrase, the orthodoxy of non-paraphrase becomes unbearable, and someone tacks up a declaration on the church door: *a poem is its ideas; poetry is idea, etc.*" The New Critics themselves have frequently doubted the value of the practice that they have followed. But William Empson, of the seven ambiguities, has humorously observed in "The Verbal Analysis," *KR* (1950): "It is not my fault, or the fault of any other analytical critic, that our equipment threatens to make us become bores; it is wonderful how many ways there are to be a bore, and almost any line of intellectual effort, however true and useful, presents this threat."

Those most pledged to explication welcome the vigor and forthrightness and good sense of the critics who attack a close reading of the texts. Explication is less in danger than other critical approaches because it constantly renews itself at the source of literature, but it too may forget that criticism by its nature is subordinate to poetry and that the mechanical adherence to formal doctrine or the ingenious proliferating of its obscurities spells ruin. Some explicators have lost their humanity, which probably can be lost in close reading as well as in other ways. Dehumanization is just as manifold in its varieties as are the ways of becoming a bore.

Let us take as a closing text a couple of sentences from "Poetry: A Note in Ontology" in *The World's Body* (1938) by John Crowe Ransom, himself a master reader of poetry and the namer of the New Criticism. "People who are engrossed with their pet 'values' become habitual killers [of literature]. Their game is the images, or the things, and they acquire the ability to shoot them as far off as they can be seen, and do." But explication is not the only kind of killing. In a recent review of "Criticism Today," *Essays in Criticism* (1956), by W. K. Wimsatt, Jr., several ways of murdering literature have been pointed out: the interpretation of a poem in terms of its contemporary audience, the insistence on the need for doing justice to over-all structures, the principle of criticism by myth and ritual origins, the limiting of myth to Christian sacramentalism, and the approach through "communication" to a pragmatic rhetorical scheme. Though in my own view these ways are fruitful—fine forms of homicide, if you will—all show some uneasiness with literature as literature, all tend to substitute something else for the business at hand. But explication, to the extent that it is honestly practiced, cannot do this. Perhaps it is not a killer after all.

And perhaps the danger of all approaches to poetry—including explication—is not so much of becoming killer as becoming the corpse. C. S. Lewis, in considering the vulnerability of theory in the face of truth, writes in *Rehabilitations and Other Essays* (1939): "I find a beautiful example proposed in the *Paradiso*

(xxviii) where poor Pope Gregory, arrived in Heaven, discovered that his theory of the hierarchies, on which presumably
he had taken pains, was quite wrong. We are told how the redeemed soul behaved; '*di sè medesmo rise.*' It was the funniest thing
he'd ever heard." But the soul in order to be redeemed has arrived
in Paradise—the man is dead. So for our unredeemed state and while
we are alive the explicational approach to poetry is not perverse or
funny (and not so perfect or so serious as its competing popes
may wish to make it) but a substantial perception. Poetry, like
religion, is a paradox, and explication has at least learned to get
along with that fact.

14

The Novel

BRADFORD A. BOOTH

CONTEMPLATING THE DEVELOP-
ment of fiction as a serious art form, Zola once remarked that the
various classes of literary production were being merged in the
novel, and would ultimately disappear within it. This has not
precisely occurred, and no doubt Zola did not intend that his
prediction should be interpreted literally. But it is well understood that the limits of the novel have been greatly expanded in the
twentieth century to embrace, if not absorb, other forms and
techniques. A century ago novels were chiefly justified by their
moral value and sustained by their entertainment value. Craftsmanship was wholly a matter of instinct, there being no codified theory
of fiction. The aesthetics of the novel, while certainly not completely lost upon such writers as Dickens, George Eliot, and
Meredith, had to wait for organization and coherent expression
until Henry James bent his fine critical intelligence to the task.
James's dedication to fiction as an art led him to attempt a systema-
tization of its principles as he practiced them. The result was so
clearly fundamental, and sank so many pilings into the shifting
sands of early critical opinion, that later writers have felt no need
to do more than add to, but not alter, the Jamesian structure. A
review of modern criticism of the novel properly and, indeed,
inevitably begins with James.

One of the results of James's critical awareness was the interest
in fiction which it generated among persons trained in poetry and
the drama. It soon became apparent to many of these people that
the purposes and techniques of the older forms could be effectively
served by the novel, and there followed, beginning with Conrad
about a half century ago, a period of experimentation in prose
fiction that perhaps reached its apogee in *Finnegans Wake*. What

James recognized in 1914 as "the new novel" was thoughtful, artistic, and often poetic. It dared to be bold and iconoclastic in form, and in its exposition of the problems of man's adjustment to society it called to its aid the hypotheses of psychology. Important movements of the twentieth century—such as naturalism, surrealism, and existentialism—are not only reflected but often had their origin in the novel and then spread to other forms. And the *rapprochement* between fiction, art, and music was never closer.

But the most significant aspect of the modern novel, that which most sharply differentiates it from the novel of the nineteenth century, is its concern with problems long considered the province of the philosopher. The Victorian novel expressed itself, for the most part, in terms of the bourgeois (or, as Mario Praz calls it, the "Biedermeier") attitude toward life, which conceives meanings and values as imposed by authority—family, church, or state. The modern novel, by contrast, viewing man as the creator of his own existence, propounds a new concept of human reality: the consciousness of experience. To understand, to assimilate, and to utilize fruitfully the full breadth of one's experience is to discover both oneself and the function of life. The distinguished novelists of the twentieth century—English, American, and continental (particularly French)—have been less concerned with a description of visible, outward reality than a study of man's inner consciousness. Proust and Kafka and Faulkner, for example, have regarded the "real" world as too chaotic to be reproduced in intelligible terms, and they have sought rather to explore the intricate, fluid world of individual consciousness. As they follow their characters' desperate quest for personal salvation, our novelists have perhaps been contributing to the old debate on the freedom of the will but from a new, non-moral point of view.

It is perfectly clear, at any rate, that the novel today is a serious form of art and that it serves notably many functions which historically it was not thought sufficiently flexible to attempt. So recently has this position been established, however, that criticism of fiction is still tentative and uncertain. But trained minds, operating from both the creative and the historical point of view, have been addressing themselves to the formidable tasks of analysis and codification. In the pursuit of their inquiries they have looked at fiction from many angles and perspectives: they have studied the social and cultural responsibilities of a novelist, charting the areas with which he may or *should* be concerned; they have approached the novel from the tangent of psychology, patiently examining the meaning of myth and symbol, and studying the current experiments in stream of consciousness; they have discussed at length the technical problems of fiction, many of which, such as point of view, have been faced up to only in our time; and they have enriched the critical literature with a series of historical and scholarly investigations—such as fresh critical surveys, biographies, bibliographies, and editions of letters—that emphasize the originality and vitality of the criticism of fiction in our time. It is primarily from these points of view that I wish to comment on recent trends and developments.

I

Literature expresses, in essence, the temper of an age in terms of imaginative art. Some of its forms, such as poetry, are, of course, highly personal and record individual reactions; others, such as the novel, while by no means relinquishing the personal approach, are more likely to shadow forth a composite view of the social and cultural milieu. Thus, fiction in the United States since World War I (and perhaps to a lesser degree fiction in England) has reflected the crosscurrents of national ideologies in the process of formation and reformation. The task of criticism is accurately to describe trends and purposes as well as to render aesthetic value judgments, and therefore much that has been lately written about the novel has dealt with its social implications.

The critical literature of the nineteenth century and of the early twentieth century falls largely in the so-called genteel tradition. Barrett Wendell, Brander Matthews, and other seaboard essayists had no enthusiasm for the protonaturalists Crane, Norris, and London. Nevertheless, Upton Sinclair, David Graham Phillips, and the "muckrakers" established themselves so firmly that Matthews was obliged in such papers as "The Economic Interpretation of Literary History" (1912) to consider what relationships might exist in these areas. After the First World War, criticism of the novel became increasingly dominated by social and political biases. V. F. Calverton in *The Newer Spirit* (1925) and in *The*

Liberation of American Literature (1932) could go so far as to say that the only novelists of importance today "who have not surrendered to the pessimism and pathology which are predominant in American literature are those who are exponents of the proletarian outlook: John Dos Passos, Michael Gold, and Charles York Harrison." Vernon Louis Parrington, whose *Main Currents of American Thought* (1927–30) had an enormous influence in shaping the critical judgment of a generation of college students was so little interested in belles-lettres that he dismissed Henry James in two pages as a novelist who represented the American "nostalgia for culture." James was "the last subtle expression of the genteel, who fell in love with culture and never realized how poor a thing he worshiped."

A critic whose work is something of a touchstone of modern social criticism of fiction is Granville Hicks. In *The Great Tradition* (1933) Hicks set up standards for the perfect Marxian novel, and in contending, in effect, that American literature has merit only to the extent that it is revolutionary, he excluded from the great tradition such writers as Hawthorne, Melville, James, and Crane. But it is interesting to note Hicks's recantation in a recent article on "Fiction and Social Criticism," *CE* (1952). He no longer holds that novels of "denunciation and exposure" constitute our great tradition. There are, he explains, two kinds of social novels—those of social protest, which inveigh against a specific evil, such as slavery, working conditions in the Chicago stockyards, or exploitation of the Okies; and those of social criticism, which are concerned with the structure of society in a broader and deeper way. It is clear that the novel of social protest, except at its best, when it enters the area of social criticism, is ephemeral; and that Hicks recognizes his error in having attached to it such an inflated value.

Hicks dates the decline of the novel of social protest from August 22, 1939—the time of the Nazi-Russian non-aggression pact. It may also be convenient to peg to the same date the change in the critical attitude toward social fiction, though in point of fact the shift began to develop a few years earlier. Hicks himself had renounced Communism by 1938. Hitler's saber-rattling, breaking in upon a mood of intense isolationism and absorption in economic and social problems, turned American attention outward; and when war came there was an immediate rededication to somewhat dusty ideals. There has been some complaint lately that after the war patriotism was allowed to harden into glorification of a shallow nationalism. In an article on "Mobilizing our Novelists" John Lydenberg called attention to articles in *Life* and in the *Saturday Review* in which novelists were criticized for not emphasizing the smiling aspects of American life. Such critics as John Chamberlain, J. Donald Adams, and Gerald W. Johnson have been implying, we are told, that our pessimistic novelists have missed the essence of American life. But it is the duty and responsibility of our novelists, unlike the Russian, who must support official doctrines, to examine the current orthodoxies with vigilant attention. Lydenberg advances the tradition of Howells, Garland, and Norris against the tradition of gentility, which leans upon the innocuous, the sentimental, the unreal. The only social cause which in recent years has stimulated novelists is racial discrimination; and however much remains to be done on that score, very little remains to be said. The present danger is that in the complacency of our prosperity we shall forget that the American novelist, from Brackenridge to Dos Passos, has functioned as collective conscience. Recent criticism has been an effective reminder.

Arthur Mizener, writing on "The Novel of Manners in America," *KR* (1950), describes two lines of interest which the fiction of our time has pursued: one is the socio-political assertion of the value of the community, the other is the aesthetic assertion of the value of the individual consciousness. Many critics seem to be convinced that the first of these had run its course and that the chief task of the novel today is to transcribe states of mind and soul, and to develop techniques that will convey nuances of feeling. Mizener holds, however, that the resources of the novel must be devoted to something more important than either the intense, personal apprehension of experience or the collective social apprehension of it—namely, "the problem of absorbing into the felt, personal awareness out of which good writing comes the huge, impersonal world presented with such deadening inhumanity by journalists and historians." This, indeed, is the problem of the novelist today.

In "The Future of English Fiction," *PR* (1948), V. S. Pritchett argues that the novelist today functions as historian. The old story concepts—hero, heroine, and villain—are dead. Now the novelist, often registering private sensibilities only, has become the historian of the crises of civilization. To this extent he is still the recorder of social and cultural changes. Toward the close of the nineteenth century a long period of individualism came to an end. A man could no longer be sustained by his own efforts, and became increasingly dependent upon large collective and technical processes. As these threatened, or seemed to threaten, his security, he was advised by many novelists to turn to Marxian solutions. When this remedy failed, there developed, particularly in the 'forties, a strong movement in the direction of the Christian tradition, with its cognizance of sin and its emphasis on values. Albert Roland in "A Rebirth of Values in Contemporary Fiction," *Western Humanities Review* (1952), comments on the strength and vigor of the neo-Thomism of Green, Mauriac, and Waugh; the existentialism of Beauvoir and Camus; and the Oriental mysticism of Huxley, Maugham, and Isherwood. In a very real sense the novelist of the twentieth century has been cultural historian, and criticism has been throughly aware of the way in which he has dramatized the social pressures and tensions of our time.

II

It has been seen that the chief characteristic of the twentieth-century novel is the writer's assumption of what Leon Edel calls the mind's-eye view. The symbolists' revolt against nineteenth-century naturalism resulted at last in an inward turning of the attention to examine not society and its varied external relationships to the individual but the human consciousness itself. It is not too much to say that the history of fiction in our time is the history of the psychological novel. In its rejection of externalized event in favor of a deliberate plunge into the experience of the mind, the psychological novel has not only added a new dimension to fiction but has revolutionized the art by providing entirely new purposes and perspectives. Criticism today fully recognizes the shift of emphasis that, beginning with Henry James, led from a careful examination of the social milieu to the study of the sensibility through which the social milieu is apprehended.

James had a quick appreciation of many facets of the Victorian novel, but he consistently inveighed against the penchant for authorial intrusion in the form of editorial asides. In his own practice he adopted a dramatic method of presentation in which he remained determinedly in the wings. The removal of the author from the scene produced two important narrative shifts: first, the reader became, of necessity, co-creator with the author; and second, the mental processes of the characters became the only links between past, present, and future. The familiar Victorian "story" gave way to the Jamesian situation—normally six characters in search of a plot—and this in turn yielded to the stream of consciousness novel, which Joyce carried to its apparent conclusion in *Finnegans Wake*.

A considerable proportion of contemporary criticism has been devoted, very properly, to identifying and defining the stream of consciousness novel, and to discussing the animating purposes and techniques of its practitioners. In 1890 William James in his *Principles of Psychology* brilliantly described the tides of thought, with its continuities and discontinuities, and hit upon the metaphor "stream of consciousness" to suggest its flux. The Victorian novelists, not so unaware of the subjective life as is sometimes assumed, understood that it might be *reported*, but they did not perceive how it might be vividly and concretely *rendered*.

In *The Psychological Novel, 1900–1950* (1955), a brilliant study of this form, Leon Edel points out that the credit for having first conceived how thought might be arrested and examined, how disruptive fancies intruding upon and interrupting the rational process might be captured, how fringes and aureoles of unconscious suggestion might be rendered intelligible in fiction, belongs not to James nor, indeed, to Dorothy Richardson but to Edouard Dujardin, who published *Les Lauriers sont coupés* in 1888. This now famous novel went quite unnoticed at the time, but in 1902 it was read by James Joyce, and its influence upon the stream of consciousness technique of *Ulysses* was freely and enthusiastically acknowledged. Dujardin's work was then reprinted and widely studied, and there came to its old and long neglected author an international fame for which he had long since abandoned hope.

The new edition of Dujardin carried a preface by the critic

Valéry Larbaud in which the extraordinary method of narration developed in *Les Lauriers* was christened interior monologue ("le monologue intérieur"). In 1931 Dujardin sought in a lecture to attribute the first use of the phrase to Paul Bourget. Wherever the precedence may rest, Larbaud gave it its present currency and alerted a generation of novelists and critics to the potential of subjective fiction so designed. Interior monologue is, of course, inseparable from stream of consciousness fiction, but a considerable critical literature has grown up about its exact definition. Dujardin, looking back at what he had done with perhaps some surprise, defined interior monologue as follows:

The internal monologue, like every monologue, is the speech of a given character, designed to introduce us directly into the internal life of this character, without the author's intervening by explaining or commenting, and like every monologue, is a discourse without listener and a discourse unspoken:

but it differs from the traditional monologue in that:

as regards its substance, it expresses the most intimate thoughts, those closest to the unconscious;

as regards its spirit, it is discourse prior to all logical organization, reproducing thought in its original state and as it comes into the mind,

as for its form, it is expressed by means of direct sentences reduced to a syntactic minimum;

thus it responds essentially to the conception which we have today of poetry.

By way of summary he added:

The internal monologue, in its nature on the order of poetry, is that unheard and unspoken speech by which a character expresses his inmost thoughts, those lying nearest the unconscious, without regard to logical organization—that is, in their original state—by means of direct sentences reduced to syntactic minimum, and in such a way as to give the impression of reproducing the thoughts just as they come into the mind.

The best and fullest discussion of interior monologue is to be found in Lawrence E. Bowling's "What Is the Stream of Consciousness Technique?" *PMLA* (1950).[1] Bowling contends that:

[1] The French text of Dujardin's definition of interior monologue is reproduced in this article.

If interior monologue is what Dujardin really means, his definition should be revised to apply to only that part of a character's interior life *farthest* from the unconscious; on the other hand, if he intends to include *all* conscious mental processes, then his definition should be made sufficiently comprehensive to include such non-language phenomena as images and sensations, and the technique which he is defining should be called not *interior monologue* but *the stream of consciousness technique.*

Dujardin's mistake lies in his assumption that the *whole* of consciousness can be rendered in language. Much that impinges importantly on the mind consists of mere sensory impressions—sights, sounds, and smells—which may make themselves felt when the mind is more or less passive; they are not susceptible of satisfactory record by interior monologue. Interior monologue, while useful for limited purposes, cannot, then, bring in a total report of the conscious and unconscious mind with all external stimuli. Bowling's conclusion is that "the stream of consciousness technique may be defined as that narrative method by which the author attempts to give *a direct quotation of the mind*—not merely of the language area but of the whole consciousness." Perhaps the most familiar example of the technique is Molly Bloom's forty-five page monologue, which brings *Ulysses* to its triumphant and soul-shattering close. It is more than interior monologue, for it presents directly and dramatically the whole of consciousness, or as much as can be apprehended and transmitted by a process that is inevitably selective.

Bowling points out that much of what is often called stream of consciousness writing is merely internal analysis. Henry James, for example, places his characters in difficult emotional situations which demand decisions profoundly affecting their lives. There may be no *plot* in the usual sense. The only action in one twenty-page chapter of *The Golden Bowl* is Adam Verver's turning a doorknob; meanwhile James examines with meticulous care Verver's state of mind as he stands at the threshold. But James does not introduce us *directly* into the interior life of Verver. He remains apart and subtly interprets what the character thinks and how he feels. This is internal analysis. It differs more in degree than in kind from the Thackerayan or Trollopian aside. Even Dorothy

Richardson intervenes between character and reader to interpret and to analyze. Faulkner, however, in *The Sound and the Fury* presents the maunderings of idiot Benjy in rigorous stream of consciousness, and Virginia Woolf in *Mrs. Dalloway* and, particularly, *The Waves* employs interior monologue consistently; both dispense entirely with internal analysis.

It might be pointed out that there has been some dispute over terminology. Bowling and others speak of the stream of consciousness *technique*, but Robert Humphrey, whose excellent study *Stream of Consciousness in the Modern Novel* (1954) is one of the two best works on this subject, in " 'Stream of Consciousness': Technique or Genre?" *PQ* (1951) contends that the phrase denotes a genre not a technique. He points out that novels in this tradition have as their essential subject matter the consciousness of one or more characters, and that "consciousness" comprehends the *whole* area of mental attention, from the "unconscious" through all levels of mind up to that of rational, communicable awareness. It is with this last area that almost all psychological fiction is concerned. But stream of consciousness fiction differs precisely in that it is concerned with the other levels as well. Therefore Humphrey defines stream of consciousness as a type of fiction "in which strong emphasis is placed on exploration of the pre-speech levels of consciousness for the purposes, primarily, of revealing the psychic being of the characters." There is no stream of consciousness *technique*, he argues; there are simply a variety of techniques which are used to present the stream of consciousness.

Another study that should be consulted by students of this genre is Melvin J. Friedman's *Stream of Consciousness: A Study in Literary Method* (1955). Happily, Humphrey's book and Friedman's are complementary rather than duplicative, and the area of overlapping is slight. Humphrey's approach is how-to-do-it, and Friedman's is historical, with emphasis not only on French antecedents but on the philosophical, psychological, and musical aspects of the subject. Friedman's study is throughly scholarly but not forbiddingly so.

Nothing has been clearer to critics in recent years than that the novel has been approaching the condition of poetry. This was inevitable as soon as James and other late Victorians began to consider fiction as a serious art form. But the development was hastened by experiments in techniques to render the stream of consciousness. In *The Waves*, for example, where the characters speak aloud no single word but merely soliloquize mentally in each other's presence, there is no apparent author, no set description of locale, no identification or qualification of speech. The novelist has, obviously, only words and images with which to create impressions and record emotions. To suggest feeling, to catch tone and mood, he must rely on metaphor, building to stunning effect by an architecture of densities, nuances, and ellipses borrowed from the language of poetry. It could scarcely be otherwise than that the novelist with such purposes and materials should turn for models to the symbolist poets and search out the devices of their imagery. To reproduce the fleeting and often chaotic images of the mind he has found it necessary to exploit all the cunning twists to which the language is susceptible; indeed, as with Joyce, he has sometimes created an idiom of his own.

The only legitimate purpose of fiction is to transform experience into art. In the nineteenth century novelists sought to do this, first, by the methods of romance and, second, by the methods of naturalism. By the 1850's or 1860's the romanticism of Scott and the sensation novelists had largely run its course, to be succeeded by the realism of Thackeray, Trollope, and George Eliot. This in turn gave way late in the century to naturalism, which developed chiefly under the influence of the French novel. But, as Charles I. Glicksberg has pointed out, the novelists soon exhausted the aspects of reality that lend themselves to such treatment: heredity, neuroticism, alcoholism, prostitution, the class war, political corruption, gangsterism, the drab life of large cities, and the like. Such work, no matter how skillfully done, is seldom likely to rise far above journalism, and the novel must not stop with reportage of fact. An art form must transmute an inchoate mass of material into a valid and ordered interpretation of life. The most significant novelists of our time have sought to do this by conceiving the novel in terms of symbol, image, and myth.

The symbolic novel attempts to discover truth not in facts only but rather in relationships. Just as the poet speaks through figures of speech, bringing both like and unlike things together for the light that one throws upon the other, the novelist calls to his aid myth and symbol to illustrate his vision of reality. But since his reality is relativistic rather than empirical he may introduce visions, dream fragments, moral volitions, introspections, subjective fancies, and free associations. The result is a multi-dimensioned reality quite confusing to the reader who is accustomed to expository statement and unadorned fact. The most familiar exemplar of the symbolic novel is Kafka, and criticism has busied itself in the last decades with exegeses of his techniques and with descriptions of his influence upon the fiction of our time. Unlike Joyce, Kafka has been perhaps more talked about than read, for his Poesque, dream-haunted symbolism, so weird and so extravagant, suggests a neuroticism that many readers find unpleasant. As Glicksberg says, "He describes vividly enough the contradictory and inscrutable aspects of life, the conflicting impulses at war in the human soul, the struggle between sin and redemption, but his creative method, which discerns a hidden intention and mystical significance in every phenomenon, results often in a Swedenborgian nightmare."

In spite of the artistic importance of symbolist fiction, it has received virtually no critical attention. There is no extended study, and the only essay devoted exclusively to the subject is William York Tindall's chapter "Supreme Fictions" in *The Literary Symbol* (1955). Fortunately, Tindall has read widely and thought long and deeply about symbolism, and his discussion is of unusual interest. He points out that all great novels are to some extent symbolic, that Dickens, Meredith, Hardy, and others developed symbols thematically in a way that anticipates the richness and precision of the technique in the twentieth century. The first novel to use symbols as extensively and as integrally as they are used today was *Moby Dick*. Flaubert, not knowing Melville, proceeded along the same lines independently in *Madame Bovary*. Tindall quotes from Conrad and Joyce, the first of the early twentieth-century symbolists, to emphasize their acknowledged debt to Flaubert.

Symbolic fiction derives in part from a reaction against naturalism. Zola, as Tindall points out, often used symbols effectively, but the authority of his manifestoes, which were at variance with his practice, canceled out the effect of his imaginative techniques, and the symbolists in poetry devised and sponsored a new type of fiction. The relationship between the symbolists and the work of Joyce and Proust has been admirably defined by Edmund Wilson in *Axel's Castle* (1931). Symbolist fiction also derives from the spreading conviction that the novel should have tighter form, a more considered style, and, above all, concentration. Baudelaire had called for "concise energy" of language, and Henry James put the matter trenchantly when he counseled, "Don't state—render." Perhaps it was his admiration for James that led Conrad to his own distinguished practice in the symbolic novel, which ushered in the great period of this form. Just before the First World War there appeared Mann's *Death in Venice*, Joyce's *Dubliners*, and the first volume of Proust's *Remembrance of Things Past*. This rich period in the history of fiction, Tindall reminds us, reached its climax in *Ulysses, The Magic Mountain*, and the completion of Proust's great work. It saw the emergence of Kafka (*The Trial*), Lawrence (*The Plumed Serpent*), and Virginia Woolf (*To the Lighthouse*). These were soon followed by formidable rivals: *A Passage to India, The Sound and the Fury*, and *Absalom! Absalom!* Finally, there was *Finnegans Wake*, which would seem to have carried the form about as far as it can go.

The author of this kind of novel, according to E. M. Forster, who prefers to call it "prophetical" rather than "symbolic," "is not necessarily going to 'say' anything about the universe; he proposes to sing." Thus, Conrad saw his novels as "an outward sign of inward feelings," which he would communicate by images.

A work of art is very seldom limited to one exclusive meaning and not necessarily tending to a definite conclusion. And this for the reason that the nearer it approches art, the more it acquires a symbolic character. This statement may surprise you, who may imagine that I am alluding to the Symbolist School of poets or prose writers. Theirs, however, is only a literary proceeding against which I have nothing to say. I am concerned here with something much larger. . . . So I will only call your attention to the fact that the symbolic conception of a work of art has this advantage, that it makes a triple appeal covering the whole field of life. All the great creations of literature have been symbolic, and in that way have gained in complexity, in power, in depth, and in beauty.

Tindall outlines three types of symbolist novel. The first two are represented by Conrad and Joyce. "Conrad's vision," he tells us, "though no less symbolist than *A Portrait of the Artist,* differs from it in structure. In Joyce's book, narrative, attended by images that enlarge it, is central; in Conrad's book, narrative and subordinate details are centered in image. Tied to narrative, Joyce's images develop thematically in time, whereas Conrad's organization, more nearly static, is spatial in effect." The third type is represented by the work of Henry Green, who has won T. S. Eliot's praise. Green's *Party Going* seems centered in the symbol of the railroad station. But what at first appears centralized is later seen to be "a system of almost equal elements, cohering not by subordination to a great image or a narrative but by glancing reflections" or refractions. Green called his novel a "conspiracy of insinuations." Tindall quotes Yeats in "The Symbolism of Poetry" admiring the way a poem "flickers with the light of many symbols." The metaphor seems appropriate to Green's method, and it is not without relevance to the over-all techniques employed by this most important group of novelists.

In "The Meanings of 'Myth' in Modern Criticism," *MP* (1953), Wallace W. Douglas remarks that *myth* is the most important and the most inclusive word in current critical literature. It is also the most difficult, for there are almost as many meanings assigned to the term as critics who have attempted elucidation. The dictionary meaning of "legend" is simply a starting point for a series of extensions that run from "illusion" through "belief" to "higher truth." Critics who approach literature from the point of view of myth treat a document as a repository of truth, of racial memories, or of unconsciously held values, and characters and action as representative of types or classes or ideals. Thus, a myth is representative in fictional form of truths or values that are sanctioned by general belief, the sanctified and dogmatized expression of basic social or class conventions and values. A myth is the living embodiment of insights, as opposed to facts or ordered knowledge, and the discussion of it will be descriptive rather than analytical. The terms of the discussion, Douglas states, "will be neither manageable words nor cataloguable phenomena, but semi-poetic devices to call attention to structural paradoxes, ironies, or tensions . . . which partly suggest the nonrational and linguistically indescribable elements of experience which lie behind the myth being described."

The most active teacher of this popular subject is Richard Chase, whose *Quest for Myth* (1949) is the standard textbook for the course. Chase takes the position that the mythopoeic mind is superior to rational or speculative reason. Primitive man, he tells us, lives in two worlds: the world of matter of fact or practical reason, and the magico-religious world of the mythopoeic faculty. Civilized man, whatever he may think, functions at these same levels; and myth is, therefore, by this anthropological analysis a defensive projection of his unconscious. It is also, in Chase's view, "literature which suffuses the natural with preternatural efficacy." Finally, he concludes, "any poem which reaffirms the dynamism and vibrancy of the world, which fortifies the ego with the impression that there is a magically potent brilliancy or dramatic force in the world, may be called myth."

The study of myth has, indeed, become one of the most pervasive occupations of the literary critic. Re-examinations of major works—from Shakespeare to Defoe, through Melville to Faulkner —have elicited the energies of many of our most practiced critics. These gentlemen have found myth everywhere, but it is perhaps a question to be asked to what extent they have conjured up the thing for which they have been looking. Nevertheless, whatever skepticism one may have about the total validity of the myth-seekers' interpretations, they have deepened our perceptions and enlarged the area of our understanding of literature.

III

A half century ago the criticism of fiction was still largely restricted to appreciative essays, celebrating a given novelist's flair for lively plot or buoyant characters or witty dialogue. Since James, critics have been increasingly (and are now, indeed, almost exclusively) concerned with fiction as a technique, exploring the mechanics of a craft which has become subject to many of the organizational and philosophical principles which have historically governed older and more fully codified literary forms. None of these has received so much thoughtful consideration as point of view, a matter which touches on many other cruces for the novelist.

Among many treatments of this subject students of fiction will probably find most comprehensive and therefore most useful Norman Friedman's "Point of View in Fiction: The Development of a Critical Concept," *PMLA* (1955).[2] Friedman presents an historical survey of critical thinking on the novelist's relationship to his material, beginning with the source of the discussion, James's prefaces. As is well known, James disapproved of the gossipy Victorian novelist, who tells the story as *he* sees it, not as one of his characters sees it. James solved the beguiling problem of finding a "center" or "focus" for his stories by framing the action not externally but within the consciousness of one of the characters. This brought about, after several centuries of chatty authorial intrusion, the disappearance of the writer. Speaking through Stephen Dedalus, Joyce in *A Portrait of the Artist* commented on what was clearly occurring: "The personality of the artist, at first a cry or a cadence or a mood [lyric] and then a fluid and lambent narrative [epic], finally refines itself out of existence [drama], impersonalizes itself, so to speak." James's theory and practice, as Friedman reminds us, was "to have the story told as if by a character in the story, but told in the third person."

The pioneer attempt to organize the theory of a consistent point of view was that of Joseph Warren Beach in *The Method of Henry James* (1918), which distinguished between James's calculated shift in focus and the Victorian novelist's arbitrary and capricious "manipulation of the puppets from without, which is so great a menace to illusion and intimacy." Three years later Percy Lubbock in *The Craft of Fiction*, a classic text, emphasized how surely the illusion of reality is dissipated by authorial intrusion, but suggested that the novelist might limit his functions in several ways: "The only law that binds him throughout, whatever course he is pursuing, is the need to be consistent on *some* plan, to follow the principle he had adopted. . . ." In 1925 James's disciple Edith Wharton advised in *The Writing of Fiction* that the novelist choose carefully and deliberately the reflecting mind, then to live inside that mind, "trying to feel, see, and react exactly as the latter would. . . ." In 1927 E. M. Forster in *Aspects of the Novel*, another standard text of the aesthetics of fiction, entered a caveat against depriving the novelist of his most distinctive and most flexible weapon, his unhampered omniscience: "All that matters

[2] This article is particularly valuable for the extensive bibliographical citations of other relevant critical studies.

to the reader is whether the shifting of attitude and the secret life are convincing."

Among many discussions of this problem in the 'thirties and 'forties, three may be mentioned. In 1932 Beach published his rigorous, incisive study of technique, *The Twentieth Century Novel*, in which he points out that the characteristic quality of the fiction of our time is that "the story tells itself; the story speaks for itself." Allen Tate in "The Post of Observation in Fiction," *Maryland Quarterly* (1944), came to the same conclusion: "The limited and thus credible authority for the action, which is gained by putting the knower of the action inside its frame, is perhaps the distinctive feature of the modern novel; and it is, in all the infinite shifts of focus of which it is capable, the special feature which more than any other has made it possible for the novelist to achieve an objective structure." Possibly the most significant recent essay on point of view is Mark Schorer's "Technique as Discovery," *Hudson Review* (1948); reprinted in *Forms in Modern Fiction* (1952), *Essays in Modern Literary Criticism* (1952), and *Critiques and Essays on Modern Fiction* (1952). Schorer examines "the uses of point of view not only as a mode of dramatic delimitation but, more particularly, of thematic definition." He contends that the devices of point of view offer a controlling medium by which the novelist may disengage his own prejudices from those of his characters and evaluate their predispositions dramatically. That such considerations are a commonplace of current criticism is the inference from the twenty-odd references which Friedman cites to this effect in the past fifteen years.

The four fundamental questions out of which can come adequate definitions of the related concepts touching on point of view are, according to Friedman, (1) Who talks to the reader? (2) From what position (angle) regarding the story does he tell it? (3) What channels of information does the narrator use to convey the story to the reader? and (4) At what distance does he place the reader from the story? The major distinction in modes of transmission of story material, that between summary narrative and immediate scene, is most fully and adequately explained in Phyllis Bentley's brief but solid study *Some Observations on the Art of Narrative* (1947). Summary (or retrospect, as Lubbock calls it—the vocabulary of the criticism of fiction is still unsettled) occurs when the novelist halts his moving world and tells us what he sees. Scene develops when narrative breaks into specific action (including scene and thought). Summary is second-hand and indirect, scene immediate and direct. When the author talks to the reader, his editorial omniscience leads away from scene.

Friedman notes a number of techniques intermediate between omniscience and the dramatic method. Some novelists have favored neutral omniscience, in which one or more of the characters are clearly projections of the author's own personality and represent his opinions. A more direct method of presentation is that of the spectator, or, to use Friedman's term, *I* as Witness. The reader sees and knows only what the spectator sees and knows. If the narrator is the chief participant, or *I* as Protagonist, the treatment must be a little more objective. In Multiple Selective Omniscience not only the author but the narrator is dispensed with, and the "story" filters entirely through the minds of the characters. In Selective Omniscience we are introduced to the mind of a single character, who is the fixed center of revelation. Finally, in the dramatic mode, we have, as in the theater, only dialogue and observed action.

Mark Schorer has shown the importance of this kind of analysis, for through a novelist's technique we discover both his purposes and the values which he is pursuing in his art. Every trained writer of fiction, seeking to produce total story-illusion, knows today that he must exercise thoughtful judgment with regard to the point of view from which his material is to be presented. Friedman likens the novelist's choice in this regard to the poet's choice of verse form and metrical pattern. The comparison is apt, for editorial omniscience is a kind of free verse, and today's more restrictive, delimiting techniques force the novelist into the acceptance of conventions quite as stringent and confining as those governing tightly structural poetry. Most critics, however, are willing to concede that in certain types of fiction, such as the satiric and the philosophical, it is not only permissible but proper that the novelist should be evident. The *sine qua non* is that his point of view should be announced at once, and that he should maintain it rigorously throughout.

Another technical problem that has been receiving a great deal of attention is the handling of time, which Henry James declared to be the stiffest responsibility facing the novelist. Time, as Thomas Mann has said, is the medium of narration, as it is the medium of life, and interest in its importance is no new thing. Indeed, every critic and historian of its place and function in the novel begins with *Tristram Shandy*, which so remarkably anticipated the fascination which this concept has had for the twentieth century. In our period, beginning with James and Conrad, it is difficult to find a major novelist who has not been acutely conscious of time values. Mann and Kafka; Proust, Gide, and Romains; Dos Passos, Wolfe, and Faulkner; Dorothy Richardson, Virginia Woolf, and Aldous Huxley—all have contributed notably, by their technical experiments in extra-medial time effects, to the now well established awareness of the meaning of time in the art of fiction. A few critics, in fact, contend that too much attention has been devoted to this aspect of the novel. Wyndham Lewis spoke with some scorn of "The Time-school of modern fiction," and Roy Campbell has remarked that "modern art reflects an obsession with time which is as ridiculous as those of the Victorians with morality."

In spite of the novelists' concern with this problem, reflected in scattered brief treatments, and incidentally in such individual studies as Edward Crankshaw's *Joseph Conrad*, critics have only recently given it extended analysis. There are now, however, two excellent inquiries: A. A. Mendilow's *Time and the Novel* (1952) and Hans Meyerhoff's *Time in Literature* (1955). Mendilow points out that time affects every aspect of fiction: the theme, the form, and the medium—language. Time is, of course, relative; and Mendilow interestingly illustrates its variability for the characters:

The hero arrives at the trysting-place by chronological time—time by the clock which is the same for everybody. He waits impatiently for what seems years by psychological time—his own private clock that measures time by values and intensity. As he waits, he recalls the various happenings that led up to this fateful rendezvous by an act of memory which is not a mechanical reconstruction or recapitulation of the past as it was but is rather an emotionally charged interpretation of events which changes and shifts as the interpreting self grows in time and is altered by it. Finally the hero greets his beloved with the pressure of all his past on the moment of his present which itself is modified by a purposiveness that thrusts towards a future big with hope.

The problems of managing these time elements within the framework of a continuous narrative challenges all a novelist's skill. He must control the tempo and maintain the established rhythms without losing grasp of his purpose and materials. If he can do this, he may attempt nothing further. At any rate, rhythm is sometimes substituted for plot, or, to use the newer terms, *formations* have replaced *forms*. In pursuit of this and related matters the student of fiction will wish to consult an excellent book by the late E. K. Brown, *Rhythm in the Novel* (1950). Mendilow in his exposition, after investigating the effect of time on theme, form and language, concludes that "In the final analysis, virtually all the techniques and devices of fiction reduce themselves to the treatment accorded to the different time-values and time-series, and to the way one is played off against another." Mendilow has loaded every rift with ore, and his treatise is solid and compact.

Meyerhoff, a philosopher, has a somewhat broader scope and purpose. He treats not only the concept of time as it has affected contemporary literature but also, and more importantly, the scientific and philosophical relationships that are involved. Actually, Meyerhoff is investigating the meaning of time in human experience; he does so in a carefully designed and closely wrought book.

Of great concern today is the still unsettled vocabulary of the criticism of fiction. The validity of such terms as *plot*, *character*, *structure*, and *form* have been widely and heatedly debated. In *The Victorian Sage* (1953) John Holloway speaks disparagingly of critics who attempt to say something vital about the novel in terms of such old-fashioned categories as *plots*, *character*, and *setting*. Queenie D. Leavis in *Fiction and the Reading Public* (1932) contends that discussion of such abstractions is pointless and profitless. In his *Introduction to the English Novel* (1951) Arnold Kettle remarks that all categories are dangerous, that one aspect of a novel is so interwoven with another that "you cannot really separate, say 'character' from 'plot,' 'narrative' from 'background.' " I. A. Richards in *Practical Criticism* (1930) and Denys

Thompson in *Reading and Discrimination* (1934) hold, in effect, that such terms are without merit in criticism, the business of which is to test the quality of an author's mind by subjecting selected passages to analysis for "sense, feeling, tone, and intention." The older concepts, it is argued, do not convey the resonance of a novel; they are merely the instruments by which a novelist expresses his sensibility. The problem remains essentially one of language. As Mrs. Leavis puts it, "the essential technique in an art that works by using words is the way in which the words are used."

At least one cautionary voice has recently been raised against such jettisoning of the older terms. Douglas Grant in "The Novel and Its Critical Terms," *Essays in Criticism* (1951), while admitting that redefinitions are in order, maintains that to discuss the novel in terms of the author's sensibility only is very dangerous. It is always difficult to know to what extent an attitude is a reflection of personal sensibility or the sensibility of the age. For this reason an examination of sensibility must be made in its proper historical context. It is reasonably clear that such an examination can be made only in accepted terms; that is, to assess fairly the purposes and techniques of the Victorian novelists it is imperative that the critic understand what they meant by the vocabulary they used.

Grant believes that criticism of fiction will continue to flounder until more exact definitions are formulated. His own thoughtful contributions toward this end are worth noting. "A novel," he says, "is a judgment on experience expressed in terms of character." He points out that the practice of the early novelists emphasizes the supreme importance of appearance and behavior. The concept of individuality generally accepted in the eighteenth and nineteenth centuries held that what a person *does* is the clue to his character. Hence the wide use of character pattern. Today it is thought that the individual is formed in large measure by forces beyond his control; his nature is best illustrated by his *reactions* to various stimuli. Character is now treated in terms of ideology and psychology, and the approach is indirect and introspective. "Character," Grant concludes, "is a symbolic personification of the attitudes and aspirations of man as they are generally but imprecisely realized in the novelist's society."

With regard to plot and structure Grant has some further pertinent and incisive remarks. The concept of character which obtained in the eighteenth and nineteenth centuries demanded a plot which would provide opportunities to illustrate the characters in action. Today the novelist (anticipated by Sterne) has been freed by a newer concept of character from dependence on plot. Action, as such, is no longer necessary, and plot has become simply the means used to confront *character* with situations provoking conflict. Structure or form is determined by the emphasis which the author places on certain aspects of experience. It has two qualities—aesthetic and moral. Structure is therefore the form that judgment takes, the moral and aesthetic order of a novel.

Students of technique will find of considerable interest and importance two little volumes by Robert Liddell: *A Treatise on the Novel* (1947) and *Some Principles of Fiction* (1953). The first of these, dealing with the elements of the novel, is the more conventional. It takes up, successively, the proper approach to criticism (a combination of the "academic" and the "practical"), the novelist's range (he must resist all temptations and exhortations to go beyond it), the novelist's values (he must be a humanist, according to T. S. Eliot's definition), the making of plot (various types are examined), the making of character (the types and sources, especially biographical and autobiographical), and background (the subordinate place, and legitimate function, of descriptive writing).

Some Principles of Fiction is a rather eccentric and iconoclastic book, but it is full of insights and shrewd observations. After discussing the subject of fiction, Liddell introduces four related questions: (1) Can a good novel be a poor work of art? (2) Can a good work of art . . . be a poor novel? (3) Is it possible to say something significant, and yet write bad prose? (4) Can prose be good when its content is insignificant? We are told that almost all the critical preconceptions that we have acquired in the second quarter of this century incline us to answer all these questions in the negative. There follows an excellent discussion of scene and summary, and informed reflections, of an amusingly haphazard nature, on dialogue. The final section, entitled "Terms and Topics," is a series of notes defining and commenting on some of the newer catch-words of the criticism of fiction. Liddell's approach is highly individual, and one often disagrees, but he is a challenging critic.

The criticism of the technique of fiction has been of late so overwhelming in sheer bulk that in brief compass one can do no more than point to a few representative writers, hoping to show something of the nature of the stimulating body of critical literature that has developed around this suddenly self-conscious art. Critics today are not only well informed on the strategy and logistics of the novel, they have contributed materially to its development by creating a climate in which sound work is recognized and appreciated.

IV

The tremendous proliferation during the last twenty-five years of such specialized critical studies as have been noted above has been paralleled by a corresponding increase in more general and perhaps more academic works. These have taken the form of histories of the novel, biographies and editions of letters, and bibliographies. In all the categories the modern tradition of exact scholarship has been brought to bear upon older, more casual work which, whatever merits it may have had as genial impressionism, was subject to extensive revision in the light of new information and more rigorous techniques of inquiry.

The most extensive survey of English fiction remains E. A. Baker's ten-volume *History of the English Novel* (1924-39), which is happily back in print after having been long unobtainable. Baker's work is chiefly descriptive rather than analytical, but it is useful as the fullest treatment of its subject. Among the one-volume histories there are a number that must be noted. R. M. Lovett and Helen S. Hughes's *The History of the Novel in England* (1932), for more than two decades the standard college text, is unexceptionable but has few positive merits and is a bit on the dull side. Pelham Edgar's *The Art of the Novel* (1933) is still of interest, for the author was a close student of James and more concerned with problems of technique than were Cross, Saintsbury, and other older historians. *The English Novelists* (1936), edited by Derek Verschoyle, is a symposium volume by first-rate British novelists and critics; but since the writers were not always authorities on the novelist to whom they were assigned, the result is an often stimulating but highly uneven work. Gordon H. Gerould's *Patterns of English and American Fiction* (1942) is a standard text which, though it has the unique advantage of following parallel developments in the two literatures, has the crippling disadvantage of trying to do too much, and is, in consequence, often thin. Edward Wagenknecht's *Cavalcade of the English Novel* (1943, revised edition 1954) is highly useful, particularly in the recent edition for its excellent bibliographies, the most comprehensive that are available. Unfortunately, however, Wagenknecht sometimes allows his prejudices to dominate his good sense. S. Diana Neill's *A Short History of the English Novel* (1952) is not entirely satisfactory, either critically or, because of a serious imbalance of material, structurally. Arnold Kettle's two-volume *An Introduction to the English Novel* (1952–53) is misnamed, for it is not a history but a series of always shrewd and often brilliant analyses of individual novels, and it is not strictly an introduction, for few who do not bring to a reading of Kettle's pages a wide background of experience with fiction and the criticism of fiction will carry away many of the fine things to be found there. Walter Allen's *The English Novel* (1955) is, to my mind, the best of the one-volume histories. Allen, who qualifies for his task by the experience of the novelist as well as that of the critic, manages his rapid survey with great skill. There is a commendable balance of space, a notable absence of bias, and a refreshing clarity of style. If there are no surprises in Allen's approach, it has the virtues of soundness and solidity.

Special mention must be made of F. R. Leavis's *The Great Tradition* (1948), the most controversial of all recent treatments of the novel. The great English novelists, we are told, are Jane Austen, George Eliot, Henry James, Joseph Conrad, and D. H. Lawrence. In this book, for reasons of unity, Leavis discusses at length only the middle three. He is very hard on Dickens, Thackeray, Trollope, Meredith, and Hardy. The principal charges against them are that they do not trouble themselves about form and method, and they do not create profoundly serious works of art. Thackeray, for example, "has (apart from social history) nothing to offer the reader whose demand goes beyond the 'creation of characters.' His attitudes and the essential substance of interest, are so limited that (though of course he provides incident and plot) for the reader it is merely a matter of going on and on; nothing has been done by the close to justify the space taken—except, of course, that time has been killed. . . ." Leavis therefore includes a chapter on *Hard Times*, as, apparently, the best of Dickens's novels, and he expresses great admiration for Disraeli, who is "so alive and intelligent as to deserve permanent currency." These are the views of an extremist, of course, but one who through his followers in *Scrutiny* exercises considerable influence on current criticism.

In American fiction there are four principal histories to be mentioned. A. H. Quinn's *American Fiction* (1936), while the first text to treat the early literature with any thoroughness, suffers badly from blind prejudice against contemporary fiction. Carl Van Doren's *The American Novel, 1789–1939* (1940), a revision of two earlier works, is slight in scope but generally sound. Alexander Cowie's *The Rise of the American Novel* (1951), though somewhat academic, is the best survey available. Edward Wagenknecht's *Cavalcade of the American Novel*, like the earlier volume on English fiction, contains valuable bibliographies, but it too is not very receptive toward the modern novel. Also to be mentioned, though it covers only a half century, is Maxwell Geismar's trilogy *The Novel in America*. This consists (in reverse order of composition) of *Rebels and Ancestors, 1890–1915* (1953), *The Last of the Provincials, 1915–1925* (1947), and *Writers in Crisis, 1925–1940* (1942). Geismar's approach is closer to that of Van Wyck Brooks than to that of Joseph Warren Beach, but he has produced a readable account of the relation of the novel to intellectual history. In addition to innumerable single volumes, studying a particular genre (for example, Ernest Leisy's *The American Historical Novel*, 1950) or sub-genre (for example, W. M. Frohock's *The Novel of Violence in America*, 1950), there is the three-volume co-operative study, *The Literary History of the United States* (1948), which includes usually first-rate chapters on the novelists.

Biographical and critical studies of the chief English novelists have been so numerous during the past twenty-five years that the process of selection from among them is entirely frustrating. The bibliography of materials relating to a major Victorian novelist, for example, may show half a dozen quite respectable biographies, an equal number of critical analyses, and literally hundreds of articles, only a small percentage of which can be dismissed as idolatrous or frivolous or incompetent. The compiler of such notes as these is reduced to utter despair as he debates how best to indicate trends and developments. Perhaps this can most readily and most usefully be done by mentioning what appears to be the best work on the best novelists.

To begin with Defoe, who has attracted much attention, the best biography is that by James Sutherland in 1938. The leading Swift scholar is Ricardo Quintana, whose *The Mind and Art of Jonathan Swift* (1936; briefer edition, 1955) is standard. There have been a number of recent psychological studies of Swift's tortured personality. Alan D. McKillop's *Samuel Richardson, Printer and Novelist* (1936) is still the fullest treatment of the author of *Pamela*, though there is much new information in William M. Sale, Jr.'s *Samuel Richardson, Master Printer* (1950). Homes Dudden's *Henry Fielding: His Life, Works, and Times* (1952), an elaborate two-volume study, is old-fashioned and rather pedantic but admirably thorough. Precisely the same things must be said of L. M. Knapp's *Tobias Smollett: Doctor of Men and Manners* (1949). Three recent studies of Sterne have not replaced W. L. Cross' standard *The Life and Times of Laurence Sterne* (revised edition, 1929). Special mention, however, must be made of James A. Work's excellent edition of *Tristram Shandy* (1940). Most of the recent work on Jane Austen has been critical (Elizabeth Jenkins, Marvin Mudrick, Andrew Wright, and others) rather than biographical, but one must take note of *Jane Austen: Facts and Problems* (1949) by R. W. Chapman, the foremost Janeite, whose edition of her works (1934) is a model. The vast amount of research on Scott has produced nothing of supernal merit, and one waits for Edgar Johnson's forthcoming biography with eager anticipation.

Among the Victorians Dickens, as expected, has received most attention. Edgar Johnson's *Charles Dickens: His Tragedy and Triumph* is one of the best literary biographies of our times. It is not often that a scholarly work achieves the status of a best seller. Reappraisals without new material have come from Una Pope-Hennessy (1946) and Hesketh Pearson (1949). Thackeray scholarship has been dominated by Gordon N. Ray, whose

Thackeray: The Uses of Adversity (1955) is the first volume of a definitive biography, The same writer published in 1952 *The Buried Life*, a study of the relationship between Thackeray's novels and his personal life. Other satisfactory studies include John Dodd's *Thackeray: A Critical Portrait* (1941), Lionel Stevenson's *The Showman of Vanity Fair* (1947), Lambert Ennis' *Thackeray: The Sentimental Cynic* (1950), and J. Y. T. Greig's *Thackeray: A Reconsideration* (1950). No first-rate biography of Trollope has recently appeared, the standard text still being that of Michael Sadleir (1927); and there is no comprehensive critical study. After many decades Wilkie Collins finally found a biographer in Kenneth Robinson, who in 1952 established the facts about Collins' iconoclastic personal life. Robinson's book was followed in the same year by Robert P. Ashley's brief biographical-critical study, and in 1957 by N. P. Davis's biography. The fascinating story of the Brontës is told and retold, chiefly by romanticists and sentimentalists, almost annually; but the book that has revolutionized Brontë scholarship is Fannie E. Ratchford's *The Brontës' Web of Childhood* (1941), which first studied exhaustively the astounding quantity of work the girls wrote about their mythical Angria and Gondal. The best of the recent biographies is probably Margaret Lane's *The Brontë Story* (1953). Studies of George Eliot that rise above the ruck of informed journalism are Joan Bennett's *George Eliot: Her Mind and Art* (1948) and Gerald Bullett's *George Eliot: Her Life and Books* (1948). Meredith has been the subject of two studies: Siegfried Sassoon's chatty and somewhat bewildered attempt in 1948, and Lionel Stevenson's fine performance in 1953. Hardy has fared well. Carl Weber's *Hardy of Wessex* (1940) presents the facts in an orderly manner. Lord David Cecil's *Hardy the Novelist* (1946) and Albert Guerard's *Hardy: The Novels and the Stories* (1949) are stimulating critical studies. Harvey Webster's *On a Darkling Plain* (1947) stresses Hardy's ideas. J. C. Furnas proved himself an excellent biographer of Stevenson in *Voyage to Windward* (1951). As has been seen earlier scholarship in Conrad has been very active. The most important biography is Gérard Jean-Aubry's *The Sea Dreamer* (1957), and there are notable critical studies by Albert Guerard (1947), Walter Wright (1949), and Thomas Moser (1957). There is a good bibliography by Kenneth Lohf and

Eugene Sheehy (1957). New studies of D. H. Lawrence have been appearing every year. The fullest factual biography is that by Harry T. Moore (1951). Rewarding critical studies include those by W. Y. Tindall (1939), Mark Spilka (1955), F. R. Leavis (1956), and Graham Hough (1957). Reginald Pound's *Arnold Bennett* (1953) recreates delightfully the literary scene in the first decades of the century. The Joyce bibliography is overwhelming. The authorized biography is that by Herbert Gorman (1939), but there are many volumes of reminiscences. Among dozens of critical studies the best introduction is Harry Levin's (1941). The standard explication of *Ulysses* is Stuart Gilbert's (1930), and *A Skeleton Key to Finnegans Wake* (1944) by J. Campbell and H. M. Robinson will guide the common reader through other Joycean mazes. Altogether, this has been an age of unparalleled critical activity.

Much interest has been shown in bibliography and in the scholarly editing of letters, such as those of Defoe by G. H. Healey (1955). But the big editorial tasks have been those of voluminous nineteenth-century writers. Sir H. J. C. Grierson's twelve volumes of Scott letters (1932–37) were followed by Gordon Ray's notable four Thackeray volumes (1945–46) and Gordon Haight's seven George Eliot volumes (1954–55), all meticulously edited. Multivolumed editions of the letters of Dickens and Stevenson are in preparation. Bibliographically, the notable achievement was Michael Sadleir's *XIX Century Fiction* (1951), an indispensable tool for scholarly research in the period.

It is not necessary to produce a detailed list of important biographical-critical works in American fiction. That function is filled more than adequately by the bibliographical volume of *The Literary History of the United States*, a reference of the first importance for all students of fiction. Attention should also be drawn to an indispensable guide to periodical literature, *Articles on American Literature 1900–1950*, edited by Lewis Leary (1954). It may suffice, therefore, merely to say a word about research in the works of the novelists who are currently attracting the most attention: Hawthorne, Melville, Mark Twain, and James.

Hawthorne continues to interest biographers, but the psychological approach of Lloyd Morris and Herbert Gorman in the 1920's, having been sadly overdone, has been replaced by more balanced evaluations. The best of these is that of Randall Stewart (1948). Mark Van Doren followed in 1949 with an excellent study giving more emphasis to criticism. Among recent works Richard H. Fogle's *Hawthorne's Fiction: The Light and the Dark* (1952) is of permanent interest. One must not forget the important section on Hawthorne in F. O. Matthiessen's *American Renaissance* (1941). Melville scholarship, as everyone knows, calls for its own chapter; but here it must suffice to note the indispensable texts. The only full biography based on new materials is that by Leon Howard (1951); it takes its origin in Jay Leyda's two-volume *The Melville Log* (1951), a chronological record of the biographical facts. In addition to Matthiessen, students will wish to read, among critical studies, at least those by Richard Chase (1949) and Newton Arvin (1950). A scholarly edition of Melville was begun a few years ago under the general editorship of Howard P. Vincent, but it seems to have come to a halt short of completion. Mark Twain studies have also flourished, but the quality of the work has been uneven. The "repressed genius" theory of Van Wyck Brooks was effectively answered by DeVoto in *Mark Twain's America* (1932). Latterly, the best studies have been those of Wagenknecht (1935), Delancy Ferguson (1943), and, on the early life, Dixon Wecter (1952). As for Henry James, American literature scholars who are not working on Melville are usually working on James. For sources the autobiographical volumes and the *Notebooks* (1947) are of the first importance. An excellent biography in progress is that of Leon Edel (*The Untried Years*, 1953). Critically, one turns after Beach to Cornelia Kelly, *The Early Development of Henry James* (1930); Matthiessen, *Henry James: The Major Phase* (1944)—that is, the last novels; Elizabeth Stevenson, *The Crooked Corridor* (1949); F. W. Dupee, *Henry James* (1951); and H. S. Canby, *Turn West, Turn East* (1951).

The energy and intelligence with which scholarship has approached literary problems in our time is clearly evident. Vigorous minds have been at work, not only evaluating and interpreting the achievements of the past but in sharing with the creative artist some of the responsibility for determining the development of the novel in the future. It has been for criticism an era of dramatic accomplishment. In its understanding of the intimate relationship between the novel and society; in its keen analyses of new psychological genres and of the intent and value of myth and symbol; in its lively awareness of technical problems, both new and old; and in its dedication to the scholarly principles of thoroughness and accuracy—in all these areas the study of the novel in the past quarter century has been pursued with skill, with devotion, and with high imagination.

15

The Drama

HENRY POPKIN

CRITICAL AND SCHOLARLY WRITING
on the drama has both benefited and suffered from the popularity
of the theater. Nearly everyone cares about the theater, and, in
fact, it sometimes seems that everyone feels obliged to write about
it. The situation is aptly mirrored by George Kelly's old farce
The Flattering Word, which reflects the familiar idea that everyone wants to be an actor. To be a drama critic is an ambition even
more easily attained. Consequently, the dramatist may, like the
poet or novelist, inspire an occasional volume or essay, but he will
also be glanced at in theater histories, actors' reminiscences, handbooks to playgoing, trade journals of show business, and theater
magazines. The most written-about literary man of our time is
surely not Eliot, Joyce, Mann, or Proust, but George Bernard
Shaw. Can Shaw have had a neighbor or an acquaintance who has
not yet gone into print on him? What other man of letters in this
century has had a biographer standing by, waiting to complete
his subject's life-story at word of his death? Hesketh Pearson
performed this ghoulish function for Shaw, publishing *G. B. S.: A
Postscript* (1950) with extraordinary promptness. Shaw's eminence as a commentator on public events can only partially explain
this interest. He belongs first to the theater, and everyone who
knows a dramatist or can pay for a ticket is entitled to make his
contribution to the history of drama. The harvest is enormous.
There may be more grain; there is certainly more chaff.

I

The theatrical reference books perfectly illustrate the perils
attendant on the theater's glory. Bernard Sobel's *Theatre Handbook and Digest of Plays* (1940, 1948) is a handy volume in which

I have very little faith. Its editor is an eminent authority on burlesque. Broadway is the center of its universe, but that would not be so bad if it were as carefully edited as Broadway's Bible, the weekly trade paper *Variety*. Although the *Handbook* is now in a presumably revised edition, it is still carelessly edited. If I consult one of its play-summaries, I know that I must recheck everything, for I can treat none of its statements as fact. Otherwise, I would have to believe that Mrs. Alving ends her son's life in *Ghosts* or that Pirandello's *Henry IV* concerns a man who thinks he is Henry II. One error in the account of Odets' *Paradise Lost* is lifted from Burns Mantle's *Best Plays*. "Guest pieces" by celebrities, including Tallulah Bankhead, seldom give thorough coverage of any theatrical tradition. But superficiality is the particular function of the editor, who thus informs us about "Tragedy": "Marlowe's idea of tragedy approximated to a degree the modern tragedy of the ordinary man at the mercy of overwhelming and inexplicable forces. . . . For the Middle Ages tragedy was a thing only of the nobility, whereas for Marlowe it dealt with individuals. The unity of these two concepts, in Shakespeare, gives us the majesty of *Macbeth* and *King Lear*."

We are in another world in Phyllis Hartnoll's *Oxford Companion to the Theatre* (1951), which is scholarly, responsible, and British in emphasis. The general articles are, for the most part, solid and authoritative. If the editor heeds the reviewers, she should be able to correct most of the factual errors in the revised edition promised for late 1957. A convenient test to apply to the new edition will be to examine the new form of some of the worst entries, like those on Bertolt Brecht and Henry James. A deficiency more difficult to correct will be the strong Soviet bias of the Russian entries, including an especially heartless note on the unfortunate director Meyerhold; at least we should be told that Meyerhold has been posthumously rehabilitated and is now officially considered to be a good director, not at all guilty of "theatrical bankruptcy."[1]

Joseph T. Shipley's *Guide to Great Plays* (1956) is more limited

---

[1] The editor did not sufficiently heed the reviewers. The second edition (1957) corrects the Brecht entry but not the James. Meyerhold's death is recorded but not his apotheosis. A revised *Theatre Handbook* is announced for 1958.

in purpose; it serves principally to record the recent New York stage history of a great number of plays. The most ambitious theatrical reference book is not yet finished. It is the *Enciclopedia dello Spettacolo* (1954–), begun under the supervision of the late Silvio d'Amico, to be completed in eight volumes. The American and British consultants of the *Enciclopedia dello Spettacolo* are, respectively, John Gassner and Allardyce Nicoll. They have themselves written histories of the drama which are serviceable reference works. Nicoll's *World Drama* (1950) is slightly longer and examines the drama in a mainly theatrical context. Gassner's *Masters of the Drama* (1949, revised 1954) displays a greater interest in general cultural tendencies and undertakes more interpretation of individual plays.

Among the more valuable secondary aids to the study of drama are *Understanding Drama*, edited by Cleanth Brooks and Robert B. Heilman (1945, revised 1948), *The Play*, edited by Eric Bentley (1951), and *The Art of the Play*, edited by Alan S. Downer (1955). *Understanding Drama* offers by far the most detailed critiques. Bentley's objections, stated in his review of the book in *KR* (1946) are valid: the editors do not show great interest in the theater or in the modern drama. Both the Bentley and Downer anthologies remedy this deficiency, but the Brooks-Heilman analyses are still unmatched.

Miscellaneous books of value to the student of drama include: *Actors on Acting*, edited by Toby Cole and Helen K. Chinoy (1949), and its companion volume, *Directing the Play*, by the same editors (1953); A. M. Nagler's *Sources of Theatrical History* (1952), a collection of documents on which theater history is based; and Barrett H. Clark's *European Theories of the Drama* (1947), a collection of dramatic criticism since Aristotle—badly in need of a modern supplementary volume. Allardyce Nicoll's *Theory of Drama* (n.d.) is a good traditional introduction to the subject.

Two recent bibliographies require to be mentioned. *Dramatic Theory: A Bibliography*, compiled by Richard B. Vowles (1956) is a useful classified list of books and articles on the subject. *A Guide to Theatre Reading*, by Roy Stallings and Paul Myers (1949), is a bit erratic, but it does list and, after a fashion, describe

the principal theater books in English since the publication of
Rosamond Gilder's *A Theatre Library* (1932).

II

Dramatic theory has sometimes been a substitute for a direct
examination of plays, but it does have a certain relevance. Of
course, many critics of the drama have gotten along splendidly
without it; certainly Eric Bentley has suffered little from his
reluctance to offer definitions of comedy, tragedy, and the like.
The British magazine *Scrutiny* was similarly reluctant; one of its
reviewers, examining a study of Sophocles, observed: "It is pleasant
to be able to say that Professor Waldock's book has one outstanding merit: nowhere does it attempt a definition of Tragedy."
L. C. Knights, long an editor of *Scrutiny*, illustrates this approach
in his essay "Notes on Comedy," reprinted in *The Importance of
Scrutiny*, edited by Eric Bentley (1948), as he concludes his remarks on Shakespeare's *Henry IV*: "No theory of comedy can
explain the play; no theory of comedy will help us to read it more
adequately."

Considerations of tragedy enjoy the authority of the first drama
critic, Aristotle. The *Poetics* is available in a variety of translations. S. H. Butcher's version, first published in 1894, includes the
Greek text and is accompanied by a lengthy commentary; it has
recently been reprinted with a new preface by John Gassner
(1951). Ingram Bywater's version, originally published in 1909,
is more crisply phrased; it has been reprinted (1920) with a preface by Gilbert Murray. L. J. Potts' version (1953) is clear and
readable, but its translation of some key terms is questionable.
Humphrey House's letter to *TLS* on February 4, 1954 conveniently states the main objections. John Crowe Ransom objects in
"The Cathartic Principle," *The World's Body* (1938), that
Butcher endeavors to elevate Aristotle, to make him more high-
minded and less a scientist than he was. Butcher's commentary is
nevertheless informative. The reader who wants his Aristotle
straight has the choice of Bywater or Potts or perhaps the two,
especially since Potts relies mainly upon Bywater's edition of the
Greek and is continually noting and justifying his departures from
Bywater's translation.

Aristotle's place among students of drama is still fairly high, although some disparagement has been heard. F. R. Leavis has made one of the most sweeping rejections of Aristotle's notes on tragedy, in "The 'Great Books' and a Liberal Education," *Commentary* (1955): "The man who leaves the university able to suppose that in the *Poetics* he has studied an illuminating treatise on the foundations of literary criticism has not used his time to real educational profit—even if he has won high educational distinction." More often, the *Poetics* is disputed on a particular point. Cedric Whitman, in *Sophocles* (1951), questioned the idea of *hamartia;* Ransom, in "The Cathartic Principle," criticized Aristotle's "scientific" bias, but he wrote more sympathetically of the *Poetics* a few years later, in "The Literary Criticism of Aristotle," for a symposium entitled *Lectures in Criticism* (1949). The case for the *Poetics* is stated modestly by F. L. Lucas, in *Tragedy* (1928); Aristotle's great virtue, according to Lucas, is asking the right questions. Greater claims are made by the University of Chicago Neo-Aristotelians. A typical statement is Elder Olson's "The Poetic Method of Aristotle: Its Powers and Limitations," in *English Institute Essays 1951* (1952); the limitations Olson sees lie principally in the fact that any method or philosophy necessarily excludes others. Aristotle, he maintains, "developed not only a permanently true but also an indefinitely operable poetic method." Another member of the same school, R. S. Crane, distinguishes in "Varieties of Dramatic Criticism," *Carleton Drama Review* (1956) between an Aristotelian and a Platonic tradition of dramatic criticism; the former holds that "the drama can be adequately discussed in terms of principles peculiar to the drama itself," while the latter invokes "other human activities or functions." This dichotomy would make most dramatic criticism Aristotelian, although Crane generously gives Shaw, T. S. Eliot, and Francis Fergusson away to the Platonic tradition.

The validity of Lucas's observation about Aristotle's asking the right questions seems borne out by the continuing examination of Aristotle's terms and concepts. The *Poetics* has become a landmark; it is as much a fact of history as the Greek drama itself. The controversies fostered by the *Poetics* have, in recent years, concerned *hamartia* (the tragic flaw) and *catharsis*. *Mimesis* has caused little difficulty lately: most critics would apparently follow

Lucas in noting that the word is more adequately translated *representation* and that it does not signify literal imitation. Philip Wheelwright, in "Mimesis and Katharsis: An Archetypal Consideration," *English Institute Essays 1951*, attributes a greater significance to *mimesis*, permitting the word to suggest participation in the object represented. Ransom, on the other hand, takes a narrower view of what Aristotle meant by *mimesis*, in "The Mimetic Principle," *The World's Body*.

Aristotle's strong emphasis on plot has not caused much criticism, in the light of the abundant attention he gives to character as a function of plot. In "The Heresy of Plot," *English Institute Essays 1951*, Reuben A. Brower endorses the Aristotelian emphasis as a corrective to our present concern with the word. The New Criticism directed us to the word, and this tendency is, in fact, reflected by Ransom in "The Literary Criticism of Aristotle."

The questions about *hamartia* have been: Does it mean sin or only error? Does the term, however translated, have any reference to tragedy? The translators have left the field open for other interpreters. Butcher renders *hamartia* as "some great error or frailty," but he qualifies these words by offering three alternatives in his commentary: first "an error due to inadequate knowledge," second "a moral . . . fault or error where the act is conscious and intentional, but not deliberate," and third, "a defect of character." Later translators are less disposed to offer a moral interpretation. Bywater translates "some error of judgement," and Potts has simply "error."

The leading interpreter of the moral view of *hamartia* has surely been A. C. Bradley in *Shakespearean Tragedy* (1904), who is explicit in his judgment of the tragic hero's fault: "The critical action is, in greater or less degree, wrong or bad." Lucas takes a moderate position, defending Aristotle but not insisting on the moral nature of *hamartia*. He finds it to be no more than "a mistake," and he permits as great a range of variation as Butcher does—from sin (in Aeschylus) to "an intellectual mistake" (in Ibsen). A more recent exponent of the moral force of *hamartia* approaches the question very differently. He is Philip Wheelwright, in *The Burning Fountain* (1954), who regards *hamartia* as a religious offence requiring a penalty and usually some sort of ritual exorcism.

The most serious criticism of Aristotle comes from those writers who have charged him with moralizing tragedy and requiring poetic justice. They include W. Macneile Dixon, *Tragedy* (1924), Cedric Whitman, *Sophocles* (1951), and Peter Alexander, *Hamlet: Father and Son* (1955). Dixon suggests that Aristotle may not have been serious or that the error may come in a student's notes. Whitman insists that Aristotle is endeavoring to impose his own ethical philosophy upon the dramatists. For Alexander, *hamartia* is an unfortunate afterthought designed to explain the more important conception of *catharsis;* it is the reverse of the truth, since the hero is ruined by his heroism, not by his frailty. Combatting *hamartia* along with other Aristotelian notions, H. D. F. Kitto, in *Form and Meaning in Drama* (1956), observes that the trouble is not always insufficient *hamartia* but sometimes too much, since "Agamemnon and Clytemnestra and Medea and perhaps Creon" possess an excess of the quality.

A few critics attempt to salvage the principle of *hamartia* without turning tragedy into a didactic drama. Bernard Knox is in effect reaching such a compromise in *Oedipus at Thebes* (1957) when he rejects the "Aristotelian formula" but concludes: "The catastrophe of Oedipus is a product not of any one quality of Oedipus but of the total man." What is to be salvaged finally is the principle of causation, the relationship between character and fate. The important thing to remember is that, in a tragedy, fate is evil, but character need be evil only in the sense that it will bring about such a fate. The catastrophe can have its inception in the excess of *hamartia* that Kitto finds in Agamemnon or in the heroic virtue that Alexander attributes to the tragic character. A line from Goethe (quoted by Dixon) expresses such a thought: "Everything we do has a result, but that which is right and prudent does not always lead to good, nor the contrary to what is bad." A similar view is taken by Clifford Leech in "Implications of Tragedy," in his *Shakespeare's Tragedies and Other Studies in Seventeenth-Century Drama* (1950): "The justice of the gods consists simply in the natural law that every act must have its consequence and that the consequence will be determined by the act and its context." Northrop Frye's formulation is similar, in *Anatomy of Criticism* (1957): "The particular thing called tragedy that happens to the tragic hero does not depend on his moral status. If it is causally related to something he has done, as it generally is, the tragedy is in the inevitability of the consequences of the act, not in its moral significance as an act."

Examining *catharsis*, both Lucas and Butcher begin with the basic circumstance that Aristotle's doctrine of *catharsis* was a necessary reply to Plato's argument against poetry in the *Republic*. If Plato charged that poetry infected its audience with the base emotions of pity and fear, then Aristotle must represent the process by which the infection is purged. Lucas considers Aristotle's case for *catharsis* no more than "an ingenious piece of special pleading" and goes on to offer an independent theory of the end of tragedy. Butcher accepts Milton's view of *catharsis* as a homeopathic treatment of Pity and Fear "to reduce them to just measure." Ransom, accepting the medical interpretation, is facetious with *catharsis* and condemns the theory as belonging to a scientist who wants to banish emotions; returning to the subject a few years later when he is more sympathetic to Aristotle, he still rejects the whole notion of *catharsis*. Wheelwright calls attention to the religious aspects of *catharsis* precisely because so little is said of them in Aristotle; the deficiency, he indicates, is Aristotle's. Kitto appropriates the term *catharsis* for his own quite independent view of the end of tragedy (as others do)—the apprehension of a coherent pattern: "We understand, as we cannot always do in life. . . . We are given the feeling that the Universe is coherent." There is an obvious kinship here to the total view of the tragic pattern earlier ascribed to Leech and Frye. Related also is Lucas' judgment that what tragedy finally offers is an experience of what is true and significant.

James Joyce's conception of the effect of pity and fear in tragedy, as expressed by Stephen Dedalus in *A Portrait of the Artist as a Young Man* (1916), has a more than curious value. He considers pity and terror to have the effect of arresting the mind. As T. R. Henn observes, in *The Harvest of Tragedy* (1956), this view is related to I. A. Richards' theory, in his *Principles of Literary Criticism* (1924); Richards, however, finds the observer to be arrested, not *by*, but *between* Pity and Fear. He translates *catharsis* "refinement" and finds it in this "balance or reconciliation of discordant qualities . . . whether Aristotle meant anything of this kind or not."

Modern considerations of *catharsis* have inevitably turned into statements of the nature and purpose of tragedy. Sometimes the critic will, like Richards and Kitto, appropriate the term *catharsis* but find his own meaning for it. Many have found, like Richards, that the essence of tragedy is in some kind of balance. Una Ellis-Fermor in *The Frontiers of Drama* (1946) discovers "the conflict of impressions; evident evil against partially hidden yet immanent and overruling good." Replying to her, Clifford Leech has located the crucial balance in the opposition of Terror and Pride. Louis Martz, "The Saint as Tragic Hero," in *Tragic Themes in Western Literature*, edited by Cleanth Brooks (1955), has preferred to speak of "the human sufferer and the secret cause," the former identified with pity and the latter with affirmation, awe, and terror. Most of these dichotomies are restatements of the opposition of life and death or of innocence and guilt.

Tragedy is the play in which man faces death, even though he may avoid it in certain Greek "tragedies." Herbert J. Muller, in *The Spirit of Tragedy* (1956), is never on firmer ground than when he finds "the ultimate source of tragedy" in "the simple fact that man must die." Henn finds it a common assumption that "death is a natural termination of the tragic fact or experience," but it is hardly necessary to seek endorsement for so elementary an observation. It may suffice to add that the Elizabethans were particularly explicit on the presence of death as the *sine qua non* of tragedy: Theodore Spencer's *Death and Elizabethan Tragedy* (1936) and J. V. Cunningham's *Woe or Wonder* (1951) supply abundant evidence on this point, and M. C. Bradbrook's *Themes and Conventions of Elizabethan Tragedy* (1935), following T. S. Eliot's hint on Othello's self-dramatization (in "Shakespeare and the Stoicism of Seneca"), comments in detail on the significant posturing of dying tragic heroes. Even the most ordinary employment of the world reminds us of the traditional and primary association of tragedy with death.

In tragedy, then, the living man encounters death and the apparently innocent man encounters guilt. Two recent articles have been especially concerned with explicating this matter. In Laurence Michel's formulation, "concocted out of a phrase of Leslie Fiedler's": "Tragedy is consummated when the dream of innocence is confronted by the fact of guilt, and acquiesces therein"—see "The Possibility of a Christian Tragedy," *Thought* (1956). Richard B. Sewall in "The Tragic Form," *Essays in Criticism* (1954) has found "the source of tragic suffering" in "the sense of simultaneous guilt and guiltlessness." But to reveal the difficult position of the "guilty" tragic hero we need do no more than recall the evanescent nature of *hamartia;* if Whitman and Alexander have not quite destroyed the conception, they have shown us how difficult it is to find, let alone define, such a quality. And if it is difficult for us, it is much more difficult for the tragic hero himself.

Few critics have questioned the hero's attainment of self-knowledge; Cleanth Brooks has made it the main point of the brief definition of tragedy in his Introduction to *Tragic Themes In Western Literature*. Kenneth Burke, approaching the problem by way of Hegel and Gilbert Murray, has found the dialectic of tragedy to be *poiema, pathema, mathema* (the act, the sufferance or state, the thing learned). Francis Fergusson, in *The Idea of a Theatre* (1949) has interpreted the triad as "Purpose, Passion (or Suffering) and Perception" and has called it the "tragic rhythm of action." His summary is endorsed by Sewall. The tragic hero perceives, or we do, but this much is implicit in what we have previously said about the recognition of a causal pattern in tragedy. The problem lies in finding the cautious path between optimism and pessimism in the hero's final state of mind.

The ultimate exaltation and enlightenment need be solely the rediscovery and assertion of the heroic personality. It is this possibility to which Alexander gives his emphasis—the mastering of disagreeables, "the sense of superiority or triumph that seems to obliterate all other considerations." This heroic exaltation is possible, not only, as Alexander implies, to the blameless, but, as Leech insists, even to the "deeply guilty," to all, in fact, who possess "a quality of mind that somehow atones for the nature of the world in which they and we live." To go further in stating the tragic exaltation is to run the danger that Muller implicitly acknowledges when he finally stumbles into quoting a Boy Scout motto. J. W. Krutch approaches this sort of exaggeration with his enthusiastic account of the joy and fortune of the tragic hero, in *The Modern Temper* (1929), even if his exaggeration is explained by his larger purpose—an effort to contrast tragic nobility with our own bleak perspectives. The problem of striking the right note has inspired at least two critical exchanges. The more noteworthy appeared in *Scrutiny* (1936 and 1944, reprinted in Bentley's *The Importance of Scrutiny*). George Santayana, in "Tragic Philosophy," represented the tragic hero as desperate and passionate but doomed to a final, unambiguous defeat. F. R. Leavis, in "Tragedy and the Medium," upheld the function of poetry, the tragic medium, in producing a "sense of heightened life" and "a recognizing of positive value as in some way defined and vindicated by death." Exchanging views in *Diogenes* (Nos. 7 and 15), Charles G. Bell and Lester G. Crocker apply different standards and come to predictably different conclusions. Bell excludes "radical pessimism"; Crocker, frequently invoking Aristotle, includes pessimistic or Christian tragedy and insists on the presence of a tragic hero.

For most interpreters the boundary of tragical optimism is Christianity. It is a boundary beyond which tragedy may not pass. The impossibility of Christian tragedy has become a sort of truism, for Karl Jaspers in *Tragedy Is Not Enough* (1953) and Herbert Weisinger in *Tragedy and the Paradox of the Fortunate Fall* (1953), as well as Richards, Lucas, Leech, Ellis-Fermor, Santayana, and Michel all make this point. Muller concedes the possibility of a Christian tragedy, but the statement must properly be seen in its context as a stick to beat T. S. Eliot, who has presumably failed to write it. Henn briefly attempts a reply to Jaspers and Ellis-Fermor, a reply which seems based on the fact that the Christian can see only the human aspect of events: "We can not *know* how the balances of judgment will be loaded." Kitto tells us that *Hamlet*, as well as Greek tragedy, is religious drama, but what he means is that the coherence of these plays gives us "the feeling that the Universe is coherent." Gilbert Murray is making a more conventional reference to religion when, in "Greek and English Tragedy: A Contrast," *English Literature and the Classics*, edited by G. S. Gordon (1912), he notes "that the English tragedy is primarily an entertainment, the Greek a religious ritual." W. H. Auden makes a quite different distinction between classical and nonclassical tragedy when, in "The Christian Tragic Hero," *New York Times Book Review*, December 16, 1945, he observes that "Greek tragedy is the tragedy of necessity" and "Christian tragedy is the tragedy of possibility." What is meant here is that fate governs in one and free will in the other; Christianity plays little direct part in the "Christian tragedy" under consideration—Melville's *Moby Dick*.

Tragedy must give the emphatic impression of the reality and significance of the event. Lucas elevates this fact into the *raison d'être* of tragedy, but even if we are more casual with this knowledge we will find it indicated in the traditional nature of Greek tragedy and in the continuing Renaissance tradition that tragedy was true. Frye embodies this view in his definition of tragedy, "The response to tragedy is 'this must be' or, perhaps more accurately, 'this does happen': the event is primary, the explanation of it secondary and variable." Leavis, in his reply to Santayana, and Ransom, in "The Literary Criticism of Aristotle," have emphasized the vital contribution of the "medium," "heroic style" to tragedy. This element is surveyed historically in Moody E. Prior's *The Language of Tragedy* (1947).

But tragedy is impossible without the complex tragic form. It is a microcosm, and tightly packed within it is the great world. In her sweeping tribute to the tragic form, Ellis-Fermor finds it at once the reflection and the proof "of a beneficent world-order," but to find this world-order "implied . . . by the presence of form" is excessive even for tragedy. Still, the chorus of Greek tragedy represents the world, and so do the analogues and subplots of Elizabethan tragedy. Lucas has made this point in principle, although he does not apply it consistently to Elizabethan drama. Henn argues this view profusely, but in detail that he never develops, listing a great variety of "minute particulars" which make up the tragic structure. Citing the use of comedy and madness in tragedy, Leech takes his illustrations from seventeenth-century drama and puts them to good use in his chapter on "The Tragic Effect." But the fullest account of the wonderful complexity of tragedy is Francis Fergusson's in *The Idea of a Theater*. The unity of *Oedipus Rex*, he maintains, is "by analogy," using the phrase that is often applied to the double-plots of Elizabethan plays. The pattern of "analogous action" is most completely illustrated in his essay on Hamlet. What Fergusson demonstrates is hard to transform into a generalization, except to say that the play is the whole play, all of it accounted for and none of it swept under the carpet.

Fergusson's book rests upon a conception of tragedy which

must be dealt with here. It is Gilbert Murray's theory of the ritual origins of tragic drama, an idea which has its roots in Nietzsche's *The Birth of Tragedy*. Murray first stated his views in an appendix to Jane Harrison's *Themis* in 1912, "Excursus on the Ritual Forms preserved in Greek tragedy." He found the origin of tragedy in the ritual observance of "the Death and Rebirth of the Year Spirit." The ceremony would include an Agon (Contest), Pathos (usually the death of the god), Messenger, Threnon (lamentation), Anagnorisis (discovery of the dead god), Theophany (resurrection), and Peripeteia ("extreme change of feeling from grief to joy"). Murray goes on to trace the continuing presence of these elements in the Greek tragic dramatists, offering Euripides as his prize example. Murray expounds these views in many more of his writings, including *Euripides and His Age* (1913), his Preface to Ingram Bywater's *Aristotle on the Art of Poetry* (1920), and *Aeschylus: The Creator of Tragedy* (1940). In an essay "Hamlet and Oedipus," in *The Classical Tradition in Poetry* (1927), he attributed resemblances between the stories of Hamlet and Oedipus to their common origin in the ritual of death and rebirth. A colleague of Murray's, F. M. Cornford, inferred a similar ritual origin for comedy and a continuing reflection of the original ritual pattern. The work of Murray and Cornford has found wide acceptance, especially among critics of literature. Theodor H. Gaster, in *Thespis: Ritual, Myth, and Drama in the Ancient Near East* (1950), identified similar rituals as the origins of drama elsewhere in the ancient world. Herbert Weisinger, in *Tragedy and the Paradox of the Fortunate Fall*, has traced back tragedy's peculiar triumph-in-death to the fortunate fall inherent in the death and rebirth of the god, making a survey of the idea and its ritual forms in pagan, Hebrew, and Christian thought. Weisinger has promised a book on literary tragedy that will further examine the ritual structure of tragedy; some of his work in progress is to be found in a recent article, "The Myth and Ritual Approach to Shakespearean Tragedy," *Centennial Review* (1957). Stanley Edgar Hyman, in "Freud and the Climate of Tragedy," *PR* (1956), constructs a theory of tragedy on Freud's "gloomy, stoic, and essentially tragic" philosophy and the ritual pattern.

But the most impressive work of literary criticism to reflect Murray's theories is Fergusson's *The Idea of a Theater*. What par-

ticularly distinguishes his use of Murray's method is his freedom
in the use of it. Murray employs the method rigidly; Fergusson
employs it along with a variety of other dramatic perspectives and,
incidentally, urges one central correction of Murray's employment
of his own method: he suggests Sophocles, rather than Euripides, as
the ideal inheritor of the ritual pattern. While Murray hunts out
the occurrences that resemble ritual events, Fergusson restores
the minute particulars to a larger pattern, resolving them as part
of a single large action that can usually be epitomized in a single
infinitive phrase (for *Ghosts*, "to control the Alving heritage for
my own life"; for *Six Characters in Search of an Author*, "to take
the stage"). The ritual method serves as a critical tool that helps
to bring about this reunification of the play, and it also puts the
play in the center of its society, reflecting a public concern as
momentous as the rebirth of the year; at least, this can be done in
interpreting *Oedipus* and *Hamlet*, but not for the "partial perspectives of the modern theatre."

Murray's theories have been under attack by classical scholars
ever since they were first stated. A. W. Pickard-Cambridge made
the most detailed criticism in his *Dithyramb Tragedy and Comedy*
(1927). He is effective chiefly when he endeavors—and fails—to
find in Greek tragedy the reappearance of ritual episodes apparently required by Murray. Similar objections have been raised
by such classical scholars as Margarete Bieber in *The History of
the Greek and Roman Theater* (1939), Moses Hadas in *A History
of Greek Literature* (1950), H. D. F. Kitto in *Form and Meaning
in Drama*, and A. M. G. Little in *Myth and Society in Attic Drama*
(1942). Werner Jaeger, in *Paideia* (1939), compliments the
"balanced judgment and great completeness" of Pickard-Cambridge. Philip Wheelwright, in *The Burning Fountain*, commends
Jaeger for warning "against over-playing the idea" of the ritual
foundations of tragedy. At the very least, these scholars have
established the necessity of a flexible application of the ritual
method. Some of the hostile scholars are, like Kitto, willing to
concede or at least to put aside the question of the ritual element in
tragedy. The matters at issue are the form of the ritual and its
influence upon "literary" drama. What seems to be in order is a
more varied approach like Fergusson's, rather than the all-or-noth-
ing argument of Murray's "Excursus."

The current critical literature on comedy is much less considerable, and most of it is repetitious. The absence of an Aristotelian
account of comedy has inspired hypotheses as to what Aristotle's
view of comedy might be. Lane Cooper has produced one such
hypothesis in *An Aristotelian Theory of Comedy* (1922), staying
very close to Aristotle's few statements on comedy and to whatever
parallels might be made to match his interpretation of tragedy. In
attributing to comedy "a catharsis of troublesome emotions like
anger and envy" or "of laughter itself," Cooper approaches
Freud's conception of "a sum of damming energy . . . released
and discharged," in *Wit and Its Relation to The Unconscious*
(1916). Northrop Frye employs Aristotle's term differently,
crediting comedy with a catharsis of sympathy and ridicule. L. J.
Potts adapts an Aristotelian idea in *Comedy* (1948); reaffirming
Aristotle's emphasis on plot, he invents for comedy a new kind
of indispensable *Mythos*, a spatial plot which exists only to gather
and to juxtapose characters—"a grouping of characters rather than
a march of events." Consequently, the Comedy of Humors is the
basic type of comedy, and everything else, including Comedy of
Manners, must be regarded as a variant.

Potts's novel theory of plot is the chief new idea in a book that
may serve to introduce us to the conventional theories of comedy.
Potts, like others before and after him, records the modesty of
comedy, the beneficent social effect of its advocacy of "balance
or proportion," and its concern with society, with sex, and with
"the abnormal but not unusual." Like most modern writers on the
subject, he will accept neither laughter nor a happy ending as a
determinant in the definition of comedy. The social function of
comedy and its "sense of proportion" are called once more to our
attention in H. T. E. Perry's *Masters of Dramatic Comedy* (1939).
Louis Kronenberger phrases some of the familiar definitions a bit
more freshly in *The Thread of Laughter* (1952), but again we are
told of comedy's modesty and of its social criticism, which reveals
"how far human beings fall short of the ideal." L. C. Knights,
fighting every step of the way against any comic theory, in "Notes
on Comedy," concedes "the breaking down of undesirable attitudes," but his main purpose is to discourage theorizing about
genres. On a simple level, James Feibleman's *In Praise of Comedy*
(1939) furnishes a handy summary of past theories of comedy and

a fresh collection of comic instances from such modern practitioners as Chaplin, Will Rogers, and the Marx Brothers; Feibleman's own theory stresses the social aspects—or, to be more exact,
the "inherently revolutionary nature" of comedy. He finds that
the perfect logic of comedy exposes the illogic of actuality, or,
to cite his italicized definition: "Comedy consists in the indirect
affirmation of the ideal logical order by means of the derogation
of the limited orders of actuality."

In *The Dark Voyage and the Golden Mean* (1949), Albert
Cook takes issue with "the socialist Feibleman." He sees comedy
as bourgeois and conservative; in his title, tragedy is represented
by the dark voyage and comedy by the golden mean. Although
he sometimes confuses a reader by the haste and plenitude of his
lists of traits and categories, Cook achieves a rather full outline of
the traditional idea of comedy. Its realm is the probable; it ritually
expels abnormality; it may exploit the subhuman, in the beast
or the machine—but most of its salient qualities are apparent from
Cook's table of contrasts with tragedy at the end of his second
chapter. The most comprehensive survey of the field of comedy
is, however, not Cook's but Northrop Frye's, in *Anatomy of
Criticism;* it rests heavily upon ritual theories but is abundantly
illustrated by literary examples.

For some relative novelty in the treatment of comedy, we are
indebted to Henri Bergson whose *Laughter* (1928) is now (1956)
available as a paperback, with George Meredith's "Essay On
Comedy" and additional material by Wylie Sypher. Bergson notes
the social usefulness of comedy but finds the basis of the comic
in "something mechanical encrusted on the living." His many developments of this pattern are immensely valuable in interpreting
Molière, but they are much less helpful with Shakespeare; E. E.
Stoll admits as much in a Bergson-inspired essay, "The Comic
Method," in *Shakespeare Studies* (1927). W. H. Auden attempts
a variation on Bergson's approach in "Notes on the Comic,"
Thought (1952), viewing the comic as "a contradiction" between
"the individual or personal" and "the universal or impersonal." As
Auden expounds his idea, the "universal" comes to resemble "the
mechanical" in Bergson, but the adjustment of vocabulary does
permit a wider employment of the basic Bergsonian notion.

Another theory of comedy can be traced to F. M. Cornford's

The Origin of Attic Comedy (1934), which proposed for comedy the same ritual origin that Murray claimed for tragedy. The chief exception is a "difference of emphasis"—comedy values character above plot, creating standard types who are mainly variations of the *Alazon* or Impostor. Cornford's ideas have been more widely applied in the interpretation of English drama than Murray's, probably because English literature has its own corroborating evidence —primitive ritual plays, interpreted and illustrated for us by R. J. E. Tiddy in *The Mummers' Play* (1923) and by E. K. Chambers in *The English Folk-Play* (1933). Tiddy points out some connections between the folk play and the professional drama of Elizabethan times. His evidence and Chambers' surely helped to popularize the ritual interpretation of English comedy. In spite of their fundamental differences, Cook and Feibleman both employ a "ritual" approach. Such an emphasis is prominent also in Frye's treatment of comedy in various essays, especially "The Argument of Comedy," *English Institute Essays 1948* (1949), which he revised for *Anatomy of Criticism*. C. L. Barber explores Shakespeare's ritual inheritance in two essays, "The Saturnalian Pattern In Shakespeare's Comedy," *SR* (1951) and "From Ritual to Comedy: An Examination of *Henry IV*," *English Stage Comedy* (1955), discovering a new and meaningful context for much of Shakespeare's comedy. Sypher interprets the "ritual" view of comedy in his appendix to Bergson and Meredith.

III

Of the general histories of English drama, two ought to be mentioned. Allardyce Nicoll's *British Drama* (1925, reissued 1927, 1932, 1947) is a conventional, faithful record of the facts of dramatic history. As a critic, Nicoll is enthusiastic and interesting but not always consistent. His pages on Yeats are devoted almost entirely to the more conventional plays; on O'Casey, however, he flies off excitedly with the judgment that *Juno and the Paycock* and *The Plough and the Stars* are "far surpassed by" the semi-expressionistic *Silver Tassie*. Alan S. Downer's *The British Drama* (1950) is very different. Instead of filling his book with long lists of plays and adding indistinguishable brief details about each, Downer has written full analyses of typical plays. His suggestive interpretations of *Lear, The Changeling, Friar Bacon and Friar Bungay, Black-Ey'd Susan,* and *Getting Married* give a fuller impression of dramatic development than Nicoll's plot-summaries. Nicoll's method is seen to better purpose in his five-volume *History of English Drama* (revised 1952–1955) where his great detail makes its impression by sheer weight. The fifth volume has not yet reappeared and must be consulted in the edition of 1946.

Recent studies of medieval drama are still overshadowed by E. K. Chambers' *The Mediaeval Stage* (1903), and Chambers has brought his history up to date in the long first chapter of his *English Literature at the Close of the Middle Ages* (1945). The most recent survey, Hardin Craig's *English Religious Drama* (1955), has the virtue of placing the English medieval plays in a European context, but it is excessively involved with Craig's special views.

Much of the scholarship in the field is devoted to a few knotty factual problems—the dating of a cycle, the nature of its origin, and the possibility of determining its author. Scholarly opinion still places the first mysteries early in the fourteenth century, in spite of Salter's efforts, in *Mediaeval Drama in Chester* (1955), to move the date forward to the last quarter of that century. The origin is in the liturgical plays, which departed out of the church and into the vernacular because of their popularity, not primarily because of any clerical hostility. The mysteries were evidently based on the liturgical plays, although few scholars will go as far as Craig in maintaining specific dependence on liturgy. Corpus Christi Day was a favorite occasion for performance, but the association of the plays with the holiday and with its procession has, in the past, been exaggerated. As for authors, none is generally agreed upon. Apart from these factual matters, two main concerns have occupied scholars—the theological and the aesthetic qualities of these plays. Karl Young supplied much of the material for study of the religious basis of medieval drama, in his *Drama of the Mediaeval Church* (1933) which is both an account and a collection of the drama that preceded secularization of the plays. G. R. Owst argues for the primacy of theology, in *Literature and Pulpit in Mediaeval England* (1933), finding inspiration for the mystery play in illustrations used by popular preachers: the plays' realism, characterization, humor, satire, and theology—all seem derived from the sermon.

The argument is sound enough, except for Owst's exclusive emphasis on sermons; few scholars will now deny that the sermon *contributed* to the mystery play. Owst has an easier task with the morality, where the sermon's influence is to be seen in the allegory, in the sharp satirical realism, and finally in "the dramatic treatment of human life and death." H. C. Gardiner, in *Mysteries' End* (1946), has provided another type of argument for the theological significance of the mystery plays. They were, he demonstrates, encouraged by churchmen and attacked by enemies of the Church. The mysteries' end in England, he concludes, was due not to any decline in popularity but to the hostility of the Puritans. Other scholars, mainly in articles, have interpreted the theological doctrine of the mysteries and found it central to them; Craig takes this view in his book.

Among those who examine the mysteries as art is A. P. Rossiter, in *English Drama from Early Times to the Elizabethans* (1950). His scholarship is a good deal more casual than Craig's or Chambers' but he makes a strong case for dramatic principles which governed from medieval times to the Elizabethan period. He provides necessary counterweight to scholars who often refuse to distinguish drama from theology, who ring a change on Owst's position by finding the drama only a form of sermon. In 1929, George R. Coffman published "A Plea for the Study of the Corpus Christi Play as Drama," *SP*, but few responded. Mary H. Marshall, in "Aesthetic Values of the Liturgical Drama," in *English Institute Essays, 1950* (1951) goes on from Young's work and finds in the liturgical plays "a formalized poetic drama" and "a complete poetic experience." Arnold Williams, in *The Characterization of Pilate in the Towneley Plays* (1950) reports the plays' consistent attention to character. Waldo F. McNeir in "The Corpus Christi Passion Plays as Dramatic Art," *SP* (1951), evidently in answer to Coffman's plea, offers a program for literary criticism of the mysteries, urging that "they are drama first, doctrine afterwards."

But we can go beyond programs to a few efforts as specific criticism. William Empson has glanced at the double-plot structure of the Second Shepherds' Play in *Some Versions of Pastoral* (1935); Homer A. Watt has closely examined the same play in

"The Dramatic Unity of the Secunda Pastorum," *Essays and Studies in Honor of Carleton Brown* (1940); John Speirs' painstaking analysis of some mystery plays, in two *Scrutiny* articles (1951 and 1952) is illuminating but is marred by an excessive emphasis on ritual origins of the action; the substance of the first article appears as "The Towneley *Shepherds' Plays*" in the Penguin *Guide to English Literature* (1954).

Scholarly opinion remains unchanged on the best-known English morality, *Everyman;* in spite of Henry de Vocht's *Everyman: A Comparative Study of Texts and Sources* (1947), it is still regarded as a translation from a Dutch play. Close study of individual moralities has revealed a more serious, more tightly woven pattern than had been suspected: Mary Philippa Coogan's *An Interpretation of the Moral Play, Mankind* (1947), for example, brings to light a complex allegory to which the comic episodes contribute. Other recent books have paused to interpret the morality play in the context of a larger subject. Thus, Willard Farnham's *The Medieval Heritage of Elizabethan Tragedy* (1936) includes two chapters on the morality as an influence on subsequent tragedy, H. H. Adams' *English Domestic or Homiletic Tragedy, 1575 to 1642* (1944) finds in the morality play an important source for one of the characteristic Elizabethan dramatic genres, and Irving Ribner's "The Tudor History Play: An Essay in Definition," *Tulane Studies In English* (1954), detects qualities of the morality in the chronicle play.

Secular dramatic traditions have been the subject of independent examination, although considerable attention has been given to their effect upon the religious drama. Craig seems inhospitable to this notion, but Chambers, Rossiter, and Salter all grant the influence of secular mimes and folk plays on religious drama. Allardyce Nicoll in *Masks Mimes and Miracles* (1931) has argued that a professional mime tradition somehow lasted from ancient Rome to the popular farces of the late Middle Ages. Such a case is hard to maintain, in the absence of any very tangible evidence, and it is therefore not surprising, as Salter points out, that Nicoll withdraws slightly from his position in two of his later books. Another kind of secular performance is recorded in Enid Welsford's *The Fool* (1935), which follows the history of the court-fool, the Lord of Misrule, the stage fool, and other buffoons from ancient times to Charlie Chaplin, with emphasis on the medieval tradition and its impact upon Elizabethan drama, mainly in Shakespeare's plays. But mimes and fools comprised only part of the secular dramatic practice. The most considerable secular activities in the medieval drama are described in two books already mentioned, A. J. M. Tiddy's *The Mummers' Play* and E. K. Chambers' *The English Folk-Play*, to which may be added a third, bringing the history down to another period, Charles Read Baskervill's *The Elizabethan Jig* (1929).

Comparatively little has been written lately on the interludes of the early Renaissance. The wonderful year for the study of the interlude was 1926, with A. W. Reed's authoritative but heavily biographical *Early Tudor Drama* and of Henry Medwall's newly discovered comedy, the charming and original *Fulgens and Lucrece*, "the earliest known English secular play," edited by F. S. Boas and A. W. Reed. Recent volumes sponsored by the University of Illinois, however, reflect an effort to restore the Renaissance conception of classical, especially Terentian, drama. They include Marvin T. Herrick's *Comic Theory in the Sixteenth Century* (1950), which interprets Terentian theory but does not establish any link with Renaissance dramatic practice; Herrick's *Tragicomedy* (1955), more devoted to theory than to practice; and T. W. Baldwin's *William Shakespeare's Five-Act Structure* (1947), in which the five-act pattern of Shakespeare's early plays is found to be derived from Terence, and which attributes to Shakespeare's act-divisions a firmness few had suspected.

Yet the most controversial classical figure has not been Terence but Seneca. Seneca had long been credited with a significant influence among the Elizabethan tragic dramatists, notably in F. L. Lucas' *Seneca and Elizabethan Tragedy* (1922) and in T. S. Eliot's "Shakespeare and the Stoicism of Seneca" (1927). The assault on Seneca began with Farnham's *Medieval Heritage of Elizabethan Tragedy*, which granted Seneca some importance but found more significance in the native medieval tradition. Farnham's pupil Howard Baker brought a powerful indictment against the Senecans in *Induction to Tragedy* (1939), in which he proposed native, mainly medieval sources for what had been regarded as Senecan rhetoric, Senecan ghosts, Senecan tyrants, Senecan structure, Senecan philosophy, Senecan plots in *Gorboduc*,

The Spanish Tragedy, and other early tragedies. Baker made his case strong enough to effect a change in the general attitude toward Senecan influence.

IV

Elizabethan studies, summarized earlier in this volume by Gerald E. Bentley, have been numerous and varied. In the last few decades, critics have shown increasing interest in the Elizabethan use of the multiple plot. The Elizabethans themselves usually justified their multiple action by saying that they were trying to satisfy all the different tastes in the audience. Occasionally they spoke of "relief" as a reason for their mixture of comedy and tragedy. Dryden defended the mixtures on this basis in his "Essay of Dramatic Poesy." This principle has been picked up by later critics including Thomas DeQuincey in his essay "On the Knocking at the Gate in 'Macbeth'. " But there are other ways of interpreting the multiple plot. As Fergusson has reminded us, Richard G. Moulton, in *Shakespeare as a Dramatic Artist* (1906), worked out causal relationships between multiple plots. The modern preference, however, is to look for parallels and contrasts. The kernel of this method is Yeats's essay on "The Emotion of Multitude," *Ideas of Good and Evil* (1903), where he speaks of the parallel plots of *Hamlet* and *Lear* as creating the impression of "multitude," of a great world whose central design we are shown. But the seminal essay for modern critics has been William Empson's "Double Plots" in *Some Versions of Pastoral*. Empson finds in the double plot "a sort of parody or parallel in low life to the serious part" which "gives the impression of dealing with life completely." Each plot comments ironically on the other, and yet both contribute to a central theme: for Green's *Friar Bacon and Friar Bungay*, "the power of beauty is like the power of magic"; for *Troilus and Cressida*, "love and war are alike"; for Middleton's *The Changeling*, "love is a madness." Empson is guilty of a few demonstrable lapses —to say "The real changeling from which the play 'derives its title' is DeFlores" is to commit several errors in one—but the essay is full of happy insights and useful suggestions for further interpretation of Elizabethan drama. Empson's way with a multiple plot is apparent in M. C. Bradbrook's *Themes and Conventions of Elizabethan Tragedy* (1935), which works out the complex patterns in more detail than Empson permits himself, and Fergusson's *The Idea of a Theater*, which provides the fullest analysis of *Hamlet's* parallel actions. A striking reminder of the play's complexity appeared the year after Fergusson's book was published, when Harry Levin reported on yet another parallel to the main action, in "An Explication of the Player's Speech," *KR* (1950). In *The British Drama*, Downer made Empson's method the basis of his section on the Elizabethans, his three chapters on "Panoramic Drama." Wylie Sypher in *Four Stages of Renaissance Style* (1955) associates the multiple plot with the spirit of the times, observing that the play of mixed action typifies evasive "mannerism," "because the pathos and laughter are both pressed as far as they can be in opposite directions without any attempt to reconcile, compromise, or accept the logic of either."

Modern scholars have endeavored to recreate the Elizabethan conception of dramatic art. Sometimes, they have proceeded upon the tacit assumptions implicit in the plays, the dramatic conventions, which have been the special concern of M. C. Bradbrook in *Themes and Conventions of Elizabethan Tragedy* and S. L. Bethell in *Shakespeare and the Popular Dramatic Tradition* (1944). E. E. Stoll, in *Art and Artifice in Shakespeare* (1933) and other books, and L. L. Schücking, in *Character Problems in Shakespeare's Plays* (1922), performed this function earlier, in a more mechanical way. Bethell, substituting a more flexible system of conventionalism, and J. I. M. Stewart, in *Character and Motivation in Shakespeare* (1949), defending Shakespeare's psychological realism, have soundly criticized Stoll's and Schücking's positions. Bethell and Miss Bradbrook recognize the Elizabethans' inconsistency, the alternation between convention and realism that so troubled T. S. Eliot (in "Four Elizabethan Dramatists," 1924).

Stage conventions are, by nature, tacit agreements. The Elizabethans also had explicit ideas of dramatic intention, and at long last, scholars have begun to study them. David Klein's *Literary Criticism from the Elizabethan Dramatists* (1910), the earliest book in the field, is a collection of quotations accompanied by some rather lame comments, but the enterprising reader might use the quotations to begin constructing his own synthesis. J. W. H.

Atkins' *English Literary Criticism: The Renascence* (1947) contains brief, orderly chapters on the playwrights' dramatic theory. Madeleine Doran's *Endeavors of Art: A Study of Form in Elizabethan Drama* (1954) is now the leading book in the field. Miss Doran covers most of the necessary subjects, with varying degrees of completeness, and she attempts some application of the dramatic principles she has formulated. Elizabethan aesthetics is set against the background of classical and Renaissance tradition, and, while this context is occasionally illuminating, it as often gives the appearance of being merely decorative. Miss Doran's book has, however, a wealth of information that should inspire further applications of the dramatists' principles to their writing. One more book of a similar purpose, but applied to one dramatic type, is J. V. Cunningham's *Woe or Wonder: The Emotional Effect of Shakespearean Tragedy*. Cunningham's exploration of the nature of tragedy and its effects ("fear, sorrow, and wonder") produces a definition of tragedy that does not take us very far from Aristotle's.

Our understanding of the Elizabethan playhouse as a flexible theater that encouraged highly conventional staging has altered remarkably little in the last few decades. Arguments against the inner stage have been presented rather effectively by George F. Reynolds in *The Staging of Elizabethan Plays at the Red Bull Theatre* (1940) and by C. Walter Hodges in *The Globe Restored* (1953). Leslie Hotson's essay on an Elizabethan "arena" theater, "Shakespeare's Arena," *SR* (1953), has won little support. George R. Kernodle's *From Art to Theatre* (1944) has, however, achieved a genuine alteration in our knowledge of theatrical conditions. Kernodle demonstrates that the popular playhouses had colorful façades which created "the atmosphere of a festival." The old conception of a bare, bleak stage seems now to be incorrect.

Ronald Watkins in *On Producing Shakespeare* (1951) and, more briefly, Alfred Harbage in *Theatre for Shakespeare* (1955) have summarized our knowledge of Elizabethan staging with a view to helping contemporary producers of Shakespeare. Harbage has also presented most of the facts about the audience in *Shakespeare's Audience* (1941). This informative volume might be supplemented by H. S. Bennett's *Shakespeare's Audience* (1944) which takes a slightly more realistic view of the possible frailties of Shakespeare's auditors. Clifford Leech's "The Caroline Audience," in

Shakespeare's Tragedies, brings the study of the audience down to the closing of the theaters.

In recent years, scholars have leaned to the view that Elizabethan acting was highly conventionalized. Harbage summarizes some of the controversy in his *Theatre for Shakespeare*, setting down M. C. Bradbrook for conventionalism and Harley Granville-Barker for realism. He might have added, on the side of formal, conventional acting, Bertram Joseph in *Elizabethan Acting* (1951) and in a chapter of the Penguin *Guide to English Literature* (1955), S. L. Bethell in "Shakespeare's Actors," *RES* (1950), and himself in a *PMLA* article, "abbreviated" in an appendix to *Theatre for Shakespeare*. On the other hand, J. R. Brown in "On the Acting of Shakespeare's Plays," *QJS* (1953) has argued that the artificial acting of which we hear so much was being replaced in Shakespeare's time by a "new naturalism." Alan S. Downer, who speaks with considerable authority as a stage historian and who promises a book on Elizabethan acting, offers contemporary evidence for realistic acting in "The Tudor Actor: A Taste of His Quality," *Theatre Notebook* (1951).

V

On the later periods of dramatic activity, the most complete source of general information is Allardyce Nicoll's five-volume *History of English Drama*. Nicoll is a theater historian first and a drama critic second, but he gives a very thorough and fair account of the literary scholarship in the fields of which he writes.

We are continually finding evidence that the break between 1642 and 1660 has been greatly exaggerated. Alfred Harbage demonstrates, in *Cavalier Drama* (1936), that Caroline dramatic traditions persisted (along with performances) into the Restoration period. The heroic drama is, in consequence, the legitimate offspring of the plays of John Fletcher. But many other sources and influences have been claimed for the heroic plays: the French romances (a source observed by Sir Walter Scott), French classical drama, and Platonic idealism. The idea of the Heroic Poem also left its mark, according to A. E. Parsons, in "The English Heroic Play," *MLR* (1938), but Nicoll omits any reference to this influence. The principal books in the field are C. V. Deane's

Dramatic Theory and the Rhymed Heroic Play (1931), which probably ascribes too much importance to Corneille while it barely mentions Platonic Love, and Bonamy Dobrée's *Restoration Tragedy* (1929), which summarizes the theoretical basis of the genre. To the theoretical expositions of the heroic play by Nicoll and Dobrée should be added a perceptive essay by Clifford Leech "Restoration Tragedy: A Reconsideration," *Durham University Journal* (1950). Leech finds that, of the tragic dramatists of the Restoration, only Dryden ever approached an understanding of tragedy. The "tragic" plays they wrote were the products of "an increasing awareness of personal inadequacy, an increasing desire to live up to extravagant ideas of conduct."

The two Restoration tragedies that belong to literary criticism and not only to literary history are Dryden's *All for Love* and Thomas Otway's *Venice Preserv'd*. They are not, properly speaking, heroic plays but belong to what might be considered a separate category of Shakespearean tragedies. Comparison between *All for Love* and its source, *Antony and Cleopatra*, has provided opportunity for much learned exploration of differences between Dryden and Shakespeare. Dobrée, in *Restoration Tragedy*, prefers Dryden's classical concentration to Shakespeare's diffuseness. Dobrée's statement of the case does not do justice to the Elizabethan panoramic technique, but it does remind us of the genuine merit of Dryden's play. F. R. Leavis, in " 'Antony and Cleopatra' and 'All for Love': A Critical Exercise," *Scrutiny* (1936) makes close comparisons and credits Shakespeare with "an immediately felt superiority in the life of the verse—superiority in concreteness, variety, and sensitiveness." Norman Suckling in "Dryden in Egypt: Reflexions on *All for Love*," *Durham University Journal* (1952) makes a less invidious comparison than either Dobrée and Leavis and decides that Dryden's play is "the greatest—perhaps the only great—classical tragedy in English," a drama with a love theme of a distinctive sort.

The recent discussions of *Venice Preserv'd* include Dobrée's in *Restoration Tragedy*, Roswell G. Ham's in *Otway and Lee* (1931) —the standard biography, coupled with a biography of Otway's contemporary, Nathaniel Lee—and Aline M. Taylor's in *Next to Shakespeare* (1950)—a stage history of Otway's two important tragedies. Dobrée straddles what he seems to think the virtue of

Otway's defect, deploring "his pity-mongering in behalf of love," praises his "reality of passion," and ranks *Venice Preserv'd* second among Restoration tragedies. Ham lists the sources and describes Otway's political troubles at the time of composition. Mrs. Taylor takes the play on Otway's terms as a study of love and friendship in which politics is a negative force. Most of *Next to Shakespeare* is concerned with relating the extraordinary stage success of *Venice Preserv'd* and *The Orphan* which flourished so long as a sufficiently flamboyant acting tradition ruled the stage but disappeared with the rise of realism in the early nineteenth century.

Restoration comedy has long been a controversial subject, but its sources have become a matter of agreement. John Wilcox establishes, in *The Relation of Molière to Restoration Comedy* (1938), that the comic writers may have borrowed freely from Molière, "but they ignored his ideas and spirit." The true inspiration came from the English tradition, especially from such plays of John Fletcher's as *The Wild Goose Chase;* the extent of the debt is recorded in John H. Wilson's *The Influence of Beaumont and Fletcher on Restoration Drama* (1928). Kathleen M. Lynch in *The Social Mode of Restoration Comedy* (1926) has examined the Restoration's inheritance from other English dramatists, including Jonson and Shirley, and from the court cult of Platonic Love.

The controversy over Restoration comedy goes back to Lamb's contention that the plays were artificial and therefore must not be subject to moral judgment. The questions of artificiality and immorality are still discussed, but another issue has arisen which Lamb had not thought it was necessary to raise—the basic question of their merit. Lamb's remarks have themselves come under examination by Walter E. Houghton, Jr., who points out, in "Lamb's Criticism of Restoration Comedy," *ELH* (1943), that Lamb's essay belongs to a larger study of acting and that he was making a plea for the artificial acting which was vanishing from the stage. At least one critic accepts Lamb's thesis without qualification—E. E. Stoll in *From Shakespeare to Joyce*, (1944).

Bonamy Dobrée, in *Restoration Comedy* (1924), contends that the comedies are realistic, critical of "acquired follies," and reflective of "a great curiosity and a desire to experiment." These views are present in Dobrée's essays on most of the dramatists, although we hear little of the "great curiosity" till the chapter on Congreve, which has a tendency to turn into rhapsody on the "constructive thinker" and on the realist who has strayed into "the Charles Lamb world of airy make-believe." To exclaim, of Mrs. Fainall, "what profound psychology is here!" is surely excessive. H. T. E. Perry in *The Comic Spirit in Restoration Drama* (1925) looks for manifestations of Meredith's Comic Spirit, and discovers plays which are satisfactorily tenuous, detached, and exalted. Miss Lynch sees in Restoration comedy the contrast between good and bad form in a "specialized society," accompanied by witty dialogue which has been heavily influenced by *précieuse* conventions: only Wycherley stands outside, criticizing the group as a whole. These defenses of Restoration comedy seem, separately or together, inadequate to the attack by L. C. Knights in "Restoration Comedy: The Reality and the Myth," *Scrutiny* (1947), who assails the comic authors of the Restoration as "insufferably dull," unrelated to "the best thought of the time," lacking in subtlety, interested in pitifully little, tiresomely cynical about marriage, and at times sentimental.

Knights' essay has awakened some controversy. Clifford Leech in "Restoration Comedy: The Earlier Phase," *Essays in Criticism* (1951), concedes the carelessness of most Restoration comedies, but defends the art of *The Man of Mode* and *The Country Wife*. Marvin Mudrick in "Restoration Comedy and Later," *English Institute Essays 1954* (1955), finds Knights "persuasive," but prefers Restoration comedy to Shakespeare's comic drama. The disapproval of Nicoll and Miss Lynch confirms him in his admiration for "Wycherly's toughmindedness": Congreve, who is not so toughminded, is rated lower, and Sheridan is "a second-rate and second-hand playwright," while Wilde manufactured "detachable epigrams." John Wain in "Restoration Comedy and Its Modern Critics," *Essays in Criticism* (1956), considers Knights "much the best writer on Restoration comedy," which is, for him, of interest as a sociological document expressing the royalist's defiance of the routed Puritan. Wain's admiration is reserved for *The Man of Mode*, which he likes especially for its honesty. F. W. Bateson, in "Second Thoughts: L. C. Knights and Restoration Comedy," *Essays in Criticism* (1957), defends Congreve and Wycherly because of their art and their social content, but without completely answering the earlier critics.

Meanwhile two books appeared that were independent of this controversy. Louis Kronenberger devotes more than half of *The Thread of Laughter* (1952) to the comedy of the Restoration and the eighteenth century. He is an appreciative reader's companion who reveals no hidden patterns but, instead, shows us the plays as they were intended and as they strike a sympathetic observer. Thomas H. Fujimura's *The Restoration Comedy of Wit* (1952) is, even Wain admits, "the best introduction to the subject." Fujimura furnishes the comic dramatists with a Hobbesian naturalistic philosophy and recommends a new conception of the genre—the substitution of "comedy of wit" for "comedy of manners." He has laid the foundation for a new appraisal of the Restoration comic dramatists, but his own chapters on Etherege, Wycherley, and Congreve do not constitute that new appraisal.

Only a few volumes on Restoration comedy require further attention. The reputation of Montague Summers, once an eminent amateur of Restoration scholarship, has collapsed and is beyond repair. His study of the drama, *The Playhouse of Pepys* (1935), is, like all his criticism, marked by undisciplined and uncritical enthusiasm. His study of the stage, *The Restoration Theatre* (1934), is filled with interesting detail, but Leslie Hotson's *The Commonwealth and Restoration Stage* (1932) and Eleanore Boswell's *The Restoration Court Stage* (1932) are more authoritative. Background is supplied by G. S. Alleman's *Matrimonial Law and the Materials for Restoration Comedy* (1942), which demonstrates the plays' dependence on reality, and by J. H. Wilson's *The Court Wits of the Restoration* (1948), which examines the activities of the literary coterie which included Etherege, Wycherley, and Rochester.

Biographies of individual dramatists have stressed the life story more than the works. Willard Connely's *Brawny Wycherley* (1930) and Laurence Whistler's *Sir John Vanbrugh* (1938) are typical. Albert S. Borgman's *Thomas Shadwell* (1928) and R. H. Barker's *Mr. Cibber of Drury Lane* (1939), dealing with less promising materials, show an effort at least to diagnose the plays and to deck them out with scholarly information. D. Crane Tay-

lor's *Congreve* (1931) is, as biography, inferior to John C. Hodges'
William Congreve: The Man (1948) which says next to nothing
about the plays. Virginia Woolf's "Congreve's Comedies," in *The
Moment and Other Essays* (1948), expresses deeply felt admiration. Stage history is faithfully recorded in Emmett L. Avery's
Congreve's Plays on the Eighteenth-Century Stage (1951), and
Ned B. Allen's *The Sources of Dryden's Comedies* (1935) is valuable for its tracing of the poet's borrowing.

VI

Historians of eighteenth-century comedy have been concerned
with defining and explaining the sentimentalism which then
dominated the stage. Ernest Bernbaum, who initiated serious study
of the subject with his *The Drama of Sensibility* (1915), found the
basis to be "confidence in the goodness of average human nature."
Nicoll in his *History* recognized sentimentalism by such traits as
"the relating of art to life" and "the deliberate enunciation of a
moral or a social problem." Joseph Wood Krutch in *Comedy and
Conscience after the Restoration* (1924, reissued 1949) finds the
identifying characteristics of sentimental comedy to be the purpose
of teaching morality, the observance of poetic justice, the presentation of ideal characters, and the avoidance of obscenity. John
Harrington Smith in *The Gay Couple in Restoration Comedy*
(1948), recommends a new term, "exemplary comedy"—which
probably says most about the distinctive feature of these plays,
"the use of characters as examples for conveying edification."

Bernbaum seems not much interested in the reasons for the rise
of sentimental drama; in his study, the dramatists simply converted
the audience. F. W. Bateson, in *English Comic Drama, 1700–1750*
(1929), offers an explanation of a sort when he associates sentimental comedy with the generally current spirit of humanitarianism. For Krutch, the key elements are the change in social life
since the Restoration and the Collier controversy. Smith takes a
different view of the matter because he follows the signs of sentimentalism in comedy further back than the others do. He has not
been alone in doing so; his predecessors include Nicoll, who
traces sentimentalism back to 1680, and DeWitt C. Croissant in

"Early Sentimental Comedy," *Essays in Dramatic Literature* (1935). Smith finds Shadwell taking the first step toward exemplary comedy in 1668 with *The Sullen Lovers*, and is convinced by the evidence of Shadwell's plays that "in determining the course which comedy would subsequently take he is the most important figure of his century." The other critical influence is, for Smith, the ladies in the audience. Collier and Steele come along later to encourage a trend that is already well under way. Of Smith's theory, it may be observed that to push back the origins is sound enough, because arbitrary, sudden beginnings are always doubtful in literary history, but to give quite so much credit to one dramatist is hazardous.

Two books examine particular aspects of the change in taste. Sister Rose Anthony's *The Jeremy Collier Stage Controversy* (1937) is very thorough but says nothing about Collier's impact on the stage, which is one of Krutch's major subjects in *Comedy and Conscience*. John Loftis, in *Steele at Drury Lane* (1952), exposes Steele's "intellectual dishonesty" in planning his career as a dramatist while he wrote his attacks on the stage; he evidently had *The Conscious Lovers* (produced, 1722) in mind "as early as 1710." Loftis employs J. H. Smith's critical terms, calling attention to the rather studied "exemplary" qualities of Steele's plays.

John Gay has been the subject of a standard biography by W. H. Irving (1940) and a study of his social philosophy in Sven Armen's *John Gay: Social Critic* (1954). His *Beggar's Opera* is the central exhibit in a study of its genre in E. M. Gagey's *Ballad Opera* (1937) and in two scholarly volumes, by F. Kidson (1922) and W. E. Schultz (1923). But for a statement, or overstatement, of its intrinsic merit, we must go to Empson's essay, "The Beggar's Opera: Mock-Pastoral as the Cult of Independence," in *Some Versions of Pastoral*. Empson savors the play's irony as he suspects it has seldom been savored before; he concludes: "It is a fine thing that the play is still popular, however stupidly it is enjoyed."

The comic dramatists of the eighteenth century have received comparatively little critical attention. Bateson, in *English Comic Drama*, grants the "second-rate" quality of most comedy of the time and relates the decline to the playgoing interests of the middle class and to the nature of the theater; he writes as appreciatively as he can of several dramatists, including Cibber, Steele, Gay, and Fielding. F. S. Boas's *An Introduction to Eighteenth-Century Drama* (1953) is little more than a collection of plot-summaries. In *The Thread of Laughter*, Kronenberger writes sympathetic chapters on Farquhar, Goldsmith, and Sheridan, but a chapter on Cibber and Vanbrugh is less generous to the former. Henry James's striking essay on *The School for Scandal*, which told him "a rather dismal tale of the poverty of the English stage," appears in *The Scenic Art* (1948). Andrew Schiller in "*The School for Scandal:* The Restoration Unrestored," *PMLA* (1956), views Sheridan's play as an attempt to recapture the qualities of Restoration comedy—a "theoretical failure" but a "practical success." Other recent articles on Goldsmith and Sheridan are essays in source-hunting, like J. H. Smith's examination of Tony Lumpkin's literary ancestors in *PMLA* (1943) and the effort by Miriam Gabriel and Paul Mueschke to establish the sources of *The Rivals* in *PMLA* (1928). The paucity of criticism testifies to the decline of dramatic quality.

Willard Connely's *Young George Farquhar* (1949) and R. Compton Rhodes' *Harlequin Sheridan* (1933) are satisfactory biographies; the former includes more material on the drama, but Rhodes has some well-informed interpretation in his edition of Sheridan's works (1928). Fielding's plays are examined in the standard biographies by W. L. Cross (1918) and F. Homes Dudden (1952). Oliver Goldsmith has been the subject of a less distinguished recent biography by William Freeman (1951). Two comic dramatists of the period have been recalled from relative obscurity: David Garrick and Arthur Murphy. Elizabeth P. Stein's *David Garrick, Dramatist* (1938) exaggerates Garrick's merit as a dramatist, but she makes an impressive case for him as the principal author of *The Clandestine Marriage* (with George Colman the Elder). Murphy's claim on our attention was stated by two books in one year, 1946—John P. Emery's *Arthur Murphy* and Howard H. Dunbar's *The Dramatic Career of Arthur Murphy*. Emery has also edited Murphy's "*The Way to Keep Him*" *and Five Other Plays* (1956). Garrick's and Murphy's plays still retain a certain interest because they avoid the sentimentalism that dominated the theater of their time. They employ the basic situations of Restoration comedy, but with less wit and less indecency.

If eighteenth-century comedy has currently declined in popularity, the tragedy of the same period has been rejected entirely. Addison's *Cato*, Congreve's *The Mourning Bride*, and Nicholas Rowe's plays are little more than curiosities now; Dobrée says the little that can be said for them in his *Restoration Tragedy*. Bertrand Bronson has included a long essay on Samuel Johnson's *Irene* in *Johnson Agonistes and Other Essays* (1946); Bronson finds that Johnson was most concerned with Irene's religious problem and with the ideal characterization of Aspasia, but he grants that the play's main interest stems from the identity of its author. The dramatic principles that underlay such works as *Cato* and *Irene* are probably best summarized by Clarence C. Green, in *The Neo-Classical Theory of Tragedy in England during the Eighteenth Century* (1934). George Lillo has won some attention as a founder of sentimental tragedy. His play, *The London Merchant*, has been defended by G. B. Rodman and attacked by G. R. Havens, both in *ELH* (1945). It is reprinted and scrutinized by Brooks and Heilman in *Understanding Drama*. To modern readers, it seems ludicrous, but it is an important sign of the times, and F. O. Nolte's *Early Middle Class Drama* (*1696–1774*) (1935) supports this point with its summary of sentimental tendencies in European drama, from Cibber's *Love's Last Shift* to an important German summation of the theory of bourgeois tragedy.

The significant recent studies of the eighteenth-century stage have had less to do with the theaters in themselves than with the effect of theater and audience upon the drama. James J. Lynch in *Box Pit and Gallery: Stage and Society in Johnson's London* (1953) explores the impact of bad taste upon dramatic writing. He ascribes ultimate responsibility to the final, full establishment of the middle class, which sponsored trivial and decadent drama. Sheridan and Goldsmith are regarded as exceptions whose success did not affect subsequent playwriting. H. W. Pedicord's *The Theatrical Public in the Time of Garrick* (1954) is a briefer survey of Garrick's audience at the Drury Lane Theatre. The playgoers, we are told, "very definitely came for entertainment values," and even their appetite for sentimentality was secondary to their desire to be amused. Alan S. Downer's "Nature to Advantage Dressed: Eighteenth-Century Acting," *PMLA* (1943) notes the four acting traditions of the time.

VII

The decline of the drama continued at even greater rate during most of the nineteenth century. Though men of letters wrote plays, they did not write for the stage, certainly not for the stage of their time. Byron, Wordsworth, Coleridge, Shelley, Keats, Tennyson (whose *Becket* was performed by Sir Henry Irving), Browning, Dickens, James, Swinburne, and Meredith all wrote plays, but none of them with any lasting effect in the theater. Shelley's *The Cenci* has been much admired—a recent tribute is St. John Ervine's "Shelley as a Dramatist" in *Essays by Divers Hands* (1936). The merits of his contemporary T. L. Beddoes, have been set forth in a biography (1935) by H. W. Donner, who later edited a volume of Beddoes' selected writings, including an interesting tragedy in the Jacobean manner. J. M. Purcell and J. M. Ariel have debated the dramatic skill of Browning's *Pippa Passes* in *SP* (1939 and 1940). Problems confronting a literary man in an unsympathetic theater are well stated by Harley Granville-Barker in "Tennyson, Swinburne, Meredith—And the Theatre" in *The Eighteenth-Seventies* (1929), and by Moody Prior in his chapter on "Nineteenth-Century Tragedy" in *The Language of Tragedy*. The whole subject is surveyed in Ernest Reynolds' *Early Victorian Drama* (1936).

The literary men were unable to fit into the theater because it had become purveyor of mere entertainment, of melodramas and "well-made plays." Most of the poets did not compromise with public demand, and, in consequence, they found themselves with no viable dramatic tradition to guide them. The issue is dramatized by the misfortunes of Henry James, who persistently tried to write for the stage and even transformed two of his novels into "well-made plays." Even the bitterest humiliation did not drive him from the theater; unfortunately, the school of Ibsen became established too late to save James for the stage, but his late play *The Other House* showed the influence of Ibsen. The whole story of James's dramatic ventures is told in Leon Edel's complete edition of James's plays (1949). His essays on the theater, collected as *The Scenic Art* (1948), reveal him as a sensitive and devoted lover of the drama who reserved most of his admiration for the French stage; some of his last essays contain discriminating comment on Ibsen and Rostand.

E. Bradlee Watson reflects the inferior quality of the dramatic literature of the time by giving more attention to the theater in *Sheridan to Robertson: A Study of the Nineteenth-Century London Stage* (1926). Allardyce Nicoll, in the fourth volume of his *History of English Drama* and in *A History of Late Nineteenth-Century Drama* (1946), gives us the most informative account of the drama in this period. M. W. Disher has written a zestful, lively history of Victorian melodrama in two books, *Blood and Thunder* (1949) and *Melodrama* (1954). Quite in the manner of the nostalgic playgoer, Disher savors every bit of blood-curdling improbability and asserts that melodrama is still a staple of the theater. George Rowell covers the ground more briefly and casually in *The Victorian Theatre* (1956).

One of the bright spots of the Victorian drama is the comic art of W. S. Gilbert. Most recent writing about him has taken as its subject the Savoy Operas in which he collaborated with Sir Arthur Sullivan. W. A. Darlington's *The World of Gilbert and Sullivan* (1950) is typical and was written chiefly with a view to explaining the operas. Kronenberger, in commenting on them, gives the ultimate credit for their success to Sullivan, but G. K. Chesterton's "Gilbert and Sullivan" in *The Eighteen-Eighties* (1930) is essentially an essay on Gilbert as "a mocker." Granville-Barker discusses Gilbert's independent work in "Exit Planché—Enter Gilbert" in *The Eighteen-Sixties* (1932).

The rise of realism, especially with the plays of Robertson, prepared the way for Ibsen and Shaw. Robertson's contribution is assessed in a study by Maynard Savin (1950). The realistic triumph is informatively treated as a matter of stagecraft by A. Nicholas Vardac, in *Stage to Screen* (1949). Realism did not doom the "well-made play." To the contrary, Robertson himself adapted Scribe, the best-known practitioner of this genre, and Ibsen, after an early attack on Scribe, adopted his methods, as Raymond Williams points out, in *Drama from Ibsen to Eliot* (1953). The case for the "well-made play" is stated by Eric Bentley in "Homage to Scribe" in *What Is Theatre?* (1956). The case against the "well-made play" is stated at great length by George Bernard Shaw, in *Our Theatres in the Nineties* (1906), a collection of reviews in which he combats the influence of Scribe and his successor Sardou. Shaw's arguments are sympathetically interpreted by Bentley who says in *The Playwright as Thinker* (1946) that Shaw opposed Scribean romanticism, "the substitution of flattering but unreal and foolish conventions for realities." But Ibsen, for whose problem plays Shaw was fighting his critical battle, had recognized the usefulness of Scribe's dramatic technique. Shaw's letters to Ellen Terry, published as *Ellen Terry and Bernard Shaw: A Correspondence* (1931), are additional documents in Shaw's campaign to establish Ibsen's plays and his own; in his letters, he tries to win the leading British actress of his time away from the popular tradition of misinterpreting Shakespeare. Shaw's quarrel with Shakespeare is continued in his Preface to *Three Plays for Puritans* (1901). Granville-Barker's "The Coming of Ibsen," in *The Eighteen-Eighties,* is a contemporary's account of this critical moment in the history of drama.

VIII

American drama had been following a similar course. The standard books are Arthur Hobson Quinn's *A History of American Drama: From the Beginning to the Civil War* (1923, revised 1943) and *A History of American Drama: From the Civil War to the Present Day* (1927, revised 1936). Quinn gives a detailed and affectionate summary of all the major figures. Quinn's admiration usually seems excessive, for these figures are major only by a local or provincial standard of judgment. The need for more acute and impersonal judgment becomes even more apparent on those few occasions when Quinn encounters a dramatist he dislikes. For instance, we are told that Clifford Odets' critical reputation is "amusing" and that *Awake and Sing* is "queer"; in passing, Quinn garbles the plot. He thinks Odets to be lacking in aspiration, and we are reminded that aspiration, conventionally conceived, is a requirement that Quinn often makes of the drama.

Constance Rourke sensitively examines the early years of American drama in an essay, "The Rise of Theatricals" in *The Roots of American Culture* (1942). She ingeniously discovers dramatic elements in Indian treaties and in the Calvinist view of the world. Her fresh comments on Royall Tyler, national types on the stage, and Junius Brutus Booth make it a cause for regret that she carries the story no further. A lively alternative to Quinn is also present in Richard Moody's *America Takes the Stage: Romanticism in American Drama and Theatre, 1750–1900* (1955), but in any of these works, the subject matter must be social history, not art. Scholarship has, however, provided us with ample tools for further study of American drama—George C. D. Odell's exhaustive *Annals of the New York Stage*, in fourteen volumes (1927–1945); Burns Mantle's *Best Plays of the Year* (1919–), which has been augmented by volumes on past decades, for a time edited by John Chapman, now being continued by Louis Kronenberger, so that it is in effect carrying forward Odell's stage history, which stops at 1891; and *America's Lost Plays*, of which Barrett H. Clark was the general editor, in twenty volumes (1940–1942).

IX

Serious books on twentieth-century drama are usually international in scope. The most influential during the last several years has been Eric Bentley's *The Playwright as Thinker*. Bentley is concerned to defend the realistic theater against various operatic, expressionistic, and purely theatrical alternatives, but his real thesis is stated in his Foreword: "the drama can be taken seriously." Accordingly, he re-examines Ibsen and Shaw, endeavors to restore such neglected dramatists as Strindberg and Wedekind, and virtually introduces two writers who were then relatively unknown—Brecht and Sartre. While Bentley is moderate and sympathetic in assessing what he then thought to be the failure in the theater of Lorca, Yeats, and other poets, he is ironically devastating in his assault on the less high-minded artistic failures of Broadway. He observes that Wilder, Odets, and O'Neill are "chiefly promising."

Bentley followed his short study of Shaw with a book which shows an increased interest in plays in performance, *In Search of Theater* (1953). Still critical of the "magical" theater, and expressing his criticism in "More than a Play?," he writes sympathetically of Yeats, an anti-realist playwright; Stark Young, an anti-realist critic; and such dominating performers as Barrault and Martha Graham. In addition, he tells us how the experience of directing plays by Lorca and O'Neill led him to a closer observation of these dramatists' distinctive qualities; his new evaluation of Lorca was more favorable. Bentley's subsequent books, *The Dramatic Event* (1954) and *What Is Theatre?* (1956), are, for the most part, collections of play reviews. They continue a quest for intelligent drama and theater which might be serious enough to withstand the test of irony, a test that Bentley is very skillful in applying. Bentley has, in the past few years, edited several volumes of plays, most of them previously unavailable; five are in paperback, in the series *The Modern Theatre*, and three are clothbound, entitled *From the Modern Repertoire*. His criticism and the books he has edited have created for Bentley a place of unquestionable importance among critics of the drama.

Although John Gassner shares a good many of Bentley's predilections, he has endeavored to vindicate the American theater, or at least a part of it. *The Theatre in Our Times* (1954) collects Gassner's pieces on a variety of subjects, and *Form and Idea in Modern Theatre* (1956) formulates the aesthetics of the modern stage. The former book shows the critic modestly, tolerantly, sympathetically working out the intellectual contexts, discovering the occasional graces, of the major modern dramatists. Gassner probably knows more than any other critic about the forces that produced the American dramatic writers of the last few decades, and his knowledge lends a special authority to his interpretation of them. He is too close to the scene ever to have dismissed the American drama as absolutely as Bentley did in *The Playwright as Thinker*, but even Bentley, astringent as he continues to be, has found more to commend, once his responsibilities as a reviewer brought him closer to the scene. Gassner's numerous anthologies include four volumes of modern American plays and a companion volume of European plays.

Ronald Peacock's *The Poet in the Theatre* (1946) urges the return of poetry to the theater. In spite of his good essays on Eliot, Yeats, and others, he weakens his case by ignoring the theater as it is, except for a few remarks on Shaw and the school of Ibsen. He is instructive even on Shaw, who is to him representative of the wrong tendency. Still, the first impression of this book is its incompleteness. Raymond Williams' thesis in *Drama from Ibsen to Eliot* is rather similar, but Williams makes a more extreme case

against naturalism; he gently takes Peacock to task for the naturalistic bias that causes him to be "glad . . . when the homely
accents of Irish peasants can be heard once more" in one of Yeats's
plays. He carefully interprets the plays of the realists, paying them
the compliment of close attention at the same time that he assails
their unpoetic language and their unimaginative conventions; he
is probably most valuable on Ibsen and Strindberg, and he is unquestionably most hostile to Shaw and O'Casey. His heroes are
the poetic dramatists, led by Eliot and Yeats, but he has little good
to say of Christopher Fry. His comment on Fry ("The result . . .
is the exact opposite of what Mr. Eliot had in mind for poetic
drama") reminds us how much both he and Peacock are indebted
to Eliot's essays on the drama.

A History of Modern Drama (1947), edited by Barrett H. Clark,
brings together a great many facts; its main function should be
that of a reference book. The many contributors all aim to defend
and, if necessary, to vindicate the drama of the nations assigned
to them. At best, the book is useful. J. W. Krutch's *"Modernism"
in Modern Drama* (1953) attacks the modern drama on the
grounds of its rejection of traditional values. Krutch says frankly,
"I speak as a moralist, not as a critic." For him, the dramatists'
efforts to explain character in the light of ideas, society, and psychology are only ways of destroying character. Pirandello is
represented as one of those who make of character "a perpetually
shifting configuration." In reply, it may be proposed that to exhibit the complexity of character is not necessarily to destroy it.
Walter Kerr's *How Not to Write a Play* (1955) is another polemic
against modern drama, this time in behalf of entertainment. Kerr
ascribes the decline of the theater to the ascendancy of Ibsen and
his school; he holds the problem play, not the movies, responsible
for Broadway's financial difficulties. This leaves unsolved the
problem of why vaudeville declined, although it was not tainted
by Ibsen. The long last chapter of Bentley's *What Is Theatre?* is
in some respects an answer to Kerr.

To call Ernest Reynolds' *Modern English Drama* (1949) the
best survey of its subject is not to say very much for it; the other
books exclusively occupied with the contemporary British theater
are mostly playgoers' jottings, like Audrey Williamson's recent
volumes. Reynolds' is a decent, sober book. A more exciting

history can be constructed from the collected reviews of Shaw in *Our Theatres in the Nineties*, of Max Beerbohm in *Around Theatres* (1930), and of James Agate in many works, beginning with *Buzz Buzz* (1918).

The senior study of modern American drama is J. W. Krutch's *The American Drama since 1918* (1939, revised 1957). It is a sympathetic appraisal, often on moral grounds (though not so exclusively as Krutch's later *"Modernism" in Modern Drama*). Krutch is surely at his best with a dramatist whose limitations he recognizes, like George S. Kaufman. Writing on others, like O'Neill, Anderson, and Behrman, he is inclined to take them on their own terms, to regard their serious aspirations as serious accomplishments; Kaufman, fortunately, shows little serious aspiration, and so Krutch can take his measure more coolly. The final chapter, added in 1957, briefly explores the possibility that Miller and Williams have been writing tragedy, that is, the possibility that their aspirations are serious. Krutch is able to attribute "tragic guilt" to *Death of a Salesman*, but the case for Williams seems to rest finally on whether a remark about *Streetcar Named Desire* has been accurately attributed to the dramatist. The book has this value: it sees O'Neill, Anderson, and a few others as they would see themselves, judging them with a seriousness that they hoped to deserve. Frank H. O'Hara's *Today in American Drama* (1939) balances between plot-summary and an effort to assign plays to traditional genres. Eleanor Flexner's *American Playwrights* (1938) is a plodding Marxist evaluation. Alan Downer's *Fifty Years of American Drama, 1900–1950* (1951) is a slim handbook, satisfactory and suggestive within its limits, but too slight to undertake detailed comment on the typical dramatists of the last quarter-century.

George Jean Nathan has collected his reviews more consistently than any other practising American drama critic. The annual *Theatre Book of the Year*, which began to appear in 1943, carried on an unofficial series which had been running for two decades. Nathan is historically important as the defender of O'Neill, O'Casey, Saroyan, and others, but he has been inhospitable to the postwar playwrights. Increasingly, too, he has been beguiled by his wit into becoming a mere funny man and not a critic. Nathan's specialty has always been disposing of trash, but he also disposes of a good deal else, especially if it clashes with one of his many prejudices. The temperate, urbane John Mason Brown has also collected his reviews, in *Broadway in Review* (1940) and other books. Stark Young is probably the most acute American critic to write regularly for any long period of time; his concern is with the whole art of the theater. Few if any can describe a performance so well as he, but he usually does justice to the play also. His chief collected volume is *Immortal Shadows* (1948), which is the subject of an appreciation by Eric Bentley in *In Search of Theater*. Mary McCarthy's *Sights and Spectacles, 1937–1956* (1956) is a collection of harsh, clever reviews that are continually turning up important patterns missed by everyone else. Francis Fergusson's "Beyond the Close Embrace," *Anchor Review* (1955), deserves attention as a study of American realism, two of its more interesting products (Odets and Williams), and a rebel against it (Wilder).

X

Oscar Wilde's standing as a dramatist rests upon one play, *The Importance of Being Earnest*, and in spite of Marvin Mudrick's objections, in "Restoration Comedy and After," his place seems secure. Wilde's biographers have so much gossip to keep them busy that they seldom bother to examine his plays. Edouard Roditi in *Oscar Wilde* (1947) finds *The Importance* contrived and trivial, but to say so much is surely to set down Wilde's intention. George Woodcock in *The Paradox of Oscar Wilde* (1950) finds abundant social criticism in Wilde's other plays; finding very little in *The Importance*, he still bestows the highest praise on it. St. John Ervine in *Oscar Wilde* (1951) rips the earlier plays to pieces with obvious enjoyment, but he can do little more than marvel at the wit of *The Importance:* "How is a bubble to be described and analysed?" St. John Hankin's "The Collected Plays of Oscar Wilde," in Hankin's edition of Wilde's *Dramatic Works* (1912) is a valuable professional appraisal. Recently *CE* (1956) printed two essays on *The Importance* (by Otto Reinert and Richard Foster) and one on *Lady Windermere's Fan* (by Morse Peckham); all three defend Wilde's dramatic methods. Among the less reverent essays are Shaw's unfavorable contemporary review, in *Our Theatres in the Nineties*, and Mary McCarthy's commentary, which reduces the play to a formula but salutes Lady Bracknell as "a goddess."

Shaw's other contemporaries have not fared so well. Henry Arthur Jones and Arthur Pinero are museum-pieces, although Bentley has taken a step toward restoring Pinero's reputation as a farceur by including one of his farces in *From the Modern Repertoire: Series Three* (1956). The definitive books on them, Richard A. Cordell's *Henry Arthur Jones and the Modern Drama* (1932) and W. D. Dunkel's *Sir Arthur Pinero* (1941), enthusiastically recount triumphs that mean little to us now.

Shaw himself is still a major industry. The best critical book is Bentley's *Bernard Shaw* (1947, revised 1957), which pays close attention both to Shaw's thought and his dramatic art—in pleasing contrast to the many who seem to regard Shaw as neither a thinker nor an artist, but only a controversialist. Bentley has written on Shaw also in *The Playwright as Thinker* and *A Century of Hero-Worship* (1944). G. K. Chesterton's *George Bernard Shaw* (1909) is still valuable because it authentically reflects the controversies in which Shaw and Chesterton engaged. Desmond MacCarthy's *Shaw* (1951) has a similar authenticity because it consists of discerning reviews written when the plays were produced. William Irvine's *The Universe of G. B. S.* (1949) is a persevering academic study which comments with varying success on every episode in Shaw's life and art. Alick West's *A Good Man Fallen among Fabians* (1950) is a Marxist assessment which is adequately summarized by its title. Louis Kronenberger's *George Bernard Shaw: A Critical Survey* (1953) collects essays by various writers and includes W. H. Auden's biographical essay, Thomas Mann's tribute, and Edmund Wilson's searching examination of Shaw's art and politics, "Bernard Shaw at Eighty." Arthur H. Nethercot, in *Men and Supermen* (1954), takes a close look at Shaw's characters; his analysis is interesting, but it can only be an extended footnote to an examination of the characters in their full dramatic contexts. The essays assembled in *G. B. S. 90*, edited by S. Winsten (1946), are not easily classified as biography or criticism, but they have at least some curiosity value.

Shaw biography has been the gathering place of eccentrics who find their own pet theories much more fun than Shaw's. In *G. B. S.:*

A Postscript, for instance, Hesketh Pearson stops to tell us that Shakespeare died of venereal disease. St. John Ervine, in *Bernard Shaw* (1956), often stops to lecture Shaw or to lecture us, but his biography contains letters and factual information unobtainable elsewhere. The biography with the most facts is now Archibald Henderson's *George Bernard Shaw: Man of the Century* (1956). For all of his critical deficiencies, Henderson gets the facts down and footnotes everything—as Ervine does not. Consider one example of his completeness. The standard procedure for critics discussing *Candida* is to quote Shaw's letter to Huneker; Henderson quotes a different Shaw letter on the play and, in the footnote, directs the reader to the Huneker letter and to yet another of Shaw's disclosures of his "secret." Henderson's completeness does not extend to Shaw's love-life, which he bowdlerizes, with the result that the names of Alice Lockett and Jennie Patterson do not appear. Shaw's biography must be supplemented by his correspondence, especially *Ellen Terry and Bernard Shaw: A Correspondence,* edited by Christopher St. John; *Bernard Shaw and Mrs. Patrick Campbell: Their Correspondence,* edited by Alan Dent (1952); and *Bernard Shaw's Letters to Granville Barker* edited by C. B. Purdom (1956).

Harley Granville-Barker is a dramatist of some interest who has not been the subject of much critical attention. C. B. Purdom's recent biography (1956) leaves criticism of the plays to quotations from contemporary reviewers and charges Barker with being too scholarly in his *Prefaces to Shakespeare.* Alan S. Downer's "Harley Granville-Barker," *SR* (1947), is the best general estimate, but the plays will repay additional study. Another meritorious dramatist of the early twentieth century has won scant attention—St. John Hankin. The reputation of a third contemporary has gone into a decline: H. V. Marrot's biography (1936) says the last brief word on John Galsworthy.

The Abbey Theatre of Dublin made notable contributions to the drama. Its story has been told many times, in Lennox Robinson's impersonal, apparently official history, *Ireland's Abbey Theatre* (1951); in Peter Kavanagh's gossipy behind-the-scenes history, *The Story of the Abbey Theatre* (1950); and in Una Ellis-Fermor's valuable critical study, *The Irish Dramatic Movement* (1939, revised 1954). The two principal founders have also given their accounts, Lady Gregory in *Our Irish Theatre* (1914) and in her *Journals* (1946), W. B. Yeats in *Plays and Controversies* (1924) and *Dramatis Personae* (1936)—reprinted as part of his *Autobiography* (1953). The general impression these sources convey is of a continual war with the public, internal dissension, and a sincere, determined effort to create a distinctively Irish drama.

Lady Gregory has not received her due as a dramatist, but Yeats's plays have increasingly become the subjects of criticism. The essays by Bentley and Raymond Williams have strengthened our impression of Yeats as a genuine dramatist, not merely a poet who strayed into the theater. Peter Ure, in *Towards a Mythology* (1946) has interpreted the Celtic legend that underlies much of Yeats's drama and has shown its significance for him. Brijit Bjersby, in *The Interpretation of the Cuchulain Legend in the Works of Yeats* (1950), has shown just what Yeats did with the myths he used. Thomas Parkinson, in *W. B. Yeats: Self-Critic* (1951), demonstrates the effect of the early plays in teaching the poet self-discipline. Of the general books on Yeats, T. R. Henn's *The Lonely Tower* (1952) is especially helpful on the plays, in its exposition of "Yeats's theory of a theatre of great speech, elimination of unnecessary action, and the stylization of what remained."

The Abbey Theatre gave two more dramatists to the world, J. M. Synge and Sean O'Casey. Synge's sources and the early versions of his plays have been the subject of recent articles by David H. Greene in *JEGP* (1947) and *PMLA* (1947, 1948); Greene has in particular established the authentically Irish nature of his sources. R. L. Collins in "The Distinction of *Riders to the Sea*," *UKCR* (1947) has argued that the play's characters are intended as abstractions. Norman Podhortetz in "Synge's *Playboy:* Morality and the Hero," *Essays in Criticism*, (1953), sees in *The Playboy of the Western World* emphasis on Christy's assertion of manhood and the problem of morality as it affects the primitive society of the play. Williams and Kronenberger have also written appreciatively of Synge's plays. O'Casey gets favorable treatment as "a baroque dramatic poet" from Gassner in *The Theatre in Our Times*; his "mechanical" effects of language are briskly assailed by Williams, but his critical standing is still high. Jules Koslow's *The Green and the Red* (1949) summarizes the plays and defends

O'Casey's social views. O'Casey has written several volumes of autobiography, of which the first was *I Knock at the Door* (1939), and a book of vehement essays, mainly on the theater, *The Green Crow* (1956). Bentley's essay, "Heroic Wantonness," in *In Search of Theater*, admiringly sums up the accomplishment of the Abbey Theatre.

The critical literature on T. S. Eliot as poet and dramatist is very extensive. Grover Smith, Jr.'s *T. S. Eliot's Poetry and Plays* (1956) is a good book to start with, because it is exceptionally full in giving Eliot's sources and in citing previous essays on the plays. Bentley has suggested that *Sweeney Agonistes* may be considered a real play and has included it in *From the Modern Repertoire: Series One* (1949), but most serious examination of Eliot as a playwright begins with *Murder in the Cathedral*. Fergusson finds in this play the pattern of ritual drama, with a peculiar "abstractness of its basic conception," and with "the demonstration of a particular theological idea" as its purpose. John Peter in "Murder in the Cathedral," *SR* (1953), commends Eliot's "simplification and intensification" of his material and concludes that this play is superior poetically and dramatically to its successors. Louis L. Martz in "The Saint as Tragic Hero," *Tragic Themes in Western Literature*, views the play as a successful solution to the difficult problem of a saint's tragedy. F. O. Matthiessen, in *The Achievement of T. S. Eliot* (1947) places *Murder in the Cathedral* and *The Family Reunion* in the context of Eliot's writings on the theater.

In *The Quest for Salvation in an Ancient and a Modern Play* (1941), Maud Bodkin compares *The Family Reunion* with Aeschylus' *Eumenides*, emphasizing the final establishment of a new order. C. L. Barber, in "T. S. Eliot after Strange Gods," *Southern Review* (1940), reprinted in Leonard Unger's *T. S. Eliot: A Selected Critique* (1948), and J. Peter, in "The Family Reunion," *Scrutiny* (1949) investigate the inadequacies of this play. The critical reputation of *The Cocktail Party* has declined since the time of its Broadway success; the measure of that decline is apparent from William Arrowsmith's two essays, "English Verse Drama: The Cocktail Party," *Hudson Review* (1950) and "The Comedy of T. S. Eliot," *English Institute Essays 1954* (1955). The former essay warmly praises Eliot's Christian symbolism; the latter compares Eliot unfavorably with Euripides. Robert B. Heilman, in *"Alcestis* and *The Cocktail Party," CL* (1953), discovers parallels that shed light on both plays. Two essays in *Accent* (1950), by Leo Hamalian and Sandra Wool, have found ritual patterns inspired by Jessie L. Weston, but it is obvious that the Christian and Euripidean patterns are first in prominence. Writing on *The Confidential Clerk* in *SR* (1954), Bonamy Dobrée discerns a didactic purpose but suspects that Eliot has succeeded better with the play as entertainment. D. W. Harding notes recurring elements in Eliot's plays, in "Progression of Theme in Eliot's Modern Plays," *KR* (1956). Eliot has himself discussed his problems as a playwright in *Poetry and Drama* (1951).

Christopher Fry has lately won a reputation with verse plays that seem at times to have too much glitter. Marius Bewley deflates the verse in *Scrutiny* (1951): *"Paradise Lost* if it were rewritten by Ogden Nash." Williams does the job more soberly and moderately in *Drama from Ibsen to Eliot.* William Arrowsmith, in "Notes on English Verse Drama: Christopher Fry," *Hudson Review* (1950), states the case for Fry but admits that his "verse is distractingly autonomous." Monroe K. Spears, on "Christopher Fry and the Redemption of Joy," *Poetry* (1951), similarly concedes that Fry's verse is not functional. His admirers seem agreed that his virtues are not precisely dramatic virtues.

XI

Eugene O'Neill is still the leading American dramatist. Barrett H. Clark's *Eugene O'Neill: The Man and His Plays* (1947) has the peculiar value of quoting significant remarks by O'Neill, often in letters to Clark, on most of the plays. Edwin A. Engel's *The Haunted Heroes of Eugene O'Neill* (1953) is now the most generally satisfactory sympathetic study of the subject. Engel works out, more fully than anyone else, the influences and issues at work in the plays, detailing the effects of psychoanalysis, or dramatic experiment, or social observation upon O'Neill's unwavering pessimism. Doris Alexander has corroborated both the pessimism in "Eugene O'Neill as Social Critic," *American Quarterly* (1954), and the "scientific" sources in "Psychological Fate in *Mourning Becomes Electra," PMLA* (1953). Evaluative essays are sharply divided. Fergusson, in an early essay, "Eugene O'Neill," in *Literary Opinion in America*, edited by M. D. Zabel (1951), found the dramatist moving from a superficial naturalism which turned up "a few muddy diamonds" to a pretentiously prophetic symbolism which divorced him from experience. "Trying to Like O'Neill," in *In Search of Theater*, tells how Bentley discovered, while directing *The Iceman Cometh*, that O'Neill is weakest as an expressionist and interpreter of ideas, strongest as a realist. Edmund Wilson in "Eugene O'Neill and the Naturalists," in *The Shores of Light* (1952), reports that O'Neill's dialogue is brilliant when it is vernacular, but at other times "tasteless and dreary." Mary McCarthy's "Eugene O'Neill—Dry Ice," in *Sights and Spectacles*, also takes a mixed view of the clumsy, inarticulate solidity of *The Iceman Cometh* and the genuine poignancy of *Moon for the Misbegotten*, but Miss McCarthy wonders in an afterthought how much of the pity of the latter play is O'Neill's own self-pity. O'Neill's uncompromising defenders are many; they include Barrett H. Clark, George Jean Nathan, and Joseph Wood Krutch, who salutes O'Neill as an author of tragic stature in *The American Drama since 1918* and in his Introduction to O'Neill's *Nine Plays* (1932). Lionel Trilling, in his Introduction to a collection of three plays (1937), defends O'Neill's quest "for the 'meaning of life' " and his "suspicion of the intellect."

Maxwell Anderson's verse is now conceded to be a serious blemish on his dramatic skill: Edmund Wilson's "Prize-Winning Blank Verse" in *The Shores of Light* is a representative comment on this matter. Thornton Wilder has probably fared best among dramatists of Anderson's generation, but H. Adler's essay on "Thornton Wilder's Theatre," *Horizon* (1945), is so enthusiastic as to be uncritical. Mary McCarthy, writing of *Our Town* and *The Skin of Our Teeth* in her *Sights and Spectacles*, is enthusiastic also, but a little more reserved. Edmund Wilson's "Antrobuses and the Earwickers," *Classics and Commercials* (1950), describes the controversy over Wilder's debt to Joyce in *The Skin of Our Teeth*. Francis Fergusson's "Three Allegorists," *SR* (1956), includes "a preliminary exploration" of Wilder's art.

The best essay on Clifford Odets is Robert Warshow's "Poet of the Jewish Middle Class," *Commentary* (1946), which examines Odets' language along with other elements in his representation of Jewish life in New York. "By Ice, Fire, or Decay?" is Kenneth Burke's study, in *The Philosophy of Literary Form* (1941), of the complexities of Odets' *Paradise Lost*.

The merit of Arthur Miller's *Death of a Salesman* is evaluated by five critics in Eric Bentley's *The Play*—Brooks Atkinson (favorable), Ivor Brown (neutral), John Mason Brown (favorable), Eleanor Clark (unfavorable), and Frederick Morgan (unfavorable). One of the more disturbing qualities of this play—its lack of specific detail—is perhaps explained in George Ross's interesting review of a Yiddish translation " 'Death of a Salesman' in the Original," *Commentary* (1951). The oversimple political allegory of a later play by Miller is given close scrutiny in Robert Warshow's "The Liberal Conscience in 'The Crucible,' " *Commentary* (1953). Bentley takes exception to the dubious political innocence of *The Crucible* and *A View from the Bridge* in *What is Theatre?* and *The Dramatic Event*. William Wiegand's "Arthur Miller and the Man Who Knows," *Western Review* (1957) is a sensible survey of Miller's whole career. Tennessee Williams is as important a dramatist; in the absence of a satisfactory full-length essay on him, the scattered remarks in Bentley's books and in Gassner's *The Theatre in Our Time* will furnish an introduction, but we may still await an essay that will find a pattern for Williams's Southern nostalgia, his romanticism, his violence, and his recurring portrayal of muscular men and dowdy women, whose archetypes are Marlon Brando and Anna Magnani. The newest playwright to arrive is Paddy Chayefsky; the main traits of his optimistic, sentimental problem plays are sketched in Gerald Weales' "Marty and His Friends and Neighbors," *Commentary* (1955).

Continental influences have been so thoroughly assimilated that little separate summation of them is required. Expressionism, a form of distortion that presents abstractions embodying the unconscious mind or, in some late manifestations, the mass mind, is traceable to Strindberg and Wedekind. Its principal impact on American drama came in the 1920's, while such expressionists as Kaiser and Toller were active in Europe. American plays of this school include O'Neill's *The Hairy Ape*, Elmer Rice's *The Adding Machine*, and *Beggar on Horseback*, by Marc Connelly and George S. Kaufman, but the watered down influence of expressionism is visible in many later plays, including Miller's *Death of a Sales-man*. C. E. W. L. Dahlström goes to the source in *Strindberg's Dramatic Expressionism* (1930) and brings back a large number of defining characteristics. William Rose, in "Expressionism in German Literature," *Men, Myths, and Movements in German Literature* (1931), traces the term "expressionism" to its earlier use in painting; the most active period in Germany, he finds, was between 1917 and 1921. A. R. Fulton, in "Expressionism—Twenty Years After," *SR* (1944), describes American expressionism from the beginning to such late, "not essentially expressionistic" instances as *Our Town*. F. J. Hoffman, in *The Twenties* (1955), rightly observes that the chief success of American expressionism was in comedy. My own "Elmer Rice: The Triumph of Mr. Zero," *Commentary* (1951) recorded Rice's decline from the comic peak of his early expressionism.

Bertolt Brecht's epic theater is, in some respects, a narrative drama, with conventions of staging that recall Elizabethan practices and with a commitment to social themes. Brecht has influenced *The Dog beneath the Skin* and other verse dramas by Auden and Isherwood, Marc Blitzstein's *The Cradle Will Rock*, and the Federal Theatre Living Newspaper productions. Epic theater is best described by Bentley in *Playwright as Thinker* and in his notes to *The Private Life of the Master Race* (1944).

16

Comparative Literature

CHARLTON LAIRD

Everyone knows what Milton Studies are—studies which somehow illumine the man or his work. Scholars usually know when they are studying Milton and when they are not, and so do readers. New materials may be discovered, new interpretations proposed, new editions issued, new techniques applied, but the area of study requires little delineation. Something similar is true of the study of genres. Critics may occasionally differ as to whether a given creative work is or is not a novel, but they seldom differ violently or seem to care much. But students of literature interested in broad approaches have no such well fenced little acres, at least not today. They do not always know whether they are studying comparative literature, world literature, general literature, or just literature, and leading comparatists do not agree as to what a scholar should be studying if he professes any of these fields. Obviously, definition is in order. Furthermore, the process of definition itself has been, consciously or unconsciously, a concern of comparatists during the past quarter century, and their differences, if not resolved, are by now clearly revealed. Noticing these differences will perhaps best distinguish what has developed in recent comparative literary studies, and even suggest the shape of much to come.

I

Since the developments of recent decades center attention upon this country, and since chauvinism is peculiarly abhorrent in a consideration of comparative study, someone other than an American may as well make the essential comparison. I propose Professor Saburo Ota of the Japan Society for Comparative Literature. He recently described the first decade of the Society, and being aware, as a matter of course, that "comparative literature," whatever its practical antiquity, acquired its formal description as a literary method mainly through scholars who lectured at or looked to Paris, he writes, "The Society's first task was thus to study the principles and methods of the Sorbonne. Copies of the *Revue de Littérature Comparée* and books by F. Baldensperger, Paul Van Tieghem, and others all helped. . . ." Thus all was started auspiciously, and only in retrospect does Professor Ota remark, "It seems strange that we did not look to the United States of America at that time."

But soon trouble brewed. Professor Ota continues:

As our work went on, the positive method of France presented difficulties. First there were relatively few cases in which such a method was applicable. There were many areas of investigation that could not be treated. Second, our study had to be limited chiefly to the Meiji Era, that is, 1869–1912, when the introduction of certain foreign authors or books could be traced fairly minutely, because the readers of foreign literature were pretty much limited to a narrow literary circle. But we see a far wider introduction and influence of foreign literatures in the present day. Thus we began to form two groups: one which closely adhered to the French school, and another which was trying to find a new method applicable to present day conditions and which was unwilling to follow blindly the pattern of the Sorbonne. The result was that the spring meeting of the society for 1954 was devoted to the discussion of the character and methodology of Comparative Literature. . . . Five persons expressed their opinions, of whom one followed the French school, keeping to strict positivism. Others insisted that we should devise a number of methods, which could be applied to the literature of different ages. The present writer, referring to Wellek's opinion, introduced the American way of comparative study.

If the lines are not so sharply drawn as Professor Ota seems to imply and if there is nothing so well-channelled in American comparative literary studies that it can confidently be called "the American way," the learned Japanese has neatly epitomized recent streams of interest. At least three American manifestations are observable: an awakened interest in literatures remote from Western Europe and often neglected by Western scholars, a search for methods of intercultural study other than those prescribed by the Sorbonne group, and an insistence that literature be studied as literature and for its impact as literature whatever may have been the "influences" on the author. These tendencies, while they are notably widespread, seem at this writing to be more observable in the United States than in most other areas and to be centering more and more in this country.

We should perhaps remind ourselves of what Professor Ota presumably means by "positivism." Concern for literatures from other than provincial approaches is of course nothing new; since before Plato men have studied writings in languages other than their own, and during the Middle Ages, when Latin provided a common medium for communication throughout western Europe, writers appeared idyllically unaware that political boundaries can be translated into literary boundaries. A commentator might distinguish between Christian and pagan writers, but scarcely between Saxons and Bavarians, or even between Italians and Frenchmen—Dante's discussion of the Provence origin of *il dolce stil nuovo* is quite another matter. Nonetheless, the broad study of literature has always presented difficulties, so much so that the field of world literature seems sometimes to be mostly composed of pitfalls. Furthermore, the pitfalls increase by something like the square or the cube of the number of languages with which the critic must deal and the cultures he must comprehend, and accordingly in a linguistically fragmented world intercultural areas have become progressively more hazardous terrain. "Positivism," then, in Professor Ota's sense might be called an attempt to define a safe and certain way among the pitfalls, to give measurable answers to intercultural literary problems.

Beginning in the late nineteenth century, perhaps as much with Professors Joseph Texte and Louis P. Betz as with anyone, and relying upon a sequence of distinguished professors—Ferdinand Brunetière, Fernand Baldensperger, Paul Hazard, Paul Van Tieghem, Jean-Marie Carré, and others—procedures were developed which were relatively certain and objective, even though limited. The comparatist in this school must be able to command at least two languages fluently. He concerns himself with evidences of transmission between these languages. As an exile in London, whom did Rousseau know? What did he and they discuss? Which of his works were translated into English, where, when, by whom? Who read these books? Which contemporary writers read French, and what evidence is there that they read Rousseau in French? Did they understand him? Were there intermediaries (reviewers, professors, lecturers, holders of soirées) who interpreted or mis-interpreted Rousseau? These researches result in an article, "Two Unpublished Rousseau Letters," which leads to a monograph, *Blake's Knowledge of Rousseau,* which grows into a two-volume study, *Rousseau and the British Muse,* which eventually is sub-merged in the comprehensive work, *Anglo-French Literary Re-lations.* These titles are hypothetical, but theoretically this process could continue until the influence of everybody and everything has been traced on everybody and everything else, insofar as editions, translations, travellers, international correspondence, internal evidence, and intermediaries permit. This procedure has its uses; the exact evidence of the manner in which Turgeniev discovered Scott tells us something about Turgeniev, about the impact of Scott, about literature and the ways specific novels came to be what they are, about the way genius is molded, about the ways of men with genres and ideas. The danger, of course, is that the comparatist of this sort may be occupied with minor figures and events which are, of themselves, relatively inconsequential. Whether A's translation of B was based upon the imperfect print-ing of 1647 rather than the excellent printing of 1643 makes no difference, except as this difference may reveal something else, for instance, the reason for C's having misunderstood B. To the comparatist, Crabbe Robinson is an important intermediary between early nineteenth-century England and Germany, but if the critic, pursuing the entrancing trails of Robinson's transmis-sion of "influences," forgets that Robinson, however important he may have been as a literary importer has minor significance as a literary figure, the critic, and perhaps his audience may forget that a work of art is after all primarily a work of art. That is, liter-ature is something more than the total of all the influences of X upon Y, and atrophy of artistic awareness would seem to be one of the occupational diseases of comparatists of the more limited sort.

Thus the Japanese scholars who fled provincialism in literary study were not alone when they found that the Sorbonne sort of *littérature comparée* applied aptly to only part of their literature and was far from final even where it worked best. That the Sorbonne formula has done great good, surely no one can deny. It introduced clarity and precision where they were sorely needed. We should be worse off without studies of the Sorbonne sort like Angela La Piana's *Dante's American Pilgrimage: A Historical Study of Dante Studies in the United States* (1948) and Werner P. Friederich's *Dante's Fame Abroad* (1950). But not all literary problems can be studied in this way. We should be worse off, also, without the Chadwicks' revealing survey, *The Growth of Literature* (1931–40), for which the methods of the Sorbonne comparatists would not have served at all. And even when the method serves, its limitations must be noted; both Goethe and Dante influenced Thoreau, and we can welcome the testimony that Thoreau knew Goethe, but that much which seems Goethe-like in Thoreau came through Emerson, who got it from Carlyle, who got some of it by mistranslation. Still, when we have exhausted all evidence of measurable influence upon Thoreau, we have still to make the most important observations about that uncommonly self-reliant Yankee, perhaps even the most important observations about what our cultural heritage did to him.

By the end of the 1920's the Sorbonne was well established as a name and a place for comparative study. A world war had made the survivors more aware of the need for international understanding. Paris had become the home of the comparatist, and doctoral candidates flocked there, especially from the politically submerged countries from the Balkans to the Scandinavian peninsula. The Sorbonne method had been well developed and several times described, especially in Paul Van Tieghem's *La Littérature comparée* (1924, third edition 1946) aptly termed "the comparatist's breviary," which was so adequate and so admirably clear that with it comparative study had a proved method. Comparative scholars had the Sorbonne manuals; they had the example of Hazard, Van Tieghem, and Baldensperger (only later did he come to Harvard). Provided they had a library, industry, and keen minds, they needed nothing more, and some of them provided nothing more. The better scholars, of course, added perspective; they never forgot that literary criticism begins after the hunt for sources and influences is over, but as source-hunting and text-establishing obsessed some nineteenth-century scholars, influence-tracing obsessed some twentieth-century critics. But not all of them. Even in the inner temple of the Sorbonne, the best scholars recognized always that the Sorbonne method was *a* method of studying literature, a method to be exploited but to be kept in its place. If Van Tieghem is the author of *Ossian en France*, which may serve as well as any other as an exemplary Sorbonne subject brilliantly developed, he is the author, culminatively, of *L'Ere romantique: Romantisme dans la littérature européene* (1948) and of *Histoire littéraire de l'Europe et de l'Amerique*, translated into English, Spanish, Serbian, Finnish, Swedish, and Danish. As M. René Bray has pointed out, "He conceived, beside the comparative study of literature, the possibility of engendering the general study of literature and of viewing literary life as a whole." If Hazard made his comparative debut with *Goethe en France* he had grown by 1935 to conceive *La crise de la conscience européenne*, translated as *The European Mind 1680–1715* (1953). If Baldensperger is thought of first as moving spirit in that key comparatist periodical, *Revue de littérature comparée*, he was interested also in the much broader problem of the relationships between literature and music (*Sensibilité musicale et romantisme*). Despite, however, this evidence of balance among the great Parisian comparatists themselves, the impact of the French school upon international study was often, and in some areas and with certain individuals deliberately, to discourage rather than to encourage synthesis in the study of literature. Thus, while all scholars must admire the great French comparatists, not all students of literature were entirely happy about the impact of *littérature comparée* as it became more and more the pattern for comparatist literary study.

By the 1920's, then, the French method, exalting a formula which I have called the influence of X upon Y, had been well described and well demonstrated, and was becoming well established. The method and its practitioners have continued to flourish, and as might be expected, have produced some of their most notable works in the second, not the first quarter century of the Parisian school—a scholar, if he is healthy and lucky, can hope for perhaps a half century of productivity. But the school was only well established when it engendered reactions.

In Russia, a lively group of critics known as the Formalists were seeking a method of studying literature which would transcend national boundaries and local mores but would transcend, also, the limitations of the Sorbonne method. The Formalists have since been efficiently throttled by the Soviets—not, as a matter of course, for being anti-Sorbonne but for being insufficiently pro-Soviet—and one hears little of them after 1930. Nevertheless, their existence was suggestive, and they had wide audiences in central Europe. How far their ripples may have traveled no one can know, not even by studying these ripples with the Sorbonne method, but one is intrigued by Professor Ota's having singled out "Wellek" as the spokesman of "the American way." Now this Wellek is Professor René Wellek, head of the Department of Comparative Literature at Yale University. Anyone who has observed his questing mind searching synthesis, essence, and order out of confusion will know that he cannot be put together out of a mingling of influences, but the following facts remain. Though he began as a student of philosophy, his dissertation was *Immanuel Kant in England, 1793–1838* (1931), an excellent study of the Sorbonne sort. After its publication Wellek, then docent at Karl University in Prague, worked with the *Cercle linguistique de Prague* which owed much to the Russian Formalists. The collapse of Czechoslovakia stranded him on this side of the Iron Curtain, where he is becoming a brilliant exponent—perhaps the most brilliant exponent now writing—of an approach to literature which makes use of the French methods but is not limited by them.

Something similar to the Russian Formalist revolt stirred in other countries. Germany, although it had its devotees of *vergleichende Literature*—a translation, in one sense, of the French term and in another of the French method—had also its dissenters who turned to *Geistesgeschichte*, literally, "history of spirit," but perhaps more accurately, "study of the temper of times, places, and peoples." To this school I shall return, for unlike the Formalists they have not been throttled, and they can be used as one corner when we endeavor to delineate current comparative interests in literature. In the Mediterranean areas the most distinguished scholars, even comparative students like Mario Praz and Benedette Croce in Italy, José Ortega y Gasset in Spain, while they have made some use of the Sorbonne procedures, have continued more interested in psychological, aesthetic, critical, and philosophic approaches to letters. Perhaps Signor Praz may be allowed to speak for them: "The future of literary history lies in a history of poetics, of directions of tastes and sensibility, not in a passive reflection or copy of the political, the social, or even the intellectual development of mankind." Croce, who earlier practiced *littérature comparée*, came more and more to believe that criticism must start with aesthetics: see *Nuovi saggi di estetica* (1948) and *Problemi di estetica* (1949). In England the Sorbonne procedures made rapid headway among scholars whose concern was one of the foreign languages—particularly French—but many of the great scholars remained insular in their interests, and others embraced a healthy concern for literature wherever they found it and for literary study wherever it led them. They thus crossed national boundaries, but not deliberately, and the result was often excellent criticism and literary history with an admirable cultural flavor but no very self-conscious comparatist methodology.

II

The United States, characteristically for what was as yet in its scholarship a European colony, was confused about the whole business. The French method was known, at least in the more alert graduate schools, but it was only scatteringly if somewhat slavishly practiced. How little it was understood may be inferred from Oscar J. Campbell's article, "What is Comparative Literature?" in *Essays in Memory of Barrett Wendell* (1926). He recommended comparative study "for the ambitious student," since "laborers in the field are as yet comparatively few, and the harvest seems to be very great." By "comparative literature" he meant mainly the Sorbonne approach, but he was certainly not relying upon the most rigid of the comparatists' dicta when he defined *littérature comparée* in Baldensperger's words as "the study of the living relationships that unite diverse literatures." Nor did he appear entirely content even with this definition, for he pointed out that it assumes that national literatures are entities, which one surmises he felt they are not.

In spite of this interest in *littérature comparée* at certain American centers, the body of the movement toward a broader understanding of literature owed little to the French school. It rested upon a native revulsion to what had been our obvious provincialism in many fields, including literary study. A great war had been fought, and won militarily but lost culturally. A great depression was staggering the country, and clearly it was international as well as national. Apparently, isolationism did not even pay. Accordingly, we furthered a widespread if floundering movement toward broader horizons, in which teachers and scholars had a part. A course in The Romantic Poets became, in effect, a course in The Romantic Movement, perhaps without change of course number or title. But there were formal changes, too. How was one to become cosmopolitan? That was a good question, but perhaps one might start by reading Confucius and Plato. Accordingly, we picked up Goethe's term, *Weltliteratur,* and courses in World Literature sprang up everywhere. But *world literature* seemed a pretentious term for a sampling of British and Continental masterpieces, savored with a few snippets out of Asia. Accordingly, with the baptismal blessings of the University of Chicago, the less ostentatious title "Great Books" has made headway, but under whatever designation, courses which deliberately flout national and linguistic boundaries have become common in all colleges and universities of any account, in many secondary schools, and in adult education.

Meanwhile, research has become more comparative, and not necessarily along the Sorbonne lines. Here one should remember that this country had a healthy, if limited tradition of broad literary study, and that "the American way" to which Professor Ota referred has strong native roots. This is not to belittle the contributions of distinguished immigrants, without whom American comparative studies could not be what they have become; Wellek at Yale, Freiderich at North Carolina, Leo Spitzer at Johns Hopkins, Horst Frenz at Indiana, the late Albert Guerard at Stanford, Napoleone Orsini at Wisconsin, Giuseppe Prezzolini at Columbia, and dozens more rely upon European backgrounds, but the native tradition need not be ignored. Henry Wadsworth Longfellow probably thought of himself primarily as Professor of Comparative Literature at Harvard, and as poet by avocation. Essentially, he was a Great Books lecturer, albeit an exalted one, importing European masterpieces, translating and popularizing them. One of his successors, the late George Lyman Kittredge, ranged so readily from language to language, from culture to culture that

he would no doubt have snorted if anybody had presumed to belittle him by calling him a "comparatist." For him philology was
comparative, as it was for the late John Matthews Manly of
Chicago; when someone asked Manly to define philology he answered, "It's life." Columbia has harbored a Department of English and Comparative Literature, where students are allowed to be
as comparative or as limited as they please, provided their material
warrants either approach. W. W. Lawrence's course in The
Middle Ages ranged freely over Europe; Roger S. Loomis's course
in Arthurian Romance was anything but Anglophile; the late
Jefferson B. Fletcher's Dante and Medieval Culture was as comparative as anyone could wish, but it owed much to Grandgent at
Harvard and nothing much to the Sorbonne. If Harvard and
Columbia were perhaps the most notable comparatist seats and
their professors some of the more notable performers, they were
not alone. Lane Cooper and Thomas F. Crane were at Cornell;
Professor Tom Pete Cross and others were at Chicago; A. R.
Hohlfeld developed the German-English studies at Wisconsin;
there were comparatists at Yale, California, Johns Hopkins, Iowa,
Michigan, New York University—but this should not become a
catalogue. On the whole they were not consciously comparatists;
they were students of literature who followed letters assuming
that, except for the barriers of language and culture, the study of
literature on a broad basis required no methods essentially different
from those pertinent to the study of national literatures.

Thus, in retrospect, and from one point of view, the last quarter
century can be characterized as America's coming of age in broad
literary studies. We have grown more concerned with such studies;
we have become more clear-headed as to what we should be doing
with them, and to a degree we are becoming the center—if there
is a center—for an attitude which endeavors to transcend the
methods and aims of the Sorbonne school.

Perhaps the joining of the issues can be most readily observed in
the *Yearbook of Comparative and General Literature*, an annual
founded in 1953 to form a "rallying point" for scholars and teachers
interested in comparative literary approaches. Its editors
announced as one of its purposes "delineation (if any) between
Comparative, General, and World Literature," but apparently
they could have omitted the *if any*, for the delineation began at

once. Henri Peyre of Yale, with a handsome preliminary bow to the Sorbonne, went on to observe that "The mistake of comparative scholars has often lain in being easily satisfied with specific monographs of a purely analytical character and in lacking the audacity to approach works of synthesis," and concluded that "the really important topics of Comparative Literature have hardly been touched." Since the Sorbonne scholars have touched a good bit of territory, this remark has implications. Alexander Gillies of Leeds also saluted the great of the Sorbonne, but he must have been relying upon the broader studies when he observed that "the study of comparative literature much more than that of national literatures brings us into contact with the real problems of the world in the past and the present." Henry W. Wells of Columbia went farther. He pointed out that "Comparative Literature demonstrates kinships which World Literature assumes," and insisted that "The student of World Literature . . . practices cosmopolitanism first, selectivism second, and in varying degrees," and that "The broader and more catholic the view of World Literature as a discipline, presumably the better."

All this was gentlemanly if lively academic discussion, but in the same issue appeared Jean-Marie Carré's preface to M. F. Guyard's *La Littérature comparée* (1951), and with that the fat was in the fire, or at least, the bite was in the typewriter. M. Carré, mentioning the earlier statements by Baldensperger and Van Tieghem, declared that *littérature comparée* needed once more to be made precise, that the movement demonstrates its worth by its progress, and that as we discipline *notre marche*, M. Guyard's book *éclairera la route*. Furthermore, he indicated the nature of the route to be illumined. *La littérature comparée* is not literary comparison, he insisted; it is a branch of literary history which does not consider literary works mainly for their original value, but is concerned especially with what each nation, each author, does when works are borrowed. "Who says *influence* says also *interpretation, reaction, resistance, combat*." In short *la littérature comparée* is not *la littérature générale*. It is not concerned with grand parallelisms and syntheses like humanism, classicism, and Romanticism, which are in danger of being at once too systematic and too vague. It should ignore *ces grandes synthéses*.

For many an American scholar that was too much, and the

next issue of the yearbook sizzled. It opened with a brief but closely reasoned statement by Wellek, who observed that M. Carré's "Preface gives an almost official blessing to what one must regard as the authoritative program." He then moved to the attack: "It seems to me that, in every way, M. Carré's concept of 'comparative literature' is obfuscating and, if it should become universal, destructive of a meaningful study of literature. It is both too narrow and too broad, falsely limited and falsely extended." A critic cannot go much farther, but he can document, and Wellek did, although his piece is too closely written to permit brief summary. Samples must suffice. He considered M. Guyard's "little chart" of subjects studied and not studied, and noted that it is both misleading and rather shockingly incomplete and inexact, and concluded, "Even if the chart were perfect it would show a mechanical conception of literary scholarship at its worst." When the Sorbonne method broadens, he added, it is no better, and thus "The concept propounded by Messrs. Carré and Guyard carries us, on the one hand, back into the old days of positivistic fragmentation, and, on the other, abolishes the clear subject matter of our study in favor of sociology and national psychology. . . . Literature is one, as art and humanity are one; and in this concept lies the future of literary studies." That is, Wellek was insisting that the concept implied in the word *literature* be not banished from *comparative literature*.

Nor was he alone. In the same issue David H. Malone of Alabama Polytechnic Institute reviewed M. Guyard's manual. He noted that M. Guyard has appropriated much of Van Tieghem's book having the same title, without even acknowledging Van Tieghem in the bibliography and has "even taken over whole sentences from Van Tieghem with only an occasional change in word order." Perhaps one should here rise to the defense of M. Guyard; surely he did not deliberately plagiarize. Presumably in preparing a work which he thought of as a manual for *littérature comparée* at the Sorbonne he made use of an earlier manual without acknowledgement, very much as the editor of a college catalogue includes much from earlier catalogues. He was probably not more than a little forgetful when he allowed the work to be printed without explanation in the "*Que sais-je?*" series. He cannot, however, be so readily defended against Professor Malone's charges of "quasi-scientific partitions" of literature and of recommending procedures in which "The path leading out of the waste land of 'arid' studies leads to comparative psychology, not to the text of a play or a poem or a novel." Thus Malone's conclusion is not much different from Wellek's: "After reading M. Guyard's *La Littérature comparée* the American student, at least, must insist that an introduction to Comparative Literature has yet to be written. Indeed, after reading this book, one feels that an Introduction to Comparative Literature *must* be written. Unless comparative literature in this country is to become the lopsided study of cultural history on the one hand or literary dilettantism on the other, such a book must, in its ultimate purpose, justify comparative literature as the best means of arriving at an understanding, appreciation, and evaluation of the individual work of literature."

To one sympathetic to what Professor Ota calls "the American way," the review appears devastating, but the discharge was apparently not enough to relieve Malone's feelings. In the next issue of the *Yearbook* he urged that we "forget that comparative literature is concerned with two or more national literatures." He observed that "A truism of almost all discussions of comparative literature is that its unique advantage lies in its insistence upon work in more than one national literature. It also should be a truism that one can be just as provincial in two languages as he can in one." For him "comparative" had best imply that to understand a work of art one always compares it with other works of art, whencever they come. That is, one should not deliberately transcend boundaries in literary study; one should ignore them as much as possible. "We should insist that comparative literature is the most rewarding field of literary study because it recognizes the full implications and responsibilities of the study of literature." Possibly this "American way" can best be summarized in the *avant propos* of *Comparative Literature*, clearly the most important American journal in the field, which reads as follows:

Its editors define comparative literature in the broadest possible manner, and accept articles dealing with the manifold interrelations of literatures, with the theory of literature, and with broad views and movements, genres, periods, and authors—from the earliest times to the present.

The essential difference may be one of temperament, although temperament formalized, recognized, and propagated. The inevitable question is perhaps this: what kind of questions do you like to ask? In the perspective of time and space all questions are inadequate and all answers wrong, but speaking generally, the more profound the question the less exact the answer. On the whole, the Sorbonne school prefers to ask relatively trivial questions, hoping that a large number of tolerably exact answers will add up to the best total answer. On the other hand, those who practice what Professor Ota characterizes as "the American way," however much they may differ in detail, feel that an inadequate question can elicit only an inadequate answer, however objectively the answer may be prepared. They say, in effect, let us be wrong if we must—and we must—but let us not be piffling. Let us ask the most profound questions we can devise, and let us ask them at once, conscious that the answers must be inadequate, but hoping that time will strengthen and age will mature them. Faced with the mystery and wonder of the world we are all either trivial or inadequate; some prefer to attempt less, hoping that they may thus approach what they envisage; others prefer to attempt all that one can be and do, knowing that some fail gloriously and some ignominiously, and that those who believe they have triumphed have all too frequently been ignorant, not only of the answer, but of the question. On the whole, the Sorbonne has preferred limited questions, and their detractors, who include many outside the United States, have preferred broader questions, hoping that the answers will be revealing if not final.

We are perhaps now ready for definitions of some terms. *Littérature comparée* is the comparative study of literature, and under the influence of the Sorbonne school it implies the recognition of national literatures and prescribes the study of the influence of something or somebody in one national literature upon something or somebody in another. It is a branch of literary history, and no more. The term *Comparative Literature* has been popularized as a translation of *littérature comparée*, which it is not very exactly, since it seems to imply a body of literature which is comparative and another body which is not. No one uses the term in this sense. In usage it is often taken to mean what the Sorbonne school means by *littérature comparée*, but it is often used, also, to identify the sort of study which I have associated above with the names of Wellek and Malone, study which asserts that literature should be studied as literature, the study impeded as little as is possible by boundaries, whether racial, temporal, political, or linguistic. In this second use the designation is practically synonymous with *General Literature*, a term advocated by the late Professor Guérard and others, but one which has attracted scanty following. *World Literature*, also, is not quite what the term might imply. It is sometimes used as a rough equivalent of General Literature, but more frequently it implies writing anywhere in the world which has gained wide currency. The Japanese *Tale of Genji* is part of World Literature because it is widely known; Arishima Takeo's *Descendants of Cain* is not, because, at least as yet, it is not widely read. Thus the term *World Literature* may imply a body of writing, if a body of writing only loosely determinable, whereas the other terms mentioned here refer to methods of study.

III

So much for the central problem in essaying broad literary studies. Here are less central problems, including some which involve methodology, for students who have been discontented with the Sorbonne formula but who recognized the value of provable and teachable practices in a broad and uncertain subject have endeavored to devise methods. Naturally, these are both vertical in time and horizontal in space, the most prominent of the first sort going under the title, History of Ideas, and of the second, *Geistesgeschichte*, to which I have already referred. Neither is without precedent. Studies extended in time with titles like *The Rise of the Novel* and *Vergil in the Middle Ages* have seemed to require no unusual techniques. Similarly, space has not deterred studies like *The Renaissance*, *The Romantic Revolt*. But both approaches, as advanced in the last quarter century, have involved methodology and ends which their practitioners feel have not previously been exploited.

The History of Ideas is perhaps the easier to describe. The name and the procedure are associated with Arthur O. Lovejoy, who had been advocating vertical studies at Johns Hopkins for many years before he brought out *The Great Chain of Being* (1936). It is an epochal book. It traces the rise during classic times of the notion that all nature consists of a great chain of creation from the inanimate rock to the pure spirit of God, and it shows how this idea grew and shifted with the centuries until it reached its height in such works as Pope's *Essay on Man*. That the book is an important study few who read it will doubt, but Professor Lovejoy presented it not merely as a study for its own sake but as an example of his procedure, which has two notable characteristics. First, he recommends giving major attention to secondary figures, on the theory that genius is likely to transcend time and place and that the writings most revealing for ideas are likely to come from those conversant but somewhat dull spirits who can do no better than reflect the fashions of the day. Second, he recommends that a broad subject like primitivism be broken into its unit ideas and their opposites, and that these units be traced as they shift in implication and importance, as they appear, transmogrify, and fade.

The method attracted immediate attention. Professor Lovejoy, with the assistance of George Boas and others, collected a very solid volume, *Materials for the History of Primitivism* (1935), which was to lay the groundwork for the study of broader subjects than that of the Chain of Being. He was instrumental in founding *The Journal of the History of Ideas,* which has become one of the most significant of our scholarly literary and philosophic periodicals, and in starting *Contributions to the History of Primitivism,* of which Lois Whitney's *Primitivism and the Idea of Progress* (1934) was the first. Meanwhile, Marjorie Nicolson, then at Smith College, was demonstrating that even undergraduates, when properly supervised, could study the history of ideas and make exciting discoveries.

The method also inspired doubts, not to say animadversions. In some ways the best brief statement of the proponents is that of Professor Nicolson, "The History of Literature and the History of Thought," *English Institute Annual, 1939* (1940), but the official statement is presumably Lovejoy's, which opens *JHI* (1940), and it was he who drew the fire, notably from his colleague, Leo Spitzer, *JHI* (1944) and from Frederic J. Teggert, *JHI* (1940), and Harold O. Taylor, *Journal of Philosophy* (1943). Their reservations are similar, that an "idea" cannot be successfully broken into "unit ideas" and their opposites, and the resulting fragments do not represent the same thing in one culture that they do in another, that the History of Ideas (with capitals) becomes more a study in the uses of words than any real history of ideas (without capitals), that "Such analysis is either philosophy considered as literary history, or literature conceived as diluted philosophy." These are the words of Professor Taylor; Professor Spitzer went farther:

I do not deny the possibility of writing the history of one idea; but in that case the idea must remain in its proper climate—that is, within the limits of one definite science or field of activity. . . . In opposition to such an *histoire des ideés*, with its bias for naturalistic and atomistic methods applied to the history of the human mind, I propose a *Geistesgeschichte* in which *Geist* represents nothing ominously mystical or mythological, but simply the totality of the features of a given period or movement which the historian tries to *see as a unity*—and the impact of which, the philosophy of the Encyclopedists and positivistic mathematicians to the contrary, does in fact amount to more than that of the aggregate of the parts. There have been, God knows, many *Fabricate* of more or less recent German make, in which the pursuit of the integration of features of detail into one whole has served as an excuse for confusion and muddled thinking so rightly condemned by Professor Lovejoy. But such writing should not be allowed to discredit the legitimate endeavors of a Burkhardt, a Dilthey, a Simmel, a Max Weber, a Tröltsch. There is nothing fraudulent or even revolutionary in a procedure which seeks to see wholes, to put one whole into relation with another, instead of marking combinations of parts detached from their wholes. This is simply the factual, the more accurate approach toward the historical problem in question.

So here we are, back to *Geistesgeschichte*, and defined as Spitzer defines it little dissent is likely from anyone who believes in broad attempts at all. But does Spitzer have much left of *Geistesgeschichte?* If it is only intelligent study by a very learned literary historian of philosophic cast who has become interested in savoring the temper of a time and place, who would object? And perhaps that is the best we can do; it has served and is serving for excellent studies. But as Spitzer in effect points out, the approach is nothing new. *Geistesgeschichte* as it is currently practiced in Germany and adjacent lands like Switzerland and Austria is something quite different, and against this Spitzer has firmly insulated himself when he calls them *Fabricate* and implies that they rest on something "ominously mystical or mythological." *Geistesge-schichte* in the more mystical sense is not content with putting together supposed relevances to construct a broadly revealing interpretation. The method relies upon the detection of a "time-spirit," which is presumed to have existed and presumed to have determined the character of all productions in all activities what-ever. Within limits, there must have been "time-spirits." Most critics would probably agree that there must be some connection between Roman love of oratory and Roman competence in government, between various Renaissance evidences of artistic efflorescence (between Italian painting and English drama, for instance), between modern American concern for function and American love of historical novels and literate non-fiction. But with any methods currently acceptable, making use of such con-cepts presents difficulties; no two investigators would describe any one "time-spirit" in the same way, and in any event such a *Geist* must be only one of a good many operatives involved. How ridiculous the use of *Geist* can become any reader of German may observe by consulting the more flamboyant writings of even such learned scholars as Fritz Strich, Helene Richter, and Herbert Cysarz. Those for whom German is an impediment may observe Wellek having fun at the expense of the approach in the *English Institute Annual, 1941* (1942), or may turn to Ronald S. Crane's review of Paul Meissner's *Die geistwissenschaftlichen Grundlagen des englischen Literaturbarocks* in *PQ* (1935). When a Teutonic scholar-critic explains that "We look for the totality behind the objects and explain all facts by this spirit of the time," most readers west of the Rhine are likely to feel that *Geistesgeschichte* has become too *vergeistigt* for any good use.

Thus a survey of methodology in comparative research will perhaps emphasize two developments in the past quarter century: first, the Sorbonne method has continued as the medium of a considerable body of significant and generally reliable research; second, a sense of inadequacy in the Sorbonne procedure has con-tributed to various attempts to find broader approaches, techniques like the History of Ideas and *Geistesgeschichte*, and a less form-ulated but perhaps more significant conviction that literature should be studied as literature, linguistic and political boundaries notwithstanding.

So much for methodology within literary bounds. But literature uses all material for its subject matter, and thus if it does not take all subjects as its province, it readily becomes involved in other provinces. Following these ramifications would take us too far afield, but the directions must be indicated. Recent decades have shown a growing interest in the relationships between literature and other areas, especially as they become involved in discussions of periods, of which Romanticism and the Baroque have occasioned some of the more incandescent prose, with the Renaissance perhaps a warm third. One should note here a shift in emphasis. Formerly, studies which bridged from one discipline into another were likely to be attempted only under provocation—to study Milton one must study his education, and to understand his education one must study the schools of his day. The result is a monograph like Donald Lemen Clark's excellent *John Milton and St. Paul's School* (1948) or T. W. Baldwin's *William Shakespeare's Small Latine & Lesse Greeke* (1944). Meanwhile, no one has seriously asked himself what are the important relationships between literature and education, although obviously they are many. To date, the best work has been done in the relationships between literature and science, with Professor Nicolson, Francis Johnson, Theodore Hornberger, Douglas Bush, and others doing sound research. Just recently the relationships between literature and music have attracted students.

A revolution in thinking about language has produced at least two productive approaches, *semantics* in vocabulary and *structural linguistics* in grammar, and this activity has encouraged writing on such subjects as "Literature and Language." The whole problem becomes involved in philosophy, notably by way of symbolism and allegory, and thus the study of literature becomes part of the study of man as a whole—a field which the literary critic may feel is outside his little plot of ground, but one which he can scarcely ignore. Particularly interesting here are the speculations of Ernst Cassirer and Suzanne Langer in what has been called "symbolic logic," and the approach employing language used by such critics as Spitzer, Erich Auerbach, E. R. Curtius, Dámaso Alonso, and Charles S. Singleton. See, for example, Spitzer's *A Method of Interpreting Literature* (1949) and his *Linguistics and Literary History* (1948).

So clearly literary in its essence, and yet so significant for primitive life that it is often associated with anthropology, is folklore. Wherever it belongs, it is clearly comparative—the folk, unconsciously, are the true comparatists—and folklorists have made great progress in recent decades. The Finnish Folklore method was well worked out by 1930, but only later did it become, with variations, standard practice throughout the world. By this method folktales are collected, broken into motifs, and studied for the pattern in time and place that these motifs display. By this process the confused welter of folk storytelling can often be reduced to revealing order. In recent decades this method has been applied, with more or less industry, to most of the world's surviving folk fiction, and folklorists have amassed comparative material which is best surveyed in Stith Thompson's *The Folktale* (1946). Professor Thompson is responsible for another of the monumental works of our day. Studying first with the Finns and later at Indiana University he produced the *Motif-Index of Folk-Literature* (revised edition 1955), which has become one of the standard tools for all students of literature.

One other development must engage us, for although it has produced little research as yet, it is healthy in almost all senses. As a people we are recovering from our notion that the Western European tradition and the world are coterminous. If we still assume, in effect if not formally, that little of consequence can come from places like Latin America and Australia; if we still incline to feel that the quantities of literature which have come from the Orient are "exotic"—I am quoting an eminent European comparatist—and are hence of lesser account, nevertheless we improve. The symptoms are everywhere: an increase in published translations from Oriental languages, the growth of Oriental institutes in research centers like Columbia, Pennsylvania, and the University of Washington; the appearance of scattered Oriental courses even in lesser places like Kentucky and Nevada; the growth of an excellent newsletter like *Literature East & West*, a labor of love edited by G. D. Anderson of New York University; a conference like that reported in *Indiana University Conference on Oriental-Western Literary Relations* (1955), or the still more recent conferences like that on Islamic studies at the University of Chicago; see *Literature East & West* (1957). If world, general, and comparative literature are still the disfavored little sisters of philology and the New Criticism, they are growing up, even in what was once that academic back country, the United States.

IV

The preceding text may already be too cluttered with titles. That it may be no more so I shall bring together here the remaining indispensable volumes, and some of the more signal works which are not indispensable for most purposes. The nature of this volume will lead me to prefer writings in English and books likely to be available in this country. Useful for languages but scatteringly read are the surveys of comparative literature by countries, building up in the *Yearbook of Comparative and General Literature* (1952—), which I shall henceforth cite as *Yb;* see, for example, Gleb Struve on the Russians, *Yb* (1955 and 1957). To keep up generally the best single item is *Yb*, which succeeded the late Arthur E. Christy's *Comparative Literature News-Letter*, a pioneer effort that never received the support it warranted, although its files are still useful. *Yb* contains general articles, appreciations of great comparatists, news of research centers, surveys of comparative literature in other lands, collegiate curricula, reviews (especially of translations), and current bibliography. More scholarly are *Comparative Literature* (hereafter referred to as *CL*) and *Revue de littérature comparée* (generally known as *RLC*), published at Oregon and Paris respectively. Comparative material appears in many other periodicals in this country and abroad, notably in the *Journal of the History of Ideas* and the *Journal of Aesthetics and Art Criticism*, and the student should not neglect the *English Institute Annual* (now *English Institute Essays*) since the Institute usually attacks problems broadly and sanely.

For bibliography the standard works are two: for comparative literature, Fernand Baldensperger and W. P. Friederich, *Bibliography of Comparative Literature* (1950), and for world literature, Hanns Wilhelm Eppelsheimer's two-volume *Handbuch der Weltliteratur* (1947–50). The first is kept down to date with supplements in *Yb*, and a revision is promised. It serves better for studies of the Sorbonne sort than for broader works, which are difficult to classify. Eppelsheimer's is a general reference work, but the bibliography is geographically the most comprehensive, even though it misses areas (Yugoslavian and some lesser bodies of writing) and many important works not in German. A third work, entitled *A Guide for Comparative Literature* in manuscript, a co-operative critical bibliography, has been more than ten years in gestation and I have been guilty of prematurely announcing in *Yb* (1952) its imminent birth. I still expect to see it in print. V. F. Hopper and B. D. N. Grebanier, *Bibliography of European Literature* (1954) is designedly brief, but useful. National bibliographies like the *Cambridge Bibliography of English Literature* include comparative items; appearing currently is the excellent *A Critical Bibliography of French Literature*, edited by D. C. Cabeen (1947–). Bibliographies of translations are scattering; perhaps the most admired is Clarissa Palmer Farrar and Austin Patterson Evans, *Bibliography of English Translations from Medieval Sources* (1946), a model for this sort of thing. Bayard Quincy Morgan has twice revised his bibliography of translations from the German, and Remigio U. Pane has made a good beginning for Spanish with *English Translations from the Spanish, 1484–1943: A Bibliography* (1944). Eppelsheimer, cited above, contains many translations into German, but translations from most languages into most languages are indifferently treated, and until something like the *Guide for Comparative Literature* appears the best way to locate available bibliographies is to consult the index of Constance M. Winchell, *Guide to Reference Books* (1951). For writing in the little-read Oriental languages see the selected bibliographies in *Literature East & West*.

To the Sorbonne concept of theory and method little has been added, although Van Tieghem's little volume *La Littérature comparée* has been revised and enlarged (1946), and there have been interesting articles in the journals; see *Yb* under Comparative Literature, and so forth, in the current bibliographies. A. Porta, *La letteratura comparata* (1951), a Van Tieghem-like manual, has not found favor. For the practice of comparative literature— mainly of the Sorbonne sort, but not exclusively so—we now have a standard work, Werner P. Friederich and David Henry Malone, *Outline of Comparative Literature from Dante Alighieri to Eugene O'Neill* (1954), which belongs in every reputable library and on every comparatist's shelves. Nothing is easier than to criticize a work of this sort adversely; much has inevitably been omitted and no two scholars would agree as to what should be noticed. Furthermore, by the definition of comparative literature used here the emphasis is on influence, not on significance; pages are given to Scott and Byron, lines to Shelley and Keats. Such comments are not, however, very pertinent in face of the obvious fact that here was a book that badly needed writing and has been well done. For some gaps see *CL* (1951).

For the broad study of literature the most engaging general book I know is Albert Guerard, *Preface to World Literature* (1940), which is charming as well as wise and informed. In many ways the most important is René Wellek and Austin Warren, *Theory of Literature* (1949). It makes no claim to special concern for comparative studies, but the comparative portions have been done by Wellek, who makes his discussion the nearest approach we have to a statement for those who believe that literature must be studied comparatively but that it must be studied first of all as literature. The volume contains excellent selected bibliographies by chapters, which happily are not restricted to writing in the Western European tradition. For factual reviews of recent volumes on theory and practice of literary study in Japan see Howard Hibbett, *CL* (1953).

Some volumes have been intended to encourage comparison by bringing together interpretations of various literatures; *The World through Literature*, edited by Charlton Laird (1951) has bibliographies and distinguished contributors. Telling observations on what might be called world literature appear in *Invitation to Learning* (1941) and *New Invitation to Learning* (1942). Important and readable are the two collections by Philo Buck, *The Golden Thread* (1931) and *The World's Great Age* (1936). Somewhat similar in intent are histories of national literatures calculated to initiate readers of English; they include J. R. Hightower, *Topics in Chinese Literature* (1950), to be supplemented with *CL* (1953); Donald Keene, *Japanese Literature: An Introduction for Western Readers* (1955); John W. Morrison, *Modern Japanese Fiction* (1955); Reynold A. Nicholson, *A Literary History of the Arabs* (1953). The following may serve such purposes although it transcends them: Carl Brockelmann, *Geschichte der arabischen Literatur* (1937–49), in two volumes and three sup-

plements. For a disillusioning review of books on Slavic literatures
see Wellek, *CL* (1950); more acceptable volumes include Waclaw
Lednicki, *Russia, Poland, and the West* (1954); Renato Poggioli,
Il fiore del verso russo (1949); Dmitry Cizevsky, *Outline of Comparative Slavic Literatures* (1952). Among the interesting collections of studies are the following: *Weltliteratur: Festgabe für
Fritz Strich* (1952); *Forschungprobleme der vergleichenden
Literaturgeschichte*, edited by K. Wais (1951), which includes
studies in English. *Letteratura comparata* (1948) has some excellent
surveys of Italian relations by countries. Not comprehensive but
useful is *France and World Literature: Yale French Studies*
(1950).

Great dictionaries, encyclopedias, handbooks, and histories of
world and comparative literature have been few in recent decades.
They were a European speciality, and wars, occupations, and
dictatorships have not been conducive to such expensive publications. One of the exceptions is *Dizionario letterario Bompiani
delle opere e dei personaggi di tutti i tempi e di tutte le letterature*
(1947–50), in nine volumes, which has been plausibly characterized
as "by far the fullest and best literary encyclopedia ever produced
in any language." Some, like Giacomo Prampolini's seven-volume
Storia universale della letteratura (1948–53), have been revised
and enlarged. Oskar Walzel's great *Handbuch der Literaturwissen-
schaft* is still theoretically in progress, but has produced little since
the accession of the Nazis. Coming out in volumes and fascicles
respectively from Stuttgart, and to be watched, are *Der Roman-
führer, herausgegeben von Wilhelm Olbrich* (1950–), restricted to
fiction, and from Vienna *Die Weltliteratur*, edited by E. Frau-
wallner and others, (1951–), a bibliographical, biographical, and
critical literary dictionary. The following are briefer, but recent
or recently revised, and limited in most instances as their titles
suggest: *Dictionary of World Literature*, edited by Joseph T.
Shipley (1953); *Cassell's Encyclopaedia of World Literature*,
edited by S. H. Steinberg (1953); *The Reader's Encyclopedia*,
edited by William Rose Benét (1948); *Columbia Dictionary of
Modern European Literature*, edited by Horatio Smith (1947);
Paul Wiegler, *Geschichte der fremdsprachigen Weltliteratur*
(1949); N. Ségur, *Histoire de la littérature européenne* (1948);
Lexicon der Weltliteratur, edited by H. Kindermann and M.

Dietrich (1951); Adolf Spemann, *Vergleichende Zeittafel der Weltliteratur vom Mittelalter bis zur Neuzeit (1150–1931)* (1951); H. W. Eppelsheimer, *Weltliteratur: Ein Versuch* (1951); and see especially both Eppelsheimer and Van Tieghem cited above. William Flint Thrall and Addison Hibbard, *A Handbook to Literature* (1936) includes genres and many literary concepts but seldom strays from the purlieus of the English language. Gonzague Truc, *Histoire illustreé de littératures* (1952) is hopelessly Francophile. There are a number of briefer student manuals, for example, *World Literature*, in two volumes in the College Outline Series, and some college anthologies have excellent apparatus, for instance the *World Masterpieces* edited by Maynard Mack and others.

There remains to mention hastily notable research involving comparative study. Down to this point I have endeavored to be relatively objective, but now I can be only eclectic and inadequate for I shall be plagued by limitations of both space and knowledge. Some few works are of such sweep and competence that they are obvious choices, notably Gilbert Highet, *The Classical Tradition: Greek and Roman Influences on Western Literature* (1949) and René Wellek, *A History of Modern Criticism: 1750–1950* (1955–) to comprise four volumes. Frederick M. Combellack, a reviewer never intimidated by great names or many volumes, calls Highet's survey "masterly and elegant," a "long and glorious story" told "superlatively well." His only reservation of consequence is that the footnotes are divorced from the text: ". . . so many of them [the footnotes] are so good that most readers will probably ruin their tempers by reading the book in two places at once. Greater worth than this hath no footnote." Two volumes of Wellek's work have appeared to date; although they, too, encourage schizophrenic reading from anyone concerned with documentation, they are so inclusive, penetrating, and learned that few will doubt that here is to be one of the one-man scholarly monuments. Moving admirably through the ages is C. S. Lewis, *The Allegory of Love* (1936). To the indispensable works I would add Hardin Craig, *The Enchanted Glass* (1936). It does not purport to be "comparative," but it is instinct with ideas both fresh and essential to comparative study, for instance, that references to great names in Medieval and Renaissance writers do not usually indicate "influence" from the writer cited but only the impact of medieval encyclopedias. Great works in related fields are often indispensable to literary study; those of Arnold J. Toynbee and Pitirim A. Sorokin scarcely require citation. Among others, I have been impressed by Herbert J. Muller, *The Uses of the Past* (1952); Crane Brinton, *Ideas and Men* (1952), reprinted in part as *The Shaping of the Modern Mind;* F. S. C. Northrop, *The Meeting of the East and West* (1946); A. L. Kroeber, *Configurations of Culture Growth* (1944).

The leaders of the Sorbonne school have perhaps been sufficiently cited earlier; others using the approach will be found in *Nea Hestia* (1948) and in various articles in *Annales du centre universitaire mediterranéen de Nice*. Marcel Bataillon should be singled out for his interest in Hispanic relations, perhaps especially *Erasme et l'Espagne* (1937). The following might be added: W. F. Schirmer, *Der Einfluss der deutschen Literatur auf die englischen im 19. Jahrhundert* (1947); E. M. Butler, *The Tyranny of Greece over Germany* (1935); Ethel Seaton, *Literary Relations of England and Scandinavia in the Seventeenth Century* (1935); Konrad Bieber, *L' Allemagne vue par les écrivains de la Resistance française* (1954); Jean-Marie Carré, *Les Ecrivains français et le mirage allemand, 1800–1940* (1947); A. Lytton Sells, *The Italian Influence on English Poetry from Chaucer to Southwell* (1955), to be continued; Ferdinand Alegría, *Walt Whitman en Hispanoamérica* (1954); Vicente Llorens Castillo, *Liberales y románticos: Una emigración española en Inglaterra, 1823–1834* (1954).

To see how much fun an essay into comparative literature can be, one might read Lawrence Marsden Price's "George Barnwell Abroad," *CL* (1950). Professor Price is just rounding off a long and distinguished career as a comparatist with revisions of two standard works: *English Literature in Germany* (1953) and *The Publication of English Humanoria in Germany in the Eighteenth Century* (1955). See also Richard Mönnig, *Amerika und England im deutschen, österreichischen und schweizerischen Schriftum der Jahre 1940–1949: Eine Bibliographie* (1951) and Anselm Schlösser, *Die englische Literatur in Deutschland von 1895 bis 1934* (1937).

Influences from abroad upon culture in this country have been lively subjects of study, especially in the journals. For a general survey of the development see Urban T. Holmes, "Comparative

Literature: Past and Future," *Studies in Language and Literature*, edited by G. C. Coffman (1945) and Victor Lange in *Forschungprobleme*, cited above. Recent book-length studies include O. W. Long, *Literary Pioneers: Early American Explorers of European Culture* (1937); Stanley T. Williams, *The Spanish Background of American Literature* (1955); Henry A. Pochmann, *German Culture in America, 1600–1900* (1957); *The American Writer and the European Tradition*, edited by Margaret Denny and William H. Gilman (1950); Stanley M. Vogel, *German Literary Influences on American Transcendentalists* (1955). Howard Mumford Jones, *America and French Culture, 1750–1848* (1927) has not been continued. Comparative studies find a large place in *The Literary History of the United States*, edited by Robert E. Spiller *et al.* (1948); it may be consulted for bibliography.

On the increase are works which deliberately study relationships between literature and related subjects. For science and literature they include many articles, a number of engaging studies by Marjorie Hope Nicolson, including *A World in the Moon* (1936) and *Newton Demands the Muse* (1946), and Douglas Bush, *Science and English Poetry* (1950). For a summary of problems in the study of literature and the arts see Wellek, *English Institute Annual, 1941* (1942), and for interesting excursions, Stephen A. Larrabee, *English Bards and Grecian Marbles* (1943); Helmut A. Hatzfield, *Literature through Art: A New Approach to French Literature* (1952); Calvin S. Brown, *Music and Literature* (1948); C. S. Brown, *Tones into Words: Musical Compositions as Subjects of Poetry* (1953); Charmenz S. Lenhart, *Musical Influences on American Poetry* (1957); *Musique et poesie au xvi° siècle* (1954); Albert Joseph George, *The Development of French Romanticism: The Impact of the Industrial Revolution on Literature* (1955); Laura Hibbard Loomis and Roger S. Loomis, *Arthurian Legends in Medieval Art* (1938). M. Carré's study of poetry and music has been cited. Bertrand H. Bronson and others have been interested in the relationships between the ballads and ballad music.

Literary periods as periods have occasioned too much controversy to permit more than a suggestion of bibliography. Again, Professor Lovejoy is at the bottom of some of it. In a symposium with Goetz A. Briefs, Eugene N. Anderson, Jacques Barzun, and Hoxie N. Fairchild in *JHI* (1941), he suggested that the concept of

Romanticism was either too broad or too narrow to have meaning, and the controversy spread. A good bit of comparative study is to be found here and there, for example, in M. H. Abrams, *The Mirror and the Lamp* (1953). The concept of the Baroque has attracted attention, especially in Germany; for full bibliography see Wellek, "The Concept of Baroque in Literary Scholarship," *Journal of Aesthetics and Art Criticism* (1946); M. V. Cerny, "Les origines européenes des études baroquistes," *RLC* (1950); and Franco Simone, *I contributi europei all' identificazione del barocco francese*, *CL* (1954). Too recent for these bibliographies, *Die Kunstformen des Barockzeitalters* (1956), edited by Rudolf Stamm, is not free from *Geistesgeschichte*, but as one reviewer observed, it "could have a stimulating effect on 'Anglo-Saxon' literary historiography if it were read in a proper spirit of cautious and speculative interest."

Of particular interest, and free from *Geistesgeschichte*, is Fritz Strich, *Goethe and World Literature*, translated by C. A. M. Sym (1949). Of first importance is Ernst Robert Curtius, *European Literature in the Latin Middle Ages*, translated by Willard R. Trask (1953). Morton W. Bloomfield, *The Seven Deadly Sins* (1952) is broadly comparative from the earliest times, but restricted to English after 1300. W. O. Sypherd, *Jephthah and his Daughters* (1948) also traces a far-flung theme, as does W. B. Stanford, *The Ulysses Theme* (1954). Comparetti's famous *Vergil in the Middle Ages* continues to attract interest with the late Frank Tenney criticizing the whole comparative approach in Comparetti and in "Spargos' industrious book *Virgil the Necromancer*" in "Changing Conceptions of Literary and Philological Research," *JHI* (1942), which, Virgil, Spargo, and Comparetti aside, is still an important article. Georg Misch has completed the second portion of his monumental survey of early autobiography, *Geschichte der Autobiographie*, II; *Das Mittelalter* (Die Frühzeit) (1955), of which the first volume appeared in 1905 and the English translation, *A History of Autobiography in Antiquity*, in 1951. A third volume is to continue the study through the Middle Ages.

Other solid contributions for early periods include the following: E. M. Butler, *The Myth of Magus* (1948), carried on, with more limited documents and less literature in *Ritual Magic* (1949);

Caroline Brady, *The Legend of Ermanric* (1943); Helen Flanders Dunbar, *Symbolism in Medieval Thought and Its Consummation in the Divine Comedy* (1929); W. R. Halliday, *Indo-European Folk-tales and Greek Legend* (1933); Lord Raglan, *The Hero* (1936); Walter Pabst, *Venus und die missverstandene Dido* (1955); Karl Hoppe, *Die Sage von Heinrich dem Löwen* (1952); Kurt Wais, *Frühe Epik Westeuropas und Vorgeschichte des Nibelungenliedes* (1953); Reta R. Bezzola, *Les Origines et la formation de la littérature courtoise en occident (500–1200)* (1944); Howard Rollin Patch, *The Other World According to Descriptions in Medieval Literature* (1950). For an excellent comparative study of the ballad, see W. T. Entwistle, *European Balladry* (1939).

Interesting for more than English are E. M. Tillyard, *The English Epic and Its Background* (1954); Douglas Bush, *Mythology and the Renaissance Tradition in English Poetry* (1932) and *Mythology and the Romantic Tradition in English Poetry* (1937); James R. Foster, *History of the Pre-Romantic Novel in England* (1949); James A. Notopoulos, *The Platonism of Shelley: A Study of Platonism and the Poetic Mind* (1949); J. J. *Rousseau en Angleterre au xviiie siècle* (1950); Clarence R. Decker, *The Victorian Conscience* (1952); Mario Praz, *La crisi dell 'eroe nel romanzo vittoriano* (1952). Of particular interest, although not deliberately comparative, are the various writings of C. M. Bowra, for example, *The Heritage of Symbolism* (1943). Broad studies, which incidentally cry out for translation, are Walter Muschg, *Tragische Literaturgeschichte* (1948); Herbert Seidler, *Allgemeine Stilistik* (1953); and Karl Vossler, *Die Dichtungsformen der Romanen* (1948). Erich Auerbach, *Mimesis: Dargestellte Wirklichkeit in der abendländischen Literatur* (1946), has been translated (1953) by Willard R. Trask. Harold Jantz offers an interesting interpretation broadly based in *Goethe's Faust as a Renaissance Man* (1951), as does Maria Rosa Lida de Malkiel in *Juan de Mena* (1950). Mary M. Colum, *From these Roots: The Ideas that Have Made Modern Literature* (1937) is interesting although less exhaustive than its title implies. Arthurian Romance has continued lively and comparative, with the trend going to the Celticists since the days of J. Douglas Bruce; see, for instance, Helaine Newstead, *Bran* *the Blessed in Arthurian Romance* (1939), Arthur C. L. Brown, *The Origin of the Grail Legend* (1943), and the numerous writings of Roger Sherman Loomis, including *Arthurian Traditions and Chretien de Troyes* (1949).

THE AUDIENCE

17

The Public Arts and the Private Sensibility

PATRICK D. HAZARD

WHAT WAS A DELIGHT HAS BECOME a problem. That, surely, is a capsule history of popular culture in our generation. In 1924, Gilbert Seldes enthusiastically announced discovery of *The Seven Lively Arts:* vaudeville, jazz, newspaper satire, movies, comic strips, revues, and the circus. In 1957, under an "objective" pro-and-con editorship, two academicians, Bernard Rosenberg and David Manning White, assembled a generally grim indictment: *Mass Culture: The Popular Arts in America.* From personal testament to collective rejection; from getting a bang out of the stuff to articulating a modish whimper. The changes behind this radical ideological shift are a microcosm of an America transformed, both in mind and material environment, by industrial technology. Moreover, any rationale for the humanities in a mass society that tries to skirt the everyday moral and aesthetic issues imposed on us by the machine is foredoomed to failure. Indeed, a good bit of the paralysis that immobilizes the humanist today comes from trying to consider the challenges of the popular arts without an adequate sense of the total situation of our society in its political, social, and economic dimensions.

But our main concern here, naturally, will be with what the public or popular arts particularly mean to us as custodians of the private sensibility. The essential issue is how we can remain faithful to the tradition of personal, private excellence we are entrusted to conserve and still encourage maturity and resist debasing tendencies in the newer collaborative forms of expression. These media more and more set the imaginative and intellectual tone of our civilization. To ignore them is simply to complicate the problem:

the media professionals with integrity need our support; the
vulgarians have to be check-reined. Further, we must come to
terms with the paradox that our society supports the publication
of both the *Kenyon Review* and *Confidential*.

The toughest question has been saved for last: Why such progress and poverty in contemporary American expression? On the
one hand, a genuine flowering of criticism and historical scholarship among a tiny elite; on the other, to use the never more apt
exclamation of Mrs. Trollope, immense exhalations of periodical
trash for the many. The task is all the more difficult because the
preceding chapters have described the largesse open to the few;
only this one remains to explain the many's concurrent poverty.

However, examining the tensions between the public arts and
the private sensibility is as important as it is difficult and neglected.
For in doing so we raise a whole series of related issues, themselves
at once crucial and unexamined: the anti-technological bias of the
humanist, audio-visualism, the legitimacy of the social sciences
as a mode of knowing about man in society, the place of vocationalism in American education, and the undeveloped potential
of the American vernacular tradition. These issues are confused
by the humanist's deep-seated prejudices. Briefly describing these
idols of our academic cave can perhaps help to exorcize them.

Thoreau gave classic expression to the humanist's anti-technological bias in *Walden* when he stated his reservations about
the Maine-Texas telegraph: "Our inventions are wont to be pretty
toys, which distract our attention from serious things. They are
but improved means to an unimproved end, an end which it was
already too easy to arrive at; as railroads lead to Boston or New
York." Which is wise enough if you mean to give a telegraph
promoter a sense of irony. But as an intramural pose, it is an invitation to smugness. Thoreau's warning to the "practical" American should not obscure for the impractical historian and critic the
fact that modern technology *can* improve ends as well as means:
material security and widespread leisure can become improved
means to the now obtainable end of universal contemplation. Ritual
denigration of the machine allows the humanist to assume an unwarranted moral superiority to a crass, materialistic civilization.
For this "ugly Carthage" makes possible research libraries and

micro-aids, scholarly journals and university presses, more university teaching jobs *and* conventions ("as railroads lead to Boston and New York"). And if we live in genteel poverty on the tattered fringe of an expense account economy, we are likewise mercifully spared the unquiet desperation of exurbia. But wheedling aside, the opinions to follow simply assume that a machine civilization is *possibly* a humane one.

Not surprisingly, our a priori distrust of the machine hobbles us in our approach to audio-visualism. Fixating our profession on the bottom rung (movable type) of the technological ladder of communication first of all makes it harder, even impossible, to reach our own proper audiences. It also impoverishes classroom use of the newer media of communication. Trite recordings, dull films, unimaginative broadcasts, and graphically stodgy textbooks are one depressing result of the humanist's superiority to mechanical teaching devices. The withdrawal of the sanity and balance of the liberal arts has polarized mass communication into bread-and-butter vulgarity and formlessness, on the one hand, and avant-garde aesthetic razzle-dazzle on the other. This semi-official resistance to mechanical interpositions between teacher and students—what I call the Mark Hopkins complex—is part of a larger disaffection of the liberal arts from mass education. Educationist-baiting has become a national pastime in English departments.

Neither ancient nor modern, however, has reason to be proud of the petty bickering poisoning the climate of opinion about education in the United States today. Nevertheless the complex of problems arising from the impact of the public arts on the content and method of the public schools provides a ready-made opportunity for honest collective bargaining between educator and humanist. It is doubtful whether there will be much progress on this crucial matter without both the traditional wisdom of the liberal arts and the idealistic commitment of the professional educator. But should both parties air their grievances across a curriculum bargaining table, they would find more to agree than disagree upon when it came to the debilitating influences of popular culture on educational achievement. Engaged in this common concern, they might even begin to face their own limitations vis-a-vis the media: the humanist's inflexibility in the face of the problematic and new; the educationist's excessive contemporamania. Rolling up their sleeves to solve a common problem, they would have to give up their childish devotion to academic scandalmongering.

The humanist's arrogant suspicion of the educator's competence is no less crippling than his petulant dismissal of intellectual competition from the social sciences. "Thou shalt not commit a social science" is part of the decalogue handed down from the Sinai of the graduate seminar room. Our professional dedication to literature of quality makes it easy for us to regard the literature of quantification as beneath serious notice. Yet, even within the humanities, the philosophers have sufficiently shown during our generation that "true" knowledge has many faces. Statistics, no less than intuition, *can* reveal a part of the truth about man. To continue to use sociology as a swear word or as synonymous with drivel is the silliest obscurantism. Without the social scientist's dedicated scanning of the shifting kaleidoscope of industrial civilization, we are partly blind. We must learn to use the new mode of apprehending reality, not unconscious of the fact that sociology can also lead to new pedantries. The humanities especially need to be in live contact with the social sciences for the same reasons they ought to be in touch with the mass media: to encourage the wise and confute the ridiculous.

The humanist can actually serve as liaison between the media and the social sciences by assuming a more imaginative role in the education of future media professionals. But the humanist's grim determination to keep the university an elegant club of eighteenth century gentlemen, oblivious to the gross concerns of men who meet payrolls, prevents the establishment of such a relationship. Because the humanities faculties have scorned mere vocationalism, they have lost touch with the new "professions" of mass communication, advertising, business management, engineering, industrial design, and related disciplines. These emergent professionals have reciprocated our superciliousness by a basic antipathy to the older disciplines which scorned their birth. It would be much more in keeping with the moral complexity of our tradition if we helped the new vocations become bona-fide professions characterized by high ethical standards and vigorous self-criticism.

Actually there is a very strangely ignored tradition within the humanities in America ideally suited to affect such a transformation. Emerson's plea in "The American Scholar" for men of ideas to lead in the development of an American vernacular is the most powerful statement of the tradition. But his ideas have deeper roots—the Puritan divine's sense of responsibility to the new Zion and Jefferson's concept of a natural aristocracy. The tradition still operates in a small way, as the progression—Emerson-Whitman-Sullivan-Wright—shows in the field of architecture. But so far in America the vernacular tradition has been published in limited editions; it is still too much the possession of an elite. It needs to be broadcast to a mass audience. Once more, the problem of the public arts seems actually to be an opportunity—for the scholar, teacher, and community to begin to work together to fulfill the ideals about public education formed by Horace Mann's generation in the first fine zeal of Jacksonianism. For the threatened annihilation of privacy by the public media makes all our little insularities suddenly obsolete. The squabbles between the humanities and social sciences, education and liberal arts, vocationalists and professionalists, should give way before a common concern: how best to meet the ambivalent possibilities of mass communication and mass production.

I

The anti-social-scientism of the humanities, some have argued, comes from the fact that social scientists have learned to shake down foundations with more finesse. This kind of academic economic determinism may account for some disaffection, but let us hope not much: it is too picayune. Another reason, considerably more persuasive, is the social scientist's ability to formulate a research project at the drop of a phenomenon—any phenomenon will do. Accustomed to a highly defined hierarchy of values in his own subject, the humanist suspects either tomfoolery or charlatanism in Ph. D.'s who can write solemn, ponderous prose about comic strips and card playing (See the *Mass Culture* reader for examples). What humanists forget is that, given a vivifying imagination, any aspect of the proper study of mankind is important and valuable—even cards and comics. Why they should forget this is curious, aware as they are that it is the poet, not the subject matter, that makes good poetry. The fecundity of social science research just complicates the perennial problem of distinguishing between the pedant (who apes a technique and goes through edifying motions) and the true scholar (who uses and refines technique to press on the frontier of man's limitless ignorance).

In point of fact, the social scientist's interest in the commonplace can remind the humanist he must constantly strike a balance between the increasing complexity of elite art and the fairly unexalted tastes of his students. It is admirable and desirable to get out on Cloud Seven so long as one stays in radio contact with the control tower. The social scientist's involvement in the ordinary here and now is a useful countervailing attraction to the humanist's commitment to the extraordinary there and then.

A decent respect for the opinions and concerns of the average educator, for example, is something the social scientist can give to the humanist. Too many liberal arts professors become interested in mass education only as a last desperate reaction to illiterate seminar papers. On the contrary, Margaret Mead's brilliant essay, "Cultural Bases for Understanding Literature," *PMLA* (1953), argues that a child's ability to think in images comes from the earliest pre-school experiences, and that therefore the English teacher and professor must experiment and explore every possible means—nursery rhymes, radio, television, toys—to help the child learn how to knit image and word together. The publication of more essays of this kind would not a whit diminish the value of *PMLA* as a journal of research; indeed, it might develop a larger audience among high school teachers who cannot afford, as professors think they can, to ignore the psychological and sociological contexts of literary teaching. And the few invaluable articles that *PMLA* does publish would enhance the literary acumen of teachers who have drifted out of the humanist orbit to read educational magazines where their *de facto* problems are considered.

Another compelling reason for interest in social science is that the social scientists have done most of the careful looking in the field of the public arts and popular culture. *Mass Culture* contains a convenient sample of their research, and its bibliographies contain still more. To start with some negative thinking, not all of this material strikes an outsider as valuable—or even useful. Irving Crespi's "Card Playing as Mass Culture" is a systematic elaboration of common sense or an uncommon lack of it. Donald

Malcolm's impatience at Crespi's fantastic circumlocution seems justified: "all those playing must be physically members of the group, seated around a common table, with attention focused on the cards." As Malcolm points out, this confirms our common sense intuition that people don't play cards by throwing them at each other across a room! Malcolm also complains of what he calls the art of the "studied avoidance of significance." As examples, he cites Bernard Berelson's "Who Reads What Books and Why?" and Leo Bogart's "Comic Strips and Their Adult Readers."

Berelson makes his point that "different kinds of people are reading different amounts of books for different reasons." He rightly condemns Professional Viewers-with-Alarm who pontificate on the Deplorable State of Reading with little more than their sour stomachs to guide them. Berelson pins down crucial terms with admirable precision: if book-reader means someone who reads one book every six months, then about half the adult population qualifies; if we mean one book a month—"the usual definition"—then 25–30 per cent are readers; one book a week, 6–8 per cent. Moreover 10 per cent of the buyers are responsible for 80 per cent of the sales. Still, in spite of the respect and gratitude one feels towards Berelson for reliable knowledge about the state of reading in America, he seems to go beyond the bare facts in his own assumptions. The grounds for his optimism about reading in America are just as unwarranted as the pessimism of the glib grumblers—with the further complication that his optimism hides behind a social science "objectivity." His description of differentiation in reading habits imperceptibly becomes a defense of mass culture: so much diversity appears to debunk the argument that mass taste is conformist. The trouble is that fifty-seven varieties of fluff are just as inane as one standard brand. There is no real individuality. The truth may be more complex than either the pose of petulance or objectivity; the former has the right judgment without adequate facts; the latter seems to use the facts to support a spurious complacency. Much the same dissatisfaction comes from reading Frank Luther Mott's "Is There a Best Seller Formula?"

On the other hand, Alan Dutscher's statistical analysis and judgments about "The Book Business in America" are enormously rewarding in spite of his conscious tone of crisis. The functional illiteracy of Americans; the desperately unprogressive distribution system; relative percentages of publishing revenue due to textbooks, reference works, juveniles, and trade books; the pressure of production costs on quality manuscripts, and the "solution" of this economic problem through reprint, book club, and movie rights: Dutscher summarizes the situation of publishing with details the humanist simply must know to survive. Similarly, Cecil Hemley's "The Problem of the Paperbacks," rejects superficial judgments about the paperback cultural renaissance by showing how the soft-cover industry is, by and large, parasitic on the hardcover publisher. One should balance these spirited essays from *Mass Culture* with Arthur Hale's "Mass Market Paperbacks" and Charles Lee's "Book Clubs" in *What Happens in Book Publishing*, edited by Chandler B. Grannis (1957). Another very useful discussion is "The Future of Books in America," a forum discussion in *The American Scholar* (Spring, 1954). It stands to reason that a humanist should at least know his own special mass medium—books—inside and out. The social scientist and the literate publisher can give him the necessary evidence.

Leo Bogart starts out by justifying his study of adult readers of comics by invoking the sociological piety about the importance of the popular arts because of their wide influence. He then devotes his article to showing how comics are not important—"a rather superficial experience," and that reading them does not provide strong compensatory gratifications and is frequently the result of chance or the absence of alternative pastimes. Bogart claims that his middle position avoids the indefensible extremes of the typical polarized positions—the negative one that comics are debasing and the positive one which claims they fill the audience's psychic needs. But as Berelson loses his way in a forest of important and incontestable facts, so Bogart misses the basic truth about comic reading: adults observe this trivial ritual when they might be gaining a real understanding of the urban world that mangles them psychologically and physically. In reacting against unsupported rejections of mass culture, some sociologists seem to support it by an "it-isn't-really-that-bad" defense. Isn't it possible to face facts *and* values with some measure of objectivity?

It would seem so from several other sociological essays in *Mass Culture*. Patricke Johns-Heine and Hans H. Gerth's "Values in

Mass Periodical Fiction, 1921–1940," traces the shift in themes from boom stories about the struggle for power of a self-made elite to depression stories about good-wife-and-mother or little man heroes. Bernard Berelson and Patricia J. Salter's "Majority and Minority Americans: An Analysis of Magazine Fiction" reveals how magazines discriminate against "non-American" types (South European, Negroes, Jews) by quietly banning them from their fiction. Siegfried Kracauer's "National Types as Hollywood Presents Them" takes content analysis a step further by exposing the film maker's phoney front of responsibility. National types vary with our foreign policy needs. Finally the White-Albert-Seeger piece, "Hollywood's Newspaper Advertising: Stereotype of a Nation's Taste," presents relevant information in an unpretentious way.

Furthermore, it is unrealistic for an outsider to criticize a discipline anyway; that is an intramural problem. One is more disposed to leave such self-criticism to the social science fraternity, moreover, after reading Leo Lowenthal's "Historical Perspective of Popular Culture," reprinted from *The American Journal of Sociology* (1950). Lowenthal deplores what he calls the applied asceticism of empirical social science, in which the shibboleth of objectivity justifies failure to place modern social phenomena in an historical and moral context. He infers that such isolation actually turns social science over to the market researchers, who are objectionable rather than objective. An important elaboration of this charge appears in Vance Packard's *The Hidden Persuaders* (1957).

Lowenthal has recently shown what he means by the historical and moral dimensions of social science research in his eighty-page study, "The Debate over Art and Popular Culture in Eighteenth Century England," in *Common Frontiers of the Social Sciences*, edited by Mirra Komarovksy (1957). He analyzes the debate in terms of five concepts: the new literary forms emerging in the period; the reactions of literati to the various audience-building devices; the gradual decline of the optimism with which intellectuals first greeted the increase of writers, readers, and reading materials; the specific criticisms which intellectuals brought to bear on the new literary products and their audiences; the search for a metaphysics for the new cultural democracy. It is uncanny how the indictment brought against popular culture in the eight-eenth century by Pope, Doctor Johnson, and Goldsmith antici-pates contemporary criticism of the mass media for crime and violence, sentimentality, novelty and variety, and mediocrity.

It is worth observing here that complementary studies of litera-ture and popular culture are being completed by Lowenthal's colleagues on the English faculties, for example, Ian Watt's *The Rise of the Novel* (1957) and Richard Altick's *The English Common Reader: A Social History of the Mass Reading Public, 1800–1900* (1957), to name two volumes that Lowenthal himself has found stimulating. Such converging inter-disciplinary interests should prepare us for Lowenthal's latest publication, *Literature and the Image of Man: Sociological Studies of the European Drama and Novel, 1600–1900* (1957). In the preface of this study of Cervantes, Shakespeare, classical French drama, Goethe, Ibsen, Knut Hamsun, and others, Lowenthal warns the reader: "As a social scientist I am here dealing with materials traditionally allocated to the humanities; and I have employed techniques of analysis other than those commonly expected in the social sciences. Against the risk of attack from both scholarly camps, I can only hope to contribute to some *rapprochement* between them." But Lowenthal's carefully stated purpose can scarcely offend rational adherents of either side: "Through an analysis of the works in-cluded in this volume, an image may be formed of man's changing relation to himself, to his family, and to his social and natural environment, from the beginning of the seventeenth to the thresh-old of the twentieth century." In the fourth part of his essay on Goethe, "World Literature and Popular Culture," it is easy to see the special value of Lowenthal's study for an understanding of the public arts in contemporary society because he shows how chang-ing social relationships alienated the man of private sensibility from his audience. Another sociologist, Hugh Dalziel Duncan, brought a powerful indictment against the academician for fail-ing to develop a tradition of criticism in the popular arts in *Language and Literature in Society* (1953). Paul Meadows, in "Popular Culture in Industrialism," *The Culture of Industrial Man* (1950), also blames the negativism of the critics for some of the aesthetic inadequacies of mass society and further claims that minority control of popular culture is due to the fact that the arts are still too expensive for most Americans. He believes the machine can solve this problem of scarcity.

David Riesman is the sociologist most famous for his brave willingness to live dangerously in that no man's land between the academic fiefs of the humanities and social sciences. His studies of popular culture, *The Lonely Crowd: A Study of the Changing American Character* (1953) and *Individualism Reconsidered and Other Essays* (1954), especially the section "Culture: Popular and Unpopular," have caused too much discussion to rate more than an other-directed nod in this essay. Our radars have picked up less known works of great value: his Antioch College Founders Day Lecture, *The Oral Tradition, the Written Word, and the Screen Image* (1956), important for hints about the way mass media are experienced in diverse ways in different cultures; *Constraint and Variety in American Education* (1956); and, finally, Riesman's and Reuel Denney's indispensable essays on leisure in *Creating an Industrial Civilization*, edited by Eugene Staley (1952), a report of a group of discussions sponsored by the ACLS and Corning Glass. John Kouwenhoven's contribution to this volume suggests the fruitfulness and feasibility of symposia on popular culture that bring together men of various disciplines to their mutual enlightenment. Other such successful programs include the Advertising Council's *Cultural Aspects of the American Society* (1953), the University of Michigan's summer session series, *The Popular Arts in America* (1953), the annual design conferences at Aspen, Colorado, and the annual symposia of the Conference on Science, Philosophy, and Religion. Two of the last group's reports, edited by Lyman Bryson and others, are particularly relevant: *Symbols and Values* (1954), especially Stanley Edgar Hyman's "The Symbols of Folk Culture," in which Mr. Hyman analyzes the absence of a folk culture in America; and *Symbols and Society* (1955), in which for example, Professor Bryson discusses name publicity as the chief prestige symbol in American life and John Ely Burchard describes the decline of the monumental in architecture. It is just such a sophisticated approach to the role of symbolism in human life that is most lacking in our examination of machine culture. Francis Fergusson's "The Human Image," *KR* (1957) suggests, in much the same spirit, how the concept of symbolism affords continuity between the works of

Hollywood and Madison Avenue and the more deep, free, and frank expression of the quarterlies.

A poet and sociologist, Reuel Denney, gives further proof of the compatibility of those two modes of knowledge, in *The Astonished Muse* (1957). This pioneer attempt to study the "aesthetics of abundance" displays an admirable catholicity; his objects of scrutiny include slavishly unimaginative "realism" in movies and television, spectator sports, hot-rodding, comic strips, science fiction, advertising, and trends in city planning and architecture. Thus Denney extends the concept of the public arts beyond the media to include man's transformations of his material environment as well as his own consciousness. He also shrewdly sees a greater evil in the media's atrophying of imagination than in overt sex and violence. But one wonders if he doesn't romanticize the hot-rodder, in a kind of urban pastoral, seeing an autonomous tinkerer under every hood. Denney also seems to demand too much information from readers who could profit most from the book. The General Reader might be as non-plussed as a waiter overhearing a conversation on popular culture at the University of Chicago Faculty Club.

Reuel Denney and Mary Lea Meyersohn have also put students of popular culture in their debt by assembling a detailed bibliography on leisure and popular culture for a special issue, "The Uses of Leisure," *The American Journal of Sociology* (1957). This issue, one of the first fruits of the Ford Foundation's Center for the Study of Leisure at the University of Chicago, contains essays of varying merit on fashion, neighborhood taverns and cocktail lounges, youth and popular music, the dialogue of courtship in popular songs, interaction in television audience participation shows, cosmetics and grooming, and the natural history of a fad.

Especially important on the problem of how popular tastes are decided is Elihu Katz and Paul Lazarfeld's *Personal Influences: The Part Played by People in the Flow of Mass Communications* (1955). The authors claim that between the media and the masses there is an important intervening variable—the influential. Media messages and taste preferences seem to be adjudicated within peer groups. If this is true, the concept of a two-step flow of communication has far-reaching implications for education in the humanities. For it means that the traditional strategy of imposing cultural choices from the top will not work as effectively as helping a peer group clarify its own tastes. Katz and Lazarfeld could be closer to the truth than Matthew Arnold.

Two sociologists of considerable value to students of popular culture are W. Lloyd Warner and C. Wright Mills. The former's *American Life: Dream and Reality* (1953) reveals the disparity between the media messages and the real possibilities of life in America; the latter's *White Collar: The American Middle Class* (1951) has a section on "The Mass Media" that balances the optimism of the Riesman-Denney school. (See also Mills' *Mass Society and Liberal Education*, 1954.) Two journalists with sociological orientation also deserve mention here. William H. Whyte, Jr.'s *The Organization Man* (1956) is particularly good in analyzing conformist tendencies in popular fiction like *The Caine Mutiny*. Daniel Bell's "The Theory of Mass Society," *Commentary* (1956), by far the sanest examination of the issues, is a necessary corrective to the thoughtful but slanted essays of Clement Greenberg and Dwight Macdonald in *Mass Culture*. Two final volumes that indicate the relevance of social science to humane study of popular culture are: *Technology and Social Change*, edited by John F. Cuber (1957), with essays on the social effects of the automobile, motion pictures, and broadcasting, as well as general essays on the relationships between technology and social change; and Colin Cherry's *On Human Communication: A Review, a Survey, and a Criticism* (1957), the first synthesis of material from many disciplines. It should not be difficult to persuade humanists to use the social sciences as background for their own kind of intuitive judgments. It is more important, even if more difficult, to convince humanists to take audio-visualism and professional education seriously. For if they will not, they damage both the liberal arts and mass education by their intransigence.

II

A recent and typical statement of the Mark Hopkins complex is Gerald Weales' article in the *Quarterly of Film, Radio, and Television* (1957):

It is the familiar quarrel between matter and method, the running warfare that has given to 120th Street—the street that separates Columbia Teachers College from the rest of the University—the title "the widest street in the world." The audio-visualizers, usually educationists, label their opponents as reactionaries and fuddy-duddies, lovers of scholarship at the expense of human beings; while the opposition, firing from the stronghold of the humanities, attack the audio-visual admirers as worshippers of gimmicks and gimcracks who sacrifice human beings to techniques.

And while their wise elders spat, students use a technology of communication barely developed beyond the little red schoolhouse level. To the humanist with the Mark Hopkins mentality, the mere suggestion that machines (recordings, films, broadcasting) can improve upon the individual sensibility of the classroom teacher is anathema. Such selective supporters of machinery (for books are also mass-produced engines for focussing attention) regard audio-visualism as nothing more than another instance of the outrageous academic inflation of the education faculties.

This a priori rejection of audio-visualism contradicts the complex and ironic heritage of the humanities. The first thing we must learn about audio-visualism is that we are ignorant. Sensible and dedicated men have been trying for over a generation to exploit the new technology for mass education. Edgar Dale's *Audio-Visual Methods in Teaching* (1954) provides the humanist with some evidence of their success. The most obvious value of Dale's book is the way it guides the teacher through a labyrinth of sources. For example, Dale informs the English and humanities teacher of many specialized tools: Milton Brooke and Henry J. Dubester's *Guide to Color Prints* (1953); William Chapman's *Films on Art* (1952); UNESCO'S *Films on Art* (1951); Isabel and Kate Munro's *Index to Reproductions of American Painting* (1948); L. B. Pitts' *Handbook on 16 mm. Films for Music Education* (1952); Sister Mary Brian's *Audio-Visual Aids for Courses in American Literature* (1953, and 1957); as well as lists of films and recordings on the standard classics. Such specific materials from Chapters 26 ("English and Reading") and 28 (" The Humanities: Art, Music and Foreign Languages") are in addition to information on general sources for films, filmstrips, and recordings.

That not all audio-visualists have slavishly narrow concepts of their specialty is evident from Edgar Dale's description and praise of the Hofstra College Shakespeare Festival. Yet in spite of Dale's obvious humanistic learning, he was singled out by *Film Culture* as a whipping boy for all the excesses of audio-visualism. This avant-garde film journal apparently was ignorant of Dale's long fight to overcome the lethargy of his humanist colleagues for an art film series at Ohio State. Such are the dangers of indiscriminate censure. There is a lot of waste motion, pretentiousness, and aimless wandering in this field; it is the pedantry of the too practical and literal minded, a pedantry just as ludicrous and subversive of educational objectives as the more highly publicized scholarly kind. (Or, for that matter, the pedantry of the avant-garde motion picture historian who comments on his projection of old scraps of valueless films as if he were displaying a new El Greco: pedantry is protean.) But no reader of Edgar Dale's monthly *The Newsletter, Bringing Information to the Teacher about the Radio, the Press, and the Motion Picture* (Bureau of Educational Research, Ohio State University) can fail to see that the humanities and audio-visualism are compatible. Doubting humanists can sample Dale's ability to relate his wide reading in both classic and contemporary literature in his "Reading and Related Media," *Adult Reading*, edited by Nelson Henry (1956).

Before one condemns the field wholesale it would be the better part of wisdom to see how many sensible things have been said by reading in the journals, for example, the National Education Association's *Instructional Materials*, and *The Audio-Visual Communication Review*, and the *Journal of Communication;* or articles listed in F. Dean McClusky's *The A-V Bibliography* (1955), and McClusky's and James S. Kinder's compilation, *The Audio-Visual Reader* (1954). Humanists won't like or respect everything they read there, but then it is possible to say the same about *PMLA*.

The main thing wrong with most audio-visual aids is their poor aesthetic quality—a condition not unrelated to the alienation of the humanities from their production and use. When a first-rate artist creates an aid, as Leonard Bernstein has done in "What Is Jazz?" (Columbia LP 919), the result is compelling, both as art and as teaching. For this recording based on the soundtrack of an "Omnibus" television program, Bernstein explains syncopation, "blue" notes, improvisation by playing a well-known tune, "Sweet Sue," several times, each time omitting one of these basic jazz ingredients.

What Bernstein does in his aural essay simply cannot be done with a book.

The National Association of Educational Broadcasters, moreover, has shown that it is equally possible for scholars to interpret their findings in ways that exploit radio's unique powers for concentrating attention. Their thirteen disc album, "Ways of Mankind," dramatizes the basic concepts of anthropology. Most useful to the humanities teacher are "A Word in Your Ear: A Study in Language," "When Greek Meets Greek: A Study in Values," and "I Know What I Like: A Study in Art." The Bernstein and NAEB recordings are important also because they bring immediately into the classrooms subjects that most teachers have little preparation or confidence to handle. The examples suggest that the biggest weakness of the audio-visualists is their failure to enlist first-rate artists and scholars in the production of aids. This would seem to be an extraordinary opportunity for two new scholarly committees: Professor Howard Mumford Jones's Committee for the Humanities in the Secondary School of the American Council of Learned Societies, and Professor Alexander Kern's Committee on New Methods of Instruction of the American Studies Association.

In a sense their earlier alienation from the public schools may be a blessing in disguise since they now can look freshly at the need for a technological revolution in American education, unencumbered by the jurisdictional disputes of the long-suffering schoolmen. The idea of a closed circuit television network connecting classrooms and the great museums and art galleries is an exciting one. Or a series of color films on major American painters. Or a series of television interviews with great living writers, similar to the several already completed by the Educational Television and Radio Center at Ann Arbor. For the Center's work, see I. Keith Tyler's essay in *Television's Impact on American Culture*, edited by William Y. Elliott (1956). Leo Martin's piece on the ETV stations and Herold Hunt's chapter on television and formal education are also worth reading. A convenient bibliography is Benjamin Shimberg's "Selected References in Educational Television," in the special television issue of *The American Psychologist* (1950). The Fund for the Advancement of Education's leadership in this area is evident in Alexander Stoddard's *Schools for Tomorrow: An Educator's Blueprint* (1957).

Another phase of audio-visualism that requires the special talents of the liberal arts is the restoration of the natural balance in the humanities upset since the sixteenth and seventeenth centuries. Then, technological reproduction of print far outstripped comparable techniques for the aural and visual arts. The long-playing record and four-color printing now make it possible to teach the entire community of the arts in their natural symbiotic relationships. Luckily, these physical developments are matched by scholarly investigations reconstructing the total cultural context of literature in America, for example, Charles L. Sanford's "The Concept of the Sublime in the Works of Thomas Cole and William Cullen Bryant," *AL* (1957); Joseph J. Kwiatt's "Robert Henri and the Emerson-Whitman Tradition," *PMLA* (1956); and Charles Hirschfield's "America on Exhibition," *American Quarterly* (1957). Paperback gatherings of the best of this new scholarship could bring these fresh perspectives quickly into the classroom. But part of the task is simply to use whatever elements we can find from the commercial mass reproduction revolution. *Paperbound Books in Print* and *Schwann's Long-Playing Record Catalog* are indispensible guides for two media. Other possibilities are suggested in my "Technological Change and the Humanities Curriculum," *College English* (1955), although that article is not sufficiently aware of the parasitic nature of these media as outlined by Cecil Hemley's essay cited above.

A final criticism that the humanist can legitimately make of audio-visualism is its lack of historical perspective. There is great need for the kind of long view of communication contained in Lancelot Hogben's *From Cave Painting to Comic Strip: A Kaleidoscope of Human Communication* (1949). Hogben's description of man's tedious and painfully slow search for simple tools of communication like the alphabet, calendar, numbers, and maps should give teachers a proper respect for heritages we take for granted. Audio-visualism needs humane perspective to keep it from degenerating into *ad hoc* tinkering, to make it more than a seminar on threading a Bell and Howell. But it seems that the humanists have only themselves to blame for what they despise in audio-visualism.

III

Many specialists in the humanities manage to ignore audio-visualism as an aberration of the Education departments. It takes a better ostrich to overlook the appearance of communication ("whatever that is" is the smart ploy) courses as "improvements" on traditional freshman rhetoric. The new courses enrage the old line English teacher because they strike him as the rank weed of Education sprouting up everywhere in his own well-tended formal garden. This is no place to try to settle the raging civil war between education and liberal arts, but we must at least recommend one of the most thoughtful analyses of the dispute—"On the Conflict Between the 'Liberal Arts' and the Schools of Education," *ACLS Newsletter* (1954). The committee report recognizes that both sides have vices and virtues.

This is something. Denigration of Education and the teachers college point of view, in fact, has become so ritualistic that it behooves partisans of the liberal arts to stop now and again to check their stereotypes. It is essential to distinguish between the real wisdom of the educator's goals and the clap-trap and clichés that all but obscure these truths in practice. The Education faculties do have serious faults: a sentimental egalitarianism that frequently hides departmental aggrandizement, an unconscionable inflation in courses, an insatiable appetite for novelty, and a paradoxically impractical pragmatism. But their real virtues are too often overlooked: a sincere regard for the problems of students as distinct from the private interests of teachers; a dedicated commitment to work with the public schools to ameliorate their various problems; and, most of all, a willingness to look at curricular problems with fresh eyes. As with most people, their vices are but defects of their virtues. Moreover, the liberal arts could easily mitigate the effects of those vices.

For example, it would make more sense for humanists to participate wholeheartedly in the creation of adequate communication curricula. Radical changes in modern communication clearly justify basic educational alterations. Yet it is a common thing to see bright English Ph. D.'s despise their first assignments as communication instructors; they yearn from the first condescending day of teaching to graduate out of the Hades of freshman courses to the Elysian fields of English major seminars. Once again we see the familiar degenerative process: humanist alienation increases the vulgarity and triviality of the thing that first repelled him.

Even without much aid from the liberal arts, teachers college committees have gone ahead and created respectable courses in communication. One of the most hopeful signs of this maturity was contained in the special "Communication and Communication Arts" issue of the Columbia *Teachers College Record* (November, 1955). (A second printing with revised bibliographies appeared in August, 1957). Edited by Professor Francis Shoemaker, it summarizes the experience of an interdivisional program in operation at Teachers College since 1943. Specialists in anthropology (Solon T. Kimball), psychology (Irving Lorge), philosophy (Philip H. Phenix), behavioral sciences (Joseph T. Klapper), and cultural history (Marshall McLuhan) discuss the special angles of vision their separate disciplines afford the student of communication. A sense of the solidity of the foundations of their courses is apparent from the items in the useful bibliography: Ruth Benedict, David Riesman, Harold Innis, Lewis Mumford, Ernst Cassirer, John Dewey, Susanne K. Langer, Harold Lasswell, and Erich Fromm. A useful part of the bibliography is called "Studies in Arts and the Newer Mediums," namely, dance, language, literature and the literary audience, music, theater and drama, visual and plastic arts, architecture, film, press, radio, and television. A final section, "Educational Extensions," is of special value and contains titles like the report of the Commission on the English Curriculum of the National Council of Teachers of English, *The English Language Arts* (1952), with an important chapter on "Mass Modes of Communication" and a useful bibliography; Earl McGrath, editor, *Communication in General Education* (1949); National Conference on Research in English, *Education and the Mass Media of Communication* (1950); and National Society for the Study of Education, *Mass Media and Education* (1954).

An important aspect of the Teachers College program is its unabashed humanistic orientation. Good evidence of their increasing humanism is the growing contribution of Marshall McLuhan of the University of Toronto to their program. *The Mechanical Bride: The Folklore of Industrial Man* (1951), a series of "close readings" of the iconography of American popular culture, was

McLuhan's way of learning the languages of his freshman students at the University of Wisconsin. McLuhan feels that the dominance of the new commercial media makes a radical rechanneling of pedagogical energies essential. To fight the ads on their own terms is impossible; a comparison of advertising and school budgets proves that. But the enormous appeal of the ads can be subtly "perverted" toward educational ends:

Carried out as an educational programme directed toward self-knowledge and self-criticism, the study of these sprightly fantasies of unrestricted appetitive life would constitute precisely that step toward moral and intellectual regeneration which we have always known must precede any sort of genuine improvement. To contemplate the products of our own appetites rather than to anathematize the people who are keen enough to exploit them—that is surely no programme which must await the setting up of committees or social machinery. It is the only form of adult education which could be called realistic and it is instantaneously practicable.

McLuhan's most recent ideas are at once more stimulating and more difficult to assess. "Sight, Sound, and the Fury," reprinted from *Commonweal* (1954) in *Mass Culture*, stresses that languages too are mass media; that the printed book was our first mass medium; that the new media of journalism, film, radio, and television are actually new art forms, that is, new modes of apprehending and codifying reality. "Every shape (gimmick or metropolis), every situation planned and realized by man's factive intelligence, is a window which reveals or distorts reality," McLuhan argues, emphasizing his conviction that through modern technology man presumes to attempt a "total transformation of man and his environment." Because the "entire urban environment has become aggressively pedagogic," nothing less than a "classroom without walls" making every person sophisticated in his patronage of the new media will preserve traditional humane values.

McLuhan has also edited *Explorations: Studies in Culture and Communication*, a journal that grew out of an interdisciplinary seminar at Toronto. McLuhan has alienated some by his recent orphic and oracular style as in "Five Sovereign Fingers Taxed the Breath," and "Media Log," *Explorations 4*, short albums of snapshots on the history of communication and its social and cultural effects, or "Classroom without Walls," *Explorations 7*, an exercise in typographical poetics. These experiments in print, however, do make *some* sense to those who have followed more orthodox Mc-Luhan, such as "Notes on the Media as Art Forms," *Explorations 2*, or his and Edmund Carpenter's "The New Languages," *Chicago Review* (1956).

Lyman Bryson is another boldly imaginative thinker who has thrived in the Teachers College atmosphere of freedom. (The failure to include Bryson in *Mass Culture* points up a glaring weakness in that collection: education, which should be central in any consideration of mass culture, is hardly mentioned.) Bryson's classic essay distinguishing between folk, elite, and popular arts appeared in his own fine anthology, *The Communication of Ideas* (1948), a landmark in our understanding of popular culture in America. The most complete explication of Bryson's ideas on a democracy of culture appears in *The Next America: Prophecy and Faith* (1952), especially Chapter 10, "Art and Democracy," and Chapter 11, "Art and the Machine." Bryson scoffs at "sentimental memories" of the good old days which he claims are much more interesting to nostalgic historians than to those who lived through them. He defends the freedom to be vulgar and states his belief that individual (even mediocre) creation is more important than passive possession of the highest tradition. But Bryson is strongest in his condemnation of "intellectualist syncretism" about the popular arts. He notes that critics who condemn radio or television wholesale would never think of doing the same thing to books. Bryson's hopes for a careful criticism of the media happily are gradually coming to pass.

IV

A "new" criticism of television from elementary school through professional training, for example, is one of the goals of the communication arts philosophy being developed at Teachers College. Louis Forsdale brought together six educators and four television professionals for a symposium, "Adapting Literary Materials to Television," published in *The English Journal* (1955/1956). The same committee proposed an annual television award from the National Council of Teachers of English as another strategy for encouraging excellence in the new medium. Oddly, when this award was proposed to the Council, a rather respected professor rose to object to such traffic with the devil! The Council has continued, however, to find ways of supporting the most mature efforts of the medium. When NBC-Television telecast Olivier's "Richard III," *The English Journal* (1956) printed a helpful reading of the play by Frank and Audrey Hodgins of the University of Illinois. NBC also distributed 100,000 copies of a similar guide written for *Scholastic Teacher* by John F. Sullivan of the University of Detroit. The response to the *English Journal* feature was good enough to warrant a monthly department, "The Public Arts," designed to help teachers support all the media at their best. *Elementary English*, moreover, has begun support of a monthly feature, "Windows on the World: The Popular Arts in the Classroom," which suggests tie-ins between book reading and the popular media. The Women's National Book Committee prepares lists of books for that purpose each month. Also useful for developing an adequate criticism of television are Gertrude Broderick's *Radio and Television Bibliography*, Bulletin 1956, number 2; Herbert L. Marx, *Television and Radio in American Life* (1953), an H. W. Wilson Reference Shelf volume; and Charles Siepmann's *Radio, Television, and Society* (1950), especially strong on comparing British, Canadian, and American systems.

The most important publishing development for the English teacher who wants to follow up Alice Sterner's essay, "We Help Create a New Drama," *English Journal* (1954) is the growing shelf of printed television plays. Paddy Chayefsky's *Television Plays* (1955) has already been given a careful scholarly analysis in Frank Wadsworth, "The TV Plays of Paddy Chayefsky," *Quarterly of Film, Radio, and Television* (1955). Unfortunately his plays are the only single collection that has really proved profitable to the publisher. Other television playwrights deserve our support: Gore Vidal's *Visit to a Small Planet* (1957); Reginald Rose's *Six Television Plays* (1956); Tad Mosel's *Other People's Houses* (1956); Horton Foote's *Harrison, Texas: Eight Television Plays* (1956); and Rod Serling's *Patterns* (1957). Also worthwhile are William Kaufman's collections, *How to Direct for Television* (1955) and *How to Write for Television* (1955), for what they reveal of television craftsmen's attitudes toward their art. Kaufman has also edited *Best Television Plays* (1957), selected by a board of college teachers presided over by Frank Baxter, John Houseman, and Joseph Wood Krutch. Random House and Ballantine have other collections about to appear. Also very interesting are symposia by the new writers in *Variety:* "Consider the Case of the TV Writer" (July 29, 1953) and "Stating the Case for the TV Writer" (July 27, 1955). Heartening, too, is the appearance of first-rate critical essays like Norman Podhoretz, "Our Changing Ideals, as Seen on TV," in an otherwise arrogant collection, *The Scene Before You: A New Approach to American Culture*, edited by Chandler Brossard (1955).

Radio should not be forgotten in the furor over her more glamorous younger sister. Robert J. Landry's "Wanted: Radio Critics," *The Public Opinion Quarterly* (1940) is still a moving plea. Gilbert Highet's radio talks for the Book of the Month Club deserve a wider audience in both aural and printed forms. *The Listener* is a mine for the teacher of English literature who wants to connect tradition and British mass culture. And it is stimulating to see how much of what was said in *Radio and English Teaching: Experiences, Problems, Procedures*, edited by Max Herzberg (1941), an NCTE publication, still holds. The tape recording and long-playing record erased two big problems—scheduling and expense. But the remarks of the editor on leisure in the machine age still have point as do his ten ways of using radio for classroom goals. Samuel Beckoff, an alert New York City English teacher, has published four pamphlets on the media, including radio, for Oxford Book Company. His practical ideas will appeal to many teachers.

There is also a well-developed "new" movie criticism designed to give the ordinary patron standards of choice. One weakness of this single-medium criticism is that it overlooks a community of interests and problems in all the public arts. Thus it becomes harder to show the continuity between the traditional humanities curriculum and popular culture. Many of these difficulties are overcome in "The Humanities Today," a monthly department in *Clearing House* published for junior and senior high school teachers of all subjects. Starting as "TV and the Newer Media," it has enlarged its scope to include movie criticism, "Screenings"; explications of poetry published in magazines and paperbacks, "Poems for Teaching"; reviews of recordings, "Transcriptions"; reprints of outstanding criticism of the popular arts in "The Critics Note-book"; as well as reviews of books on the mass media and study suggestions for forthcoming television and radio programs. The editors, Henry B. Maloney and Myles Platt, are two Detroit high school teachers who believe that their liberal arts training is ideal preparation for criticizing popular culture. The National Council of Teachers of English seems to have moved in this direction also because in *The English Language Arts in the Secondary School* (1956) the media are not studied separately but are regarded to-gether as part of a chapter on "Making Communication Arts and Skills Reinforce Each Other."

The Council gave a big push to movie criticism when it sup-ported William Lewin's doctoral study at New York University's School of Education, *Photoplay Appreciation in American High Schools* (1933). Since then, Lewin has published a great many study guides for commercial films. Recently he collaborated with Alexander Frazier on *Standards of Photoplay Appreciation* (1957), a textbook for junior and senior high schools. Like some of his study guides, the text has a tendency to give the industry the benefit of too many doubts. Lewin's best study guides, however, as that of *Julius Caesar* included in his book, are very much worth-while. Doctor Joseph Mersand's Educational Consultants on Entertainment Films from time to time publish study guides for films on the back of the free "Green Sheet," the newsletter of Joint Estimates of Current Entertainment Films, sponsored by an industry trade association. Still, perhaps the most objective sources of criticism are in our better papers and magazines, for example, Bosley Crowther of *The New York Times*, John McCarten of the *New Yorker*, Arthur Knight and Hollis Alpert of the *Saturday Review*, Marya Mannes of *The Reporter* and the anonymous re-views in *Time* and *Newsweek*. The sooner we can get students to respond to this kind of criticism the sooner we have launched them as sensitive patrons of good movies *and* good journalism.

Another sign of the growing maturity of sections of the Ameri-can audience was the statement in *America* by Bishop William A. Scully of the National Legion of Decency in the Spring of 1957 urging subscribers to the Legion oath to start supporting aestheti-cally good films. A Catholic layman, Edward Fischer, film critic for *Ave Maria*, added the warning that viewers had better prepare themselves with some reading in the history and aesthetics of the film before setting up as judges. Roger Manvell's *The Film and the Public* (1955); Stanley Reed's essay, "Guidance in Aesthetic Appreciation: The Theatre and Film," *Year Book of Education* (1956); a promised paperback on the filming of "The Devil's Disciple" by Kenneth Macgowan for Hecht-Hill-Lancaster; studies of individual policymakers like Richard Griffith's *Samuel Goldwyn: The Producer and His Films* (1956); and the articles by Hortense Powdermaker, Wolfenstein and Leites, and Herbert J. Gans in *Mass Culture* should help the neophyte to develop meaningful standards.

Progress made since Lewin's pioneer study is evident from Jack C. Ellis's doctoral dissertation for Teachers College, Columbia's interdivisional program in communication, *Approaches to Film as an Art Form: A Handbook for College Teachers* (1955). The thesis also contains a bibliography on "Film Activities in Formal Education at the Secondary Level," a list of sources for 16 mm. films, and a bibliography of books on the aesthetics, history, and criticism of the film. Part of the dissertation has been printed in *The Audio-Visual Communication Review* (1956) as "University Film Societies and Series."

Two paperback anthologies are extremely useful for teachers who would like to start their teaching of films outside the classroom: *Sixty Years of 16 mm. Film, 1923–1983: A Symposium* (1954) and *Film Society Primer*, edited by Cecile Starr (1956). The Film Council's newsletter, *Rushes*, is also valuable. For a packaged first film series, see Ernest Callenbach's *Our Modern Art: The Movies* (1955), a handbook examining thoughtfully a film in each of a dozen or so genres.

College English has also begun to show interest in the film translations of novels, printing Milton Stern's fine essay on Huston's *Moby Dick* (1956) and Frank Selbajoris's study of King Vidor's *War and Peace* (1956). The journal also published a short symposium on "Mass Culture" in 1956; five teachers told why they thought the college English curriculum had a responsibility to cultivate good taste in the popular media. Other indications that conservative academic interests are finally facing up to this issue are a special issue, "The Art of the Cinema," *Yale French Studies* (1956) and George Bluestone's liberal arts dissertation at Johns

Hopkins, *Novels into Film* (1957). Bluestone eschews the usual baiting of films for "messing up the book"; he rather contends that because the film is a special way of seeing, film translations ought to differ from fictional prototypes. He urges film creators to use the medium's special resources and avoid literal (that is, unimaginative) re-creations of novels on the screen.

Martin Kallich and Malcolm M. Marsden (English Department, South Dakota State College) have developed another imaginative connection between tradition and the newer forms of literature in their mimeographed textbook, *Varieties of Modern Drama: Radio-Television-Motion Picture* (1954). The text studies Huston's *Red Badge of Courage* through the scenario, excerpts from Lillian Ross's *Picture,* and reviews of the film. Kallich and Marsden explain their ideas in "Teaching Film Drama as Literature," *Quarterly of Film, Radio, and TV* (1956).

It is fairly evident, then, that the communication approach has many aspects, from traditional to very experimental, from grade school through graduate school. These various methods have in common the feeling that the teacher must resist vulgarity and support excellence in the media. It is essential to stress, however, that a teacher can go on the offensive tomorrow without benefit of committee. Themes and term papers are the most potent means we have for popular arts criticism, as I have tried to explain in "I Know What I Like, I Think," *Education* (1956). Another not inconsiderable value of term papers on popular culture is that such topics wipe out the assets of fraternity term paper banks. But complementary to our encouragement of standards in the patron of the media is an equally great responsibility to use the liberal arts tradition to give future media professionals an aspiration towards excellence.

V

So far we have largely muffed this opportunity. The humanities specialists' disdain of college training for the emergent professions as mere vocationalism has not served the cause of liberal education. It has simply made it more difficult for journalists, advertisers, motion picture producers, and broadcasters to aspire to professional standards. As a matter of fact the journalism schools have already led the way for the humanities. The remarkable Wilbur

Schramm, for example, assesses the growth of knowledge in "Twenty Years of Journalism Research," in a special issue, "Twenty Years of Public Opinion Research," *Public Opinion Quarterly* (1957). Schramm has also edited three books of unusual value, *Communications in Modern Society* (1948), *Mass Communication* (1949), and *The Process and Effects of Mass Communication* (1954). The Journalism and Communications Library of the University of Illinois prints a quarterly new book list; the *Journalism Quarterly* contains a similar annotated check list of articles. Textbooks for the new courses can also give the humanist non-specialist a sense of the field, for example, *The Press and Society: A Book of Readings*, edited by George L. Bird and Frederic E. Merwin (1951) and Edwin Emery and Henry Ladd Smith's history, *The Press and America* (1954).

Moreover, graduate research in the area of journalism and broadcasting is flowering. Theodore Peterson's *Magazines in the Twentieth Century* (1956), a revised doctoral dissertation at Illinois, and Sydney Head's *Broadcasting in America: A Survey of Television and Radio* (1956) are admirable introductions to their subjects characterized by a dual commitment to business realism and humanistic idealism, exactly the kind of tension that the liberal arts must actively support. Head's "Toward Professionalization" is a powerful statement of the kind of philosophy the humanities ought to encourage, instead of arrogantly deriding vocationalism.

Media professionals are also publishing works of value to the general reader, for example, Leo Bogart's *The Age of Television: A Study of Viewing Habits and the Impact of Television on American Life* (1956), a thorough compendium of facts; Erik Barnouw's *Mass Communication: Television, Radio, and Film* (1956), especially valuable for its explanation of sponsorship and the increasing complexity of mass communication; Malcolm Boyd's *The Crisis in Communication* (1957), a synthesis of media experience and Episcopalian theology; and *Television in the Making*, edited by Paul Rotha (1956), the working thoughts of a score or more of British television craftsmen. Finally, a book like Burton Paulu's *British Broadcasting: Radio and Television in the United Kingdom* deflates the liberal arts penchant for lusting after the Third Programme of the BBC instead of learning to live with our own broadcasting system. The point is that whereas we have ignored the media, they have set about developing their professional ideals; and they have had considerable success in their endeavors. There is still plenty of room for improvement, however, and the humanist's own tradition of the American vernacular seems ideally suited both to improve consumer taste and heighten professional ideals.

VI

By the American vernacular tradition John Kouwenhoven meant the unpretentious solution of new problems in our experiment in industrial democracy. In his important book, *Made in America: The Arts in Modern Civilization* (1948), Kouwenhoven showed that Americans were most creative when they unselfconsciously set out to master new materials and unprecedented situations in the American environment. The vernacular thus includes among its achievements axes and clipper ships, skyscrapers and factory buildings, jazz and Charles Sheeler's paintings. Kouwenhoven also shows how undue deference to Europe and the separation of art and technology made our "serious" culture timidly genteel and our industry unnecessarily brutal. The vernacular tradition, then, charges the humanists to help his society find new forms adequate to express the ideals of a cultural and technological democracy. As man transforms both his mind and material environment through technology, the humanist must see to it that these changes are morally and aesthetically sound.

That humanists have been slow to formulate this dual responsibility is clear from the fact that Gilbert Seldes and Lewis Mumford, both from outside the academic world, have provided what little leadership we have had. Seldes has examined the moral ambiguities involved in the technological transformation of man's consciousness through the mass media. Mumford has analyzed the crises that arise from irresponsible transformation of the natural environment. Both men have unquestionable commitments to the private sensibility. In the 1920's Seldes was an articulate defender of *Ulysses;* Mumford, a prime force in the Melville revival. As a matter of fact, their concern about the "public arts" was a function of their dedication to the values of the private sensibility. A standard objection to humanist involvement in the public arts is that such activity will compromise a prior responsibility to the private forms of expression. Seldes and Mumford have insisted that one cannot pretend to defend the private sensibility while passively witnessing the erosion of those values by negative tendencies in the public arts. Any enlightened attempt to employ the vernacular tradition for humanizing the public arts, then, must proceed from the basic insights expressed in Seldes' and Mumford's major works—the former's *The Seven Lively Arts* (1924), *The Great Audience* (1950), and *The Public Arts* (1956); the latter's *Sticks and Stones: A Study of American Architecture and Civilization* (1924); his trilogy, *Technics and Civilization* (1934), *The Culture of Cities* (1938), and *The Condition of Man* (1944); and *Art and Technics* (1952). The value of Seldes, Mumford, and Kouwenhoven becomes more apparent when their assumptions are compared with the dominant ones in the Bernard Rosenberg and David Manning White *Mass Culture* reader. The vernacular partisans are hard-headed meliorists; the Greenbergs, Macdonalds, and van den Haags are proudly eschatological. The former enjoy many levels of complexity and think a spectrum of taste is as desirable as it is inevitable; the latter like to polarize culture between the elect (themselves) and those slobs in the exterior darkness. The former see man's creative intelligence at work in both studio and factory; the latter tend to denigrate mass-produced artifacts.

One of the most comprehensive explorations of the aesthetic dimension of mass production and technological art has appeared in the sixteen issues of *Perspectives, USA* a publication intended for the enlightenment of our friends in the Atlantic community but equally pertinent to our own nationals. There one can find authoritative articles on the skyscraper (VIII); suburbia (IX); Frank Lloyd Wright (IV); mass housing (XV); graphic magazine humor (XIV); photography as an art (XV); movies (XI); the city in an automobile age (XVI); city planning (X); and changing leisure patterns (V). Most importantly, these studies of the public arts and popular culture appear side by side with equally valuable appraisals of the private sensibility in America—literature, painting, music, philosophy, religion, and social thought. This kind of "cultural pluralism" is the humanist's best strategy for fulfilling his dual obligation to elite and popular culture, to the public arts and the private sensibility. For the two spheres come into contact to mutual advantage—the private sensibility refining the baser metal of the public arts, the latter keeping the former from becoming too little related with the common life.

The humanist can very easily understand how the integrity of mass communication is related to his traditional responsibilities, for it happens in America that most teachers of the humanities or literature are also teachers of language or expression. However the humanist must make a special effort to see that integrity of mass production is equally relevant to the cause of the private sensibility in America. To that end, the *Perspectives, USA* essays will be a great help, as will the following: Rudolph Rosenthal and Helena L. Ratzka, *The Story of Modern Applied Art* (1948); Neutra's, Cheney's, and Hamlin's essays in *Art in American Life and Education*, edited by Guy Montrose Whipple (1941); Reyner Banham's "Industrial Design and the Common User," *The Listener* (1956); George Nelson, "Obsolescence," *Industrial Design* (1956); Mary Mix Foley, "The Debacle of Popular Taste," *Architectural Forum* (1957); Pierre Francastel, "Technics and Aesthetics," *Journal of Aesthetics and Art Criticism* (1953); "Textiles, USA, An Exhibition at the Museum of Modern Art," *American Fabrics* (1956); Eloise and Otto Spaeth, "Art and Industry Issue," *Art in America* (1956); L. Hilberseimer, *The Nature of Cities* (1955); and Sigfried Giedion, *Space, Time and Architecture: The Growth of a New Tradition* (1954).

Once humanists overcome their reluctance to take mass production and communication seriously, they can start to use their own ability to exist enthusiastically on many levels of American culture to great advantage. The best proof that the elite and vernacular traditions can coexist, that the private sensibility and public arts are compatible, is by example. Marshall Stearns, published specialist in medieval literature and professor of English at Hunter, has deepened an avocational interest in jazz to scholarly *expertise* in *The Story of Jazz* (1956). Barry Ulanov, on the other hand, started as a jazz critic but more recently has taken advanced studies in Renaissance literature; his book, *A History of Jazz in America* (1952), further reveals the happy interaction of elite and vernacular traditions. Similarly, Jacques Barzun's *Music in American Life* (1956), an analysis of the effects of social and economic changes on the creation, performance, and patronage of music in our country, contains the mature judgment of an accomplished cultural historian. Barzun forces us to consider the public and private arts together by showing how they share a common fate in our society.

A better case in point is Walter Terry's *The Dance in America: From the Days of the Minuet to the TV Spectacular* (1956). Terry, the *Herald Tribune* drama critic, shows how a single art can provide a connection between the public arts and the private sensibility. He not only describes Martha Graham's dance for Emily Dickinson, *Letter to the World*, and Walt Whitman's influence on Isadora Duncan and Tamiris' *Walt Whitman Suite*, but he also analyzes the influences of Hollywood, Broadway, and television on the dance. The humanist might take it as one of his jobs to provide such cross-cultural fixes in both secondary literature and in classroom anthologies. Roland Gelatt's social history of recordings, *The Fabulous Phonograph* (1955), reveals how technological innovation changes the relationship between popular and elite forms of music and their several audiences. Russell Lynes studies in *The Tastemakers* (1954) the effects of a maturing technology on both the products of the private sensibility (painting and sculpture) and public arts (mass-produced consumer goods and architecture). Though he does not share Lynes' any-browism, Bernard Rudofsky, in *Behind the Picture Window* (1955), very shrewdly shows how the public art of domestic architecture in contemporary America has dreadful effects on the private sensibility. And John Keats's *The Crack in the Picture Window* (1956), although too much a horror story, does establish a connection between transformations of mind and matter in the prefabricated suburbs. Electronic bulldozers are leveling the landscape of the American mind just as surely as their Caterpillar prototypes are conforming the physical environment. And Sir Herbert Read indicates in *A Coat of Many Colours* (1956) that a critic can say illuminating things about painting and sculpture *and* films, machines, and architecture.

But these growing resources must become risk capital in the enterprise of protecting man's freedom as he transforms the public mind, through the mass media, and the public landscape, through mass production, in an urban environment. This capital is for humanists to risk as they use the new technology of communication for their own special instrument—public education. Using these new modes of expression the humanist must create new curricula that will help student consumers resist deformations of their minds and milieus, and other courses of study that will inspire the transformers of mind and material to respect their own consciences and the freedom of their patrons. If we are content, however, to bank our risk capital—to clip the coupons of an ever lengthening bibliography—then we are at least partly to blame that the lively arts have become the ogre of mass culture. We need only to put our own best ideas to work—in the traditional forms of anthology and lecture, through the traditional strategies of themes and term papers—to prevent the most noxious elements in the public arts from destroying further the complex heritage of the private sensibility. The lethargy lost in such invigorating confrontations of elite and popular arts may be our own—and that of our students.

18

Literary Audience

LENNOX GREY

SEVENTY-FIVE YEARS HAVE PASSED
now since the publication of Alexandre Beljame's *Le Public et les Hommes de Lettres en Angleterre au Dix-huitième Siècle 1660–1744* (1881). Yet only within the past ten years has the book been published in English—with introduction, notes, and modernization of bibliography by Bonamy Dobrée and several associates, and with a reversing of the elements of the title to put the writers first, *Men of Letters and the English Public in the Eighteenth Century 1660–1744, Dryden, Addison, Pope* (*1948*).

The significance of these dates and other facts begins to come clear when put in context of other works of the past twenty-five years, and particularly studies of the past ten years, which as a whole or in part answer to the description "studies of literary audience."

The twenty-five year context includes such varied works as these from literary scholars, critics, editors, journalists:

Q. D. Leavis	*Fiction and the Reading Public* (1932)
Edward Weeks	*This Trade of Writing* (1935)
Alfred Harbage	*Shakespeare's Audience* (1941)
Levin L. Schücking	*The Sociology of Literary Taste* (1944) from the German *Die Soziologie der Literarischen Geschmacksbildung* (1931)
Alice Payne Hackett	*Fifty Years of Best Sellers 1895–1945* (1945) since extended to *60 Years of Best Sellers, 1895–1955* (1956)
Frank Luther Mott	*Golden Multitudes* (1947)
Stanley E. Hyman	*The Armed Vision* (1948)
James D. Hart	*The Popular Book* (1950)

Altogether this selected miscellany supports two complementary inferences—the first inference probably requiring no special documentation for most of us, the second possibly escaping our attention in view of the seeming miscellaneousness of the list:

(1) If these works are representative, our literary scholarship has been relatively slow in getting a comprehensive view of one important half (at least) of that reciprocal phenomenon called literature, the *audience*.

(2) But here are signs that a considerable number of vigorous workers are beginning to remedy the deficiency, partly within and partly outside the usual reaches of scholarship.

I

The dozen works chosen for focal attention here may be regarded, of course, as aspects or offshoots of *Beowulf* scholarship, Eighteenth Century scholarship, Dickens scholarship, or the history of taste, rather than as members of a coherent or potentially coherent field which may be justifiably called the study of literary audience. Certainly they have such older affinities and associations, and will keep them. At the same time they have a common restless pioneering air and a beginning of interplay, cutting across old fields, which are among the marks of an identifiable and self-conscious field. They share a combination of disarming apology and defiance that suggests a breaking away from the conventions of the older fields rather than complete identification with them or the ordinary dissent within them. Most of them (including the

---

[1] These have been selected primarily for their variety and representativeness, not necessarily as the dozen best in the sprawling field. If we extend the time-span and scope a little, we may readily add a further selective symptomatic chronology of twice as many items: See end of chapter, page 460.

present inquiry) start with the impression they are working practically *de novo*. They consistently remind us that while we commonly agree that literature is a reciprocal phenomenon, and that audiences share in the making of literature as surely as writers, patrons, publishers, and critics, we have done very little with that other shareholder, and have not done that little well. One way or another they struggle with those problems of "mass culture" which have been exploited in a good deal of pyrotechnic writing in the past ten years. They tend often to make common cause with modern spokesmen for literary criticism (which also cuts across old fields) as contrasted with or as a capstone to literary history.

Thus Mrs. Leavis:[1]

Even as I write, the bulky and authoritative volumes of . . . a . . . *History of the English Novel* are being ground out of the press. Here are recorded the plots and histories of all the well-known English novels . . .; but there is no indication that they ever had readers, much less that they played any part in shaping the human spirit and were shaped by it . . .

Harbage is no less sharp:[2]

the most brilliant criticism in English has been provoked by Shakespeare's plays. But the least brilliant of this criticism is, I believe, that which relates the plays to their audience. It is usually incidental; and it is often careless, cynical, or marked by an incredible condescension. The Elizabethan stratum of humanity is divested of mystery . . . its perceptive range simplified to "two levels of intelligence," while whole battalions of our former fellow mortals are dismissed with placid allusions to "groundlings" or a "motley crew."

Dorothy Whitelock asks:[3]

And why my title: . . . it seems to me that the contribution of the audience to the full understanding of the poem is so important that it is time that for once it should be allowed to get on to a title-page.

[1] Q. D. Leavis, *Fiction and the Reading Public* (London, Chatto & Windus, 1932), p. xiv.

[2] Alfred Harbage, *Shakespeare's Audience* (New York, Columbia University Press, 1941), p. 138.

[3] Dorothy Whitelock, *The Audience of Beowulf* (New York, Oxford University Press, 1951), p. 2.

Bonamy Dobrée's introduction to Beljame's "classic" is symptomatic on other scores: [4]

But before plunging into this work, the reader, especially if he be
a student, should perhaps ask himself what it is he is really reading
about. A book such as this is commonly regarded as a part of literary
studies, and the danger is that it may come to be accepted as a study of
literature. It cannot be too plainly stated that a knowledge of the
appurtenances of literature, of its social surroundings, of the soil in
which it flourished, will not make a fig of difference to its value for us
here and now—and it is that which matters. . . .
Nevertheless, a study of this kind has enormous value, if properly
used; it may remove certain barriers which prevent us from getting
into intimate contact with the work of literature. Of course it has its
value as a sociological study, but with such, as students of literature,
we are not primarily concerned.
Yet if we can discount the mental and moral trappings of an age,
separate them from what is essential so that they need not distract us
from our proper study of the work of art as such, a great deal has been
gained. A generation or so ago such a statement would have been
regarded as "mere aestheticism," as perhaps a good many now may
regard it, with a good deal of stress on the "mere"; but it is time to
reconsider the position in view of the danger of the study of literature
becoming a sub-department of sociology.

One of Dobrée's main criticisms of Beljame's work, apart from
its misuse by students, is the French scholar's preoccupation with
the middle class and his lack of sensitiveness to the "fluid" character
of the British class system. This question of social class in relation
to literary taste and audience is persistent.

A number of interlocking reasons for hesitation and slowness
in our studies of literary audience are fairly clear.

First of all, the field is amorphous—shifting, sprawling, hard to
document in approved scholarly ways. Studies in "taste" have
sought economically to distill a pervasive essence or *Zeitgeist*
characterizing the "public" or "audience" of a given time. Too
often these studies have become so involved in arguing or posturing about questions of "good taste" and "bad taste" that they have
given very questionable impressionistic descriptions of the varie-

[4] Alexandre Beljame, *Men of Letters and the English Public in the
Eighteenth Century, 1660–1744, Dryden, Addison, Pope,* ed. Bonamy Dobrée
(London, Routledge and Kegan Paul, Ltd., 1948), p. xiii.

ties of tastes and audiences of any given time. At the close of *The Tastemakers*, Russell Lynes declares:[5]

This book has been concerned from the start with an abstraction called taste, and yet I have not defined it. . . . I do not know what *good* taste is. I do know that taste is not constant. . . . The point is that we have a tremendously diversified basis of morality, education, and sensibility . . . conflicts of ideas and tastes that give the arts of our country vitality, and that make the museum and the corner movie houses equally important manifestations of our culture.

And Richard D. Altick's *The English Common Reader* exclaims at the start:[6]

(and this sentence ideally should be printed in bold red letters, to forestall unfounded expectations) this volume is not intended to be an examination of nineteenth-century literary taste . . . [but] to provide some of the information that obviously must be taken into account before anyone can safely interpret the popular taste of an age. . . . The lack of such knowledge inevitably makes discussion of the audience's formative influence on literature little more than idle speculation.

Significantly, a clear-cut, self-evident, focusing name for the field has not emerged, and is hard to find. If we say "literary audience," do we mean a highly literate minority, or all who can and do read some sort of literature, or (suspiciously) all who respond to literary experience in any form, from comic strip to the Old Vic *Romeo and Juliet* on television? Now, however, in a day of approved ambiguities there may even be virtue in a term susceptible of varied interpretations, suggesting various possible audiences. Here the use of the term *literary audience* takes its cue from the relative frequency among our key works. Alfred Harbage and Dorothy Whitelock use it scrupulously for listening audiences, of course. But usage has become broader than that. A recent symposium in *Perspectives USA* (1954) has been captioned "The Creative Artist and His Audience." There Robinson Jeffers, poet, and Robert Motherwell, painter, freely use the editor's caption word (Jeffers protesting, however, that poetry "does not need, though Whitman said so, 'great audiences too,' "

---

[5] Russell Lynes, *The Tastemakers* (New York, Harper and Brothers, 1954), pp. 339–341.

[6] Richard D. Altick, *The English Common Reader* (Chicago, University of Chicago Press, 1957), p. 6.

and Motherwell exclaiming concerning "The Painter and His Audience," "What a disagreeable subject!"). The novelist Saul Bellow uses the word *reader* in "The Writer and His Audience," and the musician Roger Sessions uses the term *public* in "The Composer and the Public Today." In this symposium we see both the diffusiveness of older terms and an apparent acceptance of the broader term.

Closely related to the difficulty of documentation and naming is an antipathy to certain of the more obvious tools and methods for working in the field. We have commonly resisted those offered by the sociologist, statistician, and pollster, for we fear the dangers of confusing quantity with quality. Hence, Dobrée's comments on sociology. Hence, Harbage's disarming quips about a study "bristling with statistics" and "made dismal by arithmetic," prefacing his tallies of theater sizes and the population of London; and sixteen years later John Lough's "polluted by vulgar statistics" in *Paris Theatre Audiences in the Seventeenth and Eighteenth Centuries* (1957). Simon O. Lesser's *Fiction and the Unconscious* (1957) analyzes such fears.

Related to these, in turn, are the pressures of priorities. The humanities, by definition, are concerned first of all with the expressions of the individual human spirit and only secondarily with the "mass." These individual expressions come along at a rate to command most of our attention. In *The Popular Book* Hart is careful to speak of his concern "with individual books as part of a species," and seeks tactfully to keep the individual to the fore in the midst of social considerations:[7]

in some way or another, the popular author is always the one who expresses the people's minds and paraphrases what they consider their private feelings. This combination of social history, cultural history, and literary taste, tacitly involves itself in the question, "Which came first, the chicken or the egg?"—the popular book that shaped the public interest or the public interest that shaped the book's popularity? Sometimes one can say clearly it is the first, sometimes the second; most often one can answer only in terms of a dynamic interplay of reader, writer, and the times in which both lived.

[7] James D. Hart, *The Popular Book* (New York, Oxford University Press, 1950), p. 385.

Finally, and not least significant perhaps in this limited exploratory view, is the fact that scholars and teachers (particularly
American) have been brought up with a special twist of the
Matthew Arnold tradition—where, for various reasons, we have
identified ourselves with the "Cultured" versus the "Philistine,"
but hesitate to examine the case openly, sometimes for fear we may
be contaminated and labelled "Philistine," sometimes for fear that
if we examine it in "class" terms (particularly in America) we will
be labelled undemocratic or snobbish. Harbage's thrust at a conception of Shakespeare's audience "simplified to two levels of
intelligence" points to this problem and is in harmony with a number of efforts to break through such oversimplification and to
establish sounder conceptions of audience. Such conceptions range
in this quarter century from Q. D. Leavis's academically representative "low-brow, middle-brow, and high-brow" (with the university scholar-critics at the top) to Russell Lynes's wittily
thoughtful play upon this (coupled with his critical look at W.
Lloyd Warner's "upper-upper, middle-upper, lower-upper," etc.)
and his arrival recently at an American occupational conception of

free-standing pyramids, each with its several levels [social and literary]
. . . the big-business pyramid . . . the communications and entertainment pyramid . . . the intellectual pyramid.

(with the university critic-philosophers at or near the top), and
with a new class of "upper Bohemians" who can move from one
pyramid to another as they

regard the performances and pretensions of the new aristocracies with
detached amusement . . . possibly the only cohesive class that we can
still put our fingers on.[8]

Russell Lynes's creative urbanity is probably as near as we have
come to providing a modern, twentieth-century American match
for the nineteenth century British creative urbanity of Matthew
Arnold—lacking which heretofore Matthew Arnold's persuasive
conception has held on with remarkable tenacity, both in the
distorted "Cultured" versus "Philistine," dichotomy and in the
essentially similar "intellectual" versus "vocational" and "intellectual" versus "anti-intellectual" versions of the same notion.

[8] Lynes, *op. cit.*, pp. 15–16, 29–30.

But if we have been relatively laggard in our study of literary audience on these and other accounts, it seems unlikely that we can hesitate or lag much longer. Many forces now are pressing us to overcome the old obstacles to a comprehensive and coherent study of literary audience or audiences, both within and outside the established fields of literary scholarship. Most provocative perhaps are the recent dramatizations of the conflicts between high culture and "mass culture," in such books as David Riesman's *The Lonely Crowd*, Vance Packard's *The Hidden Persuaders*, A. C. Spectorsky's *The Exurbanites*, William H. Whyte, Jr.'s *The Organization Man*, and Bernard Rosenberg and David Manning White's anthology of short pieces in *Mass Culture*, all demanding more plain scholarly prose on the subject. Workers in many fields—anthropologists like Margaret Mead, sociologists like Paul Lazarsfeld, political scientists like Harold D. Lasswell, editors like Edward Weeks (*The Atlantic Monthly*) and Russell Lynes (*Harpers*), journalist-teachers like F. L. Mott and Gilbert Seldes, library experts like Douglas Waples and Robert D. Leigh, educators like Lyman Bryson and Bernard Berelson—have been concerned with audience research in ways that would compel literary scholars to get their voices in, even if venturesome literary scholars had not been here long before.

There has been some danger that literary scholars would avoid the field, fearing the contamination of "communication" studies. Several years ago, for instance, the editor of *PMLA* warned against " 'communication arts' involving necessarily small doses of psychology, sociology, semantics, politics, librarianship, radio-listening, television-viewing, and so forth," leading to a "brand-new department" with a "catch-all social studies character." But not long after he considered comparable ways to add strength to the Humanities:[9]

Anyone seen the Humanities lately? Yesterday, history tells us, they were strong, were clear and far-extending in their influence on men. Today, try to define their influence. For that matter, try to define the Humanities. Are we in the MLA included—literary historians, new critics, linguists, and all? By what definition? . . . Perhaps symptomatically, the director of the Division of the Humanities of the Rocke-

[9] W. R. Parker, *PMLA*, LXVIII (April, 1953), p. 1.

feller Foundation is a political scientist . . . [Observe that] there exists no national council of literary scholars and authors, of art historians and artists, of musicologists and musicians . . . [Consider] the flourishing state of anthropology, psychology, sociology, and other studies that actively explore *the nature and behavior of man*. Have we students of literature been too little interested in this potential product of our own studies, which laymen sometimes expect of us? Have we been too little interested in learning something from current discoveries in these other allied fields? What do we mean by saying we are in the Humanities? If we do not redefine and rededicate our activities, humanity may tell us what we are and ask us to please to excuse the expression.

There is enough evidence of accelerating interest in literary audience for us to speculate seriously whether studies of literary audience, quantitative and qualitative, taking advantage of the resources of many fields but giving them a literary turn, may not be among the most exciting contributions to literary scholarship in the next twenty-five years, and among our most important contributions to teaching (as scholarly methods have been the chief inspirers of teaching method when they have provided exciting new findings, insights, and outlooks) in our efforts to understand and form the actual and potential literary audiences of tomorrow in our high school and college classes.

The key question for teachers is *where to take hold* for greatest economy, with the kinds of concreteness or visibility needed and always with an invitation to get to the *values* behind the facts. In our dozen or so focal works there are various inviting possibilities of essentially literary interest. Some of the most likely appear to be these—any one of which can lead to the others:

Studies of common or favored rallying points, or pivotal symbols, in the literature on audiences, such as

Dr. Johnson's and Virginia Woolf's "common reader." ("I rejoice to concur with the common reader; for by the common sense of readers, uncorrupted by literary prejudices, after all the refinements of subtility and the dogmatism of learning, must be finally decided all claim to poetical honors." *Life of Gray*)

"Philistines"

The war with "mass media" and the "mass audience"

Historical or comparative studies of differing *concepts* of the literary audience or audiences.

The conception of a "golden-age" of one homogeneous cultivated audience.

The international perspectives in the French Beljame, the British Mrs. Leavis, the American Harbage, the German Schücking.

Studies of the conflict between the "literary" outlook and method, on the one hand, and the sociological and statistical on the other—of the symbolic instance, perhaps, contrasted with the statistical total or average or percentage.

Comparative studies of the audiences of "best sellers," school classics, "rediscovered classics," *avant-garde* works.

Studies of the relations and rivalries of literary scholars, critics, teachers, and audiences—the human equations and inequations.

To maintain focus and proportion, the remainder of this modest chapter explores the dozen key works more fully, but all too briefly, with occasional reference to the secondary bibliography where that may be particularly helpful. Systematically it will consider each work under three heads: (1) focus and method of inquiry; (2) chief findings or conclusions; (3) conceptions of audience stated or implied (probably the most important consideration for the teacher). At the same time it will attempt to maintain a sense of the integrity of each work, essential to any kind of literary method. Transecting all these considerations will be a concern for the value of each work for teaching as well as for scholarship, constantly influencing what is selected and emphasized, in the effort to make clear the web of relationships with which we are concerned.

II

Q. D. Leavis's *Fiction and The Reading Public* (1932) and Alfred Harbage's *Shakespeare's Audience* (1941) provide a useful contrasting pair for the first decade of our 25 years. They stand at either end of that decade. One is British, the other American. They deal with opposite ends of the literary spectrum—the first concerned chiefly with the modern audience for fiction at the lower end of the literary scale, the second with sixteenth- and seventeenth-century audiences of the acknowledged supreme master of English literature. They differ markedly in their conceptions of the worth of audiences.

Conveniently, they provide differentiating pivotal points also for two-thirds of our dozen selected works—*Fiction and the Reading Public* as a reference center for the best-seller studies (Weeks, Hackett, Mott, Hart, Altick) and *Shakespeare's Audience* for studies concentrating on single authors and on single works (Whitelock, Ford). In turn, they help to reveal, by comparison, a third grouping of inquirers (Schücking, Hyman, Seldes, Lynes) who seek in various ways to view the whole field, with Hyman's *The Armed Vision* (1948, abridged and revised 1955) venturing a six-page historical survey of the fragmentary field incidental to his chapter on "I. A. Richards and the Criticism of Interpretation." These categories or classifications are far less important, however, than the interplay of key ideas and reference points.

From the start, Mrs. Leavis's *Fiction and the Reading Public* shows a strong concern with methods of inquiry:[10]

> The system of working adopted in this study demands some explanation. There are two accepted methods of dealing with the Novel, and neither has scope for a kind of interest in fiction that I feel to be of great urgency. . . .

> Clearly both methods, the critic's and the scholar's, need to be supplemented by a third. . . I found encouragement to pursue this kind of interest in certain hints thrown out by Mr. I. A. Richards in *Principles of Literary Criticism*—e.g. "there is some evidence, uncertain and slight, no doubt, that such things as best sellers (compare *Tarzan* with *She*), magazine verse, mantelpiece pottery, Academy pictures, Music Hall songs, County Council buildings, War Memorials . . . are decreasing in merit;" and "Best-sellers in all the arts, exemplifying as they do the most general levels of attitude development, are worthy of very close study. No theory of criticism is satisfactory which is not able to explain their wide appeal and give clear reasons why those who disdain them are not necessarily snobs."

> I soon found myself committed to a method of investigation which I prefer to describe as "anthropological." It consisted in examining all the material that seemed to bear on this question in an unbiased but inquisitive frame of mind and concentrating on registering shifts of

[10] Leavis, *op. cit.*, pp. xiii–xv.

taste and changes in cultural background, allowing such conclusions as I arrived at to emerge simply by comparison and contrast and analysis.

The exemplar of this anthropological method is identified as Robert S. and Helen M. Lynd's *Middletown* in the opening "Manifesto" of the critical journal *Scrutiny*, where Mrs. Leavis and other students of F. R. Leavis (to whom *Fiction and the Reading Public* was dedicated and whose essay "Mass Civilization and Minority Culture" contributed much) were to carry forward the recommendations of her book. Here were some portentous new forces from Great Britain and America, to go along with the traditional studies by Beljame, Collins, and others noted in the bibliography.

The three main parts of *Fiction and the Reading Public*—I, "The Contemporary Situation," II, "The Past," III, "The Significance of the Best Seller"—combine the three prevailing types of method in histories of taste and audience which may be called the *statistical*, the *historical inferential*, and the *exposition or exposé of the best seller* as indicator of taste. Since the book has notable pivotal significance, both for scholarship and teaching, but has long been out of print and is available in few libraries, it is examined here in greater detail than any other. It gives an excellent measure of where we were twenty-five years ago, for time-comparison with Harbage nine years later, Hart's *The Popular Book* nine years after that, and Altick's *The English Common Reader*, which appeared just as this manuscript was being completed.

Part I offers various sorts of statistical data on the contemporary context: library reports of 1927, showing that 11 per cent of the population used public library books; data about book clubs and other agencies in terms of social class (Times Book Club and Mudie's "upper middle-class"; Boots' "lower middle-class"; Woolworth's "working-class"); periodicals serving various reading levels ("highbrow," "middlebrow," "lowbrow") with comparative typical circulation figures (4,000; 10,000; 30,000–100,000); advertising claims for books ("*Old Pybus* by Warwick Deeping. 75,000 copies in six weeks"); the results of "a literary competition held by the *Sunday Dispatch* (net sales 1,200,767) from March 23rd to April 13th, 1930 . . . [in which] competitors were invited to send their choice (with reasons) of a post-war book which they believe will be read a generation hence, together with the names of five other such post-war books"—with some thirty replies published, and the most votes going to "respected middling novelists of blameless intentions . . . but lacking interest for the 'highbrow' reader, who complains that their works are 'academy art' [here Mrs. Leavis notes one "original competitor who backed *Ulysses, Principles of Literary Criticism*, and *The Poems of T. S. Eliot* . . . published . . . as a curiosity not a prizewinner"]; and the questionnaire returns from 25 effective replies" to Mrs. Leavis from 60 authors (1 "Highbrow"; 4 "Middlebrow" read as literature; 3 "Middlebrow" not read as literature, but not writing for the "lowbrow" market; 17 Absolute best sellers).

Part II, "The Past," is based on and extends such studies of publishing data and reader-revealing content as Beljame had provided, applying the inferential method to Nashe, Bunyan, Defoe, Aphra Behn, Steele and Addison, Fielding, Scott, Dickens, and Hardy.

Part III, "The Significance of the Best Seller," proceeds in three sections—I, "The Novel," II, "Reading Capacity," and III, "Living at the Novelists' Expense"—to annotate the earlier statement about " 'best seller' as an almost entirely derogatory epithet among the cultivated"—a statement which was to prompt Frank Luther Mott in *Golden Multitudes* to take direct exception fifteen years later.

The appendix provides a list of best sellers beginning with *Euphues*, anticipating Weeks's, Alice Payne Hackett's, Mott's, and James D. Hart's more specialized works,—even to an occasional statistical parenthesis: "1814 *Waverly*—Scott (sold 12,000 copies rapidly, considered remarkable.)" and "1852 *Uncle Tom's Cabin*—Harriet Beecher Stowe (1 million sold in England this year)."

The chief findings or conclusions about "The Contemporary Situation" are that "we now have, apparently, several publics, loosely linked together" and that "a consistent selection by the majority of the 'worst' novels ('worst' by consensus of the critical minority) has created a state exactly contrary to what . . . the innocent eighteenth-century observer might expect. . . ."

Part II, "The Past," goes on to document the view in the last chapter of Part I that

novel readers in 1760, for example . . . would be equally likely to read
any novel, or every novel, published . . . [and] even a century later
the same conditions hold . . . each class read or perfectly well might
have read the entire output of all the contemporary novelists, who all
live in the same world. . . .[11]

Like Beljame Mrs. Leavis gives Steele and Addison considerable
credit for that earlier unity:[12]

The gulf between Defoe the journalist of the bourgeois and Aphra
Behn the journalist of the court seems impossible to be bridged . . .
Steele and Addison . . . succeeded in striking a compromise, invalu-
able while it lasted.

But Dickens's books are "written for a new, a naïve public"
which developed after the "draining of the country into the
cities":[13]

The peculiarity of Dickens, as any one who runs a critical eye over a
novel or two of his can see, is that his originality is confined to recaptur-
ing a child's outlook on the grown-up world, emotionally he is not only
uneducated but also immature.

George H. Ford's *Dickens and His Readers* (1955) was to question explicitly parts of Mrs. Leavis's "depressing and disturbing"
views as they bear on Dickens, much as Harbage was to question
implicitly Mrs. Leavis's doubts about getting close to Shakespeare's
audience, and as Robert K. Webb's *The British Working Class
Reader 1790–1848* (1955) was to qualify any generalizations about
a single audience as late as 1860. All would question one or another
part of her current view that[14]

the general public—Dr. Johnson's common reader—has now not even a
glimpse of the living interests of modern literature, is ignorant of its
growth and so prevented from developing with it . . . and the critical
minority to whose sole charge modern literature has now fallen is
isolated, disowned by the general public and threatened with extinction.

Fiction and the Reading Public closes with a vision of what such
a minority might do to survive—a vision that was to have considerable consequence:

[11] *Ibid.*, p. 32.
[12] *Ibid.*, p. 120.
[13] *Ibid.*, p. 157.
[14] *Ibid.*, p. 35.

This minority has two main modes of usefulness . . . research . . .
the training of a picked few who would go out into the world equipped
for the work of forming and organizing a conscious minority . . . [and]
educational work in schools and universities . . . specifically directed
against such appeals as those made by the journalist, the middleman,
the best seller, the cinema, and advertising. . . Such a missionary
spirit, however amusing to the psychologizing observer, has played a
considerable part in history. . . .

Research in Humanities and teaching might thus be closely cor-
related, to their mutual profit. There must be a considerable number of
people at least potentially interested . . . to support . . . such a periodical as the *Calendar* (so soon defunct) but without being restricted
like the *Calendar* to literary criticism. . . .[15]

The consequence was the critical journal *Scrutiny*, published by
students of F. R. Leavis at Cambridge University, whose opening
"Manifesto" in 1932 read in part:[16]

In England during the last two decades no serious critical journal has
been able to survive in the focus in which it was conceived. . . . In
America there is *The Hound and Horn, The Symposium,* and *The
New Republic* . . . But these papers have no English counterparts,
and the ordinary man receives far less help from the better-class
journals and critics than, in a civilized community, he has a right to
expect.

Scrutiny is not to be a purely literary review . . . [but will concern
itself with] "modern affairs" at large . . . politics, for instance . . . .
a play of the free intelligence upon the underlying issues. This is to
desiderate a cultivated historical sense, a familiarity with the "anthropological" approach to contemporary affairs exemplified by *Middletown,* and a catholic apprehension of the humane values . . . . [*Scrutiny*] will direct itself especially upon educational matters. . . .

today there are anti-high-brow publics and "modernist" publics, but
there is no public of Common Readers with whom the critic can rejoice to concur. . . .

And when criticism defaults, the loss is not merely the readers . . .
the artist does depend in large measure on the prevailing standard of
taste. On occasion he may be able to ignore his age and its demands,
but in the past the relation between artist and patron . . . (. . .

[15] *Ibid.,* pp. 270, 272.
[16] F. R. Leavis, *et al. Scrutiny* (1932). Used with permission of the Editors.

person or persons . . .) has been of great importance in determining the use of talent. There is no reason to suppose that it will be otherwise in the future.

it is only a small minority for whom the arts are something more than a luxury product, who believe, in fact, that they are "the storehouse of recorded values". . . . The trouble is not that such persons form a minority, but that they are scattered and unorganized. Every year, for instance, intelligent young men and women go down from the universities and are swallowed by secondary and public schools. Their interests wilt in the atmosphere of the school common-room, and isolation makes their efforts to keep themselves informed of "the best that is known and thought in the world" unnecessarily depressing and difficult. Others beside schoolmasters are in the same position. *Scrutiny* has been founded on the assumption that a magazine in which such men and women can exchange and refine their ideas, and which provides a focus of intellectual interests, will perform a service attempted by no other paper.

The "Manifesto" sets up a network of questions to explore: What became of those aims in the years of *Scrutiny's* existence?— seventeen of which are happily represented in nearly fifty selected articles in Eric Bentley's *The Importance of Scrutiny* (1948). What do they tell us about the audience of *Scrutiny?* What bearings can we take from the quoting of Arnold, alongside Mrs. Leavis's quoting of Richards and Richards's Coleridgean concern with audience? Where, if anywhere, do the affinities of the American New Critics—also university centered—come into the picture? Are they an American counterpart of the *Scrutiny* group?— a question to be touched on in Section III.

The web of interrelating factors can be followed here only briefly, but enough can be suggested to indicate the value of *Fiction and the Reading Public* and *Scrutiny* as a pivotal instance of what may come from a study of audience:

(1) The constituency of *Scrutiny* were evidently concerned (judging from their files) with the refinements of "the best that has been thought and said" rather than with education and questions of larger audiences to be approached in a missionary spirit. Here was a very fruitful purpose in itself, of course, shared by the Leavises, which was to have considerable oblique effect on education by way of the New Critics in both England and America. But

it was only part of the Leavises' purpose, and it was at considerable remove from Matthew Arnold's basic purposes.

(2) What Arnold said basically (we may need to remind ourselves) was that nineteenth-century England was in a perilous state; that there was little to be hoped from the once splendid aristocracy, now materialized "Barbarians"; that immediate hope must rest on the middle classes, of which Arnold was a member, if they could develop a new culture, largely through a new secondary education, to overcome their current "Philistine" self-satisfaction with mechanical progress, narrow sectarianism, and narrow education, and so gain the flexibility to meet great changes lying ahead; and that hope ultimately must rest with the currently brutalized lower classes or "populace," whose elementary schools Arnold served as Her Majesty's Inspector, if the new middle-class culture could be extended in a spirit of *equality*—one of the few good things he found in America in his visit of 1884.

The hopes of *Scrutiny* were in the university minority, not in Arnold's secondary schools. To F. R. Leavis, Arnold is[17]

one of the great critics . . . compellingly alive . . . [but criticism has moved beyond him]. Arnold's distinction as a propagandist for criticism [T. S. Eliot's words in *The Sacred Wood*] cannot be questioned. At the same time perhaps, it must be admitted that these essays do not involve any very taut or subtle development of an argument or any rigor of definition. They are pamphleteering—higher pamphleteering that has lost little of its force or relevance with the passage of time.

Arnold's conceptions of the actual and potential audiences along British class lines, and his program for doing something about the middle- and lower-classes, provide the scholar, teacher, and student with very useful indexes for determining the positions of others who have sought sanction from his slogans and epithets, frequently for other ends in other contexts. In *Scrutiny*, associated with F. R. Leavis's Downing College (named for an American philanthropist and serving able sons of the working classes) there are many signs of this conception of an aristocracy of intellect—with interesting avoidance of the epithet "Philistine" in the writ-

[17] F. R. Leavis, *Education and the University* (New York, George W. Stewart, 1948), p. 89.

ings of the Leavises (including F. R. Leavis's appreciative-critical article on Arnold), with D. W. Harding's ambivalent use of "intelligent" and "civilized Philistines" in referring to the audience I. A. Richards sought to reach, and with Q. D. Leavis's attack in 1938 on Virginia Woolf's "women of our class"—"Mrs. Woolf would apparently be surprised to hear that there is no member of the class on the contributing list of this review."

Alfred Harbage's *Shakespeare's Audience* (1941), as noted, recognizes a certain hostility that may greet his method "made dismal with arithmetic." But neither arithmetic nor the study of audience seems to have obstructed a notable series of professorships at the University of Pennsylvania, Columbia University, and Harvard University, with the sanction of Shakespeare to give dignity to a study of audience.

As if aware of Mrs. Leavis's observation on Shakespeare's audience, Harbage is careful not to claim too much at first, though he declares his faith firmly later:[18]

What follows is a series of computations culminating in a guess. My only claim is that it is the most thoughtful guess thus far made. The contributory facts have to do with theater capacities, admission prices, and receipts in a period when uncertainties are fewest.

He arrives at his "guesses" in seven chapters and two appendixes: "The Evidence"; "How Many People?"; "What Kind of People?"; "Behavior"; "Quality Elizabeth Appraisals"; "Quality Modern Appraisals"; "Our Shakespeares and Our Audiences"; "Appendix A, Estimates of Attendance"; "Appendix B, Attendance Charts."

His computations lead him to the conclusions that the larger theaters could accommodate about 2,500, with an average attendance of about 1,250 at all plays; that of the 160,000 people in the London metropolitan area in 1605, about 13 per cent of the population went to the theater, or two persons in fifteen (as contrasted with 85,000,000 Americans said to go to the movies every week in 1940, or about 65 per cent, or ten persons in fifteen)—and that the cost of admission (relatively a little higher than ours) virtually assured a remarkably respectable audience of apprentices, craftsmen, merchants, wives, and so forth—the latter inferences sharply

[18] Harbage, *op. cit.*, p. 21.

at variance with those of Bradley, Chambers, and others who rely chiefly for their image of the audience on scattered Puritan and political protests against the depravity or political subversiveness of theater crowds. He goes on to summarizing conclusions about a popular audience somewhat resembling Mrs. Leavis's in its concept of a brief Golden Age, but differing radically from Mrs. Leavis's concerning mass civilization and minority culture: [19]

I should guess that the audience as a whole understood and appreciated what it bought and approved. Its approval could not have been easy to win. Unlike some other audiences existing in and near his time, Shakespeare's audience was literally popular, ascending through each gradation from potboy to prince. It was the one to which he had been conditioned early and for which he never ceased to write. It thrived for a time, it passed quickly, and its like has never existed since. It must be given much of the credit for the greatness of Shakespeare's plays. Mere coincidence will not explain why every Elizabethan play addressed to a sector of the people, high or low, learned or unlearned, is inferior in quality; why neither university, nor law school, nor guild hall, nor princely banquet house begat dramatic poetry comparable to what came from the public theaters; or why Blackfriars failed to sustain the level achieved at the Globe. The drama reached its peak when the audience formed a great amalgam, and it began its decline when the amalgam was split in two. The difference between Shakespeare and Fletcher is, in some inverse fashion, the difference between a penny and sixpence.

Harbage's and Mrs. Leavis's different conceptions of literary audiences seem, in some inverse fashion, a difference between one side of the Atlantic and the other: [20]

To grant the audience our respect is reasonable enough. The genius of Shakespeare was incredibly great, but so also is the genius of men by and large. . . . The subtleties missed by one are not missed by his neighbor. The reception of the play is a work of collaboration. Shakespeare's meanings are caught in the mesh of a thousand minds. . . .

The art of the few is great, when great it is, not because of but in spite of its exclusiveness. The qualities of artistic greatness in the literature of the few are identical with those in the literature of the many.

[19] *Ibid.*, p. 159.
[20] *Ibid.*, pp. 159–163.

But, if so, why do the theater audiences and the vast movie audiences of 1940 fail to bring forth a Shakespeare? Harbage's conclusions anticipate those of Gilbert Seldes in *The Great Audience* nine years later. Harbage writes:[21]

Audiences today in the legitimate theater are by no means a cross section of humanity. The spectators may be called, for want of a better name, intellectuals or literati. If an accidental collision at the Globe would have brought us face to face with a grocer, an accidental collision in a theater today would bring us face to face with a schoolteacher. This modern audience is by no means a bad one. The intellectual has a wide range of sympathies and much power of association. He has some knowledge of all classes and can identify himself with them imaginatively. But an audience of this kind is only a reflection of a universal audience and is likely to be regaled only with reflections of universal plays. The moving-picture clientele is truly universal. The Lord Chamberlain's Men barnstormed in the provinces and acted in Whitehall. Moving pictures are shown in the backwoods and in the presidential mansion. In theory, at least, it is to Hollywood that we should look for new dramatic triumphs. But, unluckily, the moving-picture clientele does not compose an audience at all. It does not participate in the creation of a play, and its influence upon creative artists is exercised through deputies not of its own choosing. The true audience of a moving picture is a delegation of studio critics.

The possibilities for teaching? Most obvious, of course, is the contrast of views between Mrs. Leavis and Mr. Harbage on minority and majority culture. They would probably agree, though, on Harbage's view that "mentality should not be measured in terms of caste."

For the student investigator there must be a key question: Do Harbage's and Mrs. Leavis's conceptions of audience derive directly from the evidence, or from prior belief? May each be right in his own context?

Edward Weeks's *This Trade of Writing* (1935) appeared three years after *Fiction and the Reading Public* and six years before *Shakespeare's Audience*. As the title suggests, this book by the editor-to-be of the *Atlantic Monthly* deals chiefly with desiderata for writers seeking to sell their wares, particularly during the depression of the 1930's. Chapters include "Beginners Luck,"

[21] *Ibid.*, pp. 166–167.

"How Men Write," "Women and Short Stories," "The Un-
suspected Poet," "The Meaning of Literary Prizes," "Sex and
Censorship," "Hard Times and the Author," and "The Three
Crises." The method is that of the urbane editorial reader, generally tolerant of all sorts of successful writing—amiably ironic
at times about outworn plots and situations, but generally seeking
to offend no one.

The appendix, "A Tonic for Readers," and the last two chapters, have the most to contribute to the question of literary audience. "The Tonic" contains "A Modern Estimate of the Fifty
Best Books in American Literature (1833–1933)," a list of sixty-
five "American Best Sellers—1875–1933," chronologically arranged, with estimated number of copies sold, and three lists of
"The Twenty-Five Most Influential Books Published Since 1885"
by Edward Weeks, John Dewey, and Charles A. Beard respectively.[22]

It was at the suggestion of Mr. Russell Potter, of the Columbia Institute of Arts and Sciences, that I undertook to make a modern estimate of the fifty best books published in the United States during the
years 1833-1933. . . . When the final selection of the best American
books had gone to press, the suggestion was made that I might furnish
an amusing comparison were I to list the best sellers in America during
the same period. . . . The thought then occurred to me that it might
be stimulating to try to determine which books published within the
last fifty years had most influenced human thought and action. In Mr.
Aristotle's absence, I doubt if there is living a man of sufficient knowledge and experience to make such a choice indisputable.

It is significant that such lists were considered novelties twenty-
five years ago, and that Edward Weeks avoided matters of value,
letting the lists speak for themselves as the principal findings.

The conflicting concepts of literary audience pulling on Weeks
as on most Americans appear chiefly in the last two chapters. One
view is to be found in a little anecdote in "Hard Times and the
Author:"[23]

Shortly after I had begun to serve my turn as a publisher's apprentice
I suffered the unavoidable experience of falling in love. . . . whatever

[22] Edward Weeks, *This Trade of Writing* (Boston, Atlantic Monthly
Press, 1935), pp. 261–275.
[23] *Ibid.*, pp. 202–205.

the young lady might think, her elders regarded me as unnecessarily risky. . . . their suspicions centered chiefly on the fact that I had committed myself to a bookish career . . . "Twenty-five years from now you'll find yourself at the end of a blind alley. Books are doomed."

I cite this somewhat private conversation . . . because it represents such a drear and philistine estimate of literature.

Weeks is gentle and professional about the "many books 'of ephemeral interest.' "[24]

I do not mean to say that those mediocre books dissipated our taste for the first-rate, but I think it is candid to admit that their presence lowered the tone of the book trade.

Despite the depression he is statistically optimistic about "the trade" in the long run:[25]

From 1929 to 1933 our volume of fiction (measured not by the number of new titles, but by the number of copies distributed) shrank 55 per cent; the volume of children's books shrank 38 per cent; biography, 47 per cent; books about fine arts, 70 per cent; religion and philosophy, 61 per cent.

The American Library Association estimates that between four and five million new borrowers were added to library lists during the years I have just mentioned; in that time the total circulation of public library books in the United States increased by nearly 40 per cent. The same years witnessed the enormous, unchecked, and almost immeasureable development of the circulating libraries. . . . Judging from the depression, by the time we all come to live on a four-day week our reading will really amount to something.

In the final chapter, "The Three Crises," Weeks addresses himself in part to young college graduates who are "all dressed up intellectually but have no place to go," and whom he advises "to shun the word-splitting and critical analyses which are apt to impede their action." He warns of differences between magazine and book writing in ways that suggest an American counterpart of Mrs. Leavis's view of the changing audience in *Fiction and the Reading Public*, although there is no explicit mention of her here or in the earlier chapter on little magazines.

[24] *Ibid.*, pp. 205–206.
[25] *Ibid.*, pp. 214–215.

One hundred years ago, when literature was largely the possession of a small literate minority, the few magazines of the day printed much of the best material that was to be had. But as literacy became diluted and as the public grew fond of reading, magazines became proportionately more popular . . . . they began to print, as someone [Mrs. Leavis?] has said, material suitable for a *very large* public consisting of *very simple people.* The quality of most things in life, I think, is in inverse proportion to their circulation.

In the United States magazine writing and literature have become two rather different things. . . .

I hope I imply no snobbishness when I say that their [the magazines'] selection is more often respected for its craftsmanship than for its literary genius.[26]

Almost certainly the editor of the *Atlantic* would modify some of these observations today, but taken in association with other American views they document well for their times the conflicting tendencies to follow the American version of Matthew Arnold's depreciation of "Philistines" yet to allow tolerantly for a large variety of tastes and audiences.

In the classroom and library the best book and best seller lists in *This Trade of Writing* invite lively comparisons with such earlier lists as Asa Don Dickson's *One Thousand Best Books* (1924) and *The Best Books of Our Time 1901–1925,* and articles on best sellers in *Publishers Weekly* by Irving Harlow Hart in 1921, 1925, 1927, and 1933. Concerning attitudes toward literary audience, *This Trade of Writing* invites comparison with Van Wyck Brooks's *America's Coming-of-Age* ten years earlier and Russell Lynes's *A Surfeit of Honey* twenty-two years later.

Levin L. Schücking's *The Sociology of Literary Taste* (translated by E. W. Dickes, 1944) had been published in German the year before Mrs. Leavis's *Fiction and the Reading Public.* Since they were in preparation at essentially the same time, neither took account of the other. Interestingly, the English version of Schücking's work was published in the same International Library of Sociology and Social Reconstruction (edited by Karl Mannheim) as the translation of Beljame's book four years later.

Schücking's book, Mrs. Leavis's, and Stanley E. Hyman's *The*

26 *Ibid.,* pp. 252–255.

Armed Vision provide a useful triangulation on methods and out-look. Hyman's book, which is based on the premise that "literary criticism written in English over the past quarter of a century is qualitatively different from any previous criticism" in its "organized use of non-literary techniques and bodies of knowledge to obtain insights into literature," has this to say about the other two, in the little history of studies of literary audience incidental to his study of I. A. Richards:[27]

Schücking's *The Sociology of Literary Taste* . . . . is little more than a brief literary history generalizing about the shift in status of the artist and the criteria of art and taste in modern times. It does, however, manage to suggest some of the lines of investigation that would make an actual sociology of literary taste possible; detailed study of changes in newspapers and periodicals; "inquiry into the views of particular social groups and professions"; examinations of statistics on the sales of books, including figures on reprintings of earlier literature; surveys of lending libraries, book clubs, reading groups. Unscientifically Schücking has already made such a study or series of studies in his imagination. and he announces what they "would show" . . . . Some of his intuitions and conjectures are extremely shrewd, but Schücking has neither compilations of data nor experimental records to back him up. If any concrete work has been done in the area since, I am not familiar with it. (Without the trappings of scientific sociology, Mrs. Leavis has done a much superior study of literary taste, heavily dependent on Richards, in *Fiction and the Reading Public*.)

Many of Schücking's proposals were in fact carried out by Mrs. Leavis with her "anthropological" method—but drawn from *Middletown* and Beljame (neither cited by Schücking). Schücking's chief interest for us here, along with the imaginative sociological approach which Hyman finds both relevant and repellent, is in his broad concept of British, American, French, and German publics and sub-publics.

In seven short chapters—"Contemporary Taste and the Spirit of the Age," "The Sociological Medium of Literature in the Past," "Shifting of the Sociological Position of the Artist," "Literature and the Public," "The Start of New Trends of Taste," "Means of Selection," and "Public Recognition"—Schücking questions Herder's simple idea of *Zeitgeist* or "a common formula": "the most

[27] Stanley E. Hyman, *The Armed Vision* (New York, Alfred A. Knopf, 1948), pp. 328–329.

that can be done is to distinguish groups." He uses (but questions) the historical inferential method by which "the Spirit of the Gothic period, for instance, is first deduced from its art and then rediscovered in its art." He traces the changes in status of the literary artist from opprobrium to deification, as the rising middle-class, "fallen victim to all sorts of affectation . . . aristocratized . . . narrowed by a thousand conventions . . . nurtured a secret affection for the untrammelled existence, as it saw it, of the artist . . . . almost a higher type of human being . . . . plainly visible at its extremest in France, very noticeable in England, faintest at first in Germany." He sees further separations of artist and public with the development of "art for art's sake," on the one hand, and of "naturalism" (particularly in Germany) on the other [this is the section Hyman particularly objects to], where research would show "at the beginning of the 'nineties' . . . a period during which every society, every club, every family resounded with passionate declarations . . . to the effect that for thousands of years the artist had set out to represent not the true but the lovely and noble." He observes the passing, with the First World War, of the higher official with university training, as the older "taste-upholding type," and the rise of new taste-upholding types who "possess the practical means of success and command the technical media for establishing their view—publishing firm, theater, review, and so forth . . . . sometimes . . . with a particular professional class . . . . for instance, of the type of the journalist of the great cities." He analyzes the role of education ("Of all the elements that determine taste the school probably plays the principal part") in the German universities, which "as a whole maintain strict seclusion" and which "unlike many foreign universities . . . . never dream of inviting critics of recognized standing." Schücking's concluding view of the audience lends interesting support to Mrs. Leavis in that any group which wants to become the "taste-upholding" group must campaign for its position "in a society of countless competitors where [regrettably] one can become a success only if, following the American device, one 'gets talked about.' "

In "Final Considerations" Schücking editorializes as Mrs. Leavis had—though with a different slant on Dr. Johnson's "Common Reader":

Since art does not exist in a world of absolutes and its acceptance is
dependent on the character of the accepter, and since the establishment
of a taste is thus not independent of sociological forces, which are not
always of a purely intellectual nature, the one and only criterion for
the value of that art which has ultimately triumphed lies in the permanence of its appeal. The reason is not that, as Dr. Johnson said, the public, which is the ultimate judge; comes usually, in matters over which it
ponders for long, to the right conclusions, but that art which has maintained its reputation through many centuries must have passed from
one taste-upholding type to another.

the recognition that all art rests fundamentally on the shoulders of a
particular taste-upholding type should strengthen the critical attitude
of the individual. . . .

At no time, perhaps, has this warning been more necessary than today, when, in Germany, at least . . . . people no longer have the
courage of their aesthetic convictions. Only thorough self-examina-
tion and, where required, clear-sighted organization of the laity can
help to restore it.[28]

The teaching possibilities here are fairly obvious in the Leavis-
Schücking-Hyman triangulation, not least of all in their concep-
tion of the actual and potential role of universities. Have the New
Critics perhaps changed the picture of the then-current critical
ineffectualness of universities which Van Wyck Brooks, Mrs.
Leavis, and Schücking agreed on?

With the four individual instances of Q. D. Leavis, Edward
Weeks, Alfred Harbage, and Levin L. Schücking now in mind
for international, ideational, occupational, and methodological
reference, we may conveniently cluster three of the four selected
books which were to appear—momentarily delaying further discussion of Hyman's *The Armed Vision* (1948) which was published between the last two of the cluster. These three concentrate on the phenomenon of best sellers, which had been part of the
concern of Q. D. Leavis and Edward Weeks and which was also
to be an appendix feature in Altick's *The English Common Reader.*

Alice Payne Hackett's *Fifty Years of Best Sellers, 1895–1945*
(1945), to be followed a decade later by *60 Years of Best Sellers,*
Frank Luther Mott's *Golden Multitudes: The Story of Best Sellers
in the United States* (1947), and James D. Hart's *The Popular*

---

[28] Levin L. Schücking, *The Sociology of Literary Taste,* tr. E. W. Dickes
(London, Routledge and Kegan Paul, Ltd., 1944), pp. 75–76.

Book: A History of America's Literary Taste (1950), present a kind of chain reaction, among three different kinds of observers. The first comes essentially from the publisher's point of view, by the associate editor of *Publishers Weekly*. The second is by a journalist, professor, director, and dean of journalism successively at the State University of Iowa and the University of Missouri, and Pulitzer Prize winner in 1939 for his *A History of American Magazines*. The third is a professor of English (since appointed vice-chancellor) at the University of California at Berkeley, with his degrees from Stanford and Harvard. In dealing with their views, we can gain desirable focus by seeing how each treats a specific work—Steinbeck's *The Grapes of Wrath*—chosen because Steinbeck's "literary ecology" has considerable value in opening to students the problem of scientific method, probably clearer in its application to literary audience than Mrs. Leavis's "anthropological" method.

Fifty Years of Best Sellers provides this general setting for its facts and figures, culled from *Publisher's Weekly:*[29]

These records for each year, compiled from the monthly reports of the booksellers of Amercia, make what can be imagined as a moving picture of this country's reading interests, projected against the background of national history. Sometimes the background stands out strongly and clearly, as during the two world wars, when book titles were shaped by the dramatic events of those years. Sometimes the screen shows only dimly grey shadows, as people turn to . . . escape from the monotony of passing events which have little direct impact upon themselves. . . .

Comment upon literary and social currents is, however, only incidental in this book. Its primary concern is to assemble, from many sources, the available facts about best sellers, in the expectation that future historians and researchers will find them useful.

"How many copies does a book have to sell to be a best seller?" Such a question embodies a very common misconception. "Best seller" is a purely comparative term. When one book sells more than any other book at a certain time and place, that book is the best seller at that time and place.

The compiler's general inferences from her compilation and observation appear to correspond with the following:

[29] Alice P. Hackett, *Fifty Years of Best Sellers* (New York, R. R. Bowker Co., 1945), pp. 1–4.

Professor Irving Harlow Hart, who has closely studied best-seller records, ever since they were begun in 1895, and several of whose analytical articles on the best seller are listed in the bibliography at the end of this book, found a most cheering note in the popularity of *The Good Earth*. On the basis of his own method of analyzing best-seller lists, he determined that *The Good Earth* was the most popular book in the period from 1919 to 1932 and that it was second in popularity from 1895 to 1932; whereupon he wrote, "The popularity of this book nullifies the adverse criticism of American reading taste based upon past preferences and gives the lover of literature renewed faith in the character and judgment of the reading public. . . . Evidently the American reader reads what he reads when he reads it and declines to be largely influenced by anything other than the book itself."

The observations on *The Grapes of Wrath*, which led the list of fiction best sellers in 1939, and stood in eighth place in 1940, run thus, with introductory context, in both *Fifty Years of Best Sellers* and *60 Years of Best Sellers:*[30]

The New York World's Fair opened, with exhibits from nearly all the countries of the world except Germany, and was visited by the new King and Queen of England. The Spanish Civil War ended with the surrender of the Loyalists. Late in the year Germany invaded Poland—the period of peace between two world wars had ended. A novel of the "Okies," those dispossessed by the dust storms of 1934, made John Steinbeck top best seller of the nation. Book stores sold 300,000 copies during the year.

Mott's *Golden Multitudes*, two years later, drawing its title from Shakespeare's *Henry IV*, Part I, seeks with the journalist's eye what would presumably be of widespread interest, and also brings the outlook which is transforming many of our schools of journalism into schools of communication research, dealing with the complex of "who says what to whom in what medium or channel with what effect?" Mott disclaims finality as Harbage does. "This study . . . . is in the nature of a pioneer expedition, and has the weaknesses and vulnerability of such ventures." He is sharply conscious of the problem of respectability of a study of audience as a way of studying a work—gaining comfort, however, from Jefferson's "It is rare that the public sentiment decides immorally or unwisely, and the individual who differs from it ought

[30] *Ibid.*, pp. 79–80.

to distrust or examine well his own opinion"—as contrasted with Alexander Hamilton's "The people are turbulent and changing; they seldom judge or determine right," Ruskin's "The public is just a great baby!" and Q. D. Leavis's observation that "Best seller is an almost entirely derogatory epithet among the cultivated." Mott's debated measure of what he calls an over-all best seller is that it should "have had a total sale equal to one per cent of the population of continental United States (or the English Colonies in the years before the Revolution) for the decade in which it was published," an ambiguity which James D. Hart was to comment on later. At the outset Mott identifies himself with "your sincere and convinced democrat":[31]

He believes that the people, conservators of primitive and essential truth, may be depended upon to take to their heart the really great books; therefore, that books long popular must be great books. He perceives a richness, a variety, a profusion, and an amplitude in popular literature that takes the individual reader out of his narrow routines and brings him into an awareness of humanity at large. He thinks that such a literature has far more to tell the sociologist, the historian, the philologer, and even the philosopher and the artist, than the more precious compositions for the few. In short, he is convinced that popular literature—the newspaper, the magazine, the best seller—has a special paramount importance because it is popular.

But what shocking doctrine this is for the aesthetician! He is not interested in the popular audience, nor much concerned with any audience save that of the elect. Professional literary critics, many of them interested chiefly in aesthetic values, have had a difficult time with best sellers.

He goes at *The Grapes of Wrath* as an experienced reporter:[32]

This story grew out of its author's interest in the problems . . . . of the migratory workers in his native Salinas Valley. Living with the migrants, writing about them in a series for the *San Francisco News*, helping a *Life* photographer get pictures of them, Steinbeck gathered the materials . . . . The Viking Press published the book April 14, 1939, and it took the country by storm. Its relentless commentary on the Dust Bowl and migratory-worker problem, its poignance and

[31] Frank Luther Mott, *Golden Multitudes* (New York, The Macmillan Co., 1947), pp. 1–3.

[32] *Ibid.*, p. 259.

realism, and its narrative power brought it a large and earnest audience. Critics praised it, editors discussed it, Congress took notice of it, President Roosevelt made a speech based on it, and California undertook to cope with the situation which it had brought to national attention. It was accepted as a great social document as well as a good novel.

Well over half a million copies were sold before the book went into the cheaper editions. It ranked first in the *Publisher's Weekly* summary of best sellers for 1939 and eighth the next year. Then in 1946 it became the actual best seller of the new Bantam Books series, and its grand total rose to at least a million and a quarter.

Neither Alice Payne Hackett nor Frank Luther Mott deals with Steinbeck's central ecological concept.

In *The Popular Book* Hart acknowledges his indebtedness to Mott, but takes issue with Mott's criterion for a best seller:[33]

Particularly I should like to express my appreciation for the kind aid of the only other author who has dealt in general with this subject. Professor Frank Luther Mott sent me the galley proofs of his *Golden Multitudes* when my work was half written and urged me to complete it because his interest was in "the story of best sellers in the United States" and mine in popular reading tastes, related to social pressures. His research frequently confirmed my own findings, although we differ on interpretations of popularity, for his depend on the criterion that a best seller is a book that . . . . since its publication has had a sale equal to 1 per cent of the population of the continental United States at the time it was first issued.

Avoiding quasi-statistical "controls," Hart also warns against misuse of the historical inferential method and leans toward critical instances that reveal a spectrum of readers:[34]

Concerned with individual books as part of a species, not as isolated best sellers, this investigation neither attempts to isolate the most widely read books from their times, nor to extract into a vacuum certain qualities supposedly inherent in all the books most widely read in America from colonial days to the present. To find such qualities is to discover generalizations so spacious that they apply perfectly to no popular book, but may, indeed, fit equally well the sum of America's less widely read books. If, then, on the one hand, this book does not try to deal with popular books as some have dealt with the question

[33] Hart, *op. cit.*, p. 289.
[34] *Ibid.*, pp. 284–285.

"what is an American?"—by isolating an abnormal average American, who has, say, one and three-eighths children and four-fifths of an automobile—neither does it attempt definition in terms of democracy, religion, materialism, or other vague words. . . .

Literary taste is not an isolated phenomenon. The taste of the largest number of readers is shaped by contemporary pressures more than is the taste of the highly cultivated reader, who has a deeper background of aesthetic experience and knowledge to guide him. Books flourish when they answer a need and die when they do not. The needs of the greatest reading public are various; they include clarification of ideas already in circulation; emotional statement of feelings that people are prepared to accept; popularization of desirable information heretofore obscure; satisfying appeal to forms of entertainment currently considered amusing or exciting . . . . in some way or another, the popular author is always the one who expresses the people's minds and paraphrases what they consider their private feelings. . . .

At one end this public shades off into students, teachers, and other serious and constant readers; at the other end it shades off into the people whose reading matter is usually restricted to newspapers and magazines. If a book sells 100,000 copies in 1949, it is tremendously successful; it may even be listed at or near the top of the official twenty best sellers, but the public that bought it represents less than .07 per cent of the whole American population, a population that weekly consumes some 25,000,000 "comic books" and about 10,000,000 pulp magazines. . . . The public with which this study is concerned is only the public possessed of enough wealth, education, and leisure to obtain and to read new books as they appear.

In the light of this view, which resembles Harbage's at many points, Hart sees John Steinbeck's *The Grapes of Wrath* in the context of Steinbeck's other fiction and of the response of his audience to more than the topical:[35]

Not until the publication of Steinbeck's *Grapes of Wrath*. in 1939, was a so-called proletarian novel widely enough read for the working class to be aware of it. Steinbeck was an author of the decade. His first novel was published in 1929 on the eve of the Depression, but this and two more novels together had not sold 3,000 copies. Then slowly he came to public notice with his appealing story of paisano life, *Tortilla Flat;* a proletarian novel, *In Dubious Battle,* which seemed too doctri-

[35] *Ibid.,* p. 250.

naire for wide circulation; his sentimental novella, *Of Mice and Men*, also a stage success; and, finally, *The Grapes of Wrath*, the epic of the contemporary dispossessed. This panoramic saga of migratory laborers harried across the continent created a strong sense of identity, its action centered on the warm portrayal of simple, but fully developed people, its thesis realized in homely, natural dialogue, so that readers could obtain a direct emotional apprehension of the dislocation of the times and find meaning in its affirmative philosophy: "We ain't gonna die out. People is goin' on—changin' a little, maybe, but goin' right on." A work of propaganda almost as stirring in its time as *Uncle Tom's Cabin* was in the 1850's, *The Grapes of Wrath* became the subject of impassioned discussion as the period's most popular novel representing the search for answers in terms of social values.

Taken together, the observations of these three American observers present a continuous line of development as well as a triangulation. None gets explicitly at Steinbeck's *balance of nature* or *web of life* conception, which will be considered briefly in Section III of this essay (as a "teaching instance" for use of these materials) but the aspect of search for relationships with an "affirmative philosophy" comes closer than much criticism.

Stanley Edgar Hyman's observations and reflections on literary audience in *The Armed Vision* (1948, abridged and revised 1955) appear chiefly in his respectful chapter on "I. A. Richards and The Criticism of Interpretation." Early in the chapter the Bennington College professor observes: [36]

All of Richards' work has been devoted to exploring . . . the poem-audience relationship rather than the poet-poem relationship.

Midway in the chapter he pauses to consider the history of the study of audience, finding it meagre: [37]

In a fragmentary and intuitive fashion, as in the case of so many other modern techniques, literary criticism has always been concerned with the reader's or audience's part in the communicative process of art. Plato and Aristotle both generalized about audience-reaction in their opposed psychosocial doctrines of art as harmful-stimulation-of-the-emotions and art as helpful-purgation-of-the-emotions, but neither attempted to study specific audience reactions to specific works.

[36] Hyman, *op. cit.*, p. 279.
[37] *Ibid.*, p. 299.

After a brief view of Longinus's oblique approaches, Hyman moves to the eighteenth century:[38]

Probably the first formal recognition of the need for psychological study of the audience came in the eighteenth century, culminating in Edmund Burke's essay "On the Sublime and Beautiful". . . . In pursuing art into the area of the audience, Burke was logically putting into practice the view, growing all through the eighteenth century, that criticism would profit from less conjecture and more data.

This leads to Coleridge and DeQuincey and the beginning of "general experimental testing in areas previously regarded as sacred to conjecture under the influence of the 'Coleridge tradition'," chiefly on the part of nineteenth century scientists in Germany and to "a lesser extent" in France [without mention of Beljame]. This "Coleridge Tradition" leads back to Richards and other moderns:[39]

A number of contemporary critics besides Richards have picked up one or the other aspects of this tradition: either attempting experimental laboratory forms of criticism, or studying the communicative process and reader-reactions by meaans of other techniques. Maud Bodkin's experiments with reader-introspection . . . . Frederick Lyman Wells. . . . "A Statistical Study of Literary Merit". . . . Allan Abbott and M. R. Trabue. . . . . *A Measure of Ability to Judge Poetry*. . . . Mortimer Adler . . . . using music . . . . Helene Hartley . . . . *Tests on the Interpretative Reading of Poetry*. . . .

Hyman concludes his brief exploratory history with the statement:[40]

Richards seems to have paid little attention to earlier workers in the experimental and audience-study traditions. . . . Richards' specific and conscious indebtedness is to a handful of earlier thinkers, most of them relatively eccentric philosophers and philosophic literary men. The most important of these is Samuel Taylor Coleridge.

These passages were not altered in the abridgment and revision of *The Armed Vision* for paperback publication in 1955, in which Hyman removed the excoriating chapter on Edmund Wilson

38 *Ibid.*, p. 300.
39 *Ibid.*, pp. 303–304.
40 *Ibid.*, p. 308.

and the chapter on Marxist criticism, and made various minor revisions.

Hyman's statement on Coleridge prompts a good question for student discussion: whether Coleridge's psychological interest in audience was not basically nullified by his fear of the vulgar audience—a fear which both Ford and Altick note, and a factor perhaps observable in Mrs. Leavis's quotation from Richards, concerning the decline in quality of best sellers.

Gilbert Seldes's *The Great Audience* (1950) was published the same year as Hart's *The Popular Book*. It is the second of the three books by Seldes (described as "Phi Beta Kappa . . . Harvard . . . music critic . . . theater critic . . . foreign correspondent . . . managing editor of *The Dial* . . . director of the television programs for CBS [1937–1945] . . . practicing radio and television critic [for the *Saturday Review*] . . . teacher [at Columbia University] . . .") in which, over a span of a quarter century, he has sought to plumb the cumulative meaning of what he now calls the "public arts." The dedication to Edward R. Murrow and Jimmy Durante in the *The Public Arts: A report on the movies, radio, and television—and on what the shift from the printed word to the electronic tube means to the American people* (1956) reviews Seldes's earlier books:[41]

Professionally I dedicate it to you together because the two fields in which you work are parts of one field, each essential to the other. I wasn't prophetic enough to see this when I wrote *The Seven Lively Arts* [1924] in praise of the gaiety and vigor of our popular entertainments, and I wasn't detached enough to see this when I wrote *The Great Audience* [1950] a rather ominous "out of balance" warning that these same popular arts which are also the mass media might be used to keep us complacent and perpetually immature. It would be silly for me to make excuses now for failing to see that the lively arts and the mass media are two aspects of the same phenomenon, which I now call the "public arts." . . . I didn't see that, while the Murrows and the Durantes worked on opposite sides of the street, it was the same street, that each needed the other, and the audience needed both.

In the preface to *The Great Audience*, which among the three books deals most vigorously with the question of literary values

[41] Gilbert Seldes, *The Public Arts* (New York, Simon and Shuster, Inc., 1956), p. v.

and their possible corruption by the mass arts, Seldes states at once his method, conclusions, and concept of audience: [42]

Twenty-five years ago I made a proposal that seemed modest at the time: that popular entertainment could be accepted and criticized on the same basis as the fine arts. . . . I didn't perceive then the direction American entertainment was going to take. . . . I hope this book will correct my earlier mistakes and place the popular arts more nearly where they belong.

In the traditional sense they are seldom considered as arts and are condemned because they are uncreative . . . . the work of art as an imperishable object is totally foreign to them.

The creative action of these arts begins after the movie or the radio program has been made: they create their own audience, making people over; they create the climate of feeling in which all of us live. The other arts are private and personal, they influence the lives of those who enjoy them; the effect of the public arts cannot be escaped . . . neither our indifference nor our contempt gives us immunity against them.

Have these arts any choice as to the kind of audiences they shall create? Is what they are doing now the best they can do?

At the moment it seems to me essential that the questions should be asked as publicly as possible . . . . [to] bring the whole question of our use of the popular arts to the average intelligent man, so that he can see how his daily life is affected by them even if he is not himself a part of the mass audience.

In order to ask questions properly I have examined the conditions in which our entertainments are created—the way major studios conduct the business of making and showing movies, the economics of sponsored radio and television . . . . a sort of Elementary Physics of the Popular Arts, considering their quantity, the speed with which they move, their mass and weight and duration, and I wish I had been able to discover the electromagnetic field surrounding each one of them.

The end product which they are now creating is the mass man. There is still time—but not much time—to make the popular arts serve free men trying to secure a free society.

[42] Seldes, *The Great Audience* (New York, Simon and Shuster, Inc., 1950), pp. 3-6.

Since Seldes's books are a part of Patrick Hazard's essay in this volume, the reader should refer to it for most of Seldes's other considerations. Students may very profitably consider the contrast he draws in the two major sections of the book, "The Big Audience" and "The Great Audience"; his views in the chapter on "The People and the Arts," on the "aristocratic" position of T. S. Eliot and the "Marxist" arguments of Dwight MacDonald; and his inverted pyramidal concept in *The Public Arts* that[43]

the public arts . . . are a cross-section of the classic, the folk, and the fine arts . . . fanning out from a narrow base in the classics, widening in the folk arts, and almost as broad in the . . . popular arts as the field itself. The frieze along the pediment of the Parthenon and Shakespeare's plays at the Globe Theatre were . . . public arts, and so were the ballads hawked in the streets of London after an execution. . . .

The touchstones which Seldes uses here make useful teaching contacts with Jacques Barzun's comments on the Greeks who "carved the frieze of the Parthenon" in *Of Human Freedom* (1939), Harbage's views in *Shakespeare's Audience* (1941), and various studies of eighteenth-century British reading.

The Audience of Beowulf (1951), a series of lectures delivered at the University of London by Dorothy Whitelock of Saint Hilda's College, Oxford, provides a modern instance of lively inferential British detective effort to reconstruct, from internal evidence ("I propose to use the poem of *Beowulf* to elucidate the poem of *Beowulf*"), documentary research, and archeological discoveries at Sutton Hoo, the eighth-century listeners ("both . . . veterans and . . . young men") to that highly Christianized poem, perhaps produced at the court of Offa in Mercia. In 1951, ten years after Harbage's *Shakespeare's Audience*, the concern with audience continues to call for comment:[44]

It will seem very trite and obvious to say that the effect of any work of art depends not only on the author's power and skill, but also on what is already present in the minds of its hearers, or readers, or—in the case of the visual arts—its beholders. Nevertheless, this con-

43 *Ibid.*, p. 287.
44 Whitelock, *op. cit.*, p. 2.

sideration is particularly pertinent to the poem of *Beowulf*, partly because it is far removed from us in time, so that we are not entitled to assume without investigation that an audience of the poet's day would be moved by the same things as we are . . . but still more because much of the poem is composed with a subtle technique of allusion, reminder, and suggestion, so that we cannot guess at the effect the poet was hoping to obtain unless we know something of the meaning and associations, his hints and allusions carried to those for whom he composed his poem. This is, of course, no new idea: it is implicit in most *Beowulf* scholarship, though occasionally writers have lost sight of it. Yet it seems to me that the contribution of the audience to the full understanding of the poem is so important that it is time that for once it should be allowed to get on to a title page.

Whitelock maintains that a concern for the manifold associations of the audience—associations traced in many documents—demonstrably throws new light on the form and meaning of the poem:[45]

One may reach the conclusion [she says] that the audience of *Beowulf* was a Christian company, and one which admitted that vengeance, in unavoidable circumstances and carried out in accordance with the law, was a binding duty . . . . My choice of the term *audience* has already indicated that I do not believe that *Beowulf* was composed merely for people who could read, which is almost equivalent to saying for the clergy. Nothing that is recorded of the ecclesiastics of Anglo-Saxon England lends countenance to a view that they were in the habit of composing long poems on secular themes solely for circulation among themselves. It is difficult to imagine any bishop or abbott approving the use of so much expensive parchment for a work which he would not regard as directly edifying to men of religion . . . . *Beowulf*, though it may contain elements intended for edification, is surely first and foremost literature of entertainment, and as such, intended mainly for laymen . . . . It could easily have been delivered in three sittings. It is perhaps not by accident that the second episode, the fight with Grendel's mother, begins with a neat synopsis of what has gone before; this may be intended to inform newcomers and remind the previous audience of what has happened in the first part. The third episode, the dragon fight, is intelligible in itself.

With British perspectives, Dorothy Whitelock gives useful reminders that in those days the class difference between audiences was between clerics and others. Yet they had much in common:

[45] *Ibid.*, p. 19.

it would be unsafe to argue that any part of England was in the Eighth Century insufficiently advanced in intellectual attainment for a sophisticated poem like *Beowulf* to have been composed there and appreciated.[46]

Russell Lynes's *The Tastemakers* (1954) and *A Surfeit of Honey* (1957), like Gilbert Seldes's several writings, offer another record of growing reflectiveness about American audiences and an increasing skepticism about the phenomenon called "taste." *The Tastemakers* includes Lynes's generative article "Highbrow, Lowbrow, Middlebrow" of 1949 and expands on his "The Age of Taste" in the 100th Anniversary number of *Harper's Magazine* in 1950.

In *The Tastemakers* the managing editor of *Harper's Magazine* provides text and pictures illustrating in three parts "The Public Taste," "The Private Taste," and "The Corporate Taste"—in architecture, furnishings, painting, lithographs, sculpture, reading, and theater. The method is that of Frederick Lewis Allen, former editor of *Harper's Magazine:* historical, anecdotal, and symbolic. Lynes begins and ends with the problem of the "Lawyer's Wife" ("a middlebrow") who was given $7,000 "to do over the living room" and who "can't make up her mind what to do." Along with this non-academic touch goes a thoughtfully selected bibliography (also largely of non-academic writings) with a note of thanks to "John A. Kouwenhoven and Wayne Andrews ["without involving them in any responsibility for my results"] for casting the dispassionate but sympathetic eye of scholarship on my manuscript," and a very substantial index—something commonly lacking in non-academic books.

The highbrows about whom I have been writing are mainly consumers and not creaters—editors, critics, and dilettantes. The creative artists who are generally considered highbrows—such men as T. S. Eliot, E. M. Forster, Picasso, and Stravinsky—seem to me to fall in another category, that of the professional man who, while he may be concerned with communicating with a limited (and perhaps largely highbrow) audience, is primarily a doer and not a done-by. When Eliot or Forster or Picasso or Stravinsky sits down at his work table, I do not know whether he says to himself, "I am going to create Art," but I very much doubt if that is what is in his mind. He is concerned rather with the communication of ideas within the frame of a poem, a

[46] *Ibid.*, p. 105.

novel, a painting, or a ballet suite, and if it turns out to be art (which many think it frequently does) that is to him a by-product of creation, an extra dividend of craftsmanship, intelligence, and sensibility. But when this happens he is taken up by the highbrow consumer and made much of. In fact he may become, whether he likes it or not, a vested interest, and his reputation will be every bit as carefully guarded by the highbrows as a hundred shares of Standard Oil of New Jersey by the middlebrows. He will be sold—at a par decided upon by the high-brows—to the middlebrows, who are natural gamblers in the com-modities of culture.[47]

In this same chapter Lynes reflects the fairly elaborate anthro-pological stratifications of W. Lloyd Warner of the "Yankee City Series," which prompted J. P. Marquand to his ambivalent satire on the anthropologist in *Point of No Return*—upper-upper, mid-dle-upper, lower-upper, upper-middle, and so forth. In *A Surfeit of Honey*, however, the "professional" consideration definitely takes over, and Lynes gently discounts Warner's classification:[48]

For purposes of common parlance we have a classless society, if a society that has only one class, a middle class, can be said to be class-less . . . . We have devised new ways of dividing people up that are just as effective, if a little less insulting. We have workers, white-collar workers, executives (junior and senior), managers and directors. That might be called a power system of classification. Another is low-brows, middlebrows, and highbrows. Still another is creative and non-creative workers . . . . For all our classlessness we keep assigning people to levels.

We have not, however, found a convenient system for assigning them to social levels, Dr. W. Lloyd Warner and his study of social classes to the contrary notwithstanding . . . .

Instead of being divided horizontally into levels and strata, as we are used to thinking of it, our society has increasingly become divided vertically. Instead of broad upper, middle, and lower classes . . . we now have a series of almost free-standing pyramids, each with its several levels and each one topped by an aristocracy of its own . . . the big-business pyramid . . . the communications and entertainment pyramid . . . an intellectual pyramid, another for small business, one for the underworld, one for labor . . . one for politics . . . another for sports.

[47] Lynes, *op. cit.*, pp. 316–317.
[48] Lynes, *A Surfeit of Honey* (New York, Harper and Brothers, 1957), pp. 12–20.

At the top of the intellectual pyramid, to take one that is close to being neat in its organization, there sits a small group of academics with a few novelists, poets, painters, composers, foundation executives, and university presidents who more or less assume charge of the arts and intellectual life of the nation. . . .

At the top of the intellectual pyramid the critics and philosophers today have a power that they have not had in the past in America—men like Jacques Barzun, Lionel Trilling, Reinhold Niebuhr, Norbert Wiener, David Riesman, and, of course, Oppenheimer. They outrank the artists and novelists and poets, who are a little afraid of them, and since they are scholars who can also write for the lay reader they outrank most other academics who can (though many insist otherwise) communicate only with their peers. As David Riesman pointed out some time ago (and as *Time* magazine recently reiterated) the position of the intellectual has never been stronger in America than it is today. It is popular among intellectuals to bemoan the fact that nobody pays any attention to them, that they have never before encountered such a wave of anti-intellectualism, and that they are voices crying in a wilderness. But an intellectual without a wilderness is a missionary without a cannibal. . . .

If the intellectual pyramid has a lower class, journalists and school-teachers are it. They constitute the broad base of workers which supports the rest of the structure but which gets little acclaim from the top. . . . The principal complaint of teachers these days is not that they are paid too little but that they lack standing in the eyes of the community. This may well be because they are patronized and looked down upon (though somewhat affectionately) by the upper reaches of their own kind.

But Lynes's most imaginative observation is of still another group with which he seems to identify himself:[49]

The Upper Bohemians live in a twilight zone in our society. . . . neither below the new aristocracies nor above what we conventionally think of as the middle class. Because they consider themselves to be genuinely unconcerned with the ladder of success, as most Americans see it, they regard the performances and pretensions of the new aristocracies with detached amusement. . . . They have dug themselves into the soil of our democracy and, if they will forgive the figure of speech, they perform the useful function, like earthworms, of aerating and fertilizing our topsoil. . . .

[49] *Ibid.*, pp. 29–30.

We have never had anything quite like them in America before. They are as much at home with the word-men of the communications pyramid as with the vice-president in charge of sales in the business pyramid or the professorial mentors of the intellectuals, though they feel removed from all of them . . . there is a kinship of spirit that makes them stick together as a group—possibly the only cohesive class that we can still put our fingers on.

In Bohemian society it is the convention to look upon all conventions, all codes of behavior, and all rules of taste as matters never to be taken for granted.

If the structure is not precisely as Russell Lynes pictures it, the student may well ask if Lynes's picture may not help make it so, even as Matthew Arnold's creative . . . simplifications" (to quote W. F. Connell of the University of Sydney) did earlier.

George H. Ford's *Dickens and His Readers: Aspects of Novel-Criticism since 1836* (1955) is the third of four selected studies published by university presses—Harbage's (Columbia University, 1941), Dorothy Whitelock's (Oxford University, 1951), Ford's (Princeton University, for the University of Cincinnati, 1955) and Altick's (University of Chicago, 1957).

The method and outlook are suggested by the subtitle which makes Dickens the focus of a larger context of criticism, covering three dated but nameless periods, "Part One: 1836–1848," "Part Two: 1848–1872," "Part Three: 1872–1952," and by the titles of three chapters in the last part, "The Common Reader," "The High Aesthetic Line," and "The Uncommon Reader."

Ford is explicit about his method, and pointedly concerned with the opposing outlook of the Leavises:[50]

literary history may be of service to the literary critic by providing perspective. Its role is similar to Coleridge's (as described by John Stuart Mill): to remind us that the persistence of a literary work as a source of pleasure for successive generations is a fact not to be lightly overlooked by the critic. One-sided criticism seems to stem from a fear of stodginess. To stimulate the indifferent, the critic resorts to urtication and becomes, in the process, merely eccentric. Among the most distinguished practitioners of this shock treatment is Dr. F. R. Leavis. Throughout his essays, reputations are tumbled round like

[50] George H. Ford, *Dickens and His Readers* (Princeton, Princeton University Press, 1955), p. 4.

roulette balls—a very exciting display. In *The Great Tradition* (1949), Fielding's novels are solemnly banished together with ninety-five percent of Dickens' work, excepting only *Hard Times* which is briefly discussed in an appendix. One can imagine that such startling treatment, given as a lecture, would pack a hall with fascinated undergraduates (they love the sound of smashing marble), but in print it becomes disappointing. What gives edge to one's disappointment is that Dr. Leavis demonstrates brilliantly, in a few short passages, that he can analyze a chapter of Dickens with unusual skill, his analysis providing a model of one kind of criticism much needed for future studies.

Ford shows little sympathy elsewhere with the "High Aesthetic Line," but is also cautious about the danger in research . . . that unless we are very careful we always find what we are seeking."

In the chapter on "The Limits of Explanatory Criticism," Ford expands on the problem of method:[51]

For this enquiry, the term *explanatory criticism* will mean any attempt to discuss some phase of a work of literature not by evaluating it or by impressionistic accounts of it, but by explanations of how it came to be what it is. Explanatory criticism includes biography, psychological analysis of the author, the history of ideas, and the history of taste and technique.

In compact illustration he applies these to the question of Dickens' "sincerity," his "psychology," and "predominant ideas, or predominant tastes, of the age"—using the instance of "Little Nell" and Dickens' feeling about the death of Mary Hogarth (citing "what Lionel Trilling calls . . . the symbolic representation of a painful experience, a catharsis for the artist. . . .") and the "cult of sensibility."

He points out the values and limits of the explanatory method:[52]

Explanatory criticism is useful in helping us to understand why Dickens' contemporaries were so little aware of the garishness that they encouraged him to continue in the same vein, and why Nell (together with *Pickwick Papers*) made Dickens the most popular and admired novelist in the language. These would seem to be its limits, and beyond them, the present-day admirer of the rest of Dickens' work has to grope for other ways of dealing with his sentimentality.

[51] *Ibid.*, p. 63.
[52] *Ibid.*, p. 71.

With his historical-comparative method of explanatory criticism Ford finds an abundance of admirers of Dickens at all levels, common and uncommon. He has an American tolerance of both of these levels, recognizing various sub-audiences in both, as at the start of the chapter "The Uncommon Reader":[53]

"How good it is to meet someone who enjoys Dickens, and how rarely this happens!" So begins an essay by the English novelist, Rex Warner, which appeared in 1947. In 1952, the American critic, Lionel Trilling, begins an essay with the following assertion: "No one, I think, is any longer under any illusion about Dickens. It is now manifest that he is one of the two greatest novelists of England (Jane Austen being the other)." From these contradictory statements, one might infer either that a miracle has taken place in five years, or that there exists a radical disagreement about literary preferences on opposite sides of the Atlantic. A more reasonable explanation is simply that Mr. Warner and Mr. Trilling must enjoy a different circle of acquaintances and that they must have been reading different books and magazines. . . .

In discussing the so-called common reader, I referred to the annual sale of such novels as *David Copperfield*, and librarians in England still report that Dickens is approached only by Scott in having the largest circulation of any "classic" writer. . . . A further sign of vitality has been the successful adaptation of such novels as *Great Expectations* and *Oliver Twist* into the medium of the film. The fact that the film seems a much more effective medium for his work than the stage has been raises a number of interesting enquiries which cannot, however, be pursued here.

For the student of literary audiences, one of the many interesting lines of inquiry in Ford is the recurrent sharpshooting at the Leavises' attitude, suggested before. It is relatively mild in the reference to Mrs. Leavis's "contempt of the Victorian fondness for laughter" and the "extremely depressing and disturbing reading in *Fiction and the Reading Public* in England, and *The Great Audience* by Gilbert Seldes in America [which] have analyzed the cynical exploitation of public taste . . . increasingly dominant since 1900." It continues persistently sharp in mention of F. R. Leavis: "F. R. Leavis tells us that 'The adult mind doesn't as a rule find Dickens a challenge to an unusual and sustained serious-

[53] *Ibid.*, p. 227.

ness' . . . F. R. Leavis . . . describes *Roderick Hudson* as *Martin Chuzzlewit* 'redone by an enormously more intelligent and better educated mind' . . . Arnold Kettle . . . is not troubled by Dr. Leavis's scruples concerning Dickens's 'place.' " Only in Leavis's "brilliant analysis" of *Hard Times* does he find much to praise.

Or the student may pursue Ford's view of Matthew Arnold's admiration of *David Copperfield*, as "an 'all-containing treasure-house' of English Philistinism": [54]

At the core of Dickens' didactic purposes is an ideal that all classes might simply enjoy life with kindness. Arnold hoped that all classes, but especially the middle classes (whom he tried to cajole with every persuasive device) might enjoy life intelligently and provide intelligent leadership.

Mass Culture: The Popular Arts in America (1957) by Bernard Rosenberg and David Manning White is an anthology of comment on the public arts, media, and taste—largely contemporary but with pieces from Alexis de Tocqueville and Walt Whitman among the seven in the early section, "Perspectives of Mass Culture." Seven other sections follow: "Mass Literature," "Motion Pictures," "Television and Radio," "Divertissement" (music, card playing, Broadway theater), "Advertising," and "The Overview." The whole is preceded by "The Issues Joined" in which the editors in opposed introductions, dramatize the anti-mass-culture view (Bernard Rosenberg, lecturer at the City College of New York and of The New School for Social Research) and the sympathetic-hopeful view (David Manning White, Research Professor of Journalism, Boston University).

Where earlier symposia on modern media and arts (such as those edited variously by Douglas Waples, Lyman Bryson, and Wilbur G. Schramm) have been essentially academic, this collection samples the range from popular or semi-popular to academic—fifty-one names in all, including these among others (in order of appearance): Leo Lowenthal, Dwight MacDonald, Gilbert Seldes, Clement Greenberg, *Frank Luther Mott, Bernard Berelson, Alan Dutcher, Cecil Henley, Edmund Wilson, George Orwell, Charles W. Rolo, Christopher La Farge* (those italicized are in the section on "Mass Literature"), Siegfried Kracauer, Hortense Powder-

[54] *Ibid.*, p. 99.

maker, Martha Wolfenstein, Nathan Leites, Eric Larrabee, David
Riesman, Kurt Lang, S. I. Hayakawa, Marshall McLuhan, Alan
Seeger, Paul Lazarsfeld, Robert K. Merton, and Leslie Fiedler.

Methods are of many sorts, though enough are in the social
sciences to prompt the headline "Sociologists Heave a Fat Tome
at TV" in a New York newspaper television column. The preface
cites contributing scholarship "in the humanities, English and
American civilization, journalism, the communication arts . . .
sociology, psychology, economics, and anthropology."

Since the accumulated findings and points of view toward
audience in *Mass Culture* are considered in Patrick Hazard's chapter in our own book, and since the great value of *Mass Culture*
is in bringing together scattered materials which the student would
otherwise have to search out (a value for the student which would
have been increased by an index), we may direct more specific
attention here only to the views of the two editors:

Bernard Rosenberg ("major interests . . . in sociology and
anthropology"):[55]

Shakespeare is dumped on the market along with Mickey Spillane,
and publishers are rightly confident that their audience will not feel
obliged to make any greater preparation for the master of world literature than for its latest lickspittle. . . . At its worst, mass culture
threatens not merely to cretinize our taste, but to brutalize our senses
while paving the way to totalitarianism.

It is necessary to take as holistic a view as possible . . . in a large
sociocultural context . . . [to] . . . clear the air of certain obviously
erroneous assumptions:

1. *Capitalism is responsible for mass culture.* Not at all . . .
2. *America is responsible.* . . . Hardly. . . .
3. *Democracy is responsible* . . . . common mistake . . . .

If one can hazard a single positive formulation . . . it would be that
modern technology is the necessary and sufficient cause of mass culture. . . . Meanwhile, change, followed by barbarous accommodation
proceeds at an accelerated tempo.

David Manning White ("background in literary history and
journalism"):

There can be no defense (either on aesthetic or moral grounds) for

55 Bernard Rosenberg and David Manning White, *Mass Culture* (Glencoe,
Ill., The Free Press, 1957), pp. 5–12.

certain aspects of our mass culture which are banal, dehumanizing, and downright ugly, both in form and content . . . every period of civilization has had its share of men who preyed upon the ignorance and insecurities of the largest part of the populace. . . .

Is it really true that the media have transformed the greatest part of the American population into this nebulous "mass mind" . . . ? Do the media contrive with all their cunning, Madison Avenue, grey-flanneled wit to keep Mencken's *booboisie* on the thirteen-year-old level . . . ? In his book, *The Power Elite,* the noted sociologist C. Wright Mills decries what appears to him our inevitable trend to a mass society for which the mass media must be held to account. At the end of this road . . . totalitarianism, as in Nazi Germany.

To equate sane and beneficent government with *haut culture* . . . has no real basis in man's experience.

To imply . . . some kind of mysterious compact on the part of the executives of our television networks, large book publishers, cinema studios, *et al.,* to mongrelize the sensibilities of the mass of Americans, is not only a canard but logically untrue. Admittedly, the media are Big Business. . . . Yet . . . on March 11, 1956, the National Broadcasting Company invested $500,000 to present a three-hour-long première of Sir Lawrence Olivier's Richard III . . . the number of viewers . . . 20 to 25 million. . . . Television . . . contributing the Academy-Award-Winning movie, *Marty,* originally a television play. . . . *Life* . . . gives its several million readers the initial publication of Hemingway's *Old Man and the Sea.* . . .

the book publishing business has never had a better year than 1955 . . . youngsters set a record for borrowing books from public libraries . . . 300 million paper bound books printed last year! Since 1939 we've consumed about two billion copies . . . the quality of the titles . . . constantly improving.

If I have presented a hopeful picture . . . it is because I see substantial amelioration in the uses of our mass media. There has been such a rehearsal of all that is ugly and bathetic in our popular arts by critics whose sincerity cannot be questioned that it is time that the other side of the coin be examined.[56]

If the issues here can excite fifty vigorous public spokesmen, many of whom are concerned with literature as part of our culture, it seems that they might excite college students to dig more deeply into and beyond their lecture notes and class anthology.

[56] *Ibid.,* pp. 14–21.

Richard D. Altick's *The English Common Reader: A Social History of the Mass Reading Public 1800–1900* (1957), "ten years . . . under construction," came to hand just as this essay was in final draft. It provides a substantial check on major conclusions arrived at here, fortunately reinforcing rather than altering them.

The first three of Altick's sixteen chapters cover "The Background, 1477–1800." The next thirteen cover various aspects of "The Nineteenth Century:" "The Social Background"; "Religion"; "The Utilitarian Spirit"; "Elementary Education and Literacy"; "Secondary Education"; "The Mechanics Institutes and After"; "Public Libraries"; "The Self-Made Reader"; "The Book Trade, 1800–1850"; "The Book Trade, 1850–1900"; Periodicals and Newspapers, 1800–1850"; "Periodicals and Newspapers, 1851–1900"; and "The Past and the Present." Three Appendixes give a "Chronology of The Mass Reading Public, 1774–1900," "Best Sellers," and "Periodical and Newspaper Circulation." There are an eleven-page selective Bibliography (giving "only a small fraction of the sources consulted" and omitting Harbage and Beljame, though they are included in the text and footnotes) and an eighteen-page comprehensive Index.

The method is that of social history, as the subtitle indicates and as Altick explains:[57]

Despite its enormous importance in social and cultural history, the growth of the mass reading public in England has never been systematically analyzed and documented. . . . [Footnote 1] R. K. Webb's recent monograph, *The British Working-Class Reader*, deals with only a small segment of the subject . . . though within its chosen scope it is authoritative and refreshingly corrective of received opinion.

Historians who have glanced at the development of the mass reading public have drawn for the most part upon two kinds of data: anecdotes and the records of best selling books and popular periodicals. The present writer . . . is not one to scorn either kind of information. The anecdote is often a valuable microcosm of history. . . .

Similarly, it is useful to know that the sale in monthly parts of Dickens' novels averaged about 40,000 copies and that, from the fifties onward, popular papers like the *Family Herald* and the *London Journal* had circulations reaching into six figures. . . . To describe and measure the spread of reading by such means is relatively easy. To account

[57] Altick, *op. cit.*, pp. 1–3.

for it, and to fix it against the panoramic background of nineteenth-century English history, is a more complex task.

For the mass reading public had its roots deep in the total history of the period . . . political, religious, economic, technological. . . .

Altick believes that we are too nearly at the groundwork stage in study of the reading public or audience to make judgments on the vulgarization of taste, but does not hesitate to state his faith:[58]

The impact of the mass public upon modern English literature—taking the term in the widest possible sense—is incalculable. Though a great deal has been said on the subject between Collins' day and our own, no truly serious study has yet been made of it. The widely held opinion that the coming of the democratic audience vulgarized literature may well be correct, but to test it is no part of our design. . . . Instead, one of the main purposes of this book is to provide some of the information that obviously must be taken into account before anyone can safely interpret the popular taste of an age. . . . The lack of such knowledge inevitably makes discussion of the audience's formative influence upon literature little more than idle speculation. . . .

We are beginning to understand the effect of general social conditions upon the production of literature; but the role of the reader—the consumer—has been largely neglected. Such commentary as exists on the topic is offhand and impressionistic. The present book does not pretend to be exhaustive. . . . There is room for literally hundreds of studies of topics which are here merely sketched. . . . Though the purpose of this book is first of all to present a body of data and ideas which are useful and significant in themselves, hardly less dominant is the desire to provide a preliminary map of the vast territory, still virtually unexplored. . . .

But both implicitly and explicitly he has faith that:[59]

genuine democracy resides not alone in the possession of certain social, political, and economic advantages but in the unqualified freedom of all men and women to enjoy the fruits of a country's culture, among which books have a place of high, if not supreme, importance . . . . behind all the fine-print statistical tables . . . shines the image of the ordinary man or woman at what is surely one of the happiest and most rewarding of human pursuits—the reading of the printed word.

[58] *Ibid.*, pp. 1–9.
[59] *Ibid.*, pp. 7–11.

In the closing chapter, "The Past and the Present," he sums up his findings and his view of the audience with interesting references to Coleridge, "mass audience," "so-called mass communication media," and our "two-sided attitude toward the common reader":[60]

In these closing pages, however, it will be worthwhile to review the "problem" of the mass audience as it appeared to successive generations of the "superior" classes during the nineteenth century and to consider how far their attitudes still influence our thinking today.

In the first half of the century, the implications of a democratic audience for print, viewed from above, were mainly political. Coleridge's exclamation in 1810, "These are AWFUL TIMES!" epitomized the horror he and most conservatives felt at the spread of the reading habit into, and even beneath, the lower reaches of the middle class. . . .

After the first fifteen years or so of Victoria's reign . . . people worried chiefly about the dangers of moral corruption associated with popular reading. . . .

With the fading of the moral concern, the problem of the mass reading public became predominantly one of literary culture. . . . Sharing the familiar human bent for idealizing the past . . . [observers] maintained that things were far different, and infinitely better, in the old days before reading had become democratized. The identical lament is heard today; but perhaps some comfort can be found in remembering that Coleridge had felt the same way in 1817. . . .

Equally deplorable to Victorian commentators, as . . . to many in our own time, was the growing demand for information and entertainment, in the easy-to-take, easy-to-digest form of condensations, summaries, and excerpts—the "Beauties, elegant Extracts, and Anas" of Coleridge's despair. . . .

there are few, if any, notions which we do not find echoed in modern commentary. We have inherited the same two-sided attitude toward the common reader. . . . Even those with an unswerving emotional and intellectual commitment to democracy as a political principle sometimes betray skepticism when democratic theory is applied to the problem of the reading audience. The capacities that qualify a man to vote intelligently are not the same, inferentially, as those which qualify him to be a devotee of books.

[60] *Ibid.*, pp. 367–374.

Students may very helpfully annotate and compare the range of Altick's considerations here with those of the other key studies as a kind of summation. Students interested in the role of the Leavises and Matthew Arnold may find significance in the single citation from *Fiction and the Reading Public*—"As Mrs. Leavis has observed, 'The difference that the disappearance of the Sunday book a generation ago has made, its effect on the outlook and mental capacity of the people, would repay investigation,'"—and in the recurrent references to Arnold (largely on his schoolman's views) as a microcosmic instance of Altick's documentary materials: Arnold's school-inspector's report of 1860 on the poor quality of school reading books; his approval of "a new subject introduced in 1871, 'English literature'"; "How much easier it seems to get entrance to their minds [wrote Arnold of apprentice teachers] and to awaken them by means of music or of physical science than by means of literature . . ."; Arnold's acceptance of the anthology as an appropriate means of developing taste among children in elementary schools; his protests against the high costs of new books favoring lending libraries:

for the multiplication and protection of bad literature, and for keeping good books dear. . . . The three-shilling book is our great want . . . [not] a cheap literature . . . like the tawdry novels which flare in the book-shelves of our railway-stations. . . ."

III

Viewed cumulatively, what have our selected studies told us?— beside giving us certain rough classifications ("studies of best sellers," "period studies," and the like) and a range of specific instances of varied methods and conceptions of audience.

—That the older "history of taste" is suspect?

—That the study of "audience," "public," "readers," is dramatically on the move, after long delay, if the history of Beljame's study of 1881 is significant?

—That there is a crucial issue in the progressive equation "mass media" = "mass audience" = "mass mind" (and also "Philistine" mind?) in which we all have stakes?

—That we still have a long way to go before we can claim definitive methods or set up firm categories in this field?

—But that we can mark out some key concepts of audience, and promising critical index points from which to take bearings?

The teacher and student often cannot wait, of course, for definitive methods and findings. Here is one of the chronic aggravations of educational inquiry or research as compared with the academic. Our question of "mass media" = "mass audience" must be met now with the most relevant facts, hypotheses, intuitions, and judgment we can bring to it. For it makes a difference whether we think of school audiences and other audiences deterministically as a mass (and treat them so, and perhaps make them so when they would not otherwise be so) or humanistically, as clustered or scattered communities of individual human beings (and treat them so, and perhaps make them so).

Here the most thoughtful art of teaching must enter with the pure science of scholarship and the professional science of education, searching out the facts and symbols (at once economical and expansive, as in any art) which will embody not only the matter but the meaning and spirit, at the most significant transection points we can find in the subject, in the student's experience, and in our own understanding.

Different teachers with different students will find different symbols. To date, the most effective means I have found for giving prospective teachers in a course in "Literature and the Literary Audience" (largely liberal arts college graduates) an initial image of the web of problems and possibilities here—of method, outlook, and literary application—is through a "triangulation" of John Steinbeck's *The Grapes of Wrath* (a best seller which also has literary stature), Steinbeck and Ricketts's *Sea of Cortez* (in which Steinbeck gives the "human ecological key to *The Grapes of Wrath*) and Paul B. Sears's *This Is Our World* (in which the Oklahoma-Oberlin-Yale botanist-ecologist spells out the "humanities" dimensions of his subject as well as the biological).

The opening of *Sea of Cortez* raises at once the question of the relation of old and new scientific methods and literary method, recalling Mrs. Leavis's conception of the "anthropological." (It also opens a vista in *The Grapes of Wrath* which persuades most students that they must go beyond the usual commentaries if they are to get at the art or the creative achievement in works of literature to 'which people respond. This is particularly needed for *The*

Grapes of Wrath [or *The Red Pony* for high-school use], which is commonly treated as topical, or regional, or proletarian literature, seldom as Steinbeck's effort also to see what an ecological outlook can mean for our literary view of the world, breaking through the older deterministic literary naturalism.) Not the least of the values for teaching is a certain protective irony in the first-glance parallel between Steinbeck's venturing into the Sea of Cortez and the venturing of student and teacher into literary audience.[61]

We have a book to write about the Gulf of California. We could do one of several things about its design. But we have decided to let it form itself: its boundaries a boat and a sea; its duration a six weeks' charter time; its subject everything we could see and think and even imagine. . . .

We wanted to see everything our eyes could accommodate, to think what we could, and out of our seeing and thinking, to build some kind of structure in modeled imitation of the observed reality. We knew that what we would see and record and construct would be warped, as all knowledge patterns are warped, first, by the collective pressure and stream of our time and race, second by the thrust of our individual personalities. But knowing this, we might not fall into too many holes—we might maintain some balance between our warp and the separate thing, the external reality.

"Let us go," we said, "into the Sea of Cortez, realizing that we become forever a part of it; that our rubber boots slogging through a flat of eel-grass, that the rocks we turn over in a tide pool, make us truly and permanently a factor in the ecology of the region. We shall take something away from it, but we shall leave something too." And if we seem a small factor in a huge pattern, nevertheless it is of relative importance.

Steinbeck's statement here (the passage is identified as his in *The Log from the Sea of Cortez*) touches in many ways our problems of method, interpretation of findings, attitude toward audience or audiences, and teaching. The novelist and the marine biologist walking together can be as significantly symbolic for our purposes as Edward R. Murrow and Jimmy Durante are for Gilbert Seldes.

[61] John Steinbeck and E. F. Ricketts, *Log from the Sea of Cortez* (New York, The Viking Press, Inc., 1951), pp. 1–3.

In going "wide open," of course, Steinbeck and Ricketts were not going at random. They went with a conscious ecological concern for the interrelations of living things with one another and with their environment, and with the finding of symbolic critical index or nexus points, where these interrelations might be most economically and strikingly observed. Hasn't this always been intuitively the literary method: "I am part of all that I have met," whether in Homer or Tennyson, Emerson or Thoreau? Can we see it now becoming also a conspicuous modern method in philosophy (whether our key is Whitehead or Dewey), in biological ecology (Paul B. Sears, Rachel Carson), in ecological anthropology (W. Lloyd Warner), in educational research and inquiry (E. L. Thorndike's *Your City*, 1939; Riesman), in ecological literary and cultural criticism (Krutch), and in other fields? Following William Riley Parker's suggestion, shouldn't we welcome Edward Ricketts and no less a Paul B. Sears when Sears writes in *This Is Our World* (1937), two years before *The Grapes of Wrath*?[62]

Man is within, and not above, the vast symphony of environment and all of life. . . .

The demonstration of this fact, and of man's origin in a long and earthy past, has been rocking the world for about eighty years—since the Darwinian earthquake. . . .

The intimation that man is an animal became the signal to break the ranks. If the red rule of nature was ruthless, so be it . . . morals became at best a matter of convenience. . . .

It is possible for a poison draught to contain its own antidote. For not quite fifty years, science, driving on to the bitter end with its assumptions, has been investigating the behavior of living things under natural conditions, as well as in the laboratory. . . .

It has found, to be brief, that Nature is indeed ruthless, but in her ruthlessness she plays no favorites. Justice is to be had, but it is neither for those who swagger, nor those who beg. It must be built, on Nature's terms, through understanding and painful toil. There is no event that is not numbered, that does not have its consequences. Conduct has become once more a matter of tremendous significance, continuity and destiny once more the rule of life.

[62] Paul B. Sears, *This is Our World* (Norman, Okla., University of Oklahoma Press, 1937), pp. 5–8.

Can we name other literary ecologists beside Steinbeck?—
George R. Stewart, Conrad Richter, the Louis Bromfield of Mala-
bar Farm, Donald Culross Peattie, Rachel Carson, Joseph Wood
Krutch, Alan Paton, perhaps? And perhaps more telling for the
spread of the ecological concept, do we see a tacit literary-ecology
in Hemingway and Faulkner (though subordinate to their more
personal concerns) and in other novelists whom Edward Weeks
describes as "cultivating their patches of erosion." What of such
films as Pere Lorenz's *The River* and Disney's *Nature's Half Acre*?
And thinking of points of contact with our students, what of the
ubiquitous popular elementary ecology of the Western movie,
or an ecology of urban symbols in the detective story?

There are potential dangers as well as sources of strength in any
method or outlook, of course, as Lionel Trilling's *The Liberal
Imagination* (1953) suggests here concerning a naïve kind of
primitivism or naturalistic primordialism in Theodore Dreiser:

a sensation of cosmic understanding, of an overarching sense of unity
with the world in its apparent evil as well as its obvious good . . .
is no more to be quarreled with, or reasoned with, than love itself—
indeed, it is a kind of love, not so much of the world as of oneself in
the world.

But a more likely consequence, if we teach as artists, is a sense
of humility when we face the cosmic context. Trilling shows the
balanced kind of consciousness of the artist and the audience
needed in the interplay of art, with its "variousness and possibility."

The poet, it is true, is an effect of environment, but we must remember that he is no less a cause. . . . In a concert room the audience
and its attitude are of course the environment of the performer, but
also the performer and his music make the environment of the audience.

To these symbolic "triangulations" I want to add, next time I
offer the course, at least two other symbolic instances of the
teacher's and critic's imagination at work on the questions of
audiences in their environment, to accompany the dozen key
works and others as subjects of small seminar studies. (With the
large classes here and ahead, we had better learn now to develop
small seminar groups within them.) These are Jacques Barzun's
chapter on "The Arts, the Snobs, and the Democrat" in *Of Human*

Freedom (1939), showing the historical imagination at work on our topic, and John Crowe Ransom's "The Esthetic of Regionalism," reprinted in Morton Zabel's *Literary Opinion in America* (1937), illustrating the regional-aesthetic imagination which Ransom has not repudiated as a New Critic.

There is not space here to demonstrate fully why these are useful, but a few excerpts from each may suggest the reasons.

Barzun, facing the rise of totalitarianism in the 1930's, had such things as these to say in *Of Human Freedom*:[63]

Generalities about a "whole people" are likely to be wrong. . . . Literature [in America] somehow pays its own way, although poetry and serious nonfiction are generally "carried" by cultured publishers out of the proceeds of best sellers. . . .

Discussions about art are . . . vitiated by a confusion between art of this easy-going kind, intended for daily consumption, and art of a different kind, designed for connoisseurs. . . . Contrary to current belief, the making of "consumer" art is by no means easy and by no means reprehensible. . . .

The distinction between the two types of art is a difference of density rather than of species. In the same number of bars of Beethoven and Sousa, there is, in Beethoven, *more* music. . . .

The many, including representatives of the rich, the well-born, and the able, are made acutely unhappy by repeated attempts to kindle art in their soul under forced draft, and the minority is too often badgered by the snobs striving to impose their fashionable favorite on everybody else. Either form of compulsion leaves the great majority indifferent or hostile to art, and Philistinism—if we must call it that—had better be accepted as inevitable than fought by the undemocratic methods now in use. . . .

Critical lag or backwardness is . . . harmless in the Philistines and fatal among the elite. . . .

A democracy where the individual can freely choose his cultural sustenance can safely leave to human genius the making of an art adequate to its greatness. . . . Even under artistic *laisser faire*, however, there are certain cultural duties. For the masses of the citizens

[63] Jacques Barzun, *Of Human Freedom* (Boston, Little, Brown and Co., 1939), pp. 99–119.

they are negative: hands off. For those more immediately concerned with the arts, they are more strenuous . . . taking what is offered [by the artist] for what it is worth. . . . These pragmatic attitudes toward art may be difficult to propagate. . . . But a beginning might be made through our schools. . . .

John Crowe Ransom's "The Esthetic of Regionalism," (coupled with his recent "The Concrete Universal" in *Poems and Essays*, 1955) raises a series of lively questions about American parallels to the *Scrutiny* story, suited to an introductory seminar study. Students can gain a good deal of insight into academic attitudes and literary criticism in America today by testing the following tentative hypothesis:

(1) When the militant Southern Agrarian Regionalists issued *I Take My Stand* (1930), their position had three major aspects:

—a concern with what rang true for both the regional writer and audience—with an organic integrity (but not ruling out "unorganic" elements) required both in art and in modern conceptions of regions;

—a conviction that the South was the most classically "liberal" part of America—hence the least provincial, the most universal (reflecting Matthew Arnold's terms?);

—Southern regional abhorrence of the mass of cities, and also an academic abhorrence of great cities into which the country had "drained" (comparable with that of Mrs. Leavis?).

(2) When *I Take My Stand* appeared it was widely greeted with cries of "Provincialism" from academic colleagues.

(3) With their regionalism widely repudiated within the profession (though the American reading public at all levels continued to be interested in literary regionalism), some of the regionalists muted the regionalism but held to the universal, classic, anti-mass sanctions for it—like the *Scrutiny* group outdoing the traditional scholar-critics at their own game, and thereupon winning (after lesser opposition in the struggle between literary historians and critics) a widespread academic following they could not win with regionalism.

If this hypothesis stands up under searching examination, it can be as revealing about our academic literary audience as about our Southern regionalists, become strategy-minded New Critics.

Some relevant passages in "The Esthetic of Regionalism" include:[64]

the first thing to observe is that nature itself is intensely localized, or regional. . . .

As a community slowly adapts its life to the geography of the region, a thing happens which is almost miraculous. . . . As the economic patterns become perfected and easy, they cease to be merely economic and become gradually esthetic. . . . The arts make their appearance in some ascending order, perhaps indicated like this: labor, craft, and business insist upon being transacted under patterns which permit the enjoyment of the natural background; houses, tools, manufactured things do not seem good enough if they are only effective but must also be ornamental, which in a subtle sense means natural; and the fine arts arise, superficially pure or non-useful, yet faithful to the regional nature and to the economic and moral patterns to which the community is committed. . . .

Now a city of any sort removes men from direct contact with nature . . . the cities of a machine age are peculiarly debased . . . without a history . . . without a region . . . without a character. . . .

the esthetic attitude is piety ("piety . . . directed first towards the physical region, the nature who has always given them sustenance and now gives them the manifold of her sensibilia . . . and also directed toward the historic community which has dwelt in this region all these generations and developed these patterns").

Ransom seems to hold the same ground in 1955, but with the "Universal" tactfully in capital letters and "local" in small:[65]

it seems idle for literary critics to raise the question whether, within the traversed region of nature, the unpredictable and highly particular detail of the local "manifold of sense" is going to enter precisely and without remainder into the formal Universal. That is too much to expect. We shall be glad to settle for much less than that. The sort of hospitality offered to our moral Universal by the Concrete of the natural world will need to be convincing, if it is to do us any good, but on the other hand the Universal is a mannerly and modest sort of tourist.

[64] John Crowe Ransom, "The Esthetic of Regionalism," *The American Review* (January, 1934) pp. 106–121.
[65] John Crowe Ransom, "The Concrete Universal," *Poems and Essays* (New York, Vintage Books, Inc., Alfred A. Knopf, Inc., 1955), pp. 166–167.

And as little bonus in the same article, Ransom's comment on Arnold shows where we continue to place the artist and the literary public (even as Bonamy Dobrée placed him in revising Beljame's title):[66]

The physical death of Keats at an early age is painful to us, but worse, perhaps, is the death of the poet in the living Arnold, and I for one, on the present occasion, will not be consoled by thinking of the value of the public man who emerged from the ruin. It is easy to agree that Arnold was the happiest of all the rhetoricians in our language who have dedicated themselves to the public cause; that is to say, the most engaging schoolmaster who ever teased and scolded his bad pupils into bothering about "the best that has been thought and uttered in the world."

While, then, we cannot yet be definitive about the history and statistics of taste on literary audience, can we at least bring the urgent question of mass audience and various transecting lines of force into visible focus for ourselves and our students through some such formulation as "The 'Cultured' and the 'Philistine' Seventy-five Years after Matthew Arnold; or Current Ideas about Literary Audience, and Their Effect on the Teaching of Literature?" This chapter looks toward such a study.

OTHER SELECTED STUDIES OF LITERARY AUDIENCE

A. C. Bradley, "Shakespeare's Theatre and Audience," *Oxford Lectures on Poetry* (1904).

H. F. Dilworth, *Reading Tastes as Influenced by College Admission Requirements in English* (1914).

Van Wyck Brooks, *America's Coming-of-Age* (1915).

Thomas G. Wright, *Literary Culture in Early New England* (1920).

Karl Julius Holzknecht, *Literary Patronage in the Middle Ages* (1923).

Asa Dow Dickinson, *One Thousand Best Books* (1924).

Arthur S. Collins, *Authorship in the Days of Johnson, Being a Study of the Relationship Between Author, Patron, Publisher, and Public, 1726–1780* (1927).

William S. Gray and Ruth Monroe, *The Reading Interests and Habits of Adults* (1929).

Douglas Waples and Ralph Tyler, *What People Want to Read About* (1931).

[66] *Ibid.*, pp. 162–163

W. W. Charters, *Motion Pictures and Youth* (1933).

Charles H. Compton, *Who Reads What?* (1934).

Louis B. Wright, *Middle-Class Culture in Elizabethan England* (1935).

William Charvat, *The Origins of American Critical Thought, 1810–1835* (1936).

Fred Eastman, *Books That Have Shaped the World* (1937).

Louis R. Wilson, *The Geography of Reading* (1938).

David Daiches, *Literature and Society* (1938).

Douglas Waples, *Libraries and Readers in the State of New York* (1939).

Jacques Barzun, *Of Human Freedom* (1939).

A. J. Jenkinson, *What Do Boys and Girls Read?* (1940).

James Westfall Thompson, *Ancient Libraries* (1940).

Paul F. Lazarsfeld, *Radio and the Printed Page* (1940).

Llewellyn White and Robert D. Leigh, *Peoples Speaking to Peoples* (1946).

Hadley Cantril, *The Invasion from Mars* (1947).

Lyman Bryson (editor), *The Communication of Ideas* (1948).

Lindsay Rogers, *The Pollsters* (1949).

Warren S. Tryon and William Charvat, *The Cost Books of Ticknor and Fields and Their Predecessors, 1832–1858* (1949).

George W. Norvell, *The Reading Interests of Young People* (1950).

W. H. Bruford, *Theatre, Drama, and Audience in Goethe's Germany* (1950).

Robert D. Leigh, *The Public Library in the United States* (1950).

David Riesman, Reuel Denny, Nathan Glazer, *The Lonely Crowd* (1950).

Eliot L. Friedson, *An Audience and Its Taste* (1952), Microfilm.

H. S. Bennett, *English Books & Readers, 1475 to 1557* (1952).

Bernard Berelson and Morris Janowitz, *Reader in Public Opinion and Communication* (1953).

Malcolm Cowley, *The Literary Situation* (1954).

Robert Kiefer Webb, *The British Working Class Reader, 1790–1848; Literacy and Social Tension* (1955).

A. C. Spectorsky, *The Exurbanites* (1955).

C. Wright Mills, *The Power Elite* (1956).

William H. Whyte, Jr., *The Organization Man* (1956).

Vance Packard, *The Hidden Persuaders* (1957).

John Lough, *Paris Theatre Audiences in the Seventeenth and Eighteenth Centuries* (1957).

Simon O. Lesser, *Fiction and the Unconscious* (1957).

A Selected Bibliography

A WORD IS NECESSARY TO EXPLAIN
the method of compilation and the purpose of the following listing. It is not intended as a supplement to the literary studies recommended in the essays which precede it, but is rather a final under-
lining of those works published within the last thirty years which
in the opinion of representative scholars and critics have contributed most to the understanding of literature. It sets forth, shall
we say, fifty examples of contemporary literary scholarship with
which every teacher should be acquainted.

The list was compiled as the result of a questionnaire sent to
two hundred and fifty critics and professors of literature in colleges and universities throughout the United States. Each was asked
to list the ten or fifteen scholarly or critical works published within
the past thirty years which seemed most important as contributions toward understanding the literature of the period or genre
in which he was most interested, and also to list the ten or fifteen
books which have contributed most to an understanding of literature in general. Results seemed at first disappointing because of an
apparent lack of any unanimity of opinion: close to five hundred
separate works were nominated, some by many, some by only
two or three, some by only one, and in several instances by the
authors themselves. With tabulation, however, more agreement
was discovered than had at first been apparent. Though the listing
as now compiled will certainly not satisfy every scholar or critic,
either in its inclusions or its exclusions, it does seem fairly to represent, perhaps not an impeccable, but an intelligent consensus.

Five works finally stood out so far ahead of the rest that they
deserve special mention. They are listed here, in order of date of
publication,[1] for the difference in number of nominations for each
was so slight that it seems fairest to disregard it entirely:

T. S. Eliot, *Selected Essays, 1917–1932* (New York, Harcourt,
Brace and Company, Inc., 1932; new edition, 1950).

[1] Hereafter works will be listed, not in order of relative standing according
to the number of nominations received, but only as among the first fifty.

A. O. Lovejoy, *The Great Chain of Being: A Study in the History of an Idea* (Cambridge, Harvard University Press, 1936).

C. S. Lewis, *The Allegory of Love: A Study in Medieval Tradition* (London, Oxford University Press, 1936; revised, 1938).

F. O. Matthiessen, *American Renaissance: Art and Expression in the Age of Emerson and Whitman* (New York, Oxford University Press, 1941).

Meyer H. Abrams, *The Mirror and the Lamp: Romantic Theory and the Critical Tradition* (New York, Oxford University Press, 1953).

Two among the first fifty were literary histories, one of English, the other of American literature: *A Literary History of England*, edited by Albert C. Baugh (New York, Appleton-Century-Crofts, Inc., 1941), to which, in addition to Mr. Baugh, Kemp Malone, Tucker Brooke, George Sherburn, and Samuel C. Chew contributed, and *The Literary History of the United States*, edited by Robert E. Spiller, Willard Thorp, Henry Seidel Canby, and Thomas H. Johnson (New York, The Macmillan Company, 1948), which contains essays by more than a score of contributors. Also included was *The Cambridge Bibliography of English Literature*, edited by F. W. Bateson (Cambridge, Cambridge University Press, 1940; New York, The Macmillan Company, 1941).

Outstanding achievements in the editing or establishment of texts were John M. Manly and Edith Rickert's eight-volume edition of *The Text of the Canterbury Tales: Studied on the Basis of All Known Manuscripts* (Chicago, The University of Chicago Press, 1940); F. N. Robinson's edition of *The Complete Works of Geoffrey Chaucer* (Boston and New York, Houghton Mifflin Company, 1933; revised, 1957, as *The Works of Geoffrey Chaucer*); C. H. Herford and Percy and Evelyn Simpson's eleven-volume edition of the writings of *Ben Jonson* (Oxford: The Clarendon Press, 1925–1952); George Sherburn's edition of *The Correspondence of Alexander Pope* (Oxford, The Clarendon Press, 1956); and F. A. Pottle's editions of the several, variously titled volumes in the Yale edition of the Private Papers of James Boswell, since 1951.

Literary biography during the past thirty years was found best represented by George Sherburn, *The Early Career of Alexander Pope* (Oxford, The Clarendon Press, 1934); Newman Ivey White,

Shelley (New York, Alfred A. Knopf, Inc., 1940); Ralph Leslie Rusk, *The Life of Ralph Waldo Emerson* (Boston and New York, Houghton Mifflin Company, 1949); and Lionel Trilling, *Matthew Arnold* (New York, W. W. Norton & Company, Inc., 1939; second edition, Columbia University Press, 1949).

Studies relating to periods were, for the medieval period and the English Renaissance: C. S. Lewis, *The Allegory of Love,* already mentioned; Ernst R. Curtius, *European Literature and the Latin Middle Ages,* translated by Willard R. Trask (New York, Pantheon Books, 1953); and Douglas Bush, *Mythology and the Renaissance Tradition in English Literature* (Minneapolis, University of Minnesota Press, 1932);

for the sixteenth century, including Shakespeare: C. S. Lewis, *English Literature of the Sixteenth Century, Excluding Drama* (Oxford, The Clarendon Press, 1954); Rosamund Tuve, *Elizabethan and Metaphysical Imagery: Renaissance Poetics and Twentieth-Century Critics* (Chicago, The University of Chicago Press, 1947); E. K. Chambers, *William Shakespeare: A Study of Facts and Problems* (Oxford, The Clarendon Press, 1930); and Harley Granville-Barker, *Prefaces to Shakespeare* (Princeton, Princeton University Press, 1946–1947);

for the seventeenth century: Douglas Bush, *English Literature in the Early Seventeenth Century, 1600–1660* (Oxford, The Clarendon Press, 1945); Basil Willey, *The Seventeenth-Century Background: Studies of the Thought of the Age in Relation to Poetry and Religion* (London, Chatto & Windus, 1934); Gerald E. Bentley, *The Jacobean and Caroline Stage* (Oxford, The Clarendon Press, 1941–1956); and Marjorie Hope Nicolson, *The Breaking of the Circle: Studies in the Effect of the "New Science" upon Seventeenth Century Poetry* (Evanston, Northwestern University Press, 1950);

for the eighteenth century: George Sherburn, *The Restoration and Eighteenth Century, 1600–1789,* Volume III of *A Literary History of England,* edited by Albert C. Baugh, published separately in 1948; and Walter Jackson Bate, *From Classic to Romantic: Premises of Taste in Eighteenth-Century England* (Cambridge, Harvard University Press, 1946);

for the nineteenth century: Meyer H. Abrams, *The Mirror and the Lamp,* already mentioned; John Livingston Lowes, *The Road to Xanadu: A Study in the Ways of the Imagination* (Boston and New York, Houghton Mifflin Company, 1927); Joseph Warren Beach, *The Concept of Nature in Nineteenth-Century English Poetry* (New York, The Macmillan Company, 1936; new edition, 1956); Douglas Bush, *Mythology and the Romantic Tradition in English Poetry* (Cambridge, Harvard University Press, 1937); and Jerome H. Buckley, *The Victorian Temper: A Study in Literary Culture* (Cambridge, Harvard University Press, 1951);

for American literature: in addition to F. O. Matthiessen, *American Renaissance*, already mentioned, Perry Miller, *The New England Mind: The Seventeenth Century* (Cambridge, Harvard University Press, 1939; reissued, 1954), and *The New England Mind: From Colony to Province* (Cambridge, Harvard University Press, 1953); R. W. B. Lewis, *The American Adam: Innocence, Tragedy, and Tradition in the Nineteenth Century* (Chicago, The University of Chicago Press, 1950); Henry Nash Smith, *Virgin Land: The American West as Symbol and Myth* (Cambridge, Harvard University Press, 1950); and Alfred Kazin, *On Native Grounds: An Interpretation of Modern Prose Literature* (New York, Reynal & Hitchcock, 1942).

Histories of literary criticism were René Wellek, *A History of Modern Criticism, 1750–1950* (New Haven, Yale University Press, 1955—the first two of four projected volumes), and William K. Wimsatt, Jr., and Cleanth Brooks, *Literary Criticism: A Short History* (New York, Alfred A. Knopf, Inc., 1957); and as a guide to varieties of literary scholarship, René Wellek and Austin Warren, *Theory of Literature* (New York, Harcourt, Brace and Company, Inc., 1949).

Studies which emphasize critical method or interpretation and which therefore fall readily into no chronological category, were, in addition to A. O. Lovejoy, *The Great Chain of Being*, and T. S. Eliot, *Selected Essays*, already mentioned:

Eric Auerbach, *Mimesis: The Representation of Reality in Western Literature*, translated by Willard R. Trask (Princeton, Princeton University Press, 1953).

R. P. Blackmur, *The Double Agent: Essays in Craft and Elucidation* (New York, Arrow Editions, 1935).

Cleanth Brooks, *Modern Poetry and the Tradition* (Chapel Hill, University of North Carolina Press, 1939).

Cleanth Brooks, *The Well Wrought Urn: Studies in the Structure of Poetry* (New York, Reynal & Hitchcock, 1947).

William Empson, *Seven Types of Ambiguity* (London, Chatto & Windus, 1930; second edition, revised, New York, New Directions, 1947).

Francis Fergusson, *The Idea of a Theatre, A Study of Ten Plays: The Art of the Drama in Changing Perspective* (Princeton, Princeton University Press, 1949).

F. R. Leavis, *Revaluation: Tradition & Development in English Poetry* (London, Chatto & Windus, 1949).

I. A. Richards, *Practical Criticism: A Study of Literary Judgment* (New York, Harcourt, Brace and Company, Inc., 1929).

Lionel Trilling, *The Liberal Imagination: Essays in Literature and Society* (New York, Viking Press, Inc., 1950).

Edmund Wilson, *Axel's Castle: A Study of the Imaginative Literature of 1870–1930* (New York, Charles Scribner's Sons, 1931).

Index

This is an index of subjects discussed, not of authors of discussion: T. S. Eliot's writings on Milton, for example, will be found under the heading "Milton," but discussion of Eliot as a poet or critic will be found under "Eliot."